Survey of Higher Education

About the Author

M.R. Kolhatkar, Ph.D., I.A.S. (Retd.) is a distinguished scholar—bureaucrat—jurist. After a bright academic career (M.A. Ist Class—Economics from Pune University) he was selected for the I.A.S. in 1960 in which service he held a variety of posts. For 15 years, he worked in the Education Sector including in the Union Ministry of H.R.D. and Planning Commission. After working for 5 years as a Member of the Central Administrative Tribunal, he did his Ph.D. from Mumbai University in the Faculty of Civics & Politics. He is trained abroad (Naples, Italy and EDI, World Bank, Washington DC) and has attended several international conferences including the Jomtien Conference on 'Education for All' in 1990. He has served as a visiting faculty in academic institutions and his articles have been published in learned journals. He has authored/edited two books.

Survey of Higher Education [1947-2007]

M.R. Kolhatkar

CONCEPT PUBLISHING COMPANY PVT. LTD.
NEW DELHI-110059

ISBN-13-978-81-8069-888-0

First Published 2012

Published and Printed by

Concept Publishing Company Pvt. Ltd.
A/15-16, Commercial Block, Mohan Garden
New Delhi-110059 (India)
T: 25351460, 25351794, *F*: 091-11-25357109
E: publishing@conceptpub.com W: www.conceptpub.com
Editorial Office: H-13, Bali Nagar, New Delhi-110 015, India.

Cataloging in Publication Data--*Courtesy:* D.K. Agencies (P) Ltd. <docinfo@dkagencies.com>

Kolhatkar, M. R., 1936-
Survey of higher education, 1947-2007 / M.R. Kolhatkar.
p. cm.
Includes bibliographical references (p.) and index.
ISBN 9788180698880

1. Education, Higher—India. 2. Education, Higher—Research—India. 3. India. University Grants Commission—Rules and practice. I. Title.

DDC 378.54 23

Preface

Between November 1980 and April 1993, I had an exposure to the planning, policy-making, financing and administration of education at national and state levels in the Union Ministry of Education, in Maharashtra State and in the Union Planning Commission. Earlier in 1969-71, I had worked in the area of agricultural research administration. So my bureaucratic exposure to the Education Sector as a whole was for a period of about 15 years of which one-third was directly in the area of the Higher Education. A collection of my articles on educational topics entitled *Educational Planning and National Development : Some Crucial Aspects* came out in 1997.

Since my retirement in 1993, I had been watching with dismay the crop of books in the market on education/higher education, some of which were in the nature of plagiarized collection of articles, about which I wrote in the *University News,* (43(40), 3rd October, 2005). Earlier still, I had occasion to review an official publication of the UGC brought out on the occasion of the so-called Golden Jubilee celebration of the foundation of the UGC, which review was published in the *EPW* (5th March, 2005, pp.948-950). I said in the course of the review: "A systematic survey of higher education based on original documentary sources and the best secondary literature is yet to be written". When I wrote that sentence, I did not have an inkling that I would be called on to attempt that survey.

Recently, the market has seen some good analytical books on higher education but they conspicuously lack a historical approach. This book is meant to fill a real gap in literature on higher education in India. I hope it will receive the desired welcome.

M.R. Kolhatkar

concern is how to regulate trade in educational services under Mode 1 and Mode 3.

The Present Indian Scenario *vis-à-vis* Globalization

In this background, Indian scenario is as below:

- India has a very large higher education system with 376 Universities and over 20,000 Colleges, a teaching faculty of over 5 lakh and student strength of 1.16 crore. India does not have a mass higher education system in the sense of participation of 15 per cent or more of students of relevant age group in higher education but it may do so in the decade 2010-20 (the target being to achieve 20 per cent of GER by 2020).
- There is a dualism, or rather trialism in structure, with a majority of institutions without high standards but a minority of institutions with an international brand name. (Trialism takes account of middling institutions below the level of IITs but above the level of the general run of institutions).
- Higher Technical and Medical Education is commercialized in a *political feudal* rather than a trade sense.
- The system is not open internally because private universities are not allowed to be set up (a Bill is pending in Parliament since 1995) and when State Governments enter the fray as the Government of Chhattisgarh did by allowing private universities to be notified on the basis of project reports, the Supreme Court had to step in to close them because the UGC failed to do so, another example of regulatory failure of the UGC.
- The number of Indian students going for study abroad (consumption abroad) is on the increase especially in the context of liberalization of foreign exchange regime. The flow is towards North America, Australia and Europe in that order. Press reports indicate that the Indian students outstripped the Chinese students as the largest group of overseas students in the USA, though China is expected to overtake India.

Acknowledgements

While writing the book I have substantially drawn on the resources of the Kalina and the Fort Libraries of the University of Mumbai. I am thankful for their assistance to the following – Mrs. Tilaka Joseph, I/c of the Fort Library and her technical staff, other support staff and of course, Heads of Library Department, viz. Prof. (Smt.) Vijaya Rajhansa and Dr (Mrs.) P.A. Gokhale. In addition, I have used books in the libraries of the Asiatic Society of Mumbai and the Maharashtra Regional Branch of the Indian Institute of Public Administration and I am thankful to the staff of the same.

The then Secretary, Union Department of Higher Education (Shri R.P. Agrawal) directed his staff to supply to me copies of the latest reports of the Ministry of HRD and its organizations and Shri M.K. Kumaran from the Planning Commission supplied to me material relating to the Eleventh Plan. I am thankful to them.

As in the case of all typing work, Shri Anil Lele has typed and retyped a large number of versions of various chapters of the book apart from correspondence. That he could decipher my handwriting and understand various signs and symbols in my manuscripts is a tribute to his skill. I am highly thankful to him.

I wish to thank my wife, Mrs. Sushama and my daughter Ms. Uttara who, at considerable inconvenience to themselves, allowed me to work for long hours in various libraries to complete the book.

Last but not the least, I gratefully acknowledge financial assistance provided by the Indian School of Political Economy (ISPE), Pune to the research project on which this book is based. I particularly acknowledge insightful comments provided by Prof. Dilip Chitre, Honorary Director of the ISPE which helped in improving the draft.

I am thankful to Shri Ashok Kumar Mittal of Concept Publishing Company Pvt Ltd., for readily agreeing to accept my work for publishing.

Mumbai, 30th November, 2010. **M.R. Kolhatkar**

Contents

Abbreviations

AE : Adult Education
AICTE : All India Council for Technical Education
AIIMS : All-India Institute of Medical Sciences
AIU : Association of Indian Universities (formerly IUB)
AMU : Aligarh Muslim University
ASCI : Administrative Staff College of India
AYUSH : Ayurveda, Yoga and Naturopathy, Unani, Siddha and Homoeopathy (previously called ISMH)
aka ; Also known as
BHU : Banaras Hindu University
BITS : Birla Institute of Technology and Science
CABE : Central Advisory Board of Education
CAS : Centre for Advanced Study
CAT : Common Admission Test
CBSE : Central Board of Secondary Education
CCE : Continuous and Comprehensive Evaluation
CDC : Curriculum Development Centre
CIFE : Central Institute of Fishery Education
CIEFL Central Institute of English & Foreign Languages (since renamed CUEFL)
CIIL : Central Institute of Indian Languages
CISCE : Council for Indian School Certificate Examination
COHSSIP : Coordinated Scheme for Humanities and Social Science Improvement Project
COSSIP : Coordinated Scheme for Science Improvement Project
COL : Commonwealth of Learning
CSIR : Council for Scientific and Industrial Research

CSTT	:	Commission for Scientific and Technological Terminology
CUEFL	:	Central University of English and Foreign Languages
CVCP	:	Committee of Vice-Chancellors and Principals
DEC	:	Distance Education Council
DEI	:	Distance Education Institute
DG	:	Director-General
DIET	:	District Institute of Education and Training
DU	:	Deemed University / Delhi University
EAI	:	Eradication of Adult Illiteracy
EB	:	Educationally Backward
EC	:	European Commission / Education Commission
ECCE	:	Early Childhood Care and Education
Ed.Cil	:	Educational Consultants (India) Ltd.
EE	:	Elementary Education
EFA	:	Education for All
EI	:	Educational Institute
EMIS	:	Education and Management Information System
EMRC	:	Educational Media Research Centre
Estd.	:	Established
FREE	:	Forestry Research Education and Extension (Project)
FRI	:	Forest Research Institute
F-YP	:	Five-Year Plan
GATS	:	General Agreement on Trade in Services
GB	:	Governing Body
GER	:	Gross Enrolment Ratio
GoI	:	Government of India
GoM	:	Government of Maharashtra
HEI	:	Higher Education Institute
HEPSN	:	Higher Education for Persons with Special Needs
HRD	:	Human Resource Development
IAMR	:	Institute of Applied Manpower Research
IASSI	:	Indian Association for Social Science Institutes
IARI	:	Indian Agricultural Research Institute
IASE	:	Institute of Advanced Study in Education
ICAE	:	Indian Council of Agricultural Education

ICAR	:	Indian Council of Agricultural Research
ICDS	:	Integrated Child Development Services/Scheme
ICFRE	:	Indian Council for Forestry Education & Research
ICHR	:	Indian Council of Historical Research
ICMR	:	Indian Council of Medical Research
ICPR	:	Indian Council of Philosophical Research
ICSSR	:	Indian Council of Social Science Research
ICT	:	Information and Communication Technology
IES	:	Indian Education Service
IEDC	:	Integrated Education for Disabled Children
IIM	:	Indian Institute of Management
IIP	:	Industry Institute Partnership
IIT	:	Indian Institute of Technology
IIS	:	Indian Institute of Science
IIITM	:	Indian Institute of Information Technology and Management
IIEP	:	International Institute of Educational Planning
IGNOU	:	Indira Gandhi National Open University
ILO	:	International Labour Organization
IMA	:	Indian Management Association / Medical Association
IMF	:	International Monetary Fund
INFLIBNET	:	Information and Library Network
INI	:	Institute of National Importance
ISTE	:	Indian Society for Technical Education
IPR	:	Intellectual Property Rights
ISI	:	Indian Statistical Institute
ISM	:	Indian School of Mines
ISMH	:	Indian Systems of Medicine and Homoeopathy (now called AYUSH)
ISRO	:	Indian Space Research Organization
ITI	:	Industrial Training Institute
IUB	:	Inter University Board
IVRI	:	Indian Veterinary Research Institute
JNU	:	Jawaharlal Nehru University
KOU	:	Kota Open University
KVK	:	Krishi Vigyan Kendra
MoA	:	Memorandum of Association

MoU	:	Memorandum of Understanding
MTA	:	Mid-Term Appraisal (of Five-Year Plan)
NAB	:	National Accreditation Board (of AICTE)
NAC	:	Norms and Accreditation Committee (of ICAR)
NAAC	:	National Assessment and Accreditation Council (of UGC)
NASSDOC	:	National Social Science Documentation Centre (of ICSSR)
NBT	:	National Book Trust
NCC	:	National Cadet Corps
NCERT	:	National Council for Educational Research and Training
NCHE	:	National Council for Higher Education
NCRI	:	National Council for Rural Institutes
NCTE	:	National Council for Teacher Education
NDA	:	National Democratic Alliance (Government) (1998-2004)
NDC	:	National Development Council
NDRI	:	National Dairy Research Institute
NEHU	:	North Eastern Hill University
NER	:	North-Eastern Region
NERIST	:	North Eastern Regional Institute of Science and Technology
NET	:	National Eligibility Test
NEE	:	National Entrance Examination
NF	:	National Front (Government) (1989-1991)
NGO	:	Non-governmental Organization
NIEPA	:	National Institute of Educational Planning and Administration (renamed as NUEPA in 2007)
NIC	:	National Informatics Centre / National Integration Council
NIPER	:	National Institute of Pharmaceutical Education and Research
NITTR	:	National Institute of Technical Teachers' Training and Research
NITIE	:	National Institute of Training in Industrial Engineering
NIT	:	National Institute of Technology (formerly REC)

NIFT	:	National Institute of Fashion Technology
NPE	:	National Policy on Education
NPRC	:	National Policy Review Committee
NUEPA	:	National University for Educational Planning & Administration (formerly NIEPA)
ODL	:	Open and Distance Learning
OU	:	Open University
P/NP	:	Plan/Non-Plan
PC	:	Planning Commission
PEO	:	Programme Evaluation Organization
P-G	:	Post-Graduate
P-GIMER	:	Post-Graduate Institute of Medical Education and Research
PoA	:	Programme of Action
PoER	:	Progress of Education Report (= five-yearly pre-1947 Reports)
QIP	:	Quality Improvement Programme
R & D	:	Research & Development
REC	:	Regional Engineering College
RO	:	Regional Office
s	:	Section (of Act, Bill etc.)
SAP	:	Special Assistance Programme (of UGC)
SAARC	:	South Asian Association for Regional Cooperation
SAU	:	State Agricultural University
SC	:	Supreme Court
SCs	:	Scheduled Castes
SCHE	:	State Council for Higher Education
SCTIMST	:	Sree Chitra Tirunal Institute of Medical Science and Technology
SDHE	:	State Directorate of Higher Education
SEBC	:	Socially and Economically Backward Classes
SET	:	State Eligibility Test (= SLET)
SICI	:	Shastri Indo-Canadian Institute
SLET	:	State Level Eligibility Test (= SET)
SLIET	:	Sant Longowal Institute of Engineering and Technology
SPA	:	School of Planning and Architecture
SPOA	:	State Programme of Action

STs	:	Scheduled Tribes
TA	:	Travelling Allowance
TE-QIP	:	Technical Education—Quality Improvement Programme
TTTI	:	Technical Teachers Training Institute (see also NITTR)
UEE	:	Universalization of Elementary Education
UF	:	United Front (Government) (1996-1998)
U-G	:	Under-Graduate
UGC	:	University Grants Commission (India) / University Grants Committee (UK)
UK	:	United Kingdom
UN/O	:	United Nations/Organization
UNDP	:	United Nations Development Programme
UNESCO	:	United Nations Educational, Scientific and Cultural Organization
UNFPA	:	United Nations Fund for Population Activities
UNICEF	:	United Nations Children Fund
UPA-I	:	United Progressive Alliance (Government) (2004-2009)
UPA II	:	United Progressive Alliance (Government) (2009 onwards)
UPE	:	Universalization of Primary Education
USEFI	:	United States Educational Foundation of India
UT	:	Union Territory
VA	:	Voluntary Association
VE/P	:	Vocational Education/Programme
VO	:	Voluntary Organization
WHO	:	World Health Organization
WIPO	:	World Intellectual Property Organization
WTO	:	World Trade Organization

Index to Frequently Cited Reports

- **Gajendragadkar Report** : Report of the Committee on Governance of Universities and Colleges, Part I – Governance of Universities (UGC, New Delhi, 1971)
- **Gnanam Report** : Report of the UGC Committee : Towards New Educational Management (UGC, New Delhi, 1990)
- **Hartog Report** : Auxiliary Committee Report on Review of Growth of Education in British India, Interim Report of the Indian Statutory Commission (Government of India, Calcutta, September, 1929).
- **Janardhan Reddy Report** : Report of CABE Committee on Policy (Ministry of HRD/Department of Education, Government of India, New Delhi, January 1992)
- **Jha Report** : Report of the Review Committee on the UGC (Ministry of Education and Social Welfare, Government of India, New Delhi, 1977).
- **Kothari Report** : Report of the Education Commission 1964-66 (Ministry of Education, Government of India, New Delhi, 1966) (NCERT Reprint, 1970)
- **Madhuri Shah Report** : Report of the Committee to enquire into the working of the Central Universities (UGC, New Delhi, 1983) [Chairperson Dr. Mrs. Madhuri R. Shah, then Chairman of UGC].
- **Model Act Report** : Report of the UGC Committee on Model Act for Universities (UGC, New Delhi, 1964) [Chairman Prof. D.S. Kothari].
- **Mudaliar Report** : Report of the Secondary Education Commission (Government of India, New Delhi, September 1953).

- **NPE 1968** : National Policy of Education 1968 (Ministry of Education, Government of India, New Delhi, 1968)
- **NPE 1986** : National Policy of Education 1986
- **NPE 1986/92**: National Policy of Education 1986 as modified in 1992 (Ministry of Education, Government of India, New Delhi, 1992)
- **PoA 1986** : Programme of Action, 1986 (Ministry of Education, Government of India, New Delhi, 1986)
- **PoA 1992** : Programme of Action, 1992 (Ministry of Education, Government of India, New Delhi, 1992)
- **Radhakrishnan Report** : Report of University Education Commission (Ministry of Education, Government of India, New Delhi, 1949, Reprint 1983) [Chairman : Dr. S. Radhakrishnan].
- **Ramamurti Report** : Report of the Committee for Review of NPE 1986 – final Report (New Delhi, December 1990). (Entitled : "Toward a More Humane and Enlightened Society").
- **Robbins Report** : Report of the Committee on Higher Education, U.K. (HMSO, London, 1963) [Chairman : Lord Lionel Robbins].
- **Sachar Report** (November 2006) : Report on Social, Economic and Educational Status of the Muslim Community in India (New Delhi, Cabinet Secretariat).
- **Sadler Report** : Report of Calcutta University Commission (Manager, Government Press, Calcutta, 1919). [Chairman : Prof. Michael Sadler].
- **Sapru Report** : Report of the Committee of Members of Parliament on Higher Education (Ministry of Education, Government of India, 1964)
- **Sargent Report/Plan** : Educational Development in India : Report by CABE (Government of India, New Delhi, 1944, Reprint 1964) [Chairman : Sir John Sargent]
- **Sen Committee Report** : Report of the Committee on Governance of Universities and Colleges, Part II – Teachers (1973).

1
Introduction

This introduction is in two parts. The first part is devoted to the methodology. In the second part the literature is reviewed.

Some Considerations of Method: Availability of Sources

This book builds on one strength of the author viz. initial access to original official documents including policy statements, official reports of Committees and Commissions or Task Forces appointed by the Education Ministry and its organizations and at the basic level, the Annual Reports of Ministries, Departments and Organizations. The task of collecting reports after 1993 when the author left the administrative scene has not been easy, even in this "Age of Information Society". Firstly, the reports, even if they are not secret, confidential or "for official use only" are not easy to get since there are no regular outlets for such publications. Secondly, there is a simple unwillingness to help a researcher in our petty bureaucracies, which may also be partly due to incomprehension as to what anyone can do with all that paper-work. Thirdly, the shifts in the academic centre of gravity need to be kept in view. The academic centre of gravity shifted from Western India/Bombay to Calcutta from about 1858 and quite decisively it further shifted by 1920 to the North, e.g. Allahabad and, after Independence to Delhi. Calcutta, being the Capital of India till 1911 had till then an upper hand in the matter of intellectual resources (both manpower and physical facilities). Even now, it houses the National Library. But Delhi is now the academic as well as the political capital of India in terms of the repository of books and journals and the habitat of scholars. NIEPA/NUEPA and AIU libraries in Delhi have no peers in Mumbai and Pune, so far as holdings of educational books and documents are concerned. Fourthly, the authoritarian regimes tend to suppress or distort history by keeping valuable source material out of the reach of scholars, as happened during the Stalinist period of the Soviet Union. After the Cold War, the history of Soviet Union could be re-written and revised because closed archives became available. Nearer home, it is well documented by scholars like Granville Austin (1999) and Ramachandra Guha (2007), that some official documents of the Janata period (1977-79) have been weeded out by the subsequent regime. Fifthly, Government of India has no thirty-year or any policy at all about official records, so that the National Archives reportedly do not have educational files beyond 1953 for use of the scholars. The basic point is that for various reasons, the scholars based in places in India other than Delhi, who wish to attempt to write a connected narrative history based on authentic official documents are seriously handicapped and even Delhi-based scholars could face officially erected hurdles.

Given the availability of documents, the next point is that you should be inclined to use them and you should also be astute enough to know how to use them. Not all authors who may be lucky to have such sources in ample measure possess these qualities. Take, for example, the official histories of Indian Education written under the auspices of the UGC, viz. by Kuldeep Kaur (2003) and Kavita Sharma (2003). Two simple examples will suffice. The former author erred in listing out the regional offices of the UGC by stating that the Northern regional office of the UGC is located at Gaziabad [on the strength of the authority of an author called Sharma Shaloo (2002)], whereas a reference to the relevant Annual Report of the UGC would have shown that the UGC had long ago shifted it to its own office, calling it the Northern Regional Bureau. Kavita Sharma refers to a report of a Government of India Committee on Training of Educational Administrators. She concludes the para by saying that the report was placed before the Commission on 23-2-1993 who accepted it in principle (K. Sharma, 2003: 203-04). But a curious reader would like to know as to what happened to the report. Kavita Sharma does not say it but obviously nothing happened because there is no institution (as recommended by the committee) on the ground. It is a matter of surmise, however, that any follow-up action would be reported in some subsequent report from 1994-95 onwards. And having done my own investigation and being lucky, I found in the UGC Annual Report for 1996-97 *vide* pp. 9-10, this gem of information:

> "The Commission appointed a sub-committee to consider the report which accepted the suggestions in principle and recommended that the nodal institute should be set up u/section 12(ccc) of the UGC Act."

The report goes on to say that there were second thoughts and it was felt that considering the number of non-teaching staff, a single centre may not suffice. Moreover, this single centre would be cost-intensive. Hence, planning and consultation had commenced. Till 2010, no such Centre/Institute has come up.

It should be evident that the use of available materials involves some element of sleuthing which might unearth some hitherto unknown facts. For example, G.D. Sharma, a colleague of Dr. Amrik Singh who later joined the NIEPA happened to be Secretary, UGC during the period 1996-99. He appears to have adopted a very open academic-friendly system of reporting. I report elsewhere that the detailed information regarding Regional Offices of the UGC is available only in the Annual Report 1996-97 of the UGC, which was the first year of G.D. Sharma's tenure. However, subsequent UGC Annual Reports do not give the information about Regional Offices, for reasons which one can only guess at high-level opposition, constraint of space, etc. *The fact remains that there is no escape from diligent and intelligent use of available documentation.* But given all these, one cannot excuse failure of authors like Kuldeep Kaur and Kavita Sharma who had ample availability of not only Annual Reports but as Kavita Sharma's book amply illustrates, "access to the agenda and the minutes of the proceedings of the periodical meetings of the UGC, various reports of the UGC committees and perhaps internal memoranda."

Political Dynamics and Dialectics of Policy-Making

I have adopted the method of close reading of the texts in analyzing reports and policy statements, which, in its turn, leads to the momentous finding that on one level the official reports and documents are part of an on-going dialogue among educational thinkers, e.g. Radhakrishnan, Kothari, Ramamurti, etc. and at a slightly lower level, part of a politico-administrative exchange between competing sides. The official documents are required to be read in the context of this background and it is required to be noted that policies which evolve are a resultant of a give-and-take among policy-makers. If the user of documents, though otherwise well-informed, is innocent of the above aspects, then the following types of mistakes can be committed. Thus, in the context of the the New Education Policy, Kavita Sharma talks of a Task Force being appointed under Chairmanship of Ramamurti (K. Sharma: 162) to implement Plan of Action for NPE. This statement is 'quite eroneous'. The sequence of events was as below: Rajiv Gandhi Government formulated the NPE 1986 along with its Programme of Action of the same year. It was to be reviewed optionally at the end of five years, i.e. in 1991. In 1989, after the defeat of the Congress Party, National Front Government under V.P. Singh came to power and appointed the Ramamurti Committee for review of the NPE 1986 (NPRC), even before the expiry of five years because the National Front Government considered Rajiv Gandhi Government's policy as too centralized and elitist and, in particular, was opposed to the Rural Public Schools called 'Navodaya Vidyalaya' Schools which had become part of the NPE 1986. The V.P. Singh Government, after appointing Rammamurti Review Committee, fell in 1990, without completing its term and after a brief spell of Chandra Shekhar as the Prime Minister, general elections were held and the new Congress Government under P.V. Narasimha Rao appointed the Janardan Reddy Committee called "CABE Committee on Policy" to review the Ramamurti Report which had in the meanwhile submitted its Report. The Reddy Committee's agenda was somehow to justify and retain the NPE 1986. It said that the NPE 1986 required no revision but only a few modifications but a new Programme of Action was required in the light of changed circumstances. Now, we have NPE 1986 as modified in 1992 with a new updated PoA 1992 (in place of PoA 1986) and in spite of protestations to the contrary, some decentralization did take place, e.g. in terms of the Ramamurti Committee recommendations, the Regional Offices of the UGC came up from 1994 onwards. Unless the scholar talking about NPE 1986/92 is acquainted with the political developments, and with the way Ramamurti ideas seeped into the NPE 1992, she/he can trip-up and in the process make herself/himself look absurd as pointed out by me.

There can, of course, be paradigmatic shifts of policy, as a result, e.g. of transformation of international scene. This happened at the end of Secand World War (1945) when the Western imperialism got weakened leading to the liberation of colonies or in 1989-90 when the world communism collapsed or in September-October 2008 when owing to financial distress in the USA, which is still a major player in a multi-polar world, there is an onset of what appears to be world recession and one begins to talk of the Return of Marx and Mao, as Samir Amin did in his lecture in Mumbai on 20th November, 2008 on the topic of "Beyond Liberal Capitalism in Crisis: A Socialist Perspective on the 21st Century" [*Times of India* (Mumbai Edition), 21st November, 2008].

The Pitfalls of writing Contemporary History

It may also be pointed out that in surveying higher education up to 2007 or beyond one is writing "Contemporary History", which is more difficult to write than history written at a distance of, say, more than two generations. Ramchandra Guha (2008) has recently written about the challenges of this genre. He has identified three pitfalls, viz. the scarcity of sources, the reader's prejudices and the writer's prejudices respectively. I have already written about the problem of sources and other difficulties would be evident in course of time. I have pointed out, e.g. that the Government of India archives of post-1953 period are closed to scholars and the Government Departments are reluctant to part with material. Ramachandra Guha has suggested tapping alternative sources, but above all, he has emphasized the need for writing India's contemporary history from a variety of perspectives calling it a growth area of the future—he has listed political, social, feminist, environmental, urban, agrarian, film, literary histories and many others that cry to be written. He has not written about educational history of the contemporary India, but that is implicit in his enumeration. He has also drawn a dividing line at the Emergency when contemporary history could be said to begin. I have similarly followed a bipartite divide ending at 1980 while writing about the

UGC. The point is that educational history of modern India is required to be perceived as part of a bigger enterprise of writing the master narrative of contemporary India to which mine is a small, but what, I believe, would be a vital contribution.

A 'New' Contemporary History of Higher Education

S.C. Ghosh, the JNU historian, has said that it is time, Indian educational historians began to write in the style of the New History. Apparently he had in mind 'Annalist' school of French historians. It would be worthwhile if I spell out what is meant by New History in the words of one of its leading practitioners, Peter Burke. He has argued (1997) that 'Old' and 'New' History differs in seven key levels of interpretation of the discipline:

- History of the traditional paradigm is concerned with politics; the new history, which has come to be concerned with virtually every area of the human activity, is not.
- Traditional historians think of history as essentially a narrative of events; although new historians do not entirely dismiss the narrative form, greater weight is given to structures than was previously the case.
- Traditional historians focus on 'a view from above, concentrated on the great deeds of great men', whereas new historians favour 'history from below', the view of the common person.
- Traditional History revolves around documents (empiricism); new historians however approach the history from the viewpoint that historians concerned with a greater variety of human activities, must examine a greater variety of evidence.
- Traditional approaches fail to account for the variety of questions which historians must ask, whereas new history does not.
- Traditional paradigm posits that history is objective and focuses upon the all-powerful voice of the author (the historian) in articulating the past. New historians, however, are concerned less with objectivity, while the range of approaches and needs covered in the history have resulted

in a move from the 'Voice History' to one of 'heteroglossia', (varied and opposing voices).

- Traditional history is hermetically sealed as a distinct disciplinary work, whereas the new history is inter/multi-disciplinary in approach and attitudes.

The third type of new history listed by Burke is obviously illustrated by what is called the subaltern stream of political history which is made current by Ranjit Guha in Australia and his followers. I am not aware of its examples in Indian education but the first type of educational history which focuses on 'the social' aspect of education is well illustrated by Aparna Basu in her *Growth of Education and Political Development in India (1898-1920) (1974)* (New Delhi, OUP). In her manifesto, 'Towards a new History of Indian Education', she says that in India, the history of education has mostly been concerned with descriptive accounts of the system of education activities as it has developed over the years, on government policy resolutions, Education Commission Reports, Acts and Charter.

She illustrates Naik and Nurullah as the best and most comprehensively written. She states that this type of history of education is written within a binary framework of (a) Government *vs*. Private, (b) Indigenous *vs*. Western, and (c) Imperialistic vs. National. It also introduces periodization of modern educational history. She feels that more use of private sources could lead to a more complete picture of the course of educational development. She advocates an inter-disciplinary approach with use of tools of economics, sociology, psychology and political science. She cites her own book as an example. Earlier, she had also referred to new models of educational history written in the West, by use of social material.

What Aparna Basu says is unexceptionable and doable. But there are a few caveats. What she says applies to history proper as distinguished from contemporary history. The only example of social science analysis being brought to bear on contemporary higher Indian education I can think of is Rudolphs (1972)* except that it is only

---

* Rudolph & Rudolph: *Education and Politics in India: Studies in Organised Society and Politics* (New Delhi, OUP).

partially contemporary. The title underlines the fact that the authors are concerned to bring to bear approaches of political science on the broad canvas of education and not merely higher education. The first part consisting of 80 pages is the core part, the other chapters being case studies or dealing with the colonial period. The author's conclusion at the end of first part is as below: (pp. 79-80) "The formulation and implementation of national policy for higher education in a federal system that places primary responsibility for education in the hands of the States, in the face of very limited resources, and in the context of tradition of laws that protect academic freedom and university autonomy, has been difficult, extremely complex, and tenuous in its results. Bargaining and persuasion within and between levels of public authorities and between public authorities and educational authorities has given some direction and coherence to higher education; at the same time, it must be recognized that the growth and content of higher education have been the result of a massive set of political demands and private initiatives of authoritative decisions and allocations from government based on clear priorities and strategies".

Secondly, Basu omits to mention that *in the West, there is a huge corpus of narrative history which serves as a point of departure for the authors of social history who give new interpretation of narrative history.* This applies to Western Europe (including UK) and the USA. There are institutional, university and systemic histories of American and British education and building on this corpus as a foundation they are being interpreted by tools of sociology, political science, anthropology, and economics, etc. which furnish new insights.

In India, however, the situation is curious. There is Nurullah and Naik of 1951 and a shorter edition of 1974, Naik and Nurullah but those books have not been revised. Aparna Basu's book (1984) is an attempt in the direction of a social history of a period long past. There are no contemporary histories, however, Indian education of any stage or branch—elementary, secondary, higher, or medical, agricultural etc. But our social scientists only superficially acquainted with the discourse analysis of a Continental theorist like Foucault, making a departure from the methods of analysis and interpretation advocated by Aparna Basu, go forth like Don Quixote, but lacking this basic corpus, even an intelligent reader finds it difficult to make sense of them. In this background, I wish to say that I have written a politico-administrative type of contemporary history of Indian Higher Education with a glance towards the 'social'. Thus, I have used Rekha Kaul's analysis of the phenomenon of capitation fee colleges of Karnataka, but I have avoided the post-colonialist or post-modernist jargon. I should not be understood to mean that the jargon is all there is to authors* who resort to Foucauldian approach; only that I do not tread that path and in my view, premature theorization in Indian history is not likely to be fruitful. There has to be a middle ground between the sophistication of Nita Kumar and mindless trot of authors like Kuldeep Kaur and Kavita Sharma**. I hope to occupy that ground.

Review of Literature

In Western countries and especially in the U.S. (with which India is required to be compared—both are vast and variegated nations with a federal form of government), history of higher education is an established discipline. In the U.S., Frederick Rudolph's book, *American College and University: A History*, is a landmark. His history is dated but his debt is acknowledged by his successors among whom may be mentioned the authors listed in the Annexure to this chapter. As pointed out by Frederick Rudolph, histories of higher education have been contributed by historians, by educationists, by Government bodies and by philanthropic foundations in the US like the Carnegie Commission on Higher Education and the Carnegie Council for Policy Studies in Higher Education.

The Indian Scene: The Curriculum of Education Faculty as Culprit

Thanks to the vicissitudes of curriculum framing in Indian universities, the B.Ed./M.Ed. courses in the post-Independence India apparently dispensed with historical foundations of Education, focusing instead on psychological foundations. The curriculum issued by the UGC in

---

* An example is Nita Kumar (2000, 2007).

** "My observations about these authors are illlustraive and should not be misunderstood as strictures. They had obviously to work against impossibly tight deadlines."

2001 for example under the theory Paper No. 3 for B.Ed. refers to history under the vague title-heading: "Development of Educational System in India". For the M.Ed., there is no compulsory paper on History of Education. Under special papers, the following subjects appear: (E) Comparative Education, (K) Management, Planning and Financing of Education. Thrust areas include: L.P.G. (Liberalization, Privatization and Globalization). Evidently, History of Education is not regarded as a foundational subject.

Review of Literature: Institutional Histories

Since there is no tradition of historiography of higher education in India, the treatment and coverage given to the topic of higher education in Modern India in general education histories, whether written by educationists or by historians has tended to be sketchy. Since the history-writing tradition is weak, the building blocks like institutional histories are also few. As examples may be mentioned the following:

- Centenary histories of three metropolitan universities—S.R. Dongerkery (1957) (Bombay (Now Mumbai)), University of Madras (Now Chennai) (1957) and Calcutta (Now Kolkata) University (1957).
- A Silver Jubilee history of University of Poona written by W.H. Golay (1974).
- A History of Punjab University (R.R. Seth and J.L. Mehta, 1968) (This is for 20 years).
- A 15-year Historical Survey of JNU (1986).
- A Centenary History of the Allahabad University written by M.L. Bhargava (1987).

Only the Bombay (Now Mumbai) University issued a Post-Centenary Golden Jubilee history *vide* Aroon Tikekar (2006) which was really an updated revision of the Post-Centenary Silver Jubilee history written in 1984. The AIU brought out special issues in 2007-2008 dealing with the three metropolitan universities hardly a substitute for regular histories.

The Textbooks: Educationists and Historians

The standard history of education in India is that by Nurullah and Naik (1943; 1951), who were educationists which, however, does not cover the post-Independence period Chapter 12 of "A Students' History of Education in India" (1974) by Naik/Nurullah dealing with post-1947 period is about of 75 pages of which 15 pages are devoted to higher education (pp. 430-441 and 468-472) with a 7-page annexure which gives a summary of the recommendations of Education Commission. This treatment is not at all adequate.

Let us next consider his treatment of the topics relating to higher education in J.P. Naik's last masterpiece (1982, reprinted in 1997). It is rather cursory and vague. Thus, on the topic of adoption of regional language as medium of instruction at higher education stage, he states: "The scheme for promoting literature in Indian languages has made differential progress, in different languages. It is necessary to evaluate the progress made so far and there is a fear that it may not present an all too bright a picture" (p. 84). On the topic of creation of five or six major universities and the related sub-topic of 'Centres of Advanced Study', he states that it did not find favour either with politicians or with academicians, but there is no review at all of developments in the period 1966-1979 and his short comment is: "During the past 12 years, even the idea of the 'Centre of Advanced Study' has lost the prestige and glamour it had in 1966" (pp. 134-138). In the two concluding chapters of the book, (Chapter 9: "Continuing Education Crisis" and Chapter 10: "Lessons for the Future") which account for 63 pages, the pages devoted to higher education are about 9 (pp. 193-198 and pp. 230-244). He says that the recommendations of the Education Commission were not radical enough, and his observations in the latter chapter are almost a cry of despair: "There is a first-rate crisis of management in the universities which are not even able to do their routine jobs like holding examinations in time and wherein the basic educational process itself comes to a grinding halt all too frequently" (p. 84). The famous Part VII in the National Policy on Education (1986) about 'Making the system work' meaning that all teachers should teach and all students should study might well be said to prescribe the solution for the crisis identified by Naik.

In historian Suresh Chandra Ghosh's book *The History of Education in Modern India (1757-1986)*, only one chapter is devoted to post-Independence period, viz. Chapter 18 (pp. 174-191). The revised edition which brings the story up to 2000, has a new Chapter 19 called 'the Critical years' which contains 30 pages.

Till about 1980, it was more common to describe Indian higher education in terms of discrete institutions like universities and colleges. In this tradition may be listed the following books: Robert L. Gaudino (1965): *The Indian University* (Bombay, Popular Prakashan) and Champa Tickoo (1980): *Indian Universities: A Historical, Comparative Perspective* (Bombay, Orient Longman). Gaudino, when he wrote the book, was based in Williams College in the USA and his book appears to have been written to explain the Indian University as an institution to the Americans. Tickoo's book is based on the author's doctoral dissertation for the University of London written in 1968. Tickoo says that Indian higher education system is characterized by "drift and disjointed incrementalism". The book claims to make students as a focus of its study, but again, it is not historically oriented.

Publications of Government or Semi-government Institutions

University Grants Commission (UGC)

UGC, at one time, used to have an active publications branch which used to bring out Reports of various Committees appointed by it. For some reason, it stopped this activity and, at present, the main work of the branch is to bring out Annual Reports of UGC and brochures about individual schemes. On the occasion of Golden Jubilee of India's Independence (1997) UGC brought out a Commemorative Volume on *Indian Universities: Toward Nation Building* (R.P. Singh (Ed.) 1998). It is seen that letters were sent to 224 universities requesting for write-ups on their contribution to national development since Independence. Seventy-three universities responded and the editor selected write-ups of 27 universities of which 17, i.e. two-thirds are Central Universities or Institutions of national importance, one exception being BITs Pilani. On the occasion of its Golden Jubilee, UGC commissioned two major publications on (1) a history of higher education in India (1781-2003), and (2) Fifty Years of UGC which, as pointed out earlier, are not up to the mark.

The ex-Chairmen/Vice-Chairmen/Secretaries have not written about UGC except C.D. Deshmukh (1974), the first Chairman of the UGC. Apart from referring to his decision to use UGC funds to improve pay-scales of college teachers, the autobiography mentions that the Government of India was not happy with his work and after his superannuation, he took over as the Vice-Chancellor of Delhi University. Madhuri Shah, Chairperson UGC in the period 1981-1986 has been interviewed by her biographers after one year and a few months in her career but she does not say much though she praises the capabilities of R.K. Chhabra, the then Secretary UGC (Suresh Dalal, 1995). One former Secretary of the UGC, K.L. Joshi has written two books in 1977 and 1981 respectively about higher education. In the 1977 book (at p. 266) he has opined that the British-type UGC has not functioned effectively and he has suggested a Soviet-type of Ministry of Higher Education in which UGC should be merged.

Association of Indian Universities (AIUs)

AIU is an NGO but financially assisted by the Ministry of Education. When Amrik Singh was its Secretary-General, AIU brought out a number of publications relating to "examination reforms" and 'Economics of Education' authored respectively by Dr. V. Natarajan and Dr. G.D. Sharma. Its publications in economics of education and related areas are listed in the Annexure. Under S.K. Agrawala, as Secretary-General, AIU brought out a monograph on the dismissal of the Vice-Chancellors. AIU also brought out its Golden Jubilee Institutional History in 1975, updated it to 1985 and further updated it to 2002. Under Prof. K.B. Powar as Secretary-General, AIU publication wing remained active and began to bring out collections of articles in its weekly newsletter, though the quality of some of these books left a lot to be desired. The collected articles of K.B. Powar (2002) under the title of Indian Higher Education are interesting for the sub-title ("a conglomeration of concepts, facts and practices") which appears to contest the existence of any higher education system in India.

National Council of Educational Research & Training (NCERT)

NCERT was an organization devoted to research and training in school education, but, in initial years, it interpreted its mandate quite imaginatively and began to bring out Yearbooks of Education. While a majority was devoted to school education, one is devoted to Research and another (not a year book) publication is devoted to costs and resources having a bearing on higher education. Moreover, its successive surveys of research in education of which the 6th Survey was published in 2001 deat with topics in higher education.

National Book Trust (NBT)

NBT has brought out (2005) a book on Education in India (authors: Padma Ramachandran and Vasantha Ramkumar). Its leading author is a retired IAS Officer with experience in training and the second author is an educator. It devotes about 52 out of 391 pages to higher education including professional education. Unfortunately, it relies rather heavily on Kuldip Kaur (2003) and on different plan documents and miscellaneous sources for its contents, so that there is a lack of consistency. Thus autonomous colleges and 'deemed universities' are dealt with in the same breath (p. 206, *Ibid.*). A long sentence about Secondary Education Commission and another about craftsmen training interrupts the flow of the narrative of technical education (pp. 221 and 228, *Ibid.*). There is heavy reliance on Kerala examples, perhaps because the lead author is from Kerala (pp. 212 and 233, *Ibid.*). The contents are unfortunately marred by factual inaccuracies. IIT Roorke is wrongly called IIT Kharagpur (p. 288). The Agricultural Research Institute at Pusa in Bihar (p. 235) was long back shifted to Delhi and is known as IARI. There was no single Indo-American Joint Commission for Agricultural Education and Research (p. 236), but two joint teams which reported in 1955 and 1960 respectively. The name of the famous agricultural scientist Borlaug is miss-spelt (p. 239). Not only IARI but also NDRI, IVRI (and also Central Fisheries Institute at Bombay (Now Mumbai)) are deemed universities (p. 241). There is no Central Council of Indigenous Medicine (p. 248) but a Central Council of Indian Medicine. There is a general paragraph on Universities on p. 150 in which there are a lot of factual mistakes including that IIMs, IISc., Bangalore, IARI, Delhi and Gujarat Vidyapeeth are wrongly stated to be statutory universities. As a matter of fact, IIMs are run by registered societies and the rest are deemed universities. Also, the book published in 2005 gives old (1997-98) data about the number of universities. Generally, therefore, the authors of the book lack sure-footedness implying lack of the mastery of sources.

Indian Institute of Advanced Studies (IIAS) Shimla

IIAS, Shimla is a centre of advanced research under the Education Ministry, comparable to the one at Princeton in the USA (best known for giving habitat to Einstein). Under V.K. Gokak as Director, it organized a Seminar on 'Management and Organisation of Indian Universities' and published it under the same name (S.C. Malik (Ed.), 1971). It contains many interesting articles. We come to know about Delhi-centrist UGC which sanctioned the first school of correspondence courses and continuing education for Delhi University in 1962 (p. 25, *Ibid.*). There are other interesting articles. The book also reproduces Amartya Sen's well-known Lal Bahadur Shastri Memorial Lecture of March 1970 on 'Crisis in Indian Education', where he stated provocatively that the right to higher education is the right of the educationally privileged to study further which is exercised by throwing children out of schools (p. 259), but also famously praised UGC for having *established standards of devoted work, efficient operation and un-bureaucratic promptness of a kind that is entirely rare in India* (quoted in S.C. Malik (Ed.) (1971). Subsequently, IIAS brought out (1974) J.N. Kaul's *Higher Education in India, 1951-71: Two Decades of Planned Drift*. It has subsequently (in 1975) brought out a volume called '*Higher Education and National Development*'.

NIEPA/NUEPA

NIEPA, though it is a multi-purpose body, is perhaps the most prolific source of research publications on higher education. It brings out occasional papers on financing of various sub-sectors of education. In 1983-85, it served as a Secretariat for the National Commission on Teachers II (Higher Education), chaired by Prof. Rais Ahmed. It produced 11 Monographs on a variety of issues of teacher education as listed in the Annexure. NIEPA did a lot of work for National Policy on Education (1986). Moonis Raza, ex-Director NIEPA, subsequently edited a volume on higher education in India on the occasion of the Conference of Vice-Chancellors of Commonwealth Universities held in New Delhi in 1991, which is remarkable for its analytical rigour. A notable publication earlier edited by Moonis Raza was on educational planning. It contains 19 articles some of them by foreign experts, presented at a UNESCO Conference held in 1982. Although issues of higher education planning were not specifically addressed, the articles on man-power planning and on technological forecasting bear on higher education. A Mathew's *(1990) organizational history of the Ministry of Education* deals *inter alia* with UGC and AICTE and propounds interesting hypotheses regarding promotional, institutionalization and guidance strategies followed by the Education Ministry. Its limitation is that its data are up to 1980 only.

The Volume edited by J. Veera Raghavan (1985) had many contributors from NIEPA including the editor, Moonis Raza and Y.P. Agarwal. It reflected thinking about the issues of higher education prior to the NPE 1986. The same can be said about Issues in *Development of Colleges: Quality and Resource Aspects* (1983) (New Delhi, Academic Foundation) compiled by an association with which G.D. Sharma, then based in NIEPA was associated.

Since then NIEPA has issued several publications including those on deemed universities, review of implementation of National Policy on Education 1986-92, globalization, even a compilation of articles published in its journal edited by J.B.G. Tilak etc. but the quality of some of the publications, e.g. on deemed universities and on educational policies (2002) has been not up to the mark. (The author has pointed out a major lapse *vide* p. 329 of Chapter 13).

Other Compilations

In the absence of a strong historiographical tradition in the field, the literature on higher education by non-Government publishers has tended to be edited compilations by multiple authors. Such publications first made their appearance in the 1960s, in the context of or consequent on the Education Commission of 1964. The Bombay (Now Mumbai) editors and publishers dominated the field initially, may be, because of the presence of authors like **A.B. Shah** of the Congress for Cultural Freedom (CCF). The volume edited by Shah in 1962 on a National University was published in the backdrop of language agitation in 1960 and thereafter. The subsequent volume on higher education was inspired by the Report of the Education Commission. Amrik Singh, as Secretary of the IUB makes an appearance here with a highly critical article on the universities and government in which he does not spare Dr. D.S. Kothari, Chairman, UGC. A.B. Shah's volume is not India centric. D.D. Karve writes on Indian Universities and India's Science Policy is also discussed. The Appendix contains Edward Shils' article on *On the Improvement of Indian Higher Education* (pp. 475-499).

Prof. D.M. Desai from Baroda has written (1970) *Some Critical Issues of Higher Education in India* (Bombay, A.R. Seth). This book written by a seasoned educationist does not have a historical focus. Another book of the old-world stamp is, B.D. Srivastava's *Development of Modern Indian Education* (1961) (Calcutta, Orient Longman, 2nd Edn.).

In the 1970s onwards, the centre of gravity of academic writing about higher education can be said to have decisively shifted to the North and especially to Delhi. As a harbinger of the trend, we have a jointly edited volume of **Amrik Singh and Philip Altbach** (1974) which has arranged the discussion on the problems of Higher Education under the following headings: (1) Structure and Governance, (2) Financial Aspects, (3) Education as Investment, (4) Students and Teachers, (5) language, (6) Examinations, (7) Reforms, (8) Science and Higher Education, and (9) Case Studies. Amrik Singh writes on examinations, Samuel Mathai, Secretary UGC, writes on UGC, Philip Altbach writes on Student Politics and on the problems of university reforms, Edward Shils writes on Academic profession in India and Suma Chitins on Teachers. The book's title evokes memory of the American Sociologist **Thorstein Veblen's** *Higher Learning in America.*

An exception to the shift to the North is a five volume publication with funding by IDRC, Canada edited by **P.R. Panchamukhi**. Although published in 1990, the first and the last volume are devoted respectively to an overview and to economics of education. The rest of the volumes contain 31 articles of which 8 are devoted to higher education topics (including an article on NIEPA in Vol. II by G.D. Sharma, an article on "Examination Reforms" in Vol. IV by V. Natarajan and three case-studies of SNDT, Poona and Agricultural and Rural Universities).

The period 1975-1985 incidentally coinciding with Emergency and its aftermath was bereft of any significant publications in higher education. The dry spell was broken by two books of **Amrik Singh**, one dealing with his Vice-Chancellorship of the Punjabi University, Patiala (1984); and the other containing a collection of articles (1985). The latter book was divided into three parts: Part I—The Baby-sitting Syndrome; Part II—Towards Restructuring and Part III—On Teachers and Teaching and wrapped up by a Conclusion. This book is representative of Amrik Singh's thought on higher education holding the educational establishment including the UGC and the teachers responsible for the ills of the higher education system. This is a plausible diagnosis which is stated and vindicated. At the time it was written, it needed courage to articulate the view point.

Amrik Singh and G.D. Sharma brought out two compilations in 1988 and 1989 respectively dealing with institutional and social contexts, containing analytical pieces on diverse topics, some of them quite old. J.P. Naik wrote on 'Education Commission and After', Amrik Singh's article on 'Foundation and Role of UGC' was originally written in 1981. His earlier article on 'Redeeming Higher Education' (1985) was republished here. Two authors were from Government. The social context book was divided into parts like: (1) Education and Development, (2) Towards Social Justice, (3) Management Dimension, and (4) Resources and Planning. The institutional context book was concerned with narrower academic issues: Relevance and Excellence, Teaching Profession (the Academics), The Student Body, The Dimensions of Governance and Towards Productivity. Amrik Singh in his article: "The Last Two Decades" (pp. 91-131), in the 1989 volume gives a potted history of higher education for the period 1973-1987.

The World Bank Seminar based volume edited by **Philip Altbach and Suma Chitnis** (1993), containing 12 articles, six on: Policy Perspectives and six Case Studies, is perhaps the best one. The policy perspectives include Financing (J.B.G. Tilak), Language Question

(N. Jayaraman), Access (Karuna Chanana), Examination Reforms (Mathew Zachariah) and Coordinating Agencies in Higher Education (Amrik Singh). The case studies include Scientific Research (B.M. Udgaonkar), Extension (D. Saldanha/P. Velaskar), College Development Councils (J. Indiresan), IITs (P.V. Indiresan and N.C. Nigam), The Open University (V.C. Kuldandai Swamy) and a concluding chapter by Suma Chitnis. The Altbach/Chitnis volume was weak on internal management issues and this was made up by a volume edited by **M.V. Mathur** *et al.* (1994). This contains 43 pieces, some of them all too brief. The notable contributions are by Bikas Sanyal of IIEP, Paris (Perspectives on University Management), S.K. Agrawala of AIU on Code of Professional Ethics and R.C. Mehrotra on Revision of Pay-scales of Teachers in Retrospect. That Altbach/Chitnis and Mathur/Arora/Sogani volumes represent the latest and best thoughts on higher education is attested by the fact that articles in these two volumes are lifted bodily, but without acknowledgement, in a recent compilation (Shaloo Sharma, 2002), apparently plagiarized (vide *University News* issue dated 3rd October, 2005).

NPE 1986 and PoA 1992, two major government documents are not reflected in these writings apparently because of usual publication scheduling problems. Moreover, their implementation has been affected by the agenda of LPG (Liberalization, Privatization and Globalization) consequent on the structural adjustment programme of the Government of India in 1991.

The critique of this agenda is incorporated in the volume edited by **S.C. Shukla** (1993), which however, does not specifically deal with higher education. The Shukla edited volume examines the consequences of colonial policy of education and why education has failed to act as an agent of social change and why there is disillusion since the 1990s. The second editor of the volume is well-known for her critique of phenomenon of capitation fees of professional colleges in Karnataka. **Sabyasachi Bhattacharya** edited volume called *Contested Terrain* (1998), contains articles on the colonial policy by a galaxy of contributors including S.C. Shukla, Aparna Basu, Amrik Singh, Nita Kumar, Poromesh Acharya, Uma Das Gupta, Deepak Kumar, B.R. Tomlinson and S. Irfan Habib. The only exception is an article on "Education in China in Modern Times". **Anirudh Prasad** a lawyer has written on University Education Administration and the

Law (2000) in which he has exposed the malpractices in several universities in UP including Gorakhpur.

Amrik Singh (2004)(a) volume is a compilation of 12 articles between 1974 and 2004. The Chapter 1 on 'Foundation and Role of the UGC' (1981) and Chapter 10, 'The Indian UGC'(1974) contain identical matter, the latter containing the scholarly apparatus of notes. The Chapter 5, the 'Reconstitution of UGC', originally published in Economic and Political Weekly in August 1970, in fact deals with a version of UGC Bill which was superseded as the Act was finally amended in 1972. The reference to whole-time Members of the UGC in addition to Chairman (p. 105) is anachronistic because the proposal was dropped subsequently and the 1972 amendment provided only for a full time Vice-Chairman and not other full-time member. The Chapter 2 (other professional bodies) is a revised version of author's contribution to Altbach/Chitnis volume of 1993. In Chapter 4, 'the Centre State Business', the author refers to State-level UGCs, but does not take note of the new body called State Council for Higher Education (SCHE) which is part of NPE 1986/PoA 1992. The 1984(b) volume is not a compilation of old pieces but a *de novo* publication. Its focus is on open universities and on technical education apart from some topics on school education. The author is critical of IGNOU and AICTE, appreciative of the role of NAAC and takes note of the new initiative of SCHE and says on p. 161 that they should be autonomous.

This review may be concluded by referring to two pieces of literature, published under auspices of international organizations. The first book (1965) is a National Study of Indian Universities done by **K.G. Saiyidin**, the then Adviser (Education), Government of India for UNESCO. It brings out the acceleration in the rate of increase in enrolment in higher education which was unprecedented. The second book by **G.D. Sharma** (1986), entitled "*Equity, Quality and Cost in Higher Education: A Case Study of India*" is written in a comparative framework of South Korea and Australia. Its concluding remarks are worth quoting as they sum up the plight of Post-Independence Higher Education in India:

> "Efforts have been made to promote equity; yet the equity does not seem to be within reach. Quality is recognized as the prime

requisite; however, attempts to improve quality are below the desired level. Increasing resource inputs are being provided but they continue to elude a critical minimum level. Broadly the state of affairs affirms that the slow and soft option approach has been adopted to tackle the issue of equity, quality and efficiency…".

Bibliographies and Encyclopaedias

Moonis Raza and Nirmal Malhotra brought out a comprehensive bibliography of Higher Education in India (New Delhi, Concept, 1991). It was published almost twenty years back and its entries do not go beyond 1990. NUEPA may be expected to bring it up-to-date. The available encyclopaedias of higher education except by Shakdhar of JNU apparently are commercial publications and cannot be called academic.

To sum up this Review was meant to establish the basic point that a comprehensive and critical survey of Higher Education in India in the post-Independence India is a desideratum and remains to be written till date. The succeeding Chapters would attempt the task.

The Bibliographic Annexure (pp. 29-31) contains in alphabetical order, titles of book-clusters, which are also listed in the Review of Literature.

A Note on the Organization of the Book

It can verily be claimed that this book is the first single-handed comprehensive and critical survey of higher education in modern India. The term comprehensive is used to convey that the book deals not only with higher general but also higher professional education. The colonial accounts of education (QRPE = Quinquennial Reviews of Progress of Education) invariably covered both these aspects. Unfortunately, in the post-Independence period, a divide built up amongst these branches and in particular, while engineering/ management education and teacher education continued with the Education Ministry, the Ministries of Health, Law, Agriculture and Environment and Forests dealing respectively with Medical, Legal, Agricultural and Forestry education continued to plough a lonely furrow. There is one redeeming feature that the UGC in its institutional statistics includes all universities and colleges (medical, legal and agricultural). The Kothari Commission dealt with agricultural education but was precluded by its Terms of Reference from dealing with the medical and legal education. The point is that this survey covers all these branches of higher education which have a synergy and is comprehensive in that sense.

The Introduction is followed by the Historical Background and then the author deals with Higher General Education and Research in six chapters of which four are devoted to the UGC including one on organizations allied to UGC like AIU, the NAAC, the DEC and NIEPA. The first chapter is a general chapter and the last chapter is devoted to Research Councils. The next five chapters deal with professional education in all its branches. The last three chapters deal with specific issues including medium of instruction, financing, overall coordination of higher education and the proposals of the National Knowledge Commission and the Yashpal Committee which are so much in the news now-a-days.

The review of literature may appear to skip the literature relating to Technical/Professional education. This is because there are very few general treatments of these subjects. The Annual Reports of the respective co-ordinating bodies, viz. AICTE, NCTE, BCI, MCI and ICAR and committee reports generated by them are the main sources of information. I have tried to list them comprehensively in the Bibliography.

The last chapter deals *inter alia* with the external challenge of globalization and the internal challenge of cleaning up the system as faced by higher education in India.

BIBLIOGRAPHIC ANNEXURE

AIU Publications

Ansari, M.M. (1987): *Education and Economic Development*.

Bhandarkar, S.S. (1985): *Association of Indian Universities (1925-1985)* (New Delhi, AIU).

Higher Education and Development: Golden Jubilee Seminar 1975.

Mridula (1983): *State Funding of Universities: A Study of Maintenance Grants to Universities. Internal Management in Universities (1986)*.

Sharma, G.D. (1978): *Resource Allocation in Education.*
Sharma, G.D. & Mridula (1982): *Economics of College Education: A Study of Hindu College,* Delhi.
Sharma, G.D. & Mridula (1986): *Elite in the making.*
Singh, Amrik & G.D. Sharma: *University and College Finance.*
Vashishta, K.K. (2002): *AIU (1986-2000)* (New Delhi, AIU).

Books on History of American Higher Education

Forst, James J. and Kevin Kinser (Ed.): *Higher Education in the US: An Encyclopaedia.*
Rudolph, Frederic (1968): *American College and University: A History* (N.Y., Alfred A. Knopf).
Thelin, John R. (2004): *A History of American Higher Education* (Baltimore and London, the John Hopkins University Press). Thelin in his bibliographic essay refers to the following works: Lester Good Child and Harold Webster (Ed.): *ASHE Reader in the History of Higher Education* (2nd Edn. 1997). Lawrence Veysey: *The Emergence of the American University* (1966). Roger Geiger: (1) *To Advance Knowledge: The Growth of American Research Universities 1900-1940*, (1986), (2) *Research and Relevant Knowledge: American Research Universities since World War II* (1993).

NCERT Publications

NCERT: Fourth Yearbook in Education (1974) (devoted to Research).
Pandit, H.N. (Ed.) (1969): *Measurement of Cost, Productivity and Efficiency of Education* (New Delhi, NCERT).

NIEPA Publications

NIEPA [on behalf of Central Technical Unit (CTU)]: National Commission on Teachers (Higher Education): 11 Studies on Teachers in Higher Education (no date, but most probably 1983). General Editors: Moonis Raza, G.D. Sharma, Shakti Ahmed: (1) Research design, (2) Higher Education in India: A Survey, (3) Economic Status, (4) Social Status, (5) Recruitment: Base and Procedures, (6) Mobility and Inbreeding, (7) Professional and

Career Development, (8) Work Ethos, (9) Participation in Decision Making, (10) Grievances and their Redressal, (11) Professional Values.

Raghavan, J. Veera (Ed.) (1985): *Higher Education in the Eighties* (New Delhi, Lancer-Intel/India International Centre).

Rao K. Sudha (2003): *Institutions Deemed to be Universities: Contribution to Higher and Professional Education and Research* (New Delhi, NIEPA and Banasthali Vidyapeeth, Rajasthan).

Raza Moonis (Ed.) (1991): *Higher Education in India: Retrospect and Prospect* (New Delhi, AIU).

Raza Moonis (Ed.) (1986): *Educational Planning: Long-Term Perspective* (New Delhi, Concept Publishing for NIEPA).

Raza, Moonis and Nirmal Malhotra (1991): *Higher Education in India: A Comprehensive Bibliography* (New Delhi, Concept).

Sharma, G.D. (1986): *Equity, Quality and Cost in Higher Education: A Case Study of India* (New Delhi, NIEPA).

K. Sudha Rao (Ed.) (2002): *Educational Policies in India: Analysis and Review of Promise and Performance* (New Delhi, NIEPA).

Dr. P.R. Panchmukhi's Publications

P.R. Panchmukhi (Ed.) (1990): *Studies in Educational Reforms in India*:

Vol. I : Perspective for Educational Reforms in India.
Vol. II : Educational Reforms at different levels.
Vol. III : Reforms towards equality and relevance.
Vol. IV : Medium of Instruction and examination reforms at different levels.
Vol. V : Economics of Educational Finance. (Bombay, Himalaya Publishing House).

2

Historical Background

The standard history of Education in India during the British period states that its object is to narrate the main events, which cover a period of about one hundred seventy years from the establishment of the Calcutta (Now Kolkata) Madarasa in 1781 to the attainment of freedom in 1947 [Nurullah and Naik (1951), xxii]. It is difficult to summarize what the book has to say about Higher Education in India because the book's account is divided into six chronological periods, viz. 1781-1813, 1813-1854, 1854-1900, 1900-1921, 1921-1937 and 1937-1947. For the first period, the book has nothing to say about higher education; for the period 1813-1854, the account is divided into (a) official experiments in education, and (b) non-official enterprise in education. For the relevant period, there is a section devoted to Professional and Vocational education (comprising Medical, Engineering, Agricultural and Legal education) (pp. 156-162). However, no clear picture emerges regarding initiation and progress of general higher education. In particular, it is not clear as to in which year higher education of the modern type, which can only mean English education, could be said to have begun in India. Moreover, in the remaining part of the book, while factual information is given about professional education, the significance of the evolution of co-ordinating bodies in higher education and research in this field during the first half of the 20th century, i.e. the period 1900-1947 is not sufficiently highlighted. Indian Research Fund Association (1911), precursor of the Indian Council of Medical Research, Indian Bar Council Act (1926), which created provincial Bar Councils as a preliminary to an all-India Bar, and the Medical Council of India (1933), are not referred to at all. The Imperial Agricultural

Research Institute, Pusa established in 1902 is referred to (*Ibid.*: 701), but not the Imperial Agricultural Research Council (ICAR) established in 1930 in pursuance of the recommendations of Royal Commission on Agriculture. Lastly, the book, thanks to its nationalist bias, tends to underrate the significance of the Sargent Report (1944), otherwise known as the Post-War Plan for Educational Development and altogether omits any reference to the path breaking Report of the Committee on Health survey and Development (1943-1946) presided over by Sir Joseph Bhore. This chapter on historical background, therefore, would deal with the following themes:

(1) What is the genesis of modern higher education in India?
(2) A summary account of evolution of higher general education in India including its co-ordinating body from inception till 1947 and landmarks.
(3) Evolution of professional higher education and research with special reference to their co-ordinating bodies, if any, in medical, engineering, agricultural, legal and teacher education.

Genesis of Modern Higher Education in India

The year 1781 is regarded as marking the beginning of modern education and by extension, modern higher education in India. The authority for this is provided by Nurullah and Naik and subsequently, it was fortified by the UGC when it brought out the publication *Higher Education in India (1781-2003)* [Kaur, Kuldeep (2003)] on the occasion of its Golden Jubilee. The significance of the year 1781 is that it is the year of the establishment of the Calcutta (Now Kolkata) Madarsa endowed by Warren Hastinge on behalf of the East India Company. However, it is difficult to consider Calcutta Madarsa as an institute of modern higher education. Its objective was to produce competent officers for Courts of Justice well-versed in Islamic Law (Nurullah and Naik, 56). Further on, it is stated that the Calcutta Madarsa, together with Benares Sanskrit College (founded by Jonathan Duncan in Varanasi in 1792) showed the beginning of Orientalist School of Educational Policy whose aim was to encourage classical learning in Sanskrit and Arabic on traditional lines (*Ibid*, 59). This matter, therefore, deserves further investigation.

There is a hoary tradition of historiography of modern education in India going back to Syed Mahmood, whose *History of English Education in India for the period 1781-1893* can be said to be first such account written by an Indian. It could be argued that 1781 has been the point of departure for starting a history of English education in India since Mahmood's time. However, a close perusal shows that the author himself, though starting his account in 1781, holds that the institution called Vidyalaya or Anglo-Indian 'College' represents the first effort made by natives of India themselves for the education of their children in the English language and literature. To quote: "In the beginning of 1817, the college or rather school was opened; it was the very first English Seminary in Bengal, or even in India, as far as I know." The title of the chapter itself is conclusive: "The Origin of English Education: The 'Vidyalaya' or Anglo-Indian College founded by Hindus of Calcutta in 1816" [S. Mahmood (1893), 25, 26]. Anathnath Basu (1940, p. 1) states that the first institution (in Bengal or for that matter the whole of India) to impart secondary education of modern type was founded in the year 1817 and it was founded through private efforts. Rammohun Roy, David Hare, Radhakanta Dev and others took initiative in founding the college. His reference to secondary education is to be taken to mean that the institution of higher education (College or Mahavidyalaya) combined in itself some classes of lower, i.e. secondary stage. Basu states in his subsequent, i.e. 1944 book (p. 16) as below: "While the Missionaries were at first interested in primary education, David Hare, Rammohun Roy and others were interested in education of a higher grade. Their efforts culminated in founding in 1817 the Mahavidyalaya (the Hindu College), the first college of the modern type in Asia."

The tradition of tracing the history of modern education in India to the year 1781 must, therefore, be traced to the conventions of the British rulers. It would appear that so far as educational records are concerned, the establishment of Calcutta Madarsa was the first instance of British official financial assistance for any type of educational institution in India. Philip Hartog, a professional historian besides being an officer of the IES, calls it the first important Government educational institution in India [Hartog, (1939), 7]. Interestingly, *Sharp's Selections from Educational Records (1920)* begins with an extract from the record regarding Calcutta Madarsa. But the first institution getting official assistance is not the same thing as the first institution imparting modern higher education. Therefore, one has to conclude that on available evidence, 1817 and not 1781 has to be treated as the year of genesis of modern higher education in India.

Another candidate for the honour of being treated as the first institute of higher education is the College of Fort Williams, Calcutta (Now Kolkata) established by the East India Company in 1800, for the training of Company officers, especially in Indian languages (David Kopf, 1969). The activities of the College are described in detail in Kopf's book and elsewhere and the college played an influential role in promoting the study and research in Indian languages and literature, like Hindustani, Urdu, Bengali, etc. Kopf's claim that the college initiated renaissance in the language and literature of what later on became distinctive. Bengali/Indian literary/cultural traditions could be discussed on its own merits without accepting the claim of the college to be the first Indian Institution of modern higher education. Simply stated, it was a training institution for Company officers but not an educational institution.

The Deccan College, Poona originally started as Sanskrit College in 1821 by Mountstuart Elphinstone, out of the Dakshina Funds of the Peshwas in the teeth of the opposition of the East India Company, might appear to be a close competitor for Hindu College, Calcutta (Now Kolkata) for the honour of being the first modern college in India, but the college, to start with, was an oriental college with the addition of modern subjects of Mathematics and English only in 1842 [Frazer, Nelson (1902)]. Hence, any such claim needs to be rejected*.

To reiterate, the first institute imparting modern higher education was the Hindu College, Calcutta (Now Kolkata). This claim has been recognized by the University Education Commission (Chapter I: Para 6). It is true that Hindu College does not exist under the same name at present because in 1855, it was forcibly, i.e. against the wishes of the then trustees reorganized as a non-sectarian institution and renamed Presidency College. There is no dispute that Presidency

* Pawan Agrawal's claim (2003) that Serampore College established in 1818 was the first college to impart higher education in India is not factual because it was initially founded to impart theological training [*vide* E. Daniel Potts (1967)].

College is the successor institute of the Hindu College established in 1817 (Presidency College Centenary Volume 1956).

Having established 1817 as the starting year of modern higher education in India, the role of the first modern universities in India established in 1857 can also be seen in a proper perspective. A higher educational institution should engage in the teaching of modern subjects including English, History, Geography, Science, etc. The Modern Indian Universities came to be established in 1857 [Calcutta (Now Kolkata)] on 24th January, 1857, Bombay (Now Mumbai) on 18th July, 1857 and Madras on 5th September 1857) in terms of Wood's Despatch of 1854. But the universities as set up in 1857 were not teaching institutions at all. They were primarily examining and affiliating bodies. They affiliated pre-existing colleges and subjected their students to examinations. It was only after the amendment of the Universities Act in 1904 that the Universities got the power to appoint Professors. Universities, however, began to exercise these powers only at the end of First World War. It can then be seen that while modern colleges in India go back to about 200 years (or less), the teaching universities in India are less than 100 years old.

Evolution of General Higher Education (1817-1947)

There are no readily available statistics of the number of colleges functioning at the time of establishment of the Presidency Universities. But the number may be estimated to be 19*. After the start of Quinquennial Review of Progress of Education from 1887 onwards, the data regarding the number of institutions and their enrolment is more readily and reliably available. Taking 1882 (the year of appointment of the Hunter Commission), 1901 (year of holding of the All India Education Conference by Lord Curzon), 1921 (start of Dyarchy), 1937 (start of Provincial autonomy) and 1947 (year of Independence) as representative years, an attempt is made below to

---

* Computed by author from different sources as below: Calcutta (Now Kolkata) 14 [*vide* Bruce T. McCully (1940)], Madras (Now Chennai) 02 [*vide* University of Madras (1957), 145] and Bombay (Now Mumbai) 3 [*vide* Dongerkery (1957), 6].

give progressive statistics regarding the number of colleges, universities and enrolment *vide* Table 2.1.

Table 2.1: Growth of Colleges, Universities and Students from 1882 to 1947

	1882	*1901*	*1921*	*1937*	*1947*
No. of Colleges	59+21 = 80	191 (Arts+ Professional)	129 (Arts+ Professional)	272 (Arts Colleges)	420
No. of Universities	03	04	08	16	19
No. of students enrolled	5399	23,000 (approx)	66,258	1,26,228	2,41,369

Source: Data for 1882 are drawn from McCully (p. 161), and for subsequent years from Nurullah and Naik (pp. 444, 631).

These data, which contain many gaps however, allow us to draw the conclusion that while the growth of collegiate and university institutions and enrolment was slow in the 19th century, it picked up speed in the first half of 20th century, but especially after 1921. The fall in the number of colleges between 1901 and 1921 was apparently the effect of strict Curzonian rules of affiliation. The growth of universities which was slow till 1913, gained momentum thereafter, because of the acknowledged policy of the Colonial Government as enunciated in the Policy Resolution of 1913 to have a University for each province. Thus the following four universities were set up in the period 1913-1920, viz. Banaras Hindu (1916), Mysore (1916), Patna (1917) and Osmania (1918). The following universities came up in the period 1921-1947—Lucknow (1921), Aligarh Muslim (1921), Delhi (1922), Nagpur (1923), Andhra (1926), Agra (1927), Annamalai (1929), Kerala (1937), Utkal (1943), Rajputana and Saugar (1946). The foundation of these universities in close succession can be explained with reference to the linguistic, cultural and politico-administrative factors. Thus, Banaras Hindu was set up on the demand of the Hindu community, which had collected funds for the same and which had given up its demand for having powers of affiliation of colleges all over India. Correspondingly, the Aligarh Muslim with an older founding college (1875) was set up later because the Muslim community initially was reluctant to give up its demand for all-India affiliation (Leah Renold, 2005). The Mysore University was set up by the Princely State of Kannada-speaking Mysore. The establishment of Patna University was a foregone conclusion after separation of the Hindi-speaking Bihar in 1911 at the time of nullification of the partition of Bengal. The Osmania University was set up by a 'firman' by the Nizam of Hyderabad and adopted Urdu, the official language of the Princely State, as its medium of instruction. The adoption of Urdu, an Indian language, as a medium of instruction was a novelty, notwithstanding that it was not a regionally rooted language.* Nagpur was set up by the Province of C.P. and Berar after long deliberations, going back to 1913. Andhra University, Waltair was set up to cater to the Telugu speaking population of the Madras (Now Chennai) Presidency, apparently preparing ground for a linguistic State of Andhra, which independent India conceded in 1954. Agra University was set up as a purely affiliating university to take the load of affiliation of colleges off the teaching universities of Lucknow and Allahabad which were to be made resident teaching universities. Annamalai University was set up in Madras (Now Tamil Nadu) Presidency to avail of a private philanthropic offer. Kerala University started its avatar as Trivandrum University in 1937 to cater to the Malayalam speaking population relieving the load of Madras University to which the colleges in the Princely States of Travancore and Cochin were earlier affiliated. The setting up earlier Utkal University even in war-time indicates the preparedness of the British to meet the aspirations of Oriya speaking people who were able, a little earlier (1937), to win the first unilingual State (Orissa) from the British. Two universities (Rajputana and Saugar) were established shortly after Second World War but before Independence.

Teaching and Research

As noted earlier, the main functions of the universities as set up under 1857 Acts were: (1) examination and (2) affiliation which means that they were not equipped to fulfil the traditional academic functions of teaching and research. Undergraduate teaching was done by colleges and of post-graduate teaching and research, there was very little, if at all. The Universities Act, 1904 inspired by Lord Curzon removed the legal difficulty but it was not till after First World War that a few Indian

* The establishment of Delhi University as a Central University was necessitated by the shift of Imperial Capital to Delhi.

universities began to engage in Post-graduate teaching which is a pre-requisite for research. An entrepreneurial Vice-Chancellor like Ashutosh Mukerjee of Calcutta (Now Kolkata) could make a substantial beginning with the help of donations but the Quinquennial Review for 1922-27 (p. 60), shows that the University faced some difficulties after his death. This applied to a university like BHU also which was *ab initio* set up as a teaching university with post-graduate departments. Naik and Nurullah have made the basic point that the British Government curbed the expansion of university education by emphasizing the need to maintain quality (pp. 856-867). While research saw better days in the period 1920-1937, still, the output of highly educated manpower as estimated by the Scientific Manpower Committee during the war was far less (p. 364). Three important developments prior to independence bearing on the promotion of research were: (a) establishment of Indian Research Fund Association in 1911 (dealt with under medical education), (b) the Imperial Council of Agricultural Research (1930) (dealt with under agricultural education), and (c) the registration of the Council of Scientific and Industrial Research (CSIR) in 1944, which last mentioned event, had a deep influence on the division of academic research in India as between Government laboratories and the Universities. I do not deal with CSIR because it properly forms part of the S & T sector rather than the Education sector.

An illustration of the unhelpful attitude of the Colonial Government towards scientific research is provided by the way Curzon dealt with the Tata proposal in 1898 for setting up an Indian Institute for Science. Jamsetji Tata offered to donate an annual endowment of Rs. 125,000 (8,000 Pounds/Sterling), which was a very generous sum at that time, to establish an Indian University of Science in Bombay (Now Mumbai) if the Government of India could match the funding. He envisaged three faculties: (i) scientific and technical, (ii) medical, and (iii) philosophical and educational. The last included education, ethics, psychology, Indian history and archaeology, statistics, economics and comparative philosophy. Lord Curzon was skeptical of so ambitious a scheme. He referred the scheme to one expert in London and thereafter to two experts. The upshot was delay and the scope of the scheme was reduced to a pure scientific research institute which was started only in 1911 well after Curzon left India. Successive

Quinquennial Reviews refer to it as the only non-Government Scientific Research Institute in India apart from the Bose Institute in Calcutta (Now Kolkata). An earlier Report (1917-1922) refers to establishment of the Cama Oriental Institute in Bombay (Now Mumbai) and of the Bhandarkar Oriental Research Institute (established in 1917) at Poona (p. 232). But the founding of the Gokhale Institute of Politics and Economics (1930) at Poona had not caught the attention of official chronicles.

Landmarks in the Development of Higher General Education (1857-1947)

Five landmarks may be identified in the development of higher general education between the date of establishment of metropolitan universities and attainment of independence:

(1) Curzon's legislation on universities.
(2) Calcutta (Now Kolkata) University Commission Report.
(3) Montford Reforms leading to Dyarchy (1920-1936).
(4) Eastablishment of IUB in 1925.
(5) Sargent Plan (1944).

1. Curzon's legislation on universities

Curzon (1898-1905) was greatly concerned with the lowering of the standard of universities and he appointed Mr. Raleigh (Law Member of the Viceroy's Executive Council) to head a Committee on universities which led to the amendment of the Acts of Universities in 1904 which, while streamlining the management led, according to a moderate leader like Gokhale, to curtailment of the autonomy of the universities.

2. Calcutta University Commission Report (1919) (Sadler Report)

As noted by Nurullah and Naik (1951, 501), the Commission's Report, although ostensibly dealing with Calcutta University only, was of inter-provincial significance. On the one hand, its recommendation about Calcutta University proper especially in regard to the increase of the elective element in the senate and other bodies could not be implemented in the disturbed conditions of the inter-war period and the transfer of the subject to the provincial government; on the other hand, its persuasive recommendation regarding drawing the line between the university and secondary courses was only half-heartedly taken up and could not be implemented till after independence (in the form of 10 + 2 + 3 pattern).

3. Montford reforms leading to Dyarchy (1919-1936)

Dyarchy literally means 'Dual Rule' and refers to bifurcation of functions and powers at the provincial level, the "transferred" subjects being dealt with by popularly elected Ministers and "reserved" subjects being dealt with by executive councilors, both under the Governor. For our purposes the significance of Dyarchy was that education became a "transferred" subject.

Naik/Nurulla (1974) have taken a dim view of Dyarchy especially the implications of Education being a partly "transferred" subject. It is stated in a jeering tone: "These orders created a queer position by treating education as partly all-India, partly reserved, partly transferred with limitations and partly transferred without limitations (*Ibid.*: p. 316).

These observations are based on a misunderstanding and do not, in particular, take account of the fact that basically education was a "transferred" subject and the Indian Member in-charge of Education (Sir Sankaran Nair) had fought valiantly for the outcome. Montford Report recommended primary, secondary and technical education to be transferred. The Committee on Division of functions, however, suggested transfer of Education as a whole. Sir Sankaran Nair agreed with the Committee. The Viceroy opposed transfer of secondary and higher education. The British (Home) Government, however, upheld the view of the committee on Divisions of Functions (i.e. Sir Sankaran Nair is used) and the Act provided accordingly, the limitations being transfer related to European education, Princes' education and central universities. Hartog, who was part of policy-making machinery, realised the significance of Dyarchy. The position of education as a "transferred" subject continued under the GoI Act 1935 and the Constituent Assembly made no changes in spite of Radhakrishnan

Commission's recommendation to make Higher Education a concurrent subject. The basic point is about the misreading of the scene and under-estimation of achievement of Liberal leaders by the standard histories of Indian education.

4. Establishment of IUB in 1925

Inter University Board (IUB), an association of heads of universities in India and Ceylon was established in1925. It played the co-ordinating role in relation to higher general education in India till the establishment of the interim UGC in 1953. It enjoyed a consultative status with the Central Advisory Board of Education (CABE) (estd. 1936). It brought out biannually a Handbook of Universities which was the main source of information about Indian universities. It is the parent body of the Association of Indian Universities (AIU).

5. Sargent Plan (1944)

The report was based on the recommendations of a number of Central Advisory Board of Education (CABE) reports on a variety of topics like Wardha Education scheme, Adult Education, Social science, School Buildings, Medical Inspection of School Children and Teaching of Hygiene in schools, Recruitment of Education Officers, Teacher and Technical Education, etc. These were put together by Mr. Sargent who was Education Adviser to Government of India, i.e. Union Education Secretary in modern terms. He tried to fit these reports into a Plan with the aim of building a *national system of education*. Its relevant recommendations so far as higher education was concerned were as below:

(1) Establishment of a University Grants Committee (UGC),
(2) Establishment of a National Board for Technical Education (NBTE).
(3) Central Government taking over the responsibility of funding of both higher general and technical education.

Sargent report has been criticized by standard histories as lacking ambition and being too costly. The whole criticism was aimed at the

Report having allowed about 40 years for the attainment of the goal of the UEE. The subsequent history shows that the attempt to curtail the time from 40 to 10 year (*vide* Constitutional Directive Principle in Article 45 of the Constitution) failed miserably. The goal of the UEE was not attained in 1960, not even in 1984 and it is doubtful if it would be achieved by 2015, the target date set by the UNESCO for attainment of Millennium Development Goals. The criticism of nationalist historians like Naik/Nurullah was misconceived and under-estimated the gravity of the problem. It is unfortunate that neither Radhakrishnan Report nor Kothari Report found it fit to give credit to Sargent Plan for its recommendations about the UGC and the NBTE which came to be known as AICTE!

Surveys of higher education normally omit any reference to higher education in specialized areas like medical education, technical education, agricultural/veterinary education, forestry education, legal education and teacher education. In the rest of the chapter, progress made in these specialized areas during the British period would be reviewed.

Medical Education: Its Regional and Communal Diversity

As in the other fields of higher education, medical education during the British period was characterized by co-existence of colleges proper and schools. Their connotation, however, was precise because of medical education's linkage with British organizations. As noted by Patrick Hehir, medical colleges granted to successful alumni: (1) degrees, which are registrable in the UK and in India, and (2) licences to practise which, though registerable in India are not registrable in UK. In medical schools, the standard was lower, the curriculum less elaborate and duration of training shorter. Successful students were granted a State diploma to practise which was not registrable (Patrick Hehir, 1923, p. 6). Although Hehir does not mention it, the medium of instruction in the colleges was uniformly English as required by regulations of the respective universities, whereas it would be mostly vernacular or regional in the medical schools.

A study of medical education in the British period is highly complicated, being characterized by: (1) multiplicity of colonial powers, (2) multiplicity of systems of medicine, and (3) inadequate specialization.

India has pockets of other colonial powers like the Portuguese and the French in addition to the British. The Portuguese established a royal hospital in Old Goa in 1703 and a Goa medical school was set up in 1842. However, the courses there were meant for the officers of the army of Portugal not only within India but also the other colonies of Portugal. The only vestige of this school is that, after the liberation of Goa, in 1961, it was upgraded to a medical college, which is now under Goa University. The same is the case with the medical school established by the French at Pondichery, which, in the post-Independence period, became the J.N. Institute of P-G Medical Education and Research (S.L. Bhatia, 1977).

Secondly, when the British came, India had two pre-existing systems of medicine, Ayurveda associated with the Hindus and the Unani Tibb system associated with the Muslims. In addition, the German system of Homoeopathy which was very popular in Europe in the first half of the 19th century, but which subsequently came to be treated as sectarian medicine was indigenized in India during the last third of the 19th century. Education in these three systems was not encouraged by the British but still survived and made some progress in the period 1919-1947.

As for specialization, nursing and dentistry education had a late start in the British period.

The Beginning of Medical Education in British India

The need for medical education arose because "native doctors" who were helpers and assistants of the British Medical Officers in the armed forces were required to be trained in a systematic manner. Two 'native doctors' were attached to each regiment and it was felt necessary to train them on a more systematic and scientific basis. The Medical Board, impressed with the orientalist discovery of Sanskrit and Arabic treatises devoted to medicine, proposed to Government in 1823 to establish a Medical Institution where Western and Indian medicine would be taught side by side.

Accordingly, the Native Medical Institution, Calcutta (Now Kolkata) (NMI) was established in June 1823 with a student intake of twenty which was increased in 1826 to fifty. The students received a stipend during training and were taught in Urdu or Sanskrit. European texts were translated into these languages and were also used at the Sanskrit College, Calcutta (Now Kolkata) where treatises in Ayurveda were taught and the Madrasa at Calcutta where Unani treatises were taught. Only one European doctor worked at the Institute, assisted by a Bengali pundit and other assistants and dissection was carried out only on animal bodies. John Tytler, a noted orientalist succeeded Surgeon Bretton as Superintendent, NMI in 1830. He set up a 30-bed hospital attached to the Sanskrit College. There were periodical reviews of the work of the NMI. A review of October 1834 by a Medical Commission was critical and the Governor-General approved a proposal for abolition of the NMI and its replacement by a Medical College with effect from 1st February, 1835, where English would be compulsory and European medical science would be taught. With the abolition of NMI, medical classes in Sanskrit college and in Madrasa at Calcutta were also abolished (Poonam Bala, 1991: 45-48). Vernacular teaching was revived after 1839 for medical schools and institutions meant for medical technicians. However, as a matter of policy, locations of such medical schools with vernacular instruction were shifted out of the metropolitan cities to the interior rural areas.

According to D.G. Crawford (1914, pp. 443-444), Campbell Medical School at Sealda, Calcutta (Now Kolkata) (named after Lt.- Gen. Sir George Campbell and started in 1873 with the transfer of the Bengali native doctor class from the medical college) is the direct successor of that class and also, one may say, the Native Medical Institution of 1822.

In retrospect, the abolition of NMI was a silent coup which prepared the ground for Macaulay's minute of 2nd February, 1835 and Bentinck's order approving the same. It needs to be noted that the Medical Commission which recommended abolition of NMI included C.G. Trevelyn, Dy. Secretary of the Political Department, that it was divided on the issue of the medium of instruction and the balance was apparently tilted by the presence of Trevelyn on the Committee. The Committee's reason for insistence on the knowledge of English as a *sine qua non* was as below:

"That knowledge combines with itself the circle of all the

> sciences and the incalculable wealth of printed works and illustrations, circumstances which give it obvious advantages over oriental languages, in which are only to be found the crudest elements of science or the most irrational substitution for it."

This wording is evidently that of Trevelyan and Macaulay's Minute really echoes the same thoughts, only more elaborately.

Gradually, all three Presidency towns had their medical colleges [Madras (Now Chennai) 1840, Bombay (Now Mumbai) 1845] and other universities followed suit. Medical schools grew side by side with medical colleges, which alone were recognized by the General Medical Council in London.

Indian Medical Service (IMS)

During the British period, practice in medical science had its own all-India service called the Indian Medical Service (IMS), which was the most powerful among the imperial or all-India services prior to independence. *As a matter of record, IMS and not ICS was the first covenanted imperial service dating back to 1788* (Chittabrata Palit, Achintya Dutta, 2005, p. 167). It was also the last to be disbanded and the least Indianized of the imperial services. Very few Indians managed to qualify for IMS for which training in a foreign medical institute was a prerequisite.

Inception of Medical Council

As part of Dyarchy, medical education as a subject was transferred to Provinces, but medical profession continued to be a Central subject. In 1933, the Government of India was compelled to pass an Act for coordination of medical education in India under pressure from General Council for Medical Education (GCME) of UK which derecognized all medical colleges in India with effect from 24th January, 1930 ostensibly because their standards were low (education in midwifery was particularly cited as a weak area). There were protracted negotiations with Provincial governments which were guided by the University authorities which, being autonomous, tended to mirror nationalist opinion. In a Conference held in June 1930 in which representatives not only of Provinces but also of universities in British India with medical faculty participated, it was unanimously resolved that the establishment of the All-India Medical Council is essential and the requisite legislation should be enacted. The Medical Council Act (No. XXVII of 1933) was brought into force on 1st November, 1933 and MCI was constituted on 15th February, 1934 (Jaggi, 1970, pp. 111-127).

The Act extended to British India only. The composition of the Council under the Act was as follows:

(a) One member from each Governor's Province to be nominated by the Central Government.
(b) One member from each Indian University to be elected by the members of the Senate of the University from amongst the members of the medical faculty of the University.
(c) One member from each Province where a provincial medical register is maintained to be elected from amongst themselves by persons enrolled on the Register.
(d) Four members to be nominated by the Central Government.

As was to be expected, the first President of the Council was an IMS Officer, Maj. General C.A. Sprawson. *Dr. B.C. Roy was the first Indian and that too non-IMS, to be the President of the Council in 1939.*

In its early years, the Council performed its statutory functions of establishment of a uniform minimum standard of higher qualifications in medicine for all Provinces and recognition of the medical qualifications in States and countries outside British India creditably enough. It arranged a ten-yearly programme of inspection of medical colleges. It is reported that some of the colleges were refused recognition at first inspections. The Council had a policy of upgrading medical schools into medical colleges and of encouraging existing licentiates to undergo condensed MBBS course so that as many licentiates as possible could become medical graduates. At the time of Independence, India had 17 medical colleges and 16 medical schools.

Nursing Education

Nursing education in India had a slow start so much so that higher education in the area of nursing by way of a B.Sc. degree in nursing was introduced for the first time only in 1946 (on the eve of Independence) in Delhi and Madras (Now Chennai). Prior to 1946, nursing education was of a rudimentary type, partly because nursing as a profession was regarded as inferior, being the refuge of the widows and the orphans (Bhatia, 1977, p. 213) and the Government was apathetic. At the beginning of 20th century, a number of training centres were established in Bombay (Now Mumbai), Bengal, Madras (Now Chennai) and Punjab provinces. A need was felt for standardization. The profession was dominated by nurses from the Mission Hospitals who took the lead in the matter and founded a North India United Board. There were several regional associations. In 1922, two of the major regional associations merged together to form the Trained Nurses Association of India (TNAI), which was the first national association of trained nurses. TNAI has been influential in bringing about some significant changes including Government legislation [P.K. Nandi in Girija Gupta (Ed.), 1981].

However, State Governments like Bombay (Now Maharashtra) and Madras (Now Tamil Nadu) had independently taken steps for professionalization and registration. The Bombay (Now Maharashtra) Presidency Nursing Association was established in 1909 and till 1935, it was responsible for inspection and recognition of training schools, prescribing curriculum and conducting examinations and the registration of nurses and midwives. The first Nurses Registration Act was passed by Madras (Now Tamil Nadu) in 1926; other Provinces followed including Bombay (Now Maharashtra) which passed such legislation in 1935. Since the late thirties, thought was given to the question of an all-India body which object was realized with the Indian Nursing Council Act being passed shortly after Independence viz. on 31st December, 1947.

Dental Education

Dental education had a late start in India. Sadler Commission observed that the fact that there was no dental school or hospital and no means of giving dental training in India was remarkable. It recommended that a department of dentistry should be established in connection with the Calcutta (Now Kolkata) Medical College. Separately, in Bombay (Now Maharashtra) a Government Dental College was established about 1920 and by 1945, KEM hospital of the Bombay (Now Greater Mumbai) Municipal Corporation also had a department of Dentistry attached to it. Thus, there were three Dental Colleges in India at the time of Independence. Bhore Committee recommended the establishment of a Dental Council and an Act in this regard was passed shortly after the Independence, i.e. in 1948.

*Medical Research**

As in many other areas, e.g. agriculture, India was the first country of the British Empire to set up in 1911 a dedicated organization for promotion of medical research, viz. Indian Research Fund Association (IRFA), predecessor of the present Indian Council of Medical Research (ICMR). *IRFA preceded such an organisation in UK (Medical Research Council) by two years* (Pandit, C.G. and Someswara Rao, 1961: 3).

The origin of IRFA could be traced to the 1894 resolutions of the Indian Medical Congress urging Government to establish and endow a research institution. In the meanwhile, a few laboratories had come up, e.g. Bacteriological Laboratory in Agra in 1892 (for Cholera), Pasteur Institute at Kasauli (1900) and Coonoor (1907), King Institute Guindy (for manufacture of calf-lymph) and Central Research Institute of Kasauli in 1905. In the same year, a Bacteriological Department consisting of 13 scientific workers was set up. IRFA came up in 1911 on the initiative of the then Health Member, Mr. Harcourt Butler.

In other countries medical research is carried out primarily in the colleges and universities. However, India, as a colony of UK, had its medical colleges which were a poor replica of such institutions in advanced countries and their dominant orientation was vocational. Research was carried out by officers of the IMS, very few of whom were Indian, but the available evidence indicates that the modality

* This section draws heavily on C.G. Pandit and K.S. Rao (1961).

of founding and funding a dedicated laboratory was dictated by the need for conducting research to tackle out-breaks of serious communicable diseases like plague, small-pox, Kala-azar, and environmental diseases like malarial fever, Beri Beri etc. The preferred strategy as illustrated by plague epidemic was to set up an enquiry; this enquiry was conducted through the agency of Multi-disciplinary Commissions and on the basis of the reports of the Commission further action was taken which might include setting up of a permanent institution. Thus, the sudden appearance of plague in Bombay (Now Mumbai) in 1896 and its further spread to other regions led to the deputation of Dr. W.M. Haffkine to work over this problem and subsequently to the appointment of a number of Plague Commissions by UK, India, Germany and Russia to investigate the epidemiology of this disease. Initially Haffkine worked in a room in Grant Medical College, Bombay (Now Mumbai) with a staff consisting of one clerk and three peons provided by the Bombay (Now Mumbai) Municipality. *The laboratory ultimately shifted to the Old Government House, Parel where it became the Headquarter of the Indian Plague Commission and formed the nucleus of the present Haffkine Institute.*

The primary object of the IRFA was promotion and assistance of research, propagation of knowledge and experimental measures generally in connection with the causation, mode of spread and prevention of communicable diseases. The Fund was a Government controlled Local Fund to which Government gave an annual grant-in-aid of Rs. 5 lakhs. The underlying idea was to utilize the facilities of the permanently constituted *framework* of laboratories and the scientific càdre for the promotion of research. The IRFA had two main bodies, the Governing Body which consisted of Government officers, headed by the Member-in-charge of the Department of Health of the Governor General's Executive Council and the Academic Body which was assisted and advised on all technical matters by a Scientific Advisory Board consisting of scientists of high standing and which worked with the help of a series of advisory bodies. In July 1913, the Fund started a journal (*Indian Journal of Medical Research*) and in 1914, the cadre of research staff was enlarged from 13 to 30 and renamed Medical Research Department. The Association also began to hold Annual Research Workers' Conference which proved useful as a sounding board for the thinking at that level. The activities of the Fund suffered a set back due to First World War. After the War, however, the Fund started a series of enquiries on Beri Beri, malaria and quinine, kalaazar and indigenous drugs. The first enquiry eventuated in the setting up a laboratory devoted to nutritional research, subsequently shifted to Hyderabad in 1925. The IRFA also decided to meet 25 per cent of maintenance expenditure of the School of Tropical Medicine, Calcutta (Now Kolkata).

However, consequent on financial difficulties and *recommendations of retrenchment Committee headed by Mr. Inchcape, grants to the Association were suspended in the period 1923-25*, but were resumed in 1926. The Beri Beri enquiry was expanded to cover "Deficiency Diseases" in general and resulted in the establishment of a centre for Nutritional Research at Coonoor in 1929. A Central Malaria Organisation was created. In 1928, IRFA received a donation of $ 6.48 lakhs from *Rockefeller Foundation* for setting up the Institute of Hygiene and Public Health at Calcutta (Now Kolkata) (in close proximity to the School of Tropical Medicine) and the Institute started functioning in 1932.

In March 1938, the Association was made more autonomous by converting it into a registered society under the Registration of Societies Act, 1860 so that it could receive private donations.

From 1932, Government's grant-in-aid to the Association was reduced from Rs. 5 lakhs to Rs. 1.5 lakh. It was increased to Rs. 4 lakhs in 1944 and at the time of Independence in 1947 it was Rs. 12 lakhs.

The Bhore Committee (1943-45) reviewed the functioning of the Association and observed the absence of organized medical research in Medical Colleges, referred to the lack of facilities for training young alert minds in a scientific approach to medical matters and to the throttling effect which routine work in the Institution was having on medical research. It recommended raising the grants, enlarging the scope of the association and appointment of a full-time Secretary. It also wanted the idea of a Central Institute for Medical Research to be revived.

On the eve of Independence, IRFA was a lean organisation with a limited number of research centres called laboratories. Considering the vicissitudes [Two World Wars, Retrenchment of the period

(1923-25), Depression years (1931-34)], through which it passed, it had done quite creditable work in a short period of time in a cost-effective manner. Not only had it an enviable record in the control of malaria, cholera, plague, small-pox etc., but *it had at least one Nobel laureate on its staff (Ross)*, it had established good research practices (Journals, Annual Research Workers' Conference, etc.). On the debit side, the medical research continued to be dominated by the Imperial medical Service which was more of a power group than a knowledge group, so that a *potential Nobel Laureate with continental recognition like Waldemar Haffkine came to be ill-treated* [Deepak Kumar in Chhitabrata Palit and A.K. Dutt (2005): 177-204].

Education in Indigenous Systems of Medicine (including Homoeopathy)

When the Medical College Calcutta (Now Kolkata) was established in 1835 in supercession of the Native Medical Institution, (which as noted was the first experiment in integrated medical education combining the curriculum of Ayurved/Yunani Tibb with Allopathy), it was also a set back to the education in the twin indigenous systems of medicine, viz. *Ayurveda and Unani Tibb which the British Raj chose to dub as being based on a 'false' doctrine*. Ayurveda was an indigenous system par excellence, its origin as a rational medicine going back to the Upanisadic period with the foundation texts associated with the names of *Bhelanda, Charaka* and *Sushruta* and culminating in the Puranic text of *Madhav Nidan* (8th Century). The Ayurvedic system suffered after Mulsim invasions which resulted in the import of a rival system, viz. Unani Tibb (which was a hybrid Greco-Arabic medical system that had originally drawn on Ayurveda). With the advent of the British, both the systems suffered a decline. Although the medical systems had decayed and the urban population increasingly took to the allopathic system associated with the new Rulers and which came to be called the only scientific system, Hehir has conceded that *even after hundred years of the prevalence of the modern system, i.e. by 1923, one-third of the population was being treated by these older systems* (Hehir, 1923: 96-120). This would imply that rural areas began to be penetrated by the Allopathy only from the closing years of the 19th century when India was ravaged by epidemic killers like bubonic plague, small-pox, bacterial infections etc. and modern medicine with scientists like Jenner and Pasteur revolutionized therapeutics and virtually eradicated infections as causes of mortality (S. Dahanukar and U Thatte, 1989: 24) and the populace realized that Ayurveda/Unani Tibb had no cure for such diseases.

The normal progression in medicine is from education/research in institutions to practice which may involve professionalization. In the case of the indigenous systems, in the absence of patronage of the Government from 1835 onwards, the education continued through the old channel of *Guru-Shishya parampara* (pupillage) which, in the highly traditional Indian society, took the form of hereditary transmission. In other words, medicine was practised by selected families with the father handing down his practice to his son. In Bengal, there were families of *kavirajs* and elsewhere of *vaidyas*. This was also true of *hakims* of the Unani Tibb. Keshwani has given a list of renowned *hakim* families in Delhi, Meerat, Lucknow, etc. [Keshwani, N.H. (1970), pp. 354-355]. Not that there were no institutions. Most Sanskrit Tols/Pathshalas would conduct classes in Ayurveda and many Madrasas as taught Unani medicine. Perhaps a rare instance of Government patronage of Ayurveda and Unani towards the end of 19th century was the Lahore based (now in Pakistan), Punjab University (estd. 1882) subsidizing the teaching of Ayurvedic and Unani medicine. It is reported that subsequently Ayurvedic classes were transferred to the DAV College and Unani classes to the Islamia College in 1898-99 (Hehir, 1923: *Ibid.*). Indian Princely States like Travancore-Cochin, Mysore, etc. also supported Ayurvedic education. A Government school of Ayurveda was reportedly established in Travancore in 1887 (Paul R. Brass, 1972: 342-371). An Ayurvedic College under a modern university was perhaps opened for the first time in 1925 under the Benaras Hindu University (QRPE, 1917-22:63).

Hakim Ajmal Khan established a Unani school in 1889 and upgraded it college level in 1916. The foundation stone of the college was laid by the Viceroy Hardinge in March 1916 and it was inaugurated by Mahatma Gandhi in 1921. Hakim Ajmal Khan also sought the patronage of the Muslim princely States like Rampur and Bhopal to support Yunani institutions—both schools and dispensaries

(Barbara Metcalf, 2004: 120-150). Aligarh Muslim University also established a faculty of Unani Medicine.

In the case of indigenous systems, by far the more important aspect is recognition of practice. This was greatly helped by the resolutions of the Indian National Congress (in 1922, it passed a resolution stating that Ayurvedic medicine was just as scientific as modern allopathic medicine), and the constitutional reforms which were in the air from the Montague Statement of August 1917 and the follow-up by way of Montford Report (1918), Dyarchy (1921-36) and the Provincial Autonomy (1937-46). In 1920, the Imperial Government expressed sympathy with the oriental system of medicine and mada a grant to the Unani Tibb Medical School of Delhi. The Indian Council of State (the then counterpart of Rajya Sabha) discussed in February 1921, a resolution proposing that the Government of India should recommend to every Provincial Government the desirability of having an Ayurvedic Medical College, of taking measures to develop indigenous drugs and appointing *Vaidyas* and *Hakims* in every dispensary to treat patients by indigenous methods. As health was a Provincial subject, an account of the debate was sent to Provincial governments for information and necessary action (Hehir, 1923: *Ibid.*).

While no connected account of what the State/Provincial Governments did is available, we know from the Udupa Committee Report (1959: 149-50), that the first Board in India of indigenous medicine was established in 1926 by the order of the UP Government, though it actually started functioning in the year 1931. Later on, a Bill was passed in the year 1939 but due to political reasons, it did not take effect till 1947. Madras (Now Chennai) constituted a Central Board of Indian Medicine in 1932 with 15 elected members and a nominated President. West Bengal Government also set up a Board of Indian Medicine in 1937 by Government order. Bombay (Now Mumbai) Government set up a Board in 1940 under Bombay (Now Mumbai) Medical Practitioners' Act, 1938. The Act gave the registered Ayurvedic practitioners many of the rights and privileges enjoyed by the modern medical practitioners.

It may be noted by way of comparison that the developments in the Princely States paralleled those in British India. It was earlier noted that an Ayurveda Pathshala was opened in Trivandrum in 1889.

This was followed by a system of medical grants to *Vaidyas* (Ayurvedic doctors) in 1895-96, generally, the alumni of the Pathshala being eligible for the grants. In 1917-18, an Ayurveda department was created which revised the curriculum of the Ayurveda Pathshala on an up-to-date scientific basis to suit modern equipment. Even in a progressive Princely State like Travancore, however, Western medicine continued to dominate the scene, thanks to the pressure exerted by the Missionaries (Sunitha B. Nair, 2001: 215-232).

The institutionalization of education and the professionalization and recognition of Ayurvedic practice were coupled with a strategy of mobilization through associations which represented the professional interests. Thus, the Ayurvedic Congress was founded in 1907. In the preceding year, Hakim Ajmal Khan had founded the Tibbi conference to tie Unani physicians together and to disseminate his arguments on the need to reform Unani medicine. The Hakim had the foresight to see that in spite of the inherent rivalry of the two systems, the two groups could fruitfully cooperate in the interest of the profession. In 1910, Hakim Ajmal Khan organized the all-India Ayurvedic and Tibbia conference. Thereafter, it met annually and virtually all petitions and representations to the government were couched in term of the two traditions (Paul R. Brass, *op cit.* and B. Metcalf, *op cit.*). As noted, this approach bore fruit in the inter-war period (1918-39).

Homoeopathic System of Medicine

This system which was founded by Dr. Samuel Hahnemann (1755-1843) of Saxony in Germany is based on certain principles like "let likes be cured by the like" and "use of infinitesimal dose of remedy". It was very popular on the Continent of Europe in the 1850s and the 1860s but declined thereafter and began to be treated as a sectarian practice. Its decline in its country of origin coincided with its popularization and spread first in Bengal and then in other parts of the country. Dr. Mahendra Lal Sarkar, an M.D. from Calcutta (Now Kolkata) medical College, converted to the system between 1863-1869. The system had a particular appeal in India because of its reliance on medicine rather than surgery and other principles, which were held to be in consonance with the Indian tradition of spiritualism. The homoeopathic training made use of regional languages, the system was not opposed to Ayurveda and prominent leader like Mahatma Gandhi patronized the medicine. All these factors explain the spread of a foreign system which became naturalized to India. In 1887, the first surviving homoeopathy college was established, followed by a hospital in 1892. Gradually, the system was commercialized. At the time of Independence, India had about 2-3 lakh practitioners of whom only 5,000 might be trained (Surendra M. Bharadwaj, 1981: 31-54).

Bhore Committee on Indigenous Systems

Unfortunately, Bhore Committee (1946) sidetracked the issue of recognition of these systems and utilization of its practitioners for Medical relief. There was, however, a Minute of Dissent by three members, containing a definite recommendation regarding the free utilization of service of persons trained in Indian systems for promoting public health and medical relief in India (Udup Committee Report: 2).

Bhore Committee Report

In historical literature relating to education, Bhore Report on Health Survey and Development (1943-1946) is often ignored. It is a detailed and path-breaking report providing a blue-print for post-War health planning in India based on the community health approach. Its recommendations relating to research, indigenous system of medicine and dentistry have been quoted earlier. Its other recommendations include a drastic revision and upgradation of pharmaceutical education. It suggested: (1) creation of an all-India Medical Institute, (2) establishment of post-graduate training institutions in different provincial centres, and (3) development of a number of teachers' training departments. In other words, it is comparable in its significance to the Sargent Report on General Education with the difference that Bhore Committee Report is more cohesive and its recommendations constitute an integrated framework (Sargent Report being a compilation of diverse reports).

Technical Education*

The origin of technical and especially engineering education goes back to the survey school set up in Madras (Now Chennai) in Fort St. George in 1794. However, it was the newly established (1836) North-Western Province, (later on renamed UP) that marked a definite progress. A survey school at Saharanpur was started in November 1847, and shortly thereafter, the Governor-General Lord Hardinge approved the proposal of Lt.-Governor James Thomason to establish a civil engineering college at Roorkee. It was meant to meet the needs of engineers required for the Ganga Canal. The college offered three types of courses: for engineers (duration 2 years), for overseers (duration one year) and for sub-overseers (duration 1 year) respectively. The college was under the administrative control of the P.W.D. of the local government. It was affiliated, first to Calcutta (Now Kolkata) University and from 1874 to Allahabad University. In 1894, the college was transferred from the P.W.D. to Education Department. In the meanwhile, the Madras (Now Tamil Nadu) Survey school was transformed first into an engineering school and in 1859, into a civil engineering college. Later on, the college specialized in mechanical engineering and was shifted first to Saidapet and then to Guindy (1920). By 1880, Bengal also had its engineering college at Sibpur. Poona Civil Engineering college in Bombay (Now Maharashtra) Presidency came up in 1864 and in 1879 its scope was extended to include the faculty of agriculture.

It was, however, clear that the colonial government was not interested in expanding technical education facilities in India. In 1859, a scheme of recruiting young civil engineers in England for service in the public works was initiated and between 1859-1864, 168 'Stanley' engineers (so-called after the then Secretary of State) were approved for service against only 45 from the Roorkee college. In 1869, the procedure for recruiting engineers in England for service in India was changed by establishing a civil engineering college in England at Cooper's Hill, which was in existence till 1907. Apparently, PWD's requirement for engineers was falling off. The Indian opinion, however, clamoured for expansion of technical education, especially because the in-take of existing colleges was mainly reserved for the whites.

---

* This account draws heavily on AICTE (1999:8-63).

At the beginning of the 20th century, the Government policy changed and it was decided to have one Central Technological Institute for each province. Thus, Victoria Jubilee Technical Institute (VJTI), Bombay (Now Mumbai) was declared as such in 1913 and a technological institute specializing in chemical applications in sugar and leather came up at Kanpur, thanks to the initiative of Sir Harcourt Butler, the then Lt.- Governor of the N-W Province. The Indian Industries Commission, 1916 strongly recommended that the government should actively assist in the expansion of the industry and recognized that the expansion of technical education was a logical prerequisite. Some favourable developments were: establishment of a college of engineering in BHU (Estd. 1917) establishment of School of a Mining at Dhanbad, as a Central Institution in 1920; establishment of Calcutta University College of Science and Technology in 1920 and the establishment of the University Department of Chemical Technology, Bombay (now Mumbai), in 1933. Engineering Colleges were also started in the newly set up universities of princely States of Travancore, Mysore, and Osmania. A college of the Engineering had come up at AMU, Aligarh in 1935. Second World War also gave a fillip to the setting up of new engineering colleges. In 1946-47, the number of students admitted to engineering courses was about 3,500.

The two most important pre-Independence developments in the field of technical education were: Firstly, the setting up of the All-India Council for Technical Education (AICTE) in November 1945 to supervise all higher technical education (i.e. survey, policies, standards and generally advising on new institutions). It consisted of representatives of the Central and Provincial Governments and other concerned interests. This was evidently a response to the recommendations of the Sargent Report. Secondly, the Interim Report of N.R. Sarkar Committee in 1945 recommended the establishment of four Institutes of Technology (patterned on the American MIT). These later on came to be established and became known as IITs.

Agricultural Education and Research*

Improvement of agriculture everywhere has been preceded by a

* This account draws on the Report of the Royal Commission on Agriculture in India (1928): Chapters 2 & 12.

central organization for scientific research in agriculture. It is not surprising, therefore, that agricultural education in India came into its own only after a central institution for agricultural research was set up by Lord Curzon.

The need for setting up of the Central Agriculture Department was emphasized by successive Famine Commissions. However, there was apparently a feeling that Provincial departments should be set up first. Following the recommendations of the Famine Commission of 1866 and some pressure by the Manchester Cotton trade in 1869, a composite Department of Revenue, Agriculture and Commerce at the Central level commenced to function in June 1871 and continued till 1879. The short lived department evolved a system for collection of agricultural statistics. In the meanwhile, North-Western Provinces under Lt. Governor Strachey had set up the first Provincial Directorate of agriculture in 1875 with the mandate to establish and to provide Indian agriculturists the advantage to be gained from small improvements and to make experiments with staples and industries connected therewith. The Directorate set up model farms for tobacco, silk and fruits. At the Central level, following Voeleker Report (1893), a post of Agricultural Chemist was created and in 1901, the post of Inspector-General of Agriculture for India was created. His duties included systematic studies of Indian agriculture, supervision and development of Provincial agricultural departments and establishment of improved agricultural methods. The Famine Commission of 1901 recommended strengthening of the expert staff of agriculture departments in all provinces and introduction of mutual credit associations on the lines of German cooperative societies.

The situation in the Provinces on the agricultural education front was as below: In Bombay (Now Mumbai), an agricultural class was opened in the College of Science (= College of Engineering) at Poona in 1879. In 1890, a diploma in agriculture was recognized by the Bombay (Now Mumbai) University, and in 1905 a college of agriculture was opened at Poona. In the neighbouring C.P. and Berar, there was a good model agricultural farm at Nagpur since 1883. In Madras (Now Tamil Nadu) an agricultural college was established at Saidapet in 1876. In 1901, two cotton farms were opened at Bellary and Tinnevelly. In the North-Western Province, there was an agricultural school at Kanpur. There was no separate agricultural school or college in Bengal;

Sibpur engineering college ran agricultural classes till 1910, when an independent college came into existence.

It was in this background that Lord Curzon proposed to the Secretary of State a scheme for establishment of an agricultural research institute, an experimental farm and an agricultural college at Pusa (in Darbhanga District of Bihar). In pursuance of the scheme, a research station with fully equipped laboratories, an experimental farm, an agricultural college for the training of students and a cattle farm for the improvement of local breeds of cattle were established on the Pusa Estate on 1906.

When the Royal Commission on Agriculture in India reported (1926-28), it found that the progress of the scheme was along expected lines, except for the problems caused by the First World War and financial stringency. There were agricultural colleges in all Provinces except in Bihar, Orissa and Assam. These were at Poona in Bombay (Now in Maharashtra), Coimbatore in Madras (Now Tamil Nadu)), Kanpur (UP) and Nagpur (Now in Maharashtra). In the meanwhile, an Indian Central Committee for Cotton had been brought into existence for improvement of cotton-growers in India. It followed a model of placing financial burden on the stakeholders in the crop, viz, growers, traders and processors.

The Royal Commission which had Lord Linlithgow as Chairman, two Indian scientists and two Indian farmers as Members, opted for a statutory council as a model for a research organization for Indian agriculture. The Central Government opted for a registered society which duly came into existence in 1929 known as Imperial Council of Agricultural Research (ICAR).

The Commission also reviewed progress of higher agricultural education and recommended as below:

1. The affiliation of agricultural colleges to universities is desirable,
2. Separate courses at agricultural colleges for those whose aim is employment under Government and for those who propose to farm their own land or that of others is not desirable,
3. Intermediate examination in science of the Provincial university should be made an essential qualification for admission to agricultural colleges,

4. Greater prominence should be given to agricultural economics and greater attention to instruction in farm management,
5. Miscellaneous short courses given in certain colleges (for example, for agricultural machinery handling etc.) are most valuable,
6. Research should be combined with teaching,
7. Post-graduate training at Pusa should be an essential qualification for all direct recruitment to higher posts in agricultural department.

It would be seen that the Commission's recommendations were progressive, quite in consonance with the Sadler Commission's recommendations and anticipated some future trends. Post-Linlithgow Commission, agricultural education and research continued to make progress. On the eve of Independence, the number of agricultural colleges was 17 with an enrolment of 1550 students.

Forestry Education and Training*

In 1947, there was no such thing as forestry education as an academic field. It was only practised as forestry training for forest department personnel and the immediate colonial purposes of exploitation of reserved forests.

The training of Superior Forest Service Officers was conducted at Cooper Hills (the institute which trained PWD Officers) till 1905, when it was taken over by three British universities of Oxford, Cambridge and Edinburgh. The curriculum was as below: the student took the first science courses in botany, physics and chemistry in the first year and the forestry courses and those in applied science, surveying, geology, etc. in the second and third years. During the summer vacations throughout the three years, he undertook practical courses in woods in Scotland, England and on the continent of Europe (this amounted to seven months' practical work).

---

* This account is drawn on E.P. Stebbing, Vols. 3 and 4.

At the end of the First World War, there was thinking in the Government of India that the Forest Service Probationers should be wholly trained in India at the Forest Research Institution at Dehradun subject to adequate arrangements being made. As forests were a "transferred" subject in Bombay (Now Maharashtra) under Dyarchy and became a "transferred" subject for the whole of India in 1937, it was decided in 1926 to train the Indian probationers of the Indian Forest Service at Dehradun, using the FRI building at the Chandbagh locality, the FRI itself being shifted to the "New Forests" locality. Subsequently, the recruitment to the Indian Forest Service was suspended and it was decided in 1937 that direct recruits to the Superior Forest Service of a Province should receive their training at Dehradun. The first biennial course was held at Dehradun in April 1938.

Forestry Research

Before 1900, the Indian Forest service was engaged primarily on settling, demarcating and surveying the State forests and bringing their protection on a sound footing with usually conservative exploitation thereof in the more accessible form. From 1900 onwards, a more scientific attitude towards forestry and utilization of forestry products began to develop. It was Lord Curzon who in his parting year helped the birth of the Imperial FRI at Dehradun by raising the status of the Forest School at Dehradun in March 1906.

The objective of the Institute was to make better provision for the scientific research in connection with the Indian forests. Six categories of research posts were sanctioned: Silviculturist (two posts), Superintendent, Forest Working Plans, Forest Zoologist, Forest Botanist, Forest Economist and Forest Chemist.

Initially the energies of the staff were largely devoted to training on the job, their research equipment being meagre. The Industries Commission in 1916 observed that the equipment of the Institute is wholly insufficient and there is need to increase the number of Research Officers. In 1919, the Working Plan Division was re-transferred to Inspector-General's Office. In 1922-23, the report of the Retrenchment Commission had the effect of halting further development of the institute. In 1929, the work of the Institute was reviewed by the Chunilal Mehta Committee which recommended *inter alia*, the strengthening of the staff of the Institute and future lines of research.

Legal Education

Although the British Government under the Governor-General Lord Bentinck had accepted in principle in 1835 itself, the study of laws as a separate faculty (B.B. Misra, 1978: 163-175), the law colleges in various Provinces were organized on a permanent footing only a little prior to 1857. The institutionalization of the legal education began with the Government Law School, Bombay (Now Mumbai) (estd. 1855). It was affiliated to the University of Bombay (Now Mumbai) in 1861, was re-christened as Government Law College in 1925, but continued to be a part-time institution right till 1938 (R.P. Karve, 1938). The poor condition of legal education in Bengal was commented upon by the Sadler Commission. Consequently, Calcutta (Now Kolkata) University took action to weed out commercially run law colleges and set up a high-quality Government Law College.

There was an important co-ordinating initiative during Dyarchy. At that time, the Legal Practitioners' Act, 1879 continued to regulate various grades of practitioners who were under the disciplinary jurisdiction of the High Courts. There was not only no All-India Bar but not even a Provincial Bar. Munshi Ishwar Charan moved a resolution in the Legislative Assembly in February 1921 to create an autonomous All-India Bar with power to regulate legal profession and education. Bowing before popular pressure, the Government of India set up the Indian Bar Committee in 1923 under the Chairmanship of Sir Edward Chalmers, retired Chief Justice of Patna High Court, to report, *inter alia*, on the possibility of constituting an All India Bar or Provincial Bars. The Indian Bar Council Act 1926 was passed by the Central Legislature in terms of the recommendations of the Committee. While the Act did not satisfy the nationalist opinion, yet a unification at the Provincial Bar level was achieved by merging Vakils and pleaders in the class of advocates and the Advisory Bar Councils were created in the five British Provinces of Bombay (Now Maharashtra), Bengal, Madras (Now Tamil Nadu), UP and Bihar with elected element with some powers (M.P. Jain, 1990: 680-86).

Teacher Education

Madras (Now Tamil Nadu) Presidency was in the forefront in the matter of recognising the need for taking action in regard to training of teachers for primary schools. Madras (Now Tamil Nadu) School Board Society proposed and Governor Munro approved the step in 1824. The Government initiative came later after Wood's Despatch (1854) as a result of which Presidency towns established normal schools in which Madras (Now Tamil Nadu) again took the lead (1856). Gradually, thought began to be given to the training of teachers for middle schools and for secondary schools. Again Madras (Now Tamil Nadu) University took the lead, consequent on the Hunter Commission Report (1882), in establishing a training college affiliated to the University (1886). Subsequently such colleges came up at Allahabad, Jabalpur (1890) and Rajamundry (1894). The Education Policy Resolution (1900) of Lord Curzon made clear-cut recommendations regarding curriculum and practical training of teachers. Sadler Commission (1919) recommended establishment of University Departments of Education to provide leadership and conduct research. It further wanted a professional body and registration arrangements for teachers [Sadler Report (1917): 325-328]. Sadler was far ahead of his times. The Sargent Report adopted the recommendations of a CABE Committee on teachers as below:

(1) Standard duration of training periods for different courses (pre-primary 2 years, junior basic 2 years, senior basic 3 years, graduates in high schools—one year) were laid down.
(2) Organization of refresher courses for giving in-service training to teachers was recommended.
(3) Provision of research facilities was suggested.
(4) Strengthening of teaching practice was recommended.

On the eve of Independence, there were 650 training schools and 41 training colleges. The number of teachers was 5,66,398 of whom 3,48,500 were trained teachers, constituting 61.5 per cent of the total (Progress of Education in India, 1937-1947, pp. 127-140). (The data include data for undivided Punjab and Bengal and need a slight downward adjustment to that extent.)

Part I
Higher General Education and Research

3

An Overview of Higher Education Growth, 1947-2007

This chapter attempts a review of the growth of higher general education co-ordinated by the UGC. The data relating to institutions and their enrolment presented below, however, comprise professional education including agricultural and medical.

Quantitative Expansion

In 1947-48, India had 20 Universities and 459 Colleges with an enrolment of 2,28,881 (1,83,238 in Arts and Science colleges and 45,643 in professional colleges). In 1951-52, India had 30 Universities and 488 Colleges with an enrolment of 4,17,709 (3,28,882 in Arts and Science colleges and 88,827 in professional colleges). With all the limitations of data, (due to integration of Princely States which lacked professional machinery for data collection and inclusion of intermediate students) enrolment increased by over 60 per cent in the five-year period ending 1951-52. The PoE Report states that by 1952, there was no major language area in India which did not have its own university. The new universities came up at Dharwad, Ahmedabad, Baroda, SNDT and in the then Bombay State, Poona, Rajasthan, Punjab, Gauhati, Kashmir and Roorkee (UP). The new Central University (Vishva Bharati, 1951) really represented conversion of a private into a Central University. The Central legislation in respect of a university located in the territory of a State (West Bengal) was justified by declaring it as an institution of national importance under entry 63 of the Central List of the Seventh Schedule of the Constitution.

Annexure 2.1 depicts the development of higher education in India over 60 years period 1947-48 to 2006-07. Five-yearly growth of enrolment has been given in Table 3.1 below:

Table 3.1: Five Yearly Growth of Enrolment

Years	*Percentage*	*Years*	*Percentage*
1950-51 to 1955-56	11.2	1981-82 to 1986-87	5.3
1955-56 to 1960-61	13.5	1986-87 to 1991-92	6.4
1960-61 to 1965-66	14.0	1991-92 to 1996-97	5.9
1965-66 to 1970-71	12.8	1996-97 to 2001-02	5.2
1970-71 to 1975-76	4.4	2001-02 to 2005-06	5.6
1975-76 to 1981-82	3.9	2006-07	5.3

Source: UGC Reports for various years and Moonis Raza (1991).

In the 60 year period, 1947-2007, absolute enrolment in higher education has increased hundred-fold (from 1,16,000 to 116,12,505), making India the third ranking State in the matter of higher education enrolment next only to the US and China. The number of teachers increased twenty-three fold from 21,264 in 1950-51 to 5.05 lakhs in 2006-07.

The number of universities has increased twenty-fold from 20 in 1947 to 403 in 2007-08. The number of Central Universities has increased eight-fold from 3 in 1947 to 24 in 2007-08. The State Universities have increased fifteen-fold from 17 in 1947 to 256 in 2007-08.

The 'deemed' universities increased seven-fold from 15 in 1947 to 103 in 2006, on the footing that about 15 institutions pre-dated 1947. It would be interesting to note which these 15 institutions are. This author, after a close perusal of relevant historical records, identified them as below:

(a) Three national colleges—Gurukul Kangri Haridwar, Gujarat Vidyapeeth, Ahmedabad and Tilak Maharashtra Vidyapeeth, Pune.

(b) Six institutions established by the Government: Forest

Research Institute, Dehradun (1905), IARI (first Pusa, then New Delhi) (1902); IVRI, Izatnagar (first set up in Poona in 1889 and subsequently shifted), National Dairy Research Institute, Karnal (first set in Bangalore in 1889 and then shifted), Indian School of Mines, Dhanbad (1926), Deccan College, Pune (1823).

(c) Six institutes were set up by NGOs—IISc., Bangalore, Tata Institute of Social Sciences, Mumbai (1936), Gokhale Institute of Politics and Economics, Poona (1929), Ramakrishna Mission, Calcutta (Now Kolkata) (1902), Institute of Agriculture, Allahabad; Bhatkhande Music Trust, Lucknow.

A trend since 2000 is to notify private self-financing institutions as deemed universities; the number of such deemed universities is large in Tamil Nadu and Maharashtra, but recently a few have come up in the Northern States of Rajasthan and UP as well.

There were 13 INIs in 2006-07 of which, Dakshin Bharat Hindi Prachar Sabha (Chennai, 1926) pre-dated 1947. The rest are IITs (7), All-India Medical institutions (4) and one Statistical institute. If the seven Indian Institutes of Management (IIMs), are treated as INIs, the number of INIs goes up to 20 and the number of universities goes up to 403. (*N.B.*: State-universities proper 251 + Statutory State Institutes 5 + Central Universities 24 + Deemed Universities 103 and INIs 20).

The biggest increase was in the number of colleges which increased forty-six fold from 459 in 1947 to 20,677 in 2006-07—of which constituent colleges were 525 and autonomous colleges 265, the rest being affiliated colleges. The number of colleges doubled in the period from 1997-98 (10,555 colleges) to 20,677 colleges (2006-07). The year-wise increase in the number of universities, colleges, students and teachers is given in Annexure 3.1

The structural features of the growth A however, are not encouraging. The share of under-graduate students has gone up from 83.7 per cent in 1950-51 to 88.92 per cent in 2006-07 and correspondingly the share of PG and Research students has gone down from 11.5 per cent to 9.42 per cent and from 0.83 per cent to 0.64 per cent. Arts and Allied faculty enrolment has gone up from

61.8 per cent in 1960-61 to 68.45 per cent in 2006-7 and Science & Technology faculty enrolment has fallen in corresponding years from 38.3 per cent to 31.55 per cent.

The Causal Factors of Growth

Threefold root causes of the growth in enrolment may be identified. Firstly, the 'Open Door' policy in regard to establishment of new institutions and non-selective policy in regard the admissions in Arts, Science and Commerce courses. Such an Open Door Policy was required to be followed due to pressing social, political, cultural and economic factors while only lip sympathy was paid to quality of education. Secondly, since the 1960s, the authorities have identified a new strategy of expansion, earlier called correspondence courses and which now has been re-christened as Open and Distance Learning (ODL). This system has gradually expanded and accounted for 24 per cent enrolment in 2002-03.

The growth of ODL institutions and their enrolment in the period 1962-2004 is depicted in the following Table 3.2.

Table 3.2: Growth of ODL institutions and their enrolment

Year	*Open University*	*Distance Education Institutions*	*Enrolment of DE as % of Total*
1962	—	001	—
1971	—	—	2.1
1975	—	022	—
1981	—	—	—
1982	01	034	2.6
1985	02	038	—
1990	05	046	11.5 (in 1991)
2000	09	—	—
2002	—	070	24
2004	11	104	—

Source: Composite of Table 1 and Table 2 in V.C. Kulandaiswamy: National Education Policies *vis-à-vis* Distance Education [*vide* Satish Garg *et al.*, (2006), pp. 24-38].

The third factor is privatization which was under way since 1980s, but which gathered momentum after the Structural Adjustment programme (SAP) from 1991 onwards. According to one estimate, private sector in higher education has grown to such an extent that it accounted for 43 per cent of the number of institutions and 30 per cent of enrolment by 2005-06 (Pawan Agarwal, 2009:91).

Equity Aspect of Higher Education Development

Inequities in higher education development can manifest themselves in dimensions like caste (SC/ST/OBC), class (rich/poor), regional (backward/advanced), rural/urban, community (Muslims/Hindus), sex (male/female) and handicap (now called disability).

The Indian political class, however, is particularly sensitive to the caste aspect. In pursuance of the recommendations of the Committee on SCs and STs, UGC introduced a section on SC/ST education facilities in its report in 1975-76 onwards and invited attention of universities to instructions about reservation of seats for SC/ST students. Reservation in the faculty recruitment at lecturers' level was agreed to, in principle, by the UGC in July 1975 and mechanisms were worked out July 1976. UGC also constituted a Standing Committee to monitor progress in the matter. More recently, reservation of seats in IITs/IIMs for the OBCs was implemented by a Central legislation in 2006. In the Supreme Court Judgment of April 2008 (Ramesh Thakur Case), the validity of the Act has been upheld. The question of reservation of faculty positions at Assistant Professor level in IITs/IIMs has also been broached by the Government of India. It may be noted that the State Governments have already extended reservation to reader and professor level.

Moonis Raza (1991: 53-58) has dealt at length with two select aspects of inequities in higher education, viz. the SCs and the Regional Dimension, which analysis need not be repeated. The educational backwardness of Muslims has assumed importance in the context of Sachar Report (2006). According to the NSSO data (2004-05) the share of Muslims in graduates is 6 per cent as against their share in population 20 + above at 11 per cent. They are stated to be as disadvantaged as the SCs/STs (Sachar Report: 65).

Gender disparities in higher education appear to be declining. In 1950-51 the number of girls per 100 boys was 14 which increased to

35 in 1979-80 and was 68 in 2006-07. In a conservative society like India, separate women's colleges act as a way of promoting girls' education of which there were 2260 in 2007-08 (UGC Annual Report, 2007-08: 46), the number having increased from 574 in 1979-80. A women's university was set up in Maharashtra part of Bombay Presidency as early as 1916 though it got a statutory status only shortly after Independence. Separate women's universities have been set up after independence in four more States, viz. Tamil Nadu (Mother Teresa at Kodaikanal), Andhra Pradesh (Padmavati Mahila), Karnataka (Bijapur) and there is a deemed women's university (Banasthali) in Rajasthan. The proportion of SC/ST women among college going girls is much lower.

Quality Dimension of Higher Education Development

The quality dimension of higher education assumes importance in the context of phenomenal quantitative expansion. The usage of the term standards of higher education was common till the seventies but in the eighties and in the nineties, with the recommendations of Jha Committee (1977) on accreditation and grading of universities and colleges, with NPE 1986 and with the establishment of National Assessment and Accreditation Council (NAAC) under the UGC in 1994, the usage of the term quality has become current.

The letter of Chairman, UGC dated 3rd August, 1961, establishing a Committee on Standards of University Education, is important enough to be cited in full to set forth the common perception in the matter in the 1960s:

> "Criticism, sometimes informed and sometimes uninformed, is often made of our standards of education. It is often said that during the last few years university standards in teaching and research have generally gone down noticeably largely as a consequence of the rapid increase in the number of students without corresponding expansion in the number of teachers and the laboratories and other facilities. As against this, we have to recognize that in a number of subjects in some of our universities, the present standards of teaching and research compare favourably with the best in the

advanced countries. It is apparent that the question of evaluation of standards of teaching and research has many aspects and is a very complex subject. It has been considered desirable that an objective assessment of the position should be made and measures adopted for raising standards wherever they have deteriorated."

The Chairman of the Committee was S. Govindrajulu, V-C of Sri Venkateswara University*. The members of the Standards Committee were distinguished academics. Dr. A.C. Joshi, V.C., Shri G.D. Parikh, Rector of Mumbai University, Prof. G.C. Banerjee [English Department of Bombay (Now Mumbai) University], Dr. R.C. Majumdar (Physics), Dr. George Kuriyan (Director, Delhi School of Economics), Prof. Arun Lal (Political Science), T.K.N. Menon (Education, Delhi), Dr. G.L. Dutta, VC and Dr. P.J. Philip, Jt. Secretary, UGC.

The conclusions of the Committee are worth summarizing:

(1) Standards are said to have declined from the point of view of examination results as also with reference to the expectations entertained by employing agencies and the general public.
(2) Courses of study in many universities are not related to well-defined objectives. The conditions under which teaching and learning are carried on are also far from congenial.
(3) The general opinion, however, seems to be that while the quality of the best students is as good as ever, the average product of an Indian university does not compare favourably with his counterparts in some of the well-known universities in the world.

---

* The Committee was appointed in August 1961 under Chairmanship of Prof. N.K. Sidhanta, V-C, Delhi University as Chairman, but Prof. N.K. Sidhanta died in December 1961, i.e. within four months of its appointment. The report finalized in October 1964 was signed by Prof. Govindrajulu as Chairman. Surprisingly the CABE Report on Autonomy of Higher Education Institutions (June 2005) published by NBT in 2009 calls the Report as Sidhanta Committee Report which is clearly a mistake (p.17 of CABE Report, 2005).

(4) On the other hand, many of our scholars and scientists have done outstanding work and various schemes of national development have been implemented by personnel trained in our universities.

(5) The various steps taken by the UGC have made a definite contribution to improvement of facilities in universities and colleges....(but) the resources at the disposal of the Commission have been far from adequate to deal effectively with this problem.

The Committee, *inter alia*, recommended the concept of autonomous colleges with special assistance. This concept was bodily adopted by the Kothari Commission (para 11.41) though without acknowledgement. In the matter of maintenance and coordination of standards, the Committee observed that the aim of UGC is to raise the levels of university education: Firstly, to the highest standards obtaining in our own country, secondly, to raise the best attainable in our country to international standards.

How serious is the issue of deterioration in quality of Indian Higher Education was described by the Education Commission (para 11.12):

> "There is a general feeling in India that the situation in higher education is unsatisfactory and even alarming in some ways, that the average standards have been falling and that rapid expansion has resulted in lowering quality. The examination results, the reports of Public Service Commissions, the views of employers and the assessment of teachers themselves—all seem to support this conclusion.... Many of our educationists and public men, however, have not fully realized how serious are the actual conditions—academic and physical—that obtain in the colleges and universities. Even those who are broadly aware of the situation fail to notice its poignancy because they have become used to such conditions."

The Education Commission's recommendations for improvement of quality were:

(1) Establishment of five or six major universities,
(2) Strengthening and expansion of UGC programmes of establishment of Centres of Advanced Study.

While the recommendation about major universities did not find favour with the Government, the latter scheme was given a fillip especially in the Fifth Plan (1974-79) onwards.

UGC had organized a workshop in the Indian School of Political Economy in March 1993 whose proceedings have been published. Articles by V.M. Dandekar and by Nilkanth Rath have been reproduced there. They essentially emphasize taking hard-headed measures for improving the performance and enforcing the accountability of the conventional system of higher education and supplementary measures like ODL and private universities (UGC (1993). Such measures have been taken but only half-heartedly.

In the NPE, quality aspect is dealt with under the rubric of assessment and accreditation of institutions for which the NAAC was set up. This aspect is dealt with in the chapter on organizations allied with the UGC.

ANNEXURE 3.1

Quantitative Growth of Higher Education (1947-2007)

Number of Universities and Colleges: Number of Students and Teachers (1947-48 to 2006-07)

Year	*No. of Univ.*	*No. of Colleges*	*Student Enrolment*	*% age increase over previous year*	*No. of Teachers*
1947-48	N.A.	N.A.	N.A.	N.A.	N.A.
1948-49	N.A.	N.A.	N.A.	N.A.	N.A.
1949-50	N.A.	N.A.	N.A.	N.A.	N.A.
1950-51	28	695	174000	—	21264
1951-52	30	762	199000	—	23880
1952-53	30	797	215000	—	25553
1953-54	30	824	238000	—	27680
1954-55	31	912	260000	—	30112
1955-56	32	1025	295000	—	33208
1956-57	33	1107	327000	—	36504
1957-58	37	1171	371000	—	39872
1958-59	40	1291	428000	—	43631
1959-60	40	1405	482000	—	49549
1960-61	44	1542	557000	—	55460
1961-62	46	1783	664000	—	63053
1962-63	54	1938	752000	—	66370
1963-64	55	2111	842000	—	68634
1964-65	62	2360	950000	12.8	77120
1965-66	64	2572	1067000	12.3	84676
1966-67	70	2749	1191000	11.6	93251
1967-68	70	2899	1370000	15.1	103180
1968-69	76	3112	1566000	14.3.	110943
1969-70	79	3297	1793000	14.5	119052
1970-71	84	3604	1954000	09.0	128876
1971-72	86	3896	2065000	05.7	139204
1972-73	90	4158	2168000	05.0	145524
1973-74	95	4308	2234000	03.1	156562
1974-75	102	4388	2367000	05.9	161782
1975-76	102	4508	2426000	02.5	167623
1976-77	105	4569	2432000	00.2	169615

(Contd.)

(*Contd.*)

Year	*No. of Univ.*	*No. of Colleges*	*Student Enrolment*	*% age increase over previous year*	*No. of Teachers*
1977-78	105	4375	2565000	05.5	178344
1978-79	108	4460	2618000	02.1	181659
1979-80	108	4558	2649000	01.2	188502
1980-81	112	4722	2753000	03.9	193341
1981-82	118	4886	2952000	07.3	199904
1982-83	120	5039	3133000	06.1	209017
1983-84	124	5246	3308000	07.2	216500
1984-85	125	5590	3404096	02.9	220101
1985-86	132	5816	3605029	05.9	226909
1986-87	136	6512	3757158	04.2	234388
1987-88	142	6647	4020159	07.0	241973
1988-89	144	6912	4285489	06.6	249068
1989-90	174	6949	4602680	07.4	257067
1990-91	176	7121	4924868	07.0	263125
1991-92	180	7513	5265886	06.9	270000
1992-93	187	7958	5534966	05.1	278000
1993-94	197	8210	5817249	05.1	286000
1994-95	204	8613	6113929	05.1	301000
1995-96	207	9278	6574005	07.5	310000
1996-97	214	9703	6842598	04.1	321000
1997-98	228	10555	7260418	06.1	331000
1998-99	228	11089	7705520	06.1	342000
1999-00	236	11831	8050607	04.5	351000
2000-01	245	12342	8399443	04.3	395000
2001-02	253	13150	8964680	06.7	427000
2002-03	300	15343	9516773	06.2	436000
2003-04	320	16885	9953506	04.6	457000
2004-05	343	17625	10481042	05.3	472000
2005-06	355	18064	11028020	05.2	485000
2006-07	376	20677	11612505	05.3	505000

Source: Moonis Raza (1991) and UGC Reports (1953-2007).

4

University Grants Commission (General)

Indian UGC: A Durable Entity

Indian UGC statutorily established in 1956 may be said to be a durable entity. The model on which it was founded, viz. the University Grants Committee (UGC) in the UK was wound up in 1989 and has been replaced by three British Regional Universities Funding Councils (UFCs), one each for England, Scotland and Wales, but the Indian UGC having completed 50+ years of its life was in existence at the end of 2011. Whether it would be replaced by a National Commission for Higher Education and Research (NCHER) in future, as proposed in a Central Bill introduced in Parliament in May 2010 remains to be seen.

UGC in UK

The terms of reference of UGC when it was first set up in 1919 as a Committee of the Treasury were brief, viz. "to enquire into the financial needs of university education in the UK and to advise the Government as to the application of any grants that may be made by Parliament to meet them." The placement of the Committee under the Treasury and not under the Board of Education was deliberate because the Treasury, unlike the Board of Education, had no theories or special interests in educational matters (Berdhal, 1959). Gradually, however, especially in the context of war and expansion, things began to change. UGC's terms of reference were modified in 1943 to include a statistical function—'To collect, examine and make available information relating to university education throughout the UK', and expanded further in 1946 to add a developmental function—'To assist, in consultation with the universities and other bodies concerned, the preparation and execution of such plans for the development of the universities as may from time to time be required in order to ensure that they are fully adequate to national needs'. Here, the qualifier 'national' was quite significant because it anticipated a role for the government which normally would be expected to take a view regarding such needs transcending those of an individual university.

The position of the Chairman, UGC was a full-time one since 1936. In 1943, the membership was increased from five to fifteen. In 1946, a full-time Deputy Chairman was appointed and the administrative and clerical staff was strengthened. In 1947, the responsibility for national grants to agricultural education (but not research) was transferred from the Ministry of Agriculture and Fisheries to the UGC.

It needs to be noted that the Committee of Vice-Chancellors and Principals (CVCP) in UK, corresponding to the IUB-AIU in India, came into existence in May 1918 by a resolution of an *ad-hoc* standing conference of universities. It was formally re-constituted in 1930. It has acted as a point of cohesion for university policy in Britain. CVCP has always maintained a relationship of informal co-operation with the UGC. Thanks to cooperative and joint planning with the CVCP, the UGC was able to present the Treasury in 1945 with an outline for a ten-year university development plan, which required substantially, enlarged government grants.

The Robbins Committee (1963) called UGC in UK an administrative invention, the device of interposing between the Government and institutions, a committee of persons selected for their knowledge and standing and not for their political affiliation. UGC acted, said Robbins Committee, as a buffer between the Government and the Universities and thus safeguarded their academic freedom. The Government itself respected the freedom of the UGC because it generally accepted the advice of the UGC regarding:

1. The magnitude of the total grants which it was appropriate to give to the universities as a whole,

2. Distribution of the grants between different universities, once it was made available.

The period 1946-63 could be said to be the golden period of UK-UGC.

However, there were some developments which underlined the trend towards diminution of prestige of UGC. In 1964, UGC was transferred from the Treasury to the Department of Education and Science (DES) and in 1966-67, it was required to submit to the control of PAC and C&AG. The setting up of a Government sector of Colleges of Advanced Technology (CAT), later on renamed as Polytechnics, with a coordinating body called Polytechnic and Colleges Funding Council (PCFC), meant reduction of the territory of influence of UGC, but did not affect its prestige. Later on, UGC lost control over crucial salary question within the universities. It was, however, in the 1981-1984 period when there were heavy reductions in the financial allocations of UGC by the DES that the downfall of UGC began. UGC tried to protect what it called "unit of resource" at the cost of the number of students, but this was unacceptable to both the political parties. UGC was also equivocal in its attitude towards academic tenure. In 1989, the Conservative Government under John Major decided to abolish both UGC and PCFC and to have a new body called University Funding Committee (UFC). As observed by Michael Shattock (1994), UFC would be more managerial, more subordinate to government and much less responsive to the universities; it would have more muscle to implement policy and much less to make it.

The reason for this comparative historical introduction to an account of the Indian UGC is to underline the role played by conventions in UK in inter-agency relationships, both as between UGC and the Government of the day and UGC and CVCP, conventions which are absent in India.

Indian UGC in the Making

It would be no exaggeration to say that in India, the UGC was in the air since the end of First World War. And this was so not only because of the establishment of UK-UGC in 1919, but because of the specific recommendation of the Sadler Commission (1919), in its Chapter

(Chapter L: Sections 43-55) relating to the Government and the Universities. It makes out a case that in spite of devolution to the provincial governments (consequent on the Reform of 1919 in the shape of Dyarchy), there would be important functions which the Government of India alone was in a position to perform for which it should create an independent organization. These functions included (1) Visitation (inspection) of universities, (2) Co-ordination of their development, and (3) Stimulation and promotion of research including both scientific and social scientific. Here was a blueprint for creation not only of the UGC but also of the ICSSR (which the Sadler Commission perhaps envisaged to be an integral part of UGC).

The first reference in Indian official literature to the UGC in UK appears in the Quinquennial Progress of Education Report (1927-1932) published in 1933. This appears to have prompted Dr. Amarnath Jha to move a resolution in the Inter-University Board (IUB)—predecessor of AIU, as early as in 1936 recommending the institution in each province or a group of provinces of a University Grants Committee on the same lines as the UGC of Great Britain. The Board welcomed the proposal and circulated it to the universities for their reaction. The proposal was welcomed by Agra, Allahabad, Andhra and Delhi, but not by Aligarh and Madras (S.S. Bhandarkar, 1975). Dr. Amarnath Jha's resolution was prescient because it appeared to recognize the difference in the conditions between UK, an island state, and India a colony but with the potential to become a sovereign state which, with its subcontinental size, would require UGC in every province [This is reminiscent of the NPE 86 proposal for State Council for Higher Education (SCHE)]. The Quinquennial Progress of Education Report (1932-1937) says: "In recent years, there has been a tendency to multiply facilities for every branch of study in all universities in India with the result that there is much overlapping of courses and much expenditure which ought to be avoided if there were closer co-operation between the university authorities. In the last review it was stated that considerable improvement has been made in this direction in the UK by the agency of UGC which keeps in close touch with universities and is thus in a position to give authoritative and experienced advice not only to the grant-giving authorities, but also to the universities themselves. At its meeting held in 1936, the IUB passed a resolution recommending the institution, in each province or a group of provinces, a UGC on the same lines as the UGC in UK. It would be interesting to see what practical effort the setting of such bodies in India would achieve."

This brings us to the Sargent Plan (1944), referred to in Chapter 2, which was the first official report to recommend the setting up of the UGC in India. A substantial proportion of the chapter on university development in Sargent Plan is devoted to description and criticism of universities. However, the Sargent Plan was clear that the Indian UGC should be patterned on that of UGC of UK with the difference that it should be set up by statute. It should consist of a few eminent persons not directly connected with Government (Central/Provincial) or with a particular university (thus serving Vice-Chancellors were ruled out), but they should have considerable experience of university administration. The following functions were envisaged:

1. To exercise a general supervision over the allocation of grants to universities from public funds. In the case of Central Universities, all grants for new developments would be made through Grants Committee. Provincial governments are to consult UGC for substantial new developments.
2. Grants should be in the form of 'block' grants (for a period of a year) [In the case of UK, it was for 5 years].
3. To eliminate overlapping and dispersion of efforts among universities, both provincial and central.
4. To adjust the output of the universities to the economic needs of the country.
5. To prevent undesirable, unhealthy and uneconomic competition between universities.
6. To remove all inter-provincial barriers (to counteract provincial outlook which puts obstacles in the way students getting facilities which are not available in their own areas).
7. To visit universities periodically with a view to ascertaining their needs at first hand.
8. To establish cultural contacts and to arrange for the exchange of teachers and students with foreign universities.
9. Following functions are also mentioned while judging that the IUB is not suitable to do the work of co-ordination: (a) insist much on various standards where this is absolutely

> required, (b) establishment of conditions of service of teachers including remunerations, and (c) prevention of creation of new universities, need for which has not been established (Sargent Plan, 1944: IV: 37-49).

Reacting to the Sargent Plan, the IUB stated that any kind of control or inspection is not consistent with the dignity and autonomy of the universities by which the IUB might have meant that it was opposed to any surprise inspections because it could not feign ignorance of UK-UGC practice. It had, it is, therefore, to be assumed, no objection to Quinquennial inspection connected with fixation and release of block grants (Bhandarkar, 1975: 167-168).

The advisory UGC, which was set up in 1946 and functioned between 1946-1950, was an *ad-hoc* administrative measure taken by the Central government in a period of uncertainty, as to the shape of the Constitution of the Indian dominion. It was not the statutory UGC recommended by the Sargent Plan. According to the Decennial Review (1937-1947), it was a four member body. To allay suspicions of interference on the part of provincial universities, it was agreed that to begin with, it would deal in a consultative and advisory capacity only with the central universities of Banaras, Aligarh and Delhi. The first meeting was held in February 1946. However, provincial universities of Calcutta, Andhra and Nagpur at first and Allahabad, Saugar and Annamalai subsequently sent their development schemes to the UGC. Consequently, the membership was raised to seven and the range of functions of the UGC was also contemplated to be raised. In the financial year 1946-47, Rs. 18.70 lakhs were sanctioned to three Central Universities of which Rs. 11.50 lakhs was of non-recurring nature, for capital expenses. The Budget Estimate for 1947-48 was Rs. 47.39 lakh (Decennial Review 1948: 283-284).

The Quinquennial Review of Progress of Education (1947-1952) makes no reference to the UGC at all. We, however, get the following information in Radhakrishnan Report—"again in 1947 its membership was increased and it was empowered to deal with all universities. Neither the Chairman nor the members are full-time. The members include such prominent people as the premier of a Province and the Vice-Chancellor of more than one university, the people who may be able to attend an occasional meeting of the Committee, but cannot possibly spare the time to familiarize themselves with all the universities requesting their assistance. We say this in no spirit of criticism. The Committee is still a very new body and there has been a good deal of doubt as to the way in which it should exercise its powers and duties. In particular, it has had no funds placed at its disposal by the Government. It has only been able to make recommendations to the Education Ministry, which in its turn transmit the case to the Finance Ministry; and in these circumstances, the Finance Ministry is inevitably required to judge for itself each recommendation for a grant made by the Committee. In spite of these difficulties the work of the UGC has been of considerable value" (Radhakrishnan Report: 1950: XIII. 11). Radhakrishnan Commission's comments on advisory UGC are unfair because it chooses to ignore the actual recommendations of the Sargent Plan. Jha Committee report states that advisory UGC's activities were suspended in 1950 pending consideration of the recommendations of the Radhakrishnan Report (Jha Report, 1977: 1.1).

Radhakrishnan Commission avoided any reference to UK-UGC although it had a British Member (James Duff, Vice-Chancellor of Durham University), apparently to avoid an impression of following an imperialist model. Radhakrishnan Commission differed from the Sargent Plan only in its suggestion to call the new organization as "Commission" in place of Committee. It insisted that "it be an expert body." "It was not sure about the number"—it could be "5 or 7". Assuming the number to be five, two would be officers (Finance Secretary and Education Secretary) and three would be experts. The inter-university allocation made by it within the total grant given by the Government was to be final. The audited accounts, unlike in Britain, were to be subject to scrutiny by the Finance Ministry, but there was no reference to PAC/C&AG. The Centre was to be responsible for advanced work, i.e. P-G and research work of provincial universities to the extent of 50 per cent. It is stated that within the next few years the amount spent on P-G and research should be doubled. It is further stipulated that capital grants would be 'earmarked' by the Commission for particular projects. It insisted that the Members of the Commission must be people of very high reputation, both for wisdom and integrity, without any political, regional or communal consideration and they would be assisted by a

Panel of experts in each subject, who should visit universities and report on them. It would have been helpful if the Radhakrishnan Commission had opined regarding the membership or otherwise of Vice-Chancellors who were barred by the UK-UGC, on the ground of conflict of interest. "They should be", added Radhakrishnan Report, "elder Statesmen of the University World. Their status should be equivalent to that of the Federal PSC. They should be debarred from subsequent holding of any university office. At least one member should be a Scientist and one member a Humanist." This was a wholesome stipulation emphasizing the need for balance between physical-biological sciences and social sciences/humanities. The Commission does not favour any duties other than allocation of grants. The Commission is particular about the duty of visitation "as often as they can". The Commission feels that the UGC being available for consultation and advice would itself cast a great burden on it.

It would thus be seen that with all its rhetoric, Radhakrishnan Commission did not give much guidance regarding organization of the Indian UGC. Bhandarkar (1975) the historian of IUB does not specifically deal with the reaction of IUB to Radhakrishnan Report's take on the UGC.

From Radhakrishnan to the passing of the UGC Act (1949-1956)

The statutory UGC came into existence in 1956; this delay in giving statutory shape to the UGC did not bode well for the nascent UGC. Amrik Singh [2004(a): 32-48] has called it a forgotten chapter in the history of higher education, which he has unearthed by research and which enables one to appreciate the nature of forces at work. The Central Government appears to have focused on giving effect to the powers vested in the Central Government contained in entry 66 of Central List, Schedule VII of the newly adopted Constitution about "co-ordination and determination of standards in institutions for higher education or research and scientific and technical institutions". The provisions of a draft bill entitled: "The Universities (Regulation of Standards) Bill" included, *inter alia*, the following (Bhandarkar, 1975: 112-115):

(1) There would be a Central Council of University Education—at least one-third members of which would be V-Cs.
(2) No university under a State Act would be recommended unless Central Government, by a notification, makes a declaration to that effect.
(3) Central Council would have powers to direct the university to take such action as may be specified.
(4) In case of non-compliance with its directions, Central Council would advise Central Government to derecognize any degree of such a university for purpose of employment under the Central Government.

The Bill was circulated to the States and Universities. None of the State Governments except one opposed the Bill. But universities persistently opposed the Bill and the lead in the matter was taken by the IUB and a prominent part was played by Dr. A.L. Mudaliar, Chairman of IUB's Standing Committee who happened to be signatory of the Radhakrishnan Report. According to Bhandarkar, Mudaliar's main contention was that the composition of the Council, viz. the number and qualifications of members was not spelt out in the main Act, but was left to the Rules. He also said that the IUB regarded itself as the co-ordinating body for universities in India, considering any new Council to be a usurper of this function. A perusal of Mudaliar's Dadabhai Naorojee Lecture is rewarding in this regard because it shows Mudaliar's evident lack of enthusiasm for Radhakrishnan Report and the advisory UGC under C.D. Deshmukh (A.L. Mudaliar, 1960: 40, 44-45).

Amrik Singh's detailed account shows that in the special meeting held in September 1952 between the Government and the Vice-Chancellors, the staunchest opponents were Mudaliar and V.K.R.V. Rao. Other members like Hansa Mehta and R.K.S. Chetty were constructively critical. Thus, R.K. Shanmukham Chetty (V-C, Annamalai, but more importantly, former Union Finance Minister), suggested that Government had mixed up its priorities. A grant-giving body should be established first and then its powers defined. He conceded that when the Central Government funds a major part of finances, it must have some voice. But Mudaliar and V.K.R.V. Rao were staunch opponents. Mudaliar stated that the Bill has not realized the implications of the likely clash between the new authority and the IUB which had existed for 24 years and had already exerted to put up standards. V.K.R.V. Rao suggested that the Standing Committee of IUB should act as a liaison between the UGC and the universities, implying that the real power should vest in the IUB, the grant giving UGC acting only as a funnel of funds.

Amrik Singh points out that Humayun Kabir who felt like a 'culprit in the dock' made some points but could not carry conviction. Ultimately, the Government withdrew the proposed Bill and decided to set up a University Grants Commission which combined the powers of grants giving and co-ordination and determination of standards as envisaged in the Constitution, but the functions and powers of the UGC did not include the two crucial powers of (1) issuing direction to any university to take a specified action and (2) derecognizing the degrees. Amrik Singh says that the Medical Council (existing since 1933) had the power to derecognize degrees.

The present author feels that the Central Government ought to have squarely met the challenge of V.K.R.V. Rao and Mudaliar who were such vocal opponents of the Draft Bill. Basically, the Government spokesman had not done his homework by way of mastery of canonical reports—Sadler, Sargent and Radhakrishnan. Firstly, the Sadler Commission had clearly distinguished between co-ordination of development of universities (by reducing overlap) and standards which at any given time are unique. One determines and maintains standards, and seeks to enhance them; one does not co-ordinate them. Secondly, Dr. Mudaliar was a medical doctor and was associated not only with the Madras University (of which he was a V-C for over 25 years), but also the Medical Council of India, since its inception in 1933. He was well aware that the MCI was the co-ordinating body for Medical education and had the power to derecognize medical degrees, notwithstanding the existence of IUB. It was improper on his part, not to be frank on this point. Incidentally S. Gopal has pointed out another example of Mudaliar's inconsistency. He was signatory of the Radhakrishnan Report, but he went back and criticized its recommendations about admission on merit (S. Gopal, 1989: 211). Thirdly, Sadler Plan had clearly spelt out why IUB could not act as an authoritative co-ordinator being a purely advisory body, lacking authority to enforce standards, and lacking the power of purse. Being a membership organization of universities, it could not arbitrate among them. Fourthly, Radhakrishnan Commission was also well aware of IUB's limitations. It had said, "The Board has acted as an advisory body, but its influence has not been as potent as might have been. The universities have not always been inclined to follow the advice given by the collective voice of the V-C's which in effect the Board had become" (Radhakrishnan Report: 15). Fifthly, IUB as such and its office bearers, following the wholesome British traditions, should have refrained from holding forth on university autonomy which belongs to an individual university. IUB was just an administrative association of universities. This has been well brought out by Eric Ashby (1963: 70-71). Therefore, the Chairman of the Standing Committee or for that matter any other office-bearer of the IUB like V.K.R.V. Rao were bound to act under a self-denying ordinance. They should have made clear in what capacity they were speaking. Eric Ashby has emphasized that CVCP in UK observes this distinction scrupulously. Sixthly, the UK-UGC is acknowledged by every academic authority as a model but there is not adequate awareness that it is the strict rule of composition of UK-UGC that no serving Vice-Chancellor is ever nominated as a Member. It is in deference to the conflict of interest which would arise if the serving Vice-Chancellors were to be associated with the duty of allocation of grants. (This point was emphasized by the Sapru Committee (1964) and almost all parliamentary committees thereafter in India and led to a major amendment of the UGC Act in 1971). Seventhly, and this is a subtle point made by the Robbins Committee, the very act of funding involves judgment as to co-ordination and standards. Says the Robbins Committee: "It is recognized that subvention involves allocation and that allocation may involve co-ordination and certain controls; and it is not felt that such measures need be an improper encroachment on legitimate academic freedoms" (Robbins Report: para 725).

Finally, both the Central Government as well as the IUB missed one basic point that unlike the UK which was a unitary country, India was a federal polity and a mechanism to give representation to end to ensure participation of State Governments was absolutely necessary. Thus, State Government representatives were unjustly kept out of the management of the UGC. What is more, it was not felt necessary to associate them with the UGC in any annual consultative role.

The Steps leading to the establishment of the UGC in 1953-56

In April 1953, the Ministry of Education convened a Conference of State Education Ministers and Vice-Chancellors of Universities, which recommended a single body carrying the functions of (1) grants and (2) co-ordination and standards (Jha Report: 1.11). Although the grants function does involve a judgment as to co-ordination and standards, for legal purposes, this specification was felt necessary; the decision also ensured that the granting body would not be able to devote itself effectively to the other functions.

In 1952, the Government issued a resolution setting up an interim UGC which was formally inaugurated by the then Union Education Minister Maulana Abul Kalam Azad on 28th December, 1953. Its functions were:

(1) To advise Government on the allocation of grants-in-aid from public funds to Central Universities,
(2) To advise Government on the allocation of grants-in-aid to other universities and institutions of higher learning whose case for such grants may be referred to the Commission by Government, and
(3) To advise Universities and other Institutions of higher learning in respect of any question referred by the Government to the Commission (Report of UGC, December 1953 to March 1957).

It would thus be evident that the interim Commission was to advise the Government regarding grants to central universities. Other functions were contingent. A perusal of the report of the interm body for a little over 2 years shows that the Commission became active in the last year after C.D. Deshmukh joined as its Chairman.

In the meanwhile, the UGC Bill was introduced in Parliament in September 1954 and was referred to a Joint Select Committee. The Bill, as amended by the Joint Select Committee was passed by the

Lok Sabha on 28th November, 1955 and it was passed by the Rajya Sabha on 7th December, 1955. The Bill was piloted by Dr. M.M. Das, Parliamentary Secretary to Education Minister in the first phase and was piloted jointly by Dr. M.M. Das and Dr. K.L. Srimali, Dy. Minister in the second phase. Dr. M.M. Das in his speech in Lok Sabha on 22nd November, 1956 had pointed out that the report of the Joint Select Committee had reduced the UGC to a mere advisory consultation body, having no powers to enforce its recommendations or decisions (Jha Report: 1.12). Factually, the then Education Minister Maulana Azad, did not attend parliamentary proceedings and this was pointed out by vigilant members. The presiding officers saved Dr. Das and Maulana Azad from embarrassment.

A lost opportunity

Thus in 1956 India lost an opportunity of establishing a strong standards-oriented UGC with a federal slant. UGC Act has been amended only thrice after 1956 till 2011 as will be noted below: 1972, 1984 and 1985. Thereafter, the proposal to amend UGC Act has been hanging fire. The following sentence has been ritualistically repeated in successive Annual Reports of UGC including for 2006-07: "An amendment to the UGC Act is under consideration of the Government of India to meet emerging challenges in higher education." As is well-known, Indian Parliament has been suffering from legislative fatigue for the last several years and one cannot hazard a guess as to when the UGC Act would be amended and what its contents would be.

The Correct Date of Foundation of the UGC

In the author's view, the year of foundation of UGC should be taken to be 1956 and not 1953. The authority of Education Commission (1966: 1367) supports the date 1956 "on the recommendation of the University Education Commission, the UGC was established under an Act of Parliament in 1956". There is also internal evidence by way of nomenclature (the body set up in 1953 was called Interim UGC) and composition, *vide* Table 4.1.

In support of the author's contention that interim UGC was not the regular UGC which came into existence only in November 1956, the composition of the Commission is compared in the Table 4.1 at two points of time.

Table 4.1: Composition of the UGC

No.	*Composition as on 28th December, 1953*	*No.*	*Composition as on 31st March, 1957*
1.	Dr. Shanti Swarup Bhatnagar, Secretary to Government—Chairman	1.	Dr. C.D. Deshmukh—Chairman (w.e.f. 28-5-57)
2.	Dr. A.L. Mudaliar, V-C, Madras	2.	Dr. A.L. Mudaliar, V-C, Madras
3.	Acharya Narendra Dev, V-C, BHU	3.	Prof. N.K. Sidhanta, V-C, Calcutta
4.	Sir N.S. Wadia, V-C, Bombay	4.	Shri G.C. Chatterji, V-C, Rajputana
5.	Dr. J.C. Ghosh, V-C, Calcutta	5.	Dr. M.S. Thacker, Director, Scientific & Industrial Research
6.	Dr. Zakir Husain, MP & V-C, AMU	6.	Dr. Zakir Husain, MP
7.	Pandit H.N. Kunzru, MP	7.	Pandit H.N. Kunzru, MP
8.	Shri K.G. Saiyidin, Ministry of Education	8.	Shri K.G. Saiyidin, Ministry of Education
9.	Shri K.R.K. Menon, Ministry of Finance	9.	Shri S. Ratna, Ministry of Finance

Source: Relevant UGC Reports.

It would be seen that the idea to have an independent Chairman, maximum three V-Cs, three eminent persons and maximum two officers could not be implemented in 1953, when the Chairman was a bureaucrat (Secretary to Government, Ministry of Natural Resources) and the number of V-Cs was disproportionate (5). Incidentally, Dr. Bhatnagar worked as Chairman from 28th December, 1953 to 1st January, 1955 (when he died). He was succeeded by Humayun Kabir, Secretary Education who worked from 2nd January, 1955 to 22nd February, 1956. Pandit H.N. Kunzru officiated as Chairman from 23rd February, 1956 to 27th August, 1956, when C.D. Deshmukh, ICS (retd.) and former Union Finance Minister took over as Chairman. Incidentally, Dr. M.S. Thacker Member in 1957, was not a bureaucrat but a scientist, classified as an eminent person.

A second lost opportunity?

If 1956 is the correct date of foundation of UGC, then it has to be held that the Golden Jubilee celebration of UGC in 2003 was premature. Apparently time for preparation was short and two hastily compiled publications[1] were brought out which were not up to the mark, giving one a sense of another lost opportunity.

The Legal Framework of the UGC

The Legal framework of the UGC may be considered first, followed by Administrative framework, under the following headings:

(1) Composition of the Commission
(2) Functions and Powers of the Commission
(3) Rules made by the Ministry
(4) Regulations made by the UGC
(5) Guidelines issued by the Commission

Composition of the Commission

In November 1956, the Commission consisted of 9 Members including an independent Chairman (full-time), three eminent academic persons, three Vice-Chancellors and two Officers of Central Government. This was amended with effect from 17th June, 1972 to provide for 12 members. Since 1972, the Commission consists of:

1. A full-time Chairman and a full-time Vice-Chairman appointed by the Central Government
2. Ten other members appointed by the Central Government of whom:
   (a) Two are officers of the Central Government to represent that Government

1. These two publications are referred to in Introduction in the course of discussion, but are listed below for ready reference: (1) Kuldeep Kaur (2003): *Higher Education in India* (1781-2003): Policies, Planning and Implementation [UGC, New Delhi and Centre for Research in Rural & Industrial Development (CRRID), Chandigarh]. (2) Dr. Kavita A. Sharma (2003): *Fifty Years of UGC* (New Delhi, UGC).

(b) Four are teachers, and
(c) The remaining are persons (i) who have knowledge and experience in agriculture, commerce, forestry and industry or (ii) are members of learned professions like engineering, medicine, law etc. or (iii) are vice-chancellors of universities or (iv) are persons who are educationists of repute or have obtained high academic distinctions.

It would be seen that the major amendments are in respect of—

(i) appointment of a full-time Vice-Chairman,
(ii) deletion of Vice-Chancellor as a category and replacement of the same by teachers as a category,
(iii) introduction of a broad category consisting of specialists in functional areas, professionals, vice-chancellors and educationists.

There is an interesting history to this change. The Sapru Committee (1964) (which was a Committee of MPs to review higher education) took the view that it is undesirable to appoint a serving V-C as a member of the UGC to avoid divided loyalties (since universities are the grantees of UGC assistance) and to ensure independence of the Commission. The precedent of UK-UGC was cited. The Sapru Committee also recommended that the number of members should be increased to 15 of whom 5 should be full-time members (Sapru Report: 28, 44). The 102nd Report of Estimates Committee of Parliament (1970) reiterated this recommendation. Accordingly, UGC Act was amended in June 1970 to provide that no serving V-C would be eligible for appointment as a member of UGC. The amendment Act also provided for increase in the number of members to 12 of whom 3 would be full-time. However, before the amendment could be brought into force, there were general elections and a new Government came into power, which amended the Act as indicated w.e.f. 17th June, 1972. The justification given was as below:

1. The Education Commission had recommended in 1966 that the UGC should not be deprived of the services of eminent

persons merely on the ground that they happen to be V-Cs and that Government should have as large an area as possible from which to select members.

2. Secondly, the appointment of a full-time Vice-Chairman was considered preferable to the appointment of three full-time members. The distinction between full-time and part-time members would have been invidious and the present strength of the Commission was considered adequate.

Jha Committee (1977) recommended enlargement of the Commission's composition from 12 to 18 by adding six members as below: (1) Two college teachers, (2) One person from the field of secondary education, (3) One expert in the field of rural higher education, (4) One expert in the field of non-formal education, and (5) Secretary, Planning Commission as an *ex-officio* member. The Janata Government which considered Jha Committee Report did not accept the recommendation as such, but the spirit of it so that these could be the relevant fields and, there could be an Advisory Committee consisting, *inter alia*, of such members which could meet twice a year. In other words, Janata Government wanted a Senate type advisory body for the UGC as in the case of Universities. Even so, the Janata Government did not recommend inclusion of any representative of State Governments as such in the context of India being a federal polity.

The 66th Report of the Estimates Committee (1989) referred to Sapru and succeeding reports and expressed unhappiness about the Government's virtual rejection of the recommendation about the V-Cs not at any time becoming members of UGC to avoid conflict of interest. It urged the Government to strengthen UGC appropriately in the context of NPE 1986/92. Any action on this recommendation of the Estimates Committee which is generally binding on the Government apparently got linked up with the proposed amendments to the UGC Act.

The Missing Federal Dimension

Apropos the composition, although UGC is primarily to assist the numerous State universities, there is no provision for the appointment of a State Government representative, as there is a provision for two Central Government officers who normally happen to be Union Education Secretary and Union Finance Secretary. This point has been flagged in general terms earlier, but a legal analysis of provisions would help the debate. As a matter of fact, the text of the Act or the scheme of the Act does not exclude the appointment of State Government representatives so long as their number does not exceed two and so long as they are within the parameters of S.5(c) of the UGC Act. The proviso to S.5(c) says: "provided that not less than one-half of the number chosen under this clause (author's note which allows nomination of four members from diverse fields) shall be from among persons who are not officers of the Central Government or of any State Government". The clause implies that not more than 2 (i.e. ½ of 4) shall be officers. In other words, all four can be non-officials but not more than two can be Central/State officials. This being the position, Central Government had appointed Prof. Kireet Joshi, a Special Secretary to Government of India (Education Department) as a UGC member in addition to Union Education Secretary and Union Finance Secretary in the years 1982-85. This was not challenged, and rightly so, because the incumbent was an educationist. So, nothing in the Act prevents the Central Government from appointing two State Government officers as members, so long as they are professionals or experts of various categories [listed in Section 5(c)]. An Education Secretary of State Government, so long as he is an educationist or has obtained academic distinctions or is an engineer etc. can be appointed. There is every justification for two State Government officers (one Director of Education and One Secretary of education) to be appointed as Members to preserve the true spirit of co-operative federalism. Incidentally, other apex bodies do have State Government representatives on their executive committee, e.g. AICTE/NCTE etc. Unfortunately, State Governments have not gotten wise to the point and have not lobbied and vested interests (which regard teachers alone as educationists and deny the label to educational administrators even of long standing), have ensured that the Central Government does not even think of the matter, not to say act.

Functions and Powers of the UGC including Rules, Regulations and Guidelines

The UGC's functions and powers are extensive. They include the funding of institutions, establishment and maintenance of inter-university centres, advisory and regulatory functions and penal powers. The regulatory functions include collection of information, conduct of inspections and specification and definition of standards in respect of which the UGC can make regulations. The penal powers of the UGC include [*vide* SS 12(B), 14, 22, 23, 24], the power to withhold grants, the power not to make a grant and, the power, to launch a prosecution for unauthorized use of the term university. However, the UGC has not been known to have used its regulatory and penal powers extensively. Firstly, the penalty is ridiculously low (fine of Rs. 1000). Secondly, Central Government/UGC have been slow in framing rules and regulations, e.g. Rules regarding supplying information by the Universities to the UGC were framed as late as 1979 and "fitness-to-receive-grants" rules, which are part of the armour of the UGC to enforce Section 12(B) [so numbered from 1-10-1984 but earlier S. 12(A)], in respect of many new types of universities have either not been framed or framed belatedly. The first Open University in the country was set up in 1982 (Andhra Pradesh) but fitness rules for OU's were framed only in 1989. Even by 2005, "fitness-to-receive-grants" rules had not been framed in respect of Law Universities and Animal Husbandry Universities. Thirdly, UGC has not been conducting inspections of universities. Fourthly, UGC has not used its power to withhold grants from universities. Its inaction was sought to be justified by the Kothari Commission on the ground that UGC can become an effective instrument of upgradation of standards only if it follows the method of persuasion rather than coercion (Kothari Report: 13.74). Amrik Singh in his article in a compilation (1974: 75) was scathing: "Notwithstanding what the Education Commission has said by way of an apologia for the UGC, the UGC would discharge its functions better if it practised a judicious mixture of persuasion and coercion rather than only persuasion. The danger now is that unless the UGC shows leadership of a decisive and vigorous kind, it will soon get blunted as an instrument of academic change and progress." The

Rudolphs (1972: 402-03), had a different take, noting that the reluctance to use negative sanctions dates back in India to pre-Independence days, and apart from the minor point that D.S. Kothari doubled both as Chairman UGC and Chairman Education Commission, with an interest in shielding the UGC, there was no reason why the UGC inspection teams representing professional rather than bureaucratic interests could not have been set up so that they were not seen as a threat to the autonomy of the universities.

Most of UGC's regulatory and penal functions/powers directly impact respective education institutions but since these institutions are owned/operated or substantially aided by the Centre and/or the States, they bring UGC in an encounter with them, which is reviewed below.

UGC and the Central Government

The Central Government can create any Central University/Institution without consulting the UGC. It can also fund certain universities directly rather than through the UGC (thus the IGNOU is directly funded by the Education Ministry and the Central Agricultural University in Manipur by the Ministry of Agriculture). The Central Government has powers to issue directives to the UGC on questions of policy relating to national purposes and also to require the UGC to furnish to it returns and information (S. 20 and S. 21 of UGC Act). Moreover, the Central Government by appointing a review committee [known as Jha Committee] to review the work of the UGC in 1974, as insisted upon by the 114th Report of PAC (April 1970), has created a precedent.

The case of deemed universities to be notified u/s 3 of the UGC Act shows that, the advisory functions of the UGC *vis-à-vis* the Centre are of an on-going nature. For the financing of Delhi Colleges and Central Universities, the Central Government, i.e. Ministry of Education has effectively made the UGC its agent, but the Central Government remains responsible to Parliament for the proper administration of the Central Universities including the visitorial functions like appointment of a Vice-Chancellor, approval of its statutes, and visitations, i.e. inspections including *ad-hoc* inquiries/ investigations. The separation of visitorial powers from the funding function has created tension areas in the relationship of the UGC with the Central Government as documented in the Madhuri Shah Report. Notwithstanding the areas of friction, the Central Government has not hesitated to enlarge powers of the UGC's by the 1984 amendment, enabling the UGC to set up, after its prior approval, inter-university centres (IUCs). Since 1985, the UGC has set up six inter-university centres.

UGC and the State Governments

A major amendment to the UGC Act bearing on the State Universities and Colleges took place in 1972. It was the result of prodding by the UGC in regard to State governments' tendency to establish universities without adequate justification and preparation. The original intention was to put a straightforward ban on opening of new universities and colleges, but it has got enacted in the following form:

> "No grant shall be given by the Central Government, the Commission or any other organization receiving any funds from a Central Government, to a university which is established after the commencement of the University Grants (Amendment) Act, 1972 unless the Commission has after satisfying itself as to such matters as may be prescribed, declared such a university to be fit for receiving grants."

The provision came into effect on 17th June 1972. It did not affect the tendency of State Governments to establish new universities at places and at times they wished. It only denied them UGC funds for a few years unless they complied with rules as to "fitness to receive grants" referred to earlier. These rules essentially required a minimum investment, and compliance with the recommendations of the Gajendragadkar Committee on governance of universities and colleges.

The very existence of an academic regulatory body like the UGC in a federal country like India raises the problem of the triangular relationship between the UGC, the universities (which include colleges), and the State Governments and the need to devise necessary working mechanisms. The first Chairman of the UGC, C.D. Deshmukh, identified this problem and observed that it would be necessary for certain conventions to be established by agreement between the State and the Central Government and between the Universities and the UGC (*vide* p. 9 of UGC Report for 1953-56). This was a clear hint of the need for institutionalization. However, the UGC in its successive annual reports merely made a grievance of the State Governments not consulting it before establishing new universities or recognizing new colleges. It did not realize that in the absence of a direct relationship as in the case of the Centre, there was a need for a participatory forum and institutional arrangements to support the forum, through which discussion, deliberation and dialogue between the parties concerned can be conducted and co-operation actualized. This was all the more necessary because the numbers involved were, even then, large and were bound to increase. A two-fold inter-locking strategy comprising (a) "aggregation" of interests of the institutions (e.g. a State level organization for State universities and colleges, and State Ministries and Directorates) and (b) a supportive decentralist instrumentality of outreach (e.g. by way of regional offices) was clearly indicated. UGC, however, decentralized its operations in relation to certain collegiate schemes only from 1994 onwards and so far State UGCs are concerned, UGC first opposed them and when the NPE 1986/92 made a clear-cut recommendation for their establishment under the name of SCHEs, UGC has merely temporized.

Guidelines for Colleges

On the eve of Independence, India had 459 Arts and Science Colleges with an enrolment of 1,83,238 which number had gone up in 2006-07 to 20,677 colleges, accounting for a total enrolment of 116.13 lakh of which 90.24 per cent was at the under-graduate level and 67.14 per cent at post-graduate level. Hence, the importance of UGC's approach to affiliation system including appreciation of the role of State Governments in the matter. On this point, the Kothari Commission's views were as below:

> "Affiliation of colleges is an academic matter which should be granted by the universities. But since each affiliation creates eligibility for aid, they should consult the State

Government in respect of all private colleges before a final decision is taken" (Kothari Report, para 13.53).

UGC signally failed to evolve any guidelines till it was prodded by the Public Accounts Committee (*vide* its 73rd Report: 95 April 1978). The UGC formulated the guidelines in December, 1987, according to which the university is to constitute a Committee on which the State Government is to be represented to consider the applications for affiliation with reference to the need for a new college and send its recommendation to the State Government which is to give its views as far as financial implications are concerned. However, the UGC failed to follow up implementation especially when private professional colleges began to question the very role of State Governments and it were the Law Commission (*vide* its 160th Report (1988) on the amendment of he AICTE Act) the Supreme Court which had to bail out the State Governments.

As for autonomous colleges, whose establishment was recommended by Kothari Commission, UGC circulated its first edition of guidelines in 1973 envisaging autonomy to deserving colleges to frame curricula, courses of studies and their own systems of evaluation. In 1986, only 21 colleges had become autonomous (PoA 1986, V.7). In spite of the NPE 1986 target of 500 colleges for the Eighth Plan, which actually covered the years 1992-1997, the number of autonomous colleges was only 265 by the end of the Tenth Plan, *vide* p. 87 of UGC Annual Report for 2006-07. UGC issued revised guidelines for autonomous colleges in 2006. Evidently, the scheme has not taken off (The anecdotal evidence suggest that there is opposition of teachers' unions and the management, and there is also delay in framing ordinances), but the UGC has not bothered to go into the problem in any depth.

UGC has issued guidelines in several other subjects like working days, code of professional conduct for university and college teachers etc. These guidelines have no force of law but they have persuasive value. UGC has also issued what are called Notifications regarding revision of pay-scales from time to time. These have the force of law and have come in for interpretation by the superior judiciary. Unfortunately, while the UGC has brought out a compilation of UGC

Act 1956 (as modified up to 20-12-1985) and Rules and Regulations under the Act, they do not include all regulations issued including, e.g. service conditions. The contents of the compilation are listed in Annexure 4.1. UGC also needs to bring out an up-to-date compilation of guidelines on important subjects as distinguished from guidelines for the successive Five Year Plans.

The Administrative Framework of the UGC

Under this head, are considered trends in appointment of Chairman/ Vice-Chairman/Secretary. The following have worked as Chairmen of UGC from 1956:

(1) C.D. Deshmukh from August 1956 to 14th January, 1960.
(2) Dr. V.S. Krishna from 14th January, 1961 to 16th February, 1961.
(3) Dr. D.S. Kothari from March 1961 to 14th January, 1973.
(4) Prof. George Jacob—15-1-73 to 28-9-74.
(4-A) Vacant from 29-9-1974 to 20-1-1976; apparently Prof. Satish Chandra, Vice-Chairman, officiated.
(5) Prof. Satish Chandra—21st January, 1976 to 4th February, 1981.
(6) Dr. Madhuri Shah—5-2-81 to 4-2-86.
(7) Prof. Yashpal—7-3-86 to 16-3-1991.
(8) Dr. Manmohan Singh—16-3-1991 to 21-6-1991.
(9) Prof. G. Ram Reddy—17-10-1991 to January 1994.
(10) Dr. (Mrs.) Armaity Desai—7-2-1995 to 27-4-1999.
(11) Dr. Hari Gautam—22-7-1999 to 6-4-2002.
(12) Prof. Arun Nigvekar—17-6-2002 to 20-4-2005.
(13) Prof. Sukhdeo Thorat from May 2005 to April 2010.
(13-A) Prof. Ved Prakash, Vice-Chairman officiating as Chairman since May 2010 till date.

Note: Dates taken from Annual Reports.

Except for C.D. Deshmukh, an ICS Officer and former Governor, RBI and former Union Finance Minister, all others have been academics. But the appointments appear to have been dictated by the predilections of the Education Minister holding office at the time of the occurrence of the vacancy, subject to the approval of the Cabinet Committee on Appointments (CCA) presided over by the PM. Thus, C.D. Deshmukh was succeeded by Dr. V.S. Krishna, a Physicist whose untimely death provided an opportunity to Prof. D.S. Kothari (a Physicist from Delhi University and concurrently Hon. Adviser, Defence Research and Development Organization). Prof. George Jacob was reportedly a dynamic person who became Chairman after the 1972 amendments and re-organization of UGC, but his tenure was short and there appears to have been some pre-meditation in appointing Prof. Satish Chandra, an Aligarh historian as Vice-Chairman (when Prof. Nurul Hasan, also an Aligarh historian was the Minister of State for Education). The post of Chairman remained vacant for over 15 months. Apparently, Prof. Satish Chandra officiated as Chairman in the interim though the Annual Reports observe an 'omertà' on this point. Dr. Madhuri Shah's initial administrative experience was as Education Officer of the Bombay (Now Mumbai) Municipal Corporation; however, she was well-qualified in higher education—she had not one but two Ph.Ds [one from Bombay (Now Mumbai) and one from London], and she had also experience in higher education as V-C of the SNDT Women's University. (Incidentally, while working as Chairman, UGC she was also appointed as Chairman of the Review Committee of NCERT). Prof. Yashpal was a space-scientist. Prof. Ram Reddy and Armaity Desai were distinguished social scientists and competent administrators. During Dr. Hari Gautam's time (which coincided with the NDA regime) inclusion of astrology in the university curricula became a matter of debate. Prof. Sukhdev Thorat was an economist and Prof. Ved Prakash is an educationist with specialization in evaluation.

There was a convention that Chairman and Vice-Chairman should belong to different streams as between Science/Art. This convention, which had authority in Radhakrishnan Report (para XIII.18), used to be observed rather meticulously in earlier times. Thus, when Prof. Satish Chandra, a historian was chairman, Prof. B. Ramchandra Rao, a scientist was Vice-Chairman. When Dr. Madhuri Shah, an educationist was Chairman, she had Prof. Ramchandra Rao and Prof. Rais Ahmad (both scientists) as Vice-Chairmen. When Prof. Yashpal (a scientist) was Chairman, he had Prof. K. Sachidananda Murthy, a philosopher, as Vice-Chairman. This convention appears to have been breached when Prof. S.K. Khanna, an engineer was appointed as Vice-Chairman during Prof. Yashpal's tenure. However, when Prof. Ram Reddy, a political scientist, took over as Chairman, the balance could be said to have been restored. When Dr. Armaity Desai, a sociologist was Chairman, she had Dr. N.C. Mathur, a scientist as her Vice-Chairman. Of late, however, this convention is not being followed. Thus, Dr. Hari Gautam, a medical doctor had Prof. Arun Nigvekar (a physicist) as Vice-Chairman. When Prof. Arun Nigvekar became Chairman, he had Prof. V.N. Rajshekharan Pillai (a Scientist) as Vice-Chairman. Thereafter, an economist Chairman (Prof. Thorat) has a legal scholar (Prof. Mool Chand Sharma) as a Vice-Chairman. There appear to be two reasons for the breach of convention. There is firstly, no institutional memory either in the Ministry or in the UGC which is supposed to advise the Ministry. Secondly, even if the convention comes to be pointed out, the powers that be may choose not to adhere to it. This tendency to break conventions can be said to be symptomatic of the current administrative malaise.

UGC Secretaries

Secretary UGC is the lynchpin of the administration of the UGC. The first Secretary, Shri Samuel Mathai was groomed in the IUB. His successor Dr. K.L. Joshi (1963-67) was an outsider, having been Chief of Education Division of Planning Commission in 1955-63. He was succeeded by Shri R.K. Chhabra, an insider, who had a long inning (1971-1983). Thereafter, there has been a succession of outsiders—Prof. S.K. Khanna, an outsider/engineer, Shri Y.N. Chaturvedi, an IAS Officer with experience in the Ministry of Education (1991-93), Inderjeet Khanna, an IAS Officer (1993-96) and Dr. G.D. Sharma (1996-99), an educational economist trained in the Research Division of AIU under Dr. Amrik Singh and subsequently faculty in NIEPA. Between 1999 and till November 2002, the post was held by departmental officers. From 6-11-2002 to 2005 Prof. Ved Prakash held the post. According to Annual Report 2007-08, Shri R.K. Chauhan a departmental officer worked as Secretary since 18-4-2008. Currently Ms N.A. Kazmi is the Secretarty of the UGC.

There is a well-known tension between insiders and outsiders, especially in an organization like the UGC where officers with Ph.D.

are being appointed directly as Joint secretaries. The issue is difficult to resolve. It is true that an outsider may take time to know the ropes but an insider may lack a vision and may have a history of friends or otherwise in the organization. This tension is not peculiar to the UGC. Some alternation between an insider and an outsider would be good for the health of an organization like the UGC, so long as the selected candidate from the outside is meritorious, is acquainted with the education sector and prepared to get immersed in the procedures and the culture of the organization.

ANNEXURE 4.1

Contents of UGC Compilation of Rules and Regulations

1.0 UGC Act, 1956 as Modified upto the 20th December, 1985.
2.0 UGC Inspection of Universities Rules, 1960.
3.0 UGC Rules regarding Fitness of Universities, 1974-88.
4.0 UGC Returns of Information by Universities Rules, 1979.
5.0 UGC Fitness of Institutions for Grants Rules, 1975.
6.0 Recognition of College in Terms of Regulations, 1974 framed under the UGC Act.
7.0 UGC (Establishment and Maintenance of Institutions) Regulations, 1985.
8.0 UGC Regulations, 1985 regarding the Minimum Standards of Instruction for the Grant of the First degree.
9.0 UGC Regulations, 1991 regarding Minimum Qualifications for Appointment of Teachers in Universities and Colleges.
10.0 List of Degrees specified for the purpose of Section 22 of the UGC Act.
11.0 UGC rules, 1996 regarding Fitness of Health Sciences and Medical Universities for receiving grants.

5

University Grants Commission (1956-1980)

Introduction

The performance of the UGC as a quasi-autonomous governmental organization (Quango) would now be reviewed chronologically. An alternative approach of reviewing it according to a scheme of themes like funding, co-ordination, standards etc. as is done by Kuldeep Kaur (2003) would tend to become artificial, functions and funding being interrelated. The chronological axis is preferable. As a Quango, the UGC is deeply affected by the changing socio-political developments, which in their turn, are determined by the rhythm imposed by the political arrangements chosen by India (a parliamentary democratic federal constitution which sees a change of regime after every General Election) and by the periodicity of socio-economic planning in terms of Five Year Plans. The official historian of UGC, Kavita Sharma (2003) has chosen the chronological approach with the following chapters; Formative Years (1953-63), The Decade of Expansion (1963-73), The Decade of Consolidation (1973-83), Breaking New Ground (1983-93) and Looking Back (1993-2003). Irrespective of the titles, it is a neat 10 year division in five parts starting from 1953 and does not make much sense to the author. The working of the UGC would be reviewed for two successive periods of 1956-1980 and 1980-2007. Nineteen-Eighty is a convenient breaking point because firstly, it was in that year, that the Congress Party under Indira Gandhi came back to power after an interlude of more than two years of the Janata Rule. Secondly, it marked the beginning of the Sixth Five Year Plan. Thirdly, 1980 marked the opening of a new administrative era involving some type of relaxation, the rise of activist judiciary etc. The terminal year 2006-07 marks the end of the Tenth Plan. So broadly the first part would cover the years from the Second Plan period to Fifth Plan period and the second part would cover the next five plan periods, viz. Sixth to Tenth Plans.

Within the long second part, the author concedes the significance of the watershed year 1991, the year initiation of liberalization. The review of UGC's functioning in the year 1956-1980 is greatly facilitated by the availability of at least three official reviews of UGC's work, viz. (a) the Jha Committee (1977), (b) the Satish Chandra Committee on Programmes (1981) and the 73rd Report of PAC (March 1978). Of these three reports, not much background is required for the PAC Report which, as is the practice, is based on the material provided by the audited accounts of the UGC. The Jha Committee was appointed, as pointed out earlier, even in the absence of a provision in the UGC Act, in pursuance of the recommendation made by the Public Accounts Committee in its 114th Report (April 1970, para 2.12). The Committee noted in its Report that it is not convinced by the argument of the Ministry that there is no provision in the Act to undertake a review of the working of the Commission. It stated that the absence of a provision in the Act need not preclude Government from undertaking a review of this type of organization. Incidentally, the Government took four years to take a decision on the recommendation, perhaps because of the political situation (Bangladesh War—December 1971 and General Elections—in 1972 etc.). The Satish Chandra Committee was constituted by the UGC itself in terms of a directive issued by the Ministry under Section 20 of UGC Act, on 18th October, 1978. The directive spelt out terms of reference also. It was to be: (a) a comprehensive *review* of the various programmes being implemented by the UGC and (b) the *impact* they have made on the fulfilment of the statutory responsibility of the Commission. Reading between the lines, one can sense that the UGC was not happy about the directive. In the Foreword to the Report it is stated,

"Jha Review Committee had already carried out a critical examination of the structure and functioning of UGC. *The Commission had already decided upon an in-depth examination of its programmes when the Government's directive for the review arrived...* . To save time, its composition was enlarged and its scope of activities was expanded to conform to the objectives Government had in mind." The directive was issued on 18th October, 1978 when the Janata Government was in power. The Chairman, UGC was an appointee of the previous Government. The UGC constituted by the earlier Congress Government might not have given heed to the hints thrown by the Education Secretary, who was a Janata appointee and hence the directive might have been issued. The Foreword was written on 1st January 1981 when the new (Congress) Government had been in power for about a year and therefore, a grievance could be made about the purposelessness of the directive.

Before considering these reviews, it may be useful to consider first the policy environment and then the UGC's leadership and its clientele during this period.

Policy Environment: 1956-1980

The policy environment of the UGC in this period may be considered in the following order: (1) Radhakrishnan Report, (2) Scientific Policy Resolution, 1958, (3) Central Planning, (4) Kothari Report, (5) NPE 1968, and (6) UGC's Policy Statement of 1978.

The Radhakrishnan Report 1949 was a landmark and the UGC itself was set up in terms of the report but a perusal of the Annual Reports of the UGC does not show any enthusiasm to go back to its recommendations and cull out action points. This may partly be because the report drafted, well prior to the commencement of the Constitution, might have been regarded as outdated. Even otherwise, some of its recommendations, e.g. about Rural Universities were rather vague. Above all, there was a vogue for 'science' as the solvent of most problems and accordingly, the Scientific Policy Resolution (SPR) of March 1958 was the policy resolution to be issued by the Government of India even prior to any policy resolution on education. The aims of the SPR were to foster research, to ensure adequate supply of manpower, to encourage training programmes and to encourage dissemination and discussion of knowledge in an atmosphere of scientific freedom. This covered almost all objectives of higher education. However, the policy of the Central Government was to conduct high-end research in national laboratories and therefore, the UGC, dealing with universities and colleges, was regarded as a minor actor in the area of scientific research.

We then come to the Central Planning framework which provided funds. Here, we find a focus on creation of engineering manpower for making a success of various irrigation, power and industrial projects. So the allocations made for the UGC were on an incremental basis rather than showing any substantial step-up.

A lot was expected from the Education Commission Report 1966 but when the report came out, there was a planning crisis leading to a three year Plan Holiday (1966-69). The NPE 1968 devoted only 2 paragraphs to higher education which reiterated current platitudes. In fact, UGC does not appear to have followed up the recommendations of Education Commission as observed by the Public Accounts Committee (1978). Finally, UGC itself brought out a policy statement of higher education in 1978 whose innovation was to add the third dimension of extension to the existing two-fold functions of higher education, viz. teaching and research. But this policy statement was associated with the short-lived Janata regime (1977-79). Thus, the direction of policy for the UGC during this first period lacked any particular focus and encouraged *ad hoc* responses to emerging situations and to academic fashions (e.g. general education).

UGC (1956-1980)

Leadership—During this period, C.D. Deshmukh, D.S. Kothari, Dr. George Jacob and Prof. Satish Chandra worked as Chairmen and Samuel Mathai, K.L. Joshi, P.J. Philip and R.K. Chhabra worked as Secretaries. After 1972 when the post of the Vice-Chairman was created, Prof. Satish Chandra and Prof. B. Ramchandra Rao worked as Vice-Chairmen. The Commission was Headless for the period from 28-9-1974 (when Prof. George Jacob retired) till 21-1-1976 when

Prof. Satish Chandra, already working as Vice-Chairman took over as Chairman of UGC (*vide* Annual Report 1975-76).[1]

Clientele—UGC gave financial assistance to: (1) the Central Universities and Delhi/BHU Colleges (both development and maintenance grants), (2) State Universities and Colleges affiliated to State Universities—mainly development grants, and (3) the Deemed Universities—selective assistance, some on par with the Central Universities and the others on par with the State Universities. The number of Central Universities increased during this period from four (BHU, AMU, Delhi and Vishvabharati) to seven. The number of Central Universities was thus quite small. The number of deemed Universities increased from 0 to 12, but it was still small. The number of Delhi colleges, however, increased from five in 1956 to 54 (Madhuri Shah Report, p. 131) and moreover, the number of State universities increased from 35 in 1956 to 91 in 1972 (when the amendment to the UGC Act putting restriction on grants to State universities was enforced), to 112 in 1980. The number of State Colleges increased from 1107 in 1956-57 to 4722 in 1980-81. Thus the increase in the number of Delhi colleges was eleven-fold, State Universities three-fold and State colleges more than four-fold during this short period. The Commission's funds were limited. The maintenance grants of Central Universities and of Delhi colleges were the first charge on the Commission's resources. The rest of funds could be used for various development schemes. The Commission was charged with the duty of co-ordinating development and of determination and maintenance of standards, which are normally measured in terms of inputs, process (teaching and learning) and outcome (students' success in examinations, their ability to get absorbed in the job market and

1. The following dates are significant. Prof. Nurul Hasan took over as Minister of State: 24-3-1972; Amendment to the UGC Act, providing for the post of full-time Vice-Chairman takes effect: 17-6-1972; Prof. Satish Chandra took over as Vice-Chairman: 15-1-1973. Prof. Satish Chandra completed 3 years as Vice-Chairman: 15-1-1976. Prof. Satish Chandra took over as Chairman: 21-1-1976. The facts as ascertained from the UGC Annual Reports speak for themselves. Apparently, the post of Chairman was consciously kept vacant, and when the Vice-Chairman completed three years, he took over as Chairman UGC in terms of rules.

the merit of the teachers). The input measure is the most common and the easiest to handle when it comes to disbursing grants in a given period. The Commission, therefore, appears to have used the funds to provide the universities and colleges with increased inputs in the form of buildings for hostels, libraries and laboratories and equipment for laboratories and books for libraries. The UGC had also to address the need to raise low salaries of the teachers which the Radhakrishnan Commission had identified as a factor in the demoralization and denigration of teaching community as early as 1948 (Radhakrishnan Commission Report: 41-51). The Commission interpreted the goal of improving pay-scales of teachers in such a manner that they compare favourably with those of provincial services. As the Commission had observed: "The teacher is the cornerstone of the arch of education; he is no less, if not more, than books and curricula, buildings and equipment, administration and the rest." (*Ibid.*: 43). The UGC, therefore, simultaneously tried to standardize qualifications of teachers on the basis of recommendation of a Committee appointed by it and also implemented revised salary scales for the teaching staff of universities, for which it assisted 14 State universities to the extent of 80 per cent of increased costs (UGC Report, 1953-57: 13).

The Eligibility of Affiliated Colleges for UGC Assistance

A Strategic Decision

The 1957-58 Annual Report of the UGC shows that the UGC had initially decided, as a matter of principle, to give assistance only to universities or to a few P-G Departments of some colleges by treating them as departments of universities. But the UGC apparently realized that the problem of raising standards of higher education in India cannot be solved unless affiliated colleges are brought under its purview. The mandate of the UGC, by definition, is to assist universities. C.D. Deshmukh, with his administrative acumen, solved this tricky problem by noting the inclusive definition of the universities under section 2(f) of the UGC Act. S.2(f) defines a "university" to include an institution recognized by the UGC in consultation with the university concerned. So the UGC framed regulations under Section 2(f) read with Section 26(d) which latter section empowers UGC to specify institutions or class of institution which may be recognized by the Commission under Section 2(f) of the Act. In the latest compilation, the rules framed by the UGC in 1957-58 are not incorporated because they have been superceded by the rules enforced from 12th July, 1984 (pp. 41-42 of the compilation), but apparently they required the colleges to produce: (a) proof of affiliation to a university, (b) proof of its being run by a registered society/trust, (c) a duly executed bond regarding proper utilization of UGC grants, and (d) balance-sheet and annual accounts of the institutions.

Thus, by an imaginative feat of administrative engineering, colleges were made eligible for UGC grants within one year of the foundation of the statutory UGC. Revised pay-scales were extended to affiliated colleges under the Universities of Poona, Calcutta (Now Kolkata), Bombay (Now Mumbai) and Osmania, under a formula of UGC bearing 50 per cent of increased expenditure for male teachers and 75 per cent for female teachers (UGC AR, 1957-58: 4). These universities received grants only after they agreed to bear the balance. Further, not only were three metropolitan universities given centenary grants but also seven colleges which had completed more than 100 years (UGC AR, 1957-58: 6). The number of colleges recognized by the Commission for financial assistance (other than Government colleges) was 718 in 1958/59 (UGC AR 1958-59: 4).

Deemed Universities

The UGC Act has, *vide* section 3, an innovative provision for notifying certain institutions as deemed universities. UGC had requested M.C. Mahajan, former C.J.I., to suggest guidelines in this regard, but he declined, stating that UGC was in a better position to frame them (UGC AR 1953-54). Some informal guidelines appear to have been framed in 1958, which were based on the premise that there are institutions which, for historical and other reasons are not universities and yet are doing work of a high standard in an academic field and at the university level and that granting of the status of a deemed to be a university would enable them to develop ideals belonging to the area of higher education and research. Indian Institute of Science

(IISc.), Bangalore and IARI, New Delhi were notified in 1958 as Deemed Universities. Thereafter, in succession, following institutions were so notified: Gurukul Kangri (Hardwar), Jamia Millia, New Delhi (1962), Gujarat Vidyapeeth, Ahmedabad (1963), TISS, Bombay (Now Mumbai) and Birla Institute of Technology & Science (BITS), Pilani (1964), Indian School of Mines, Dhanbad (1967), Central Institute of English and Foreign Languages, Hyderabad (1973), Gandhigram Rural Institute, TN (1976) and School of Planning and Architecture New Delhi (1979).

It would be seen that of the 11 Deemed Universities notified between 1958 and 1979, three were 'national' institutions set up prior to independence, one was a Gandhian Rural Institute, two related to humanities/social sciences (TISS and CIEFL), and the rest were S & T institutions—three of them set up prior to independence (IISc., School of Mines and IARI). The UGC was responsible for funding eight institutions.

Funding by UGC: Jha Committee Analysis

A statement showing Plan and Non-Plan grants released by the UGC during the 2nd to the 5th Plan was worked out by the Jha Committee as below:

Table 5.1: Plan and Non-Plan grants by UGC

Plan & Years	*Plan Grant (Rs. in Cr.)*	*Non-Plan Grant (Rs. in Cr.)*
Second Plan (1956-61)	Rs. 20.49 Crore	Rs. 8.36 Crore
Third Plan (1961-66)	Rs. 46.59 Crore	Rs. 18.14 Crore
Annual Plans (3 Years) (1966-69)	Rs. 34.15 Crore	Rs. 19.13 Crore
Fourth Plan	Rs. 110.61 Crore	Rs. 50.00 Crore
Fifth Plan	Rs. 197.33 Crore	N.A

N.A. = Not Available.

Source: Second and Fourth Plan. Jha Report; Fifth Plan; UGC Annual Report 1979-80.

This statement would show that the Commission has been receiving increased funding in successive plans. The same is distributed by the Commission among various universities and colleges on the basis of the development proposals received by the

Commission. An analysis done by the Jha Committee shows that the average development grant per institute as well as per student per annum works out as follows:

Table 5.2: Development of Grant per Institute and per Student

Universities/Colleges	*Per Institution (in lakhs of rupees)*	*Per Student in Rs.*
1. Central Universities	88.57	1192
2. State Universities	12.03	337
3. Delhi Colleges	02.90	319
4. Colleges of other Universities	00.15	23

Source: Jha Committee Report, p. 57.

It is clear that UGC grants to Central Universities and Delhi Colleges as compared with State universities and non-Delhi colleges are at a far higher level (about 4 times in the case of universities, about 14 times in the case of colleges) which is only partly explained by the fact that they are paid by the UGC maintenance grants in addition to development grants and that in regard to development grants, they are not required to make a matching contribution. But this distorts the picture. The Jha Committee recommended that maintenance grants to Central Universities and their affiliated colleges should be separately budgeted, separately operated upon and dealt with in a separate report on maintenance activities as distinct from development activities (Jha Report: 63). The Government in its Resolution dated 30-4-1979 on the Jha Report accepted various recommendations but the UGC does not appear to have taken any corrective steps. The Commission simply gives the information in a separate Chapter, but that does not serve the purpose the Jha Committee had in view.

The Jha Committee reviewed several aspects of UGC's work other than funding and made appropriate recommendations, some of which have been incorporated in the NPE, 1986/92 its two PoAs of 1986 and 1992 and even some subsequent reports. These recommendations of Jha Committee are enumerated below:

(1) A high-level coordinating body with heads of different organizations dealing with higher education and research (Chapter II.1) [vide para 5.34 of the NPE 1986/92 and *vide*

NKC's recommendation regarding establishment of an Independent Regulatory Authority in Higher Education (IRAHE)].

(2) A co-ordinating body for higher education at the State level (Chapter II.1) [This was incorporated in NPE *vide* para 5.30 as State Council for Higher Education (SCHE)].

(3) A national examination for selection of Lecturers and Research Fellowship (Chapter II.9) [This is the origin of NET/SLET examinations also endorsed by Mehrotra Committee on Pay-scales (1986)].

(4) A suitable organization should be set up for studies and research in various aspects of higher education (Chapter V.1). As pointed out subsequently, UGC appointed a Committee to work out details but the matter remains under examination.

(5) UGC should undertake accreditation and grading of University Departments and Colleges (Chapter V.10). [There is no mention of this in NPE 1986. PoA 1986 devotes paras 5.27 and 5.28 to this aspect without quoting NPE paras. So this indirectly became part of NPE. PoA 1992 para 11.12.4 says that UGC resolved in March 1992 to set up a National Accreditation and Assessment Board which actually came up in 1994].

(6) The UGC should evolve a system of periodic review of its working and organization at least once every 10 years (para VI.15) [This recommendation was accepted by Government, but neither the Government, nor the UGC acted on it after 1981. UGC lacks a culture of self-assessment. The crop of institutional reviews which were done in 2003-04 *et seq.* were a follow-up of the Report of High level Expenditure Commission of the Government of India. They were set up because otherwise, the institutions in question would have faced closure. The Yashpal Review on UGC/AICTE (February 2008) appears to be a belated follow-up of Expenditure Commission recommendations].

In passing, it may be considered as to why the Jha Committee does not have as much recall as, e.g. Radhakrishnan Report or Kothari Report or in other words why it is not considered a canonical report although its recommendations were substantial and solid. The present Author's assessment is as below:

(1) Its Chairman was an academic bureaucrat, rather than an internationally renowned scholar like S. Radhakrishnan, nor was it surrounded by the hype associated with the Kothari Commission in 1964, as the first review of the whole area of education in India.

(2) The second reason why it is not politically correct to quote from it is that it is associated with the Emergency. It had submitted an interim report to the Government suggesting making education as a Concurrent Subject. But the high powered Swaran Singh Committee of the Congress Party did not condescend to acknowledge its inputs, much less accept them.

(3) Thirdly, its spirit is centralist. It opposed establishment of regional offices of UGC since it judged that they would promote regionalism in a pejorative sense. Its recommendations in regard to State level UGC were ambiguous.

(4) But fourthly and above all, it fell by the *wayside* apparently because it had no links with the then ruling establishment in Education Sector in Delhi, which was predominantly leftist and which had its outposts in Rajasthan, (Jaipur, Udaipur) and West Bengal [Calcutta (Now Kolkata)].[1]

The Satish Chandra Committee Report (1981)

The background to the appointment of this Committee has been detailed earlier. It was a high-powered Committee, presided over by the Chairman UGC and including Secretary (Education) as a member. It had a wide membership but its recommendations are required to be considered in the context of the fact that it was essentially an internal committee. Annexure V of the Committee Report (reproduced as Annexure 5.1 to this Chapter) lists out 65 on-going programmes of the UGC under different heads like universities, colleges, faculty, research, student welfare and academic-cultural. The scope was vast

1. The author hopes to establish this hypothesis by evidence in his future writings.

but the Committee set up sub-committees which undertook field visits to universities and colleges according to zones and can be said to have made a moderately competent job of its allotted task. The Committee presumptively considers itself to be a continuation for the period April 1975 to 1980 of the work started by the Jha Committee which reviewed the functioning of UGC for the period August 1956 to March 1975. This comparison was inappropriate on two counts: (a) the Committee's work was limited to a review of programmes only and (b) the Committee's review by its own choice covered only 10 years: 1969-70 to 1978-79.

The Satish Chandra Committee endorsed the formulations about higher education in the Policy Frame for development of Higher Education in India (printed as an Annexure to its Report), first published in February 1978 during the Janata period, as well as 'Approach to development during the Sixth Plan' which was issued by the successor Government in 1980. According to the Committee, the framework sought to make educational system more flexible and dynamic and enabled us to move in the direction of providing opportunities for life-long learning to every individual. *Significantly,* however, the Committee failed to mention the emphasis the policy frame had placed on extension as the third dimension of the multi-functionality of the university system. To quote the policy frame: "If the university system has to discharge adequately its responsibilities to the entire educational system as a whole, it must assume extension as the third important responsibility and give it the same status as research and teaching. *This is a new and extremely significant area which should be developed as the basis of high priority.*"

The Committee writing in 1980, echoes the findings of the Standards Committee of 1965: the picture is one of achievements and failures. The general impression is that the best students are as good as ever and that contents of courses are also of a high level. Outstanding work is being done by some of the University Departments and a number of teachers have been receiving recognition from well-known centres of learning. The outturn of Ph.D. and research output by way of publications has gone up significantly. On the other hand, instruction in some universities has not kept pace with modern developments. There is a resistance to change and innovations on the part of teachers and an atmosphere of growing violence and intimidation on the part of students, teachers and in some cases even employees. There is also a lack of trust between the students and teachers. The potentialities of students are not fully developed and utilized by our universities and colleges. The demand on the system is far greater as compared to the inputs and availability of resources. Thus, the Committee echoed for education sector what Myron Weiner had said regarding Indian polity in his book: *Politics of Scarcity* (1962).

The Satish Chandra Committee, quoting its Western Regional Sub-Committee observed that the over-all performance was around 60 per cent of the expected target, that the institutions in the South were comparable but that less progress had been made by State universities in the Eastern and Northern Zones. In terms of courses, universities which had been relatively free from student agitations and politicization of teachers have performed better. Analysis of expenditure between 1969-70 to 1973-74 and between 1974-75 to 1978-79 showed that the order of priority had shifted from expenditure on staff, building and infrastructural facilities in favour of equipments, books and journals. The Committee found it difficult to measure the impact of its schemes on the college development sector because of the major role of State governments in the sector but stated that but for UGC assistance, no worthwhile development would have taken place in some States.

Regarding the scheme of Centres of Advanced Study (CAS) started in 1963-64 and the Scheme of Departments of Special Assistance (DSA) started in 1972-73, (the basic philosophy of which is to concentrate the available resources and expertise on building centres of excellence on a selective basis), the Committee observes that it has made the maximum impact, but also acknowledged that some centres had not functioned as national centres and that seven under-performing centres had been taken out with effect from 1st April, 1974. As for College Science Improvement Programme (COSIP) started in 1970-71 and College Humanities and Social Sciences Improvement Programme (COHSSIP) started in 1974-75 in which 177 colleges and 40 Departments and 176 colleges and 15 Departments respectively had participated, the Committee noted the general impression that these have made a meaningful and important contribution to the improvement of standards of under-graduate education, but that interaction between colleges and the Departments of University Leadership Programmes (ULP), is not as wide as envisaged. The Committee underlines the point made by the Jha Committee that there is a need for a co-ordination mechanism in between the States, Universities and the UGC. The Committee suggested the need for a five-yearly review of the programmes. Unfortunately, this recommendation of the Committee does not appear to have been implemented.

The Public Accounts Committee (PAC) on UGC (1978)

The report of the PAC is much more critical of the functioning of the UGC though its approach tends to be piecemeal rather than holistic.

Quality Improvement Programme

It noted sizable shortfall in the expenditure during the Fourth Plan period (1969-74) on the 'Quality improvement and other special programmes' (e.g. support for research) as against excess expenditure on general development programmes (PAC, para 5.35), which the Committee attributed to the *lack of systematic progressing* of the programmes by the Commission. The Committee also noted that the scheme of correspondence courses could not be implemented by the Commission during the Fourth Plan period with the energy and zeal that it deserved. Only 11 universities could start the scheme with a paltry expenditure of Rs. 12 lakh as against the target of 20 universities and an outlay of Rs. 1 Crore. The progress in the first three years of the Fifth Plan was also poor. The Commission did not frame proper guidelines for U-G and P-G programmes in correspondence education prior to 1972. Expert Committees could visit only six universities.

In regard to the CAS and DSA, the PAC made the startling discovery that although as early as in August 1968, the Commission had accepted the recommendation of the Standing Advisory Committee of the CAS to replace the scheme of CAS by the scheme of DSA, no action was taken to follow-up the decision until 1972, thus involving low utilization of funds (Rs. 4 crore as against the outlay of Rs. 8 crore). Regarding COSIPs, the PAC noted that there was delay in the completion of the first phase by several colleges, that there was delay in constitution of regional committees (for approval of the work of colleges), due to severe shortage of staff and there was a thinking to set up State level committees. The PAC similarly observed delay in implementation of the scheme of preparation of university level books by Indian authors, which was suggested by the Education Commission.

Disparities in Development Assistance to Universities

The PAC highlighted disparities in the matter of development assistance as between central and state institutions much more sharply than the Jha Committee. The Committee found that out of development grants totalling Rs. 165.39 crore released by the UGC in the seven-year period from 1969-70 to 1975-76, the share of the central universities and deemed universities (10 in number) was 27.2 per cent as against 46 per cent of all state universities (104 in number). Even after excluding grants on account of special factors like (a) grants paid to medical colleges and hospitals attached to central universities, viz. BHU and Delhi, (b) Campus development and student amenities, and (c) schemes getting assistance on cent-per-cent basis, in the case of central universities and sharing basis in the case of state universities, the share of central universities was still disproportionately high at 41 per cent against 59 per cent of state universities. The Development grants made during the same period to Delhi colleges were similarly high (10% out of a total of Rs. 37.92 crores). The Committee also found considerable disparity in the quantum of grants released to state universities *inter se*, as well as in releasing grants to colleges as between different states or as between different universities. The Committee found similar disparities in respect of central universities *inter se*, underlining a tendency to adopt an *ad hoc* approach.

Visiting Committees

The PAC also noted that the Commission did not follow a uniform procedure in regard to the visiting committee on the basis of whose recommendations plan schemes of universities for different plan periods are finalized. Thus, in regard to both the Fourth Plan and the Fifth Plan, as many as 10 universities were not visited at all, time spent by the visiting committees at some universities was too short and the process of choosing members was not transparent. There were delays in submission of reports of the Visiting Committees before the Commission (as long as 5 years) and in some cases, the schemes not recommended by the Visiting Committees were approved by the UGC Office.

Pathology of UGC Administration

PAC report has noted quite a few cases of administrative laxity and at least one case of mal-administration on the part of UGC as illustrated below:

(1) There was delay in notification of important rules under section 25(2)(e) and (f) requiring the universities to furnish returns and information relating to financial position of the university. All the rules and regulations relating to the standard of teaching and examinations in the universities prepared by Commission in 1974 remained under discussion till 1979 (para 1.57).

(2) Failure to finalize regulations regarding association of outside experts with Commission's work *vide* section 26(1)(b) read with section 9 (para 1.58).

(3) Regulations under section 26(1)(e) and (f) of the Act defining qualifications for appointment of university teachers and minimum standards of instruction for grant of a degree not framed (para 1.59).

(4) Chairman, Secretary and other staff undertook foreign tours under cultural and bilateral exchange programmes (para 3.8), which was highly improper.

(5) Failure to notify regulations u/section 27 regarding delegation of powers to Chairman, V-C and officers. They continued to function under a resolution of 1956, which permits unlimited delegation so that the Chairman with his officers could be said to have usurped the powers of the Commission (para 4.21).

(6) PAC also faulted UGC for not using the power of withholding grants to any university (para 1.58).

(7) PAC noted that the number of universities and colleges had increased from 103 and 455 in 1972-73 to 115 and 4569 in 1976-77, but that UGC had not used its powers under new section 12-A conferred on UGC specifically to prevent mushroom growth of universities and colleges.

(8) When a new Chairman (evidently Prof. Jacob who succeeded Dr. D.S. Kothari on 15-1-1973) raised a query on 7-12-1973 about two Delhi-based firms of architects having managed to corner over 200 building projects costing Rs. 3.22 crore in the universities and colleges spread over 7-8 States, it came to light that there was a suspicion in the matter as early as in November 1969 but nothing was done except to issue a circular to the universities and a press-note in May 1970 and even when a recurrence came to the notice of the Commission in 1972, nothing was done till the new Chairman assumed office. When the new Chairman asked the Secretary to look personally into the matter on 4th July, 1974, Secretary stated that there were no *mala fides*. As was noted, Chairman Prof. Jacob retired in September 1974 and the Commission was headless till January 1976. *PAC had a strong impression of collusion on the part of officers of the Commission with the two Architects* and it desired the Ministry to investigate the matter. Ministry's reply to the recommendation of the PAC is unfortunately not available (Paras 8.34 and 8.35). [NB: This last item raises an issue of mal-administration with a whiff of possible corruption.]

UGC 1956-1980—A Preliminary Assessment

Having reviewed the functioning of UGC with the help of two critical (Jha Report and PAC Report) and one internal Report (Satish Chandra Report), a preliminary assessment is attempted below. Marina Pinto (1984) has mined this gem of praise for the UGC from Amartya Sen (1971) which initially appeared as part of Lal Bahadur Shastri Memorial Lecture delivered at Hyderabad on 10th and 11th March, 1970:

> "UGC could be singled out for having established standards of devoted work, efficient operations and un-bureaucratic promptness of a kind that is entirely rare in India."

Amartya Sen was making the point that there is a crisis in Indian education (not merely higher education but education as a whole) but that it could not be attributed to administrative neglect. He was referring to the UGC as a public body under the Ministry of Education which had a galaxy of distinguished men to run its affairs. It is not at all possible to agree with this impressionistic assessment.

Marina Pinto who has devoted an entire chapter to UGC in her book (1984, pp. 63-107) has the following to say with which the author is inclined to agree:

(1) In the First decade of its existence (1956-1966), UGC did exhibit signs of diffidence and uncertainty. It is only in the 1970s that it has shown greater zest for work and academic leadership.
(2) The UGC is not autonomous. It could at best be described as a semi-independent body. It is just an appendage of the Government.
(3) The UGC does not give sufficient attention to colleges.
(4) On the whole, the working of the UGC Committees (e.g. on Standards, on Colleges, on General Education, on Legal Education, Teacher education etc.) has not been satisfactory. Their suggestions have remained on paper (They are only partly implemented and their follow-up is poor).
(5) UGC by 1980 has grown into a gigantic organization and is showing signs of increasing bureaucratization. There must be a very substantial decentralization—else the system will collapse.

Since the focus of Marina Pinto is on federalism, she rightly blames the UGC for underestimating federal complexities. She pinpoints what according to her is Achilles' Heal of the UGC: A dire need is felt for a co-ordinating body that links UGC, State Governments and State Universities, so that planning and financing of higher education is streamlined. There should be some co-ordinating body at the State level. It could be in the form of State UGCs or at least regional offices of the Central UGC.

If one has to put the matter in a more comprehensive manner, the UGC by 1980 had taken the following progressive steps:

(1) UGC made colleges affiliated to State universities eligible for financial grants which was a great feat of administrative engineering (1958).

(2) From 1973 onwards, UGC began to promote autonomous colleges which were conceived as a panacea for the ills of the system of affiliation which is a colonial legacy.

(3) It had taken some measures for improving standards in terms of investment inputs, first in terms of physical infrastructure (buildings, equipments) and later on, in terms of books and journals, support for research etc. Its showpiece in the matter of standards for the universities was CAS and in the matter of colleges, COSIP.

(4) Its action in 1956-57 and 1966 to revise teachers' salaries was well-meaning and well-deserved.

(5) J.P. Naik (1960) had identified "the clearing house function of collecting ideas and broadcasting ideas and information", as one of the exclusive federal functions in the field of education, which also had statutory sanction in the UGC Act [Section 12(6)]. During the period it tried its best. Thus it began to bring out an annual statistical publication called—*University Development in India: Basic Facts and Figures*, containing data relating to colleges and universities, collected on census basis, as against the data on the same subject collected by the Ministry from the field officers of State Directorates of Education. In the 1970s it brought out fairly regularly a *Bulletin of Higher Education* for dissemination of information about schemes useful to the colleges and universities. Its academic periodical: *Journal of Higher Education* started in 1975 to promote scholarly studies of higher education as well as to discuss problems and policies of Higher Education used to bring out three issues annually (Monsoon, Autumn and Spring). Important topics discussed in the journal related to the equality of educational opportunities with special reference to SCs/STs, examination reforms, and restructuring of courses of higher education. Reports of Committees appointed from time to time were published and disseminated.

(6) Generally, while the UGC was administratively weak and

was not fortunate to have requisite decisive academic leadership during the 1960s and 1970s, *it was on the whole a functioning machine which did not entirely lack a soul.*

On the negative side are to be set the following actions/defaults of the UGC:

(1) UGC not only did not use its powers of withholding grants and of conducting inspections of the universities but went to the extent of justifying its inaction on the ground that persuasion was a better method than coercion and that visiting committees for Five Year Plans were a substitute for inspections. Rudolphs observe that D.S. Kothari headed both the Education Commission and the UGC and was thus speaking and judging for himself (Rudolphs, 1972: 402).

(2) In 1975, salary scales were dramatically upgraded with retrospective effect from 1973 in terms of the Report of the Sen Committee (1974). Firstly, parity was brought about between under-graduate and post-graduate teaching and salary scales were brought on par with Class I officers of the Government of India. This was done in the face of opposition from the State Governments under pressure from the trade unions of college teachers, who constituted 80 per cent of the teaching force. [Annual Report of UGC, 1975-76: 61-64 and Amrik Singh (1989)].

(3) UGC also clung to its Centralist policy, opposing establishment of Regional Offices or any mechanism like the State UGC, by whatever name called, which could have ensured a better rapport with the State Governments and the State universities.

(4) UGC (apart from the C.D. Deshmukh—initiated move to make colleges eligible for financial assistance and promotion of autonomous colleges) largely neglected colleges. It did not lay down any guidelines for affiliation much less any regulations and did not follow up the suggestion of the Kothari Commission of having a survey of small colleges so as to consolidate them and a classification scheme for colleges (*ibid.*, 12.25, 11.41). Moreover the idea of

autonomous colleges did not take off and in 1980 there were only 19 of them. The UGC did not investigate the reasons.

(5) The problem of grants to Delhi Colleges which was inherited by the Commission from the Government was allowed to fester and no objective principles were framed and followed nor any attempt made to transfer the colleges to Delhi Administration. An indirect result was close contact between the UGC administration and the Delhi colleges which made the UGC vulnerable to pressure from unions of college teachers and non-teaching staff of Delhi University colleges (DUTA etc.). This detracted from the position of the UGC as an all-India standard-setting body.

(6) The Building Scandal in the Commission involving collusion between two Delhi Architects and Commission staff highlighted by the PAC underlined a seamy side of the Commission's working which was not nipped in the bud, but simply put under the carpet.

UGC: The Expanding Powers

Finally, as observed by A. Mathew (1980: 86) during this period UGC's powers expanded and its capacity increased as a result of the conscious policy followed by the Ministry:

> "Initially UGC was only an agency which implemented the programmes drawn up by the Ministry. Beginning from the Third Plan, UGC was entrusted with complete responsibility of implementing the programmes envisaged by the Ministry. From the Fourth Plan onwards, the UGC was given the freedom to perceive and articulate the programmes by itself. In this sense, UGC became more autonomous from the Ministry from its initial phase of being directly under the guidance of the Ministry. From the Fifth Plan period, the UGC not only began to evolve the strategies and priorities of higher education in relation to the plan schemes at the national level on its own, but also worked out the programmes to achieve the objectives of higher education. This shows a transformation in the function of UGC from working directly under the

guidance and control of the Ministry to an agency relatively autonomous, perceiving and carrying out programmes, but within the broader objectives of the Ministry and national plans. Hence, the organizational changes that took place in the UGC can be seen as part of the process of institutionalization followed by the Ministry."

UGC: The Expanding Space

Another way of looking at the matter is to look at the higher education space occupied by the UGC. It could be argued that it expanded from 1956 to 1980 because (a) new central universities and deemed universities were brought under the purview of the UGC as the disburser of maintenance grants, (b) Ministry tended to withdraw from the space occupied by the UGC as pointed out by A. Mathew (*supra*). No doubt, the Ministry of Education created new grant-giving bodies like ICSSR (1969), ICHR (1973), ICPR (1977,1980) and also the centres like Indian Institute of Advanced Studies, Shimla (1965) which were directly funded by the Ministry and which supplemented the role of the UGC in the giving of grants for promotion of research. But these were small institutes with limited funds, with the UGC involved in their management and not *vice versa*. Hence the place occupied by the UGC in Higher Education space was larger in 1980 than in 1956.

ANNEXURE 5.1

On-going Programmes of the University Grants Commission as in 1980

I. Development of Universities

(i) General Development (Staff, Equipment, Academic buildings, Books and Journals)
(ii) Centres of Advanced Study and Departments of Special Assistance
(iii) University Centres for Post-graduate Studies
(iv) Area Studies
(v) Guest House
(vi) Establishment of Chairs
(vii) Development of Computer Facilities
(viii) Central Instrumentation Facilities
(ix) Collection and Preservation of Manuscripts
(x) Appointment of Development Officers
(xi) Centenary Grants
(xii) Infrastructural Facilities (Hostel, Staff Quarters, Library buildings, Laboratory facilities)
(xiii) Development of Museums
(xiv) Unassigned Grants
(xv) Development of Wild Life and Research
(xvi) Development of Expertise in the field of Archaeology and Museums in the Universities
(xvii) Establishment of Archival Cells in the Universities

II. Development of Colleges

(i) General development (Rs. 3-5 lakh scheme, viz. Academic

buildings, Classrooms, Laboratories, Hostels, Staff quarters, Books and Journals and Equipment)

(ii) COSIP/COHSSIP

(iii) Development of Post-graduate Studies in Science

(iv) Development of Post-graduate Studies in Humanities and Social Sciences

(v) Development of Autonomous Colleges

(vi) Centenary Grants

(vii) Assistance towards Restructuring of Courses

III. Faculty Improvement Programmes

(i) Seminars, Summer Institutes and Workshops

(ii) National Fellowships

(iii) National Associateships

(iv) Visiting Professorships, Fellowships and Faculty

(v) Research Associateships

(vi) Teacher Fellowships

(vii) National Lecturers

(viii) Utilisation of Services of Retired Teachers

(ix) Travel Grants

(x) Career Awards to Young Scientists

(xi) Sabbatical Leave

IV. Support for Research Work

(i) Advanced Research Projects in Humanities and Social Sciences

(ii) Short-term Research Projects in Humanities and Social Sciences

(iii) Major Research Projects in Science

(iv) Minor Research Projects in Science

(v) Core Support for Research

(vi) Research Scholarships and Fellowships

(vii) Financial Assistance to Teachers for Research Work

(viii) Publication of Theses and Learned Research Works

V. Student Welfare Programmes

(i) Student-Aid-Fund
(ii) Non-Resident Student Centres
(iii) Study Homes
(iv) Book Banks
(v) Health Centres
(vi) Employment Information, Career-advising and Vocational Guidance Bureaus
(vii) Construction of Gymnasium
(viii) Development of Play-fields
(ix) Appointment of Trained Coaches
(x) Canteens

VI. Academic and Cultural Programmes

(i) Correspondence Courses
(ii) Adult/Continuing Education and Extension
(iii) Cultural and Bilateral Exchange Programmes
(iv) Examination Reforms
(v) Collection and Preservation of Manuscripts
(vi) National Integration Samitis
(vii) Planning Forums
(viii) Science Education Centres
(ix) Regional Library Centres
(x) College Development Councils
(xi) Gandhian Studies/Gandhi Bhavans
(xii) Book-Writing

Source: Satish Chandra Report, 1981.

6

University Grants Commission (1980-2007)

Introduction

This chapter deals with the functioning of the UGC between 1980 to 2007. A consideration of UGC's leadership and clientele would be followed by an assessment of policy environment and an account of structural changes of funding policies, etc. As there are no official reviews of the work of the UGC for this period, except for the 66th Report of the Estimates Committee (1988-89) which has been considered in the section regarding policy environment, it appeared convenient to survey the UGC schemes and programmes in successive Five Year Plan periods, including the recommendations of the Eleventh Five Year Plan, followed by reflections on the salient features of this period.

Leadership

Prof. Satish Chandra retired as Chairman on 4th February, 1981 and was succeeded by Dr. Madhuri Shah, hailed from Bombay (Now Mumbai) and her need to touch base frequently might explain her reported heavy reliance on the Secretariat of the UGC (then led by Shri R.K. Chhabra, Secretary UGC since 1971 who retired in 1983) during her tenure. She chaired a Committee to review the functioning of the Central Universities. She can be credited with starting Women's Study Centres in the University system. Her Vice-Chairman was Prof.

Rais Ahmed who was a physicist and had a versatile background, having worked as Director of the NCERT earlier. He subsequently chaired the National Commission on Teachers II. Prof. Yashpal (1986-91), who succeeded Dr. Shah was a space scientist, and established many inter-university centres especially in S & T area. The issue of lack of co-ordination between the UGC and the IGNOU arose during his tenure. That issue was sorted out during Prof. G. Ram Reddy's tenure (1991-94), who also gave a push to the scheme of regional offices and the NAAC. Dr. Armaity Desai (1995-1999) presided over the introduction of innovations like NET/SLET. She was sympathetic to the idea of SCHE which, however, was not pushed by her successors, Dr. Hari P. Gautam (1999-2002) and Prof. Nigvekar (2002-2005). Prof. S.K. Khanna, an engineer from Roorkee University has the unique distinction of having worked as Secretary UGC for 6 years (1984-1990), before becoming its Vice-Chairman for 3 years (1990-1993). He then went on to become the Chairman, AICTE. Two Vice-Chairmen (Dr. H.P. Gautam and Prof. Nigvekar) went on as to become Chairmen, UGC. (Earlier, such honour was had by Prof. Satish Chandra). During Prof. Hari Gautam's time, UGC introduced the scheme of universities with a potential for excellence, but his tenure is also known for implementation by the UGC of the Ministry's directive regarding introduction of courses in astrology. Prof. Thorat (Chairman 2005-2010) was known to emphasize access and equity aspects of higher education.

The Clientele

There has been a phenomenal increase in the number of universities and colleges in this 27 years period as displayed in the table below:

Table 6.1: Number of Universities and Colleges

Year	*Central Univer-sities*	*INIs*	*Deemed Univer-sities*	*Quasi-Univer-sities****	*State Univer-sities*	*Total Univer-sities*	*Colleges*
1980-81	7	9	11	3	101	131	4722
2006-07*	20	13	109	7	229	378	20,677
2007-08**	24	31	103	7	251	416	20,677

* *Source*: Annual Report of UGC, 2006-07.

** *Source*: Annual Report of Union Department of Higher Education, 2007-08.

*** IIMs.

The number of centrally funded institutions has gone up from 30 in 1980-81 to 79 in 2007-08 (24 Central, 31 INIs, 11 Deemed and 7 Quasi Universities). Not all the funding is by the UGC. In 1980-81, UGC funded seven Central Universities, viz. BHU, AMU, Delhi, Vishvabharati, JNU, NEHU, and Hyderabad and eight Deemed Universities. The new Central universities which came up after 1980 were: IGNOU (1985), Pondicherry (1985), Jamia Millia, New Delhi (1988) (by conversion of a Deemed University), Manipur Central Agricultural University (1994), Assam (Silchar) (1994), Tezpur (1994), Nagaland (1995), Babasaheb Bhimrao Ambedkar, Lucknow (1996), International Hindi at Wardha (1997), Urdu at Hyderabad (1997), Allahabad 2001 (by conversion of a very old State university (established 1887), Manipur, Tripura and Arunachal Pradesh (by conversion of respective State Universities). The Central Agricultural University at Manipur is funded by the Agriculture Ministry and IGNOU, Hindi and Urdu Universities are maintained by the Education Ministry. Thus 20 out of 24 Central universities are funded by the UGC. Four new INIS have been added, which are all funded by agencies other than (the UGC [IIT at Roorkee (2001), IIT at Guwahati (1994), Medical Science (Chitra Thirunal Institute at Thiruvananthapuram) and National Pharmaceutical Institute (1998) at Mohali]. The position in regard to deemed universities is complicated. UGC gives 100 per cent maintenance grants to the following—(i) I.I.Sc., Bangalore, (ii) Gurukul Kangri, Hardwar, (iii) Gujarat Vidyapeeth, Ahmedabad, (iv) TISS, Mumbai, and (v) Gandhigram Rural, Gandhigram. Some deemed universities have since become regular Central, Universities, viz. Jamia Millia, New Delhi and CIEFL, Hyderabad. UGC gives fixed maintenance grants to three deemed universities: Jamia Hamdard, New Delhi, Banasthali, Rajasthan and S.C. SVM Kanchipuram. 18 NITs which were deemed universities in 2006-07 have since become INIs by virtue of requisite Act having been passed. As a result, the number of INIs has shot up from 13 in 2006-07 to 31 in 2007-08. Correspondingly, the number of deemed universities has got reduced from 109 to 91, but since some new deemed universities apparently were notified with in terms their number has increased to 103 in 2007-08.

The number of State universities increased from 101 in 1980 to 251 in 2007 (more than two-fold) and the colleges affiliated to them increased from 4,722 to 20,677 (four-fold increase). One reason for this growth is in the proliferation of single faculty universities. In the earlier period, about 30 Agricultural universities came up in a big way with the support of ICAR. Also, a Sanskrit University had come up in Bihar (Darbhanga, 1961) in the face of the opposition of the UGC which opposition was confirmed by the Education Commission (Kothari Report, para 8.49). During this period, six more language universities (regional plus Sanskrit) came up—Orissa (Sanskrit, 1981), Tamil Nadu (Tamil, 1981), Andhra Pradesh (Telugu, 1985), Karnataka (Kannada, 1992), Kerala (Sanskrit, 1994), Maharashtra (Sanskrit, 1999). What is more, even the Central Government ignored the earlier dogmatic opposition of the UGC and set up universities for Urdu and Hindi apart from deemed universities for Sanskrit (two at Delhi and one at Tirupati). Single faculty universities in engineering, health sciences, veterinary sciences and women's and open universities (which latter two were multi-faculty and did not face opposition from the UGC) were established by the State Governments in addition to agricultural. As noted, from 17th June, 1972, State Governments had the obligation to seek recognition from the Central Government to become eligible for Central assistance. It would, therefore, be useful to consider the data regarding State universities and colleges eligible for Central assistance. These are presented below:

Table 6.2: Central Assistance to State Universities and Colleges

Year	*State Universities*		*Colleges*	
	Total	*Eligible for Central Assistance*	*Total*	*Eligible for Central Assistance*
1980	101	N.A.	4722	N.A.
2007	256	162	20,677	5661

Thus, though the total number of State universities and especially colleges has gone up substantially, the number eligible for the UGC assistance has not gone up to the same extent. In fact, the amendment made in June 1972 has the unintended but stringent effect that colleges otherwise eligible, i.e. u/s 2(f) of the UGC Act may become ineligible if the affiliating university of the college is affected by S.12(B). This may be illustrated by an example. As is well known, Maharashtra

State set up a sub-regional University at Amravati (1983), by shifting jurisdiction of the four ex-Berar districts from Nagpur University to the new Amravati University. In 1983, the affiliated colleges in these four districts which might have been eligible u/s 2(f) were, for a transitory period, affected by non-eligibility u/s 12(B) till Amravati, the new university, was recognized u/s 12(B). Thus, the amendment of the UGC Act, 1971 had this unintended effect which reduced financial burden of UGC. It is thus that the UGC Report for 2006-07 states that though 6352 colleges are recognized u/s 2(f), only 5661 colleges are eligible to receive assistance u/s 12(B) (UGC AR, 2006-07: 5). This works out to about 20 per cent of eligible colleges.

Policy Environment

During this period, the Policy Environment faced by the UGC underwent substantial changes. Firstly, two National Commissions on Teachers were appointed by the Ministry in 1983 and reported in 1985. One of the Commissions was specifically for Teachers in higher education. Chaired, as noted, by Prof. Rais Ahmed, it did indeed make a good job of it, thanks to research support by NIEPA now NUEPA. Secondly, NPE 1968 was replaced (after wide consultation by way of "Challenge of Education" Document 1985) by NPE 1986 accompanied by a PoA 1986. Many new ideas in relation to Higher Education were thrown up in the PoA. The conventional wisdom is that NPE 1986 was meant to actualize real objectives of the Kothari Report (NPE 1968 being based on the Report of the MPs Committee which had cut out the essence of the wholesome recommendations of the Kothari Report like major universities, selective admission etc.); however, the present author's perception is that the Kothari Report was far too much focused on the one hand, on early universalization of elementary education and eradication of adult illiteracy and on the other, on Science & Technology initiatives, and in the matter of Higher Education, it had tended either to toe the conventional anti-Provincial, anti-decentralization line of the IUB or it was pedestrian. The innovations in higher and technical education in the NPE 1986 proper were accordingly, rather limited to policy decisions which were a *fait accompli* or were in the air for a long time [e.g. statutory status for AICTE, which was decided in 1981, promotion of ODL (Open & Distance Learning), which was being advocated since 1970 and for which a national university was rather belatedly established in 1985, just prior to promulgation of the policy]. The radically new innovations came up as a part of the POA 1986 which, without acknowledgement, draws heavily on the Jha Committee Report (1977) and the Report of National Commission on Teachers II. Innovations attributable to the Jha Committee are: (1) Accreditation and grading (assessment) of universities (which led to the NAAC), (2) A State level coordination body which came to be called State Council for Higher Education (SCHE), and (3) a Super-Co-ordinator (National Council for Higher Education). Innovations attributed to Teachers' Commission are: (1) statutory status for NCTE, (2) NET (National Eligibility Test), (3) Academic Staff Colleges, and (4) A code of ethics for teachers.

The second phase of the change of policy environment was the review of NPE 1986 by Ramamurti Committee in 1990, and the review of Ramamurti Committee Report by Janardan Reddy Committee in 1992. This phase was occasioned by political changes in the form of the accession of the V.P. Singh Government to power in 1989. Although Janardan Reddy Committee on record stated that the recommendation of Ramamurti Committee for a revision of the policy was not justified, in practice it was compelled to accept the thrust towards decentralization, the establishment of regional offices of the UGC being the crucial manifestation of this changed approach.

The third aspect of policy environment was the CABE Committee Report (April 1992) on the Report of the Gnanam Committee (1990) which was appointed by the UGC itself to suggest a revised management structure in the context of the NPE 1986. Gnanam Committee Report was a sprawling in-house document of the UGC containing 20 Chapters spread over 265 pages, and 24 annexures spread over 90 pages. The chapters themselves contained a lot of historical material and gathered ideas from diverse sources including the Madhuri Shah Report on the Central Universities, *but its summary was a synthetic document in the sense that the summary of recommendations" covering 34 pages did not evolve organically out of reasoned discussion in individual chapters and logical recommendations flowing therefrom, but was drafted by another author as an independent summary of consensus*. The Ministry decided to refer it to the CABE which appointed a Committee under Chairmanship of Karsandas Soneri (Education Minister, Gujarat) to examine it. This CABE Committee Report which dissented in many respects from the Gnanam summary, therefore, provides a policy environment for higher education in the 1990s and beyond. As this report is apparently not in the public domain, I have referred to it on the basis of hearsay. All recommendations of the Committee referred to in the following paragraphs may be read with this qualification in mind. The Committee consisted, apart from four Education Ministers (Gujarat, Maharashtra, Orissa and UP) of seven academics including the then Chairman UGC, Prof. G. Ram Reddy and Dr. Malcolm Adisheshaih, a seasoned academic/bureaucrat.

- *The Committee did not accept the recommendation that the Government of India may circulate a Model Bill on State Councils of Higher Education* (Item 27). Presumably the Committee was not opposed to guidelines and of course, the Committee was not opposed to SCHE as such, but the Committee apparently did not accept Central Government's prerogative of preparing models for States to follow.
- On a related issue, *the Gnanam Committee's recommendation that the Central Government should enact a law setting out the basic structure of university governance was not accepted by Soneri Committee.*
- The Committee did not concede financial autonomy to State universities which, it wanted, should approach State Governments for approval of any expenditure outside the States' budget.
- The Committee did not accept the recommendation that the Statute making power should rest with the universities.
- In the matter of *affiliation of colleges*, the Committee did not agree to leave the final decision to the Universities *but wanted them to obtain the concurrence of State Governments* in regard to provision of grants to the colleges which were to be affiliated.
- The Committee did not agree to the Gnanam Committee's proposal to leave matter of co-ordination and standards

entirely to the UGC and Central Government. They wanted the UGC to consult State/Central Governments regarding new universities. They also wanted the UGC to be bound by a time limit of 3 months when State Government consults the UGC about State University Legislation.

- The Committee did not agree that the role of the UGC should be advisory and persuasive. They wanted the UGC to enforce standards regarding recruitment and qualification of teachers, the number of working days etc.
- They wanted SCHE at State level to be an advisory agency for the Chancellor.
- While agreeing with the proposal to establish regional offices of UGC, it wanted that some of the schemes implemented by the UGC should be transferred to State universities.
- The Committee wanted statutes to cover the code of ethics not only for teachers but also Vice-Chancellors and Principals.
- It did not agree to the Academic Council being the ultimate authority in matters within its purview.
- Not agreeing to the proposal to dispense with election to university bodies it favoured the formulation that election should be kept to the minimum.
- It wanted a Students' Council and Student Unions with voluntary membership to be provided for in the University Acts.
- It did not want the powers of the Police to be fettered when there was breach of law on the university campus.
- *It wanted UGC to prepare revised guidelines for conferring deemed university status.*

Apparently, the difference between the Gnanam Committee and the Soneri Committee essentially turned on the role of state Governments in a federal and democratic polity, the State governments' responsibility for law and order and in the matter of conceding unfettered legislative powers (statute making power) to the universities. It was apparently agreeable to guidelines, but not to a model or binding laws about the State universities and State Councils for Higher Education. Most interestingly, it apparently wanted the UGC to be more proactive in minimum standards regarding qualifications and working hours of teacher, etc.

The fourth aspect of change of policy environment was judicial activism. As the Education Ministry began to drag its feet on proposals for reforms (e.g. regulation of capitation fees proposed by a UGC Committee in 1986) which amounted to a virtual abdication of its duty by the Executive Branch of the Government, the higher judiciary (HCs/SC) stepped into the breach by entertaining PILs and in general by judicial activism. The UGC and higher education institutions generally, therefore, began to follow the lead given by the judiciary as in the case of the Unnikrishnan judgment on capitation fees (1993) and in the matter of the guidelines against ragging, in the matter of elections to Students' Council and even in curricular matters (e.g. introduction of environmental science in the courses of study).

The fifth and final aspect of change of policy environment coincided with the NPE Review. On a very broad view, the Ramamurti review of NPE in 1990 and Janardan Reddy Report on Policy (1992) as a counter point to the Ramamurti Report were political epiphenomena which were subsumed under the more fundamental shift in the direction of economic policy incorporated in the Union Budgets in 1991-92 and 1992-93. The economic difficulties which required the Union Government to agree to a structural adjustment programme entailed, in the education field, a thrust towards liberalization and privatization because of financial stringency. The innovations suggested in the NPE 1986/1992 and PoA 1986/1992 were implemented but some of them after a time lag, some of them in a piecemeal manner and some fell by the wayside. One had to pay lip service to the NPE but the hard reality of financial stringency was overwhelming and the push towards privatization was difficult to resist.

Structural Changes in the UGC and in the UGC-State Government Interface

It was noted earlier that a scholar, who had studied UGC in the context of the paradigm of cooperative federalism in India, had suggested State UGCs as a solution to the thorny problem of the triangular relationship between the UGC, the State Governments and State Universities (Marina Pinto, 1984: 174-185). The 1960s version of the UGC-type bodies in UP, Bihar, MP etc. were regarded as too complicit with the State governments and therefore, could not ensure reconciliation of accountability required by State financing with the autonomy of State UGCs. A possible alternative or rather a supplementary mechanism suggested by A.L. Mudaliar as early as in February 1960 was regional offices of the UGC (Mudaliar, 1960). It was also noted that the UGC as well as the Central Government were opposed to both the ideas. However, the UGC swore by the idea of the visiting committees for finalization of Five Year Plans for various reasons. In the period under review, visiting committees declined in importance. However, the idea of Regional offices of UGC came to be accepted and were set up in the 1990s and the State Councils of Higher Education (SCHEs) became part of the NPE though only a few major States accepted them. How did this come about? The following paragraphs attempt an answer.

Visiting Committees: Decline in importance

At one stage, Visiting Committees consisting of UGC Officers and the Experts appointed by the UGC and representatives of State governments to examine Five Year Plans of individual universities were considered as a promising avenue for tripartite association of State Governments, State Universities and the UGC (Kothari Report 13.93; Gajendragadkar Report: 34, PAC Report (1977): 110-118, Estimates Committee Report: 53-60. The available evidence shows that State Governments were not associated with the Visiting Committees except during the Fifth Five Year Plan (1974-79). For the Sixth Plan (1980-85) the Visiting Committees were constituted very late. For the Seventh Plan (1985-90), because of the delay in finalization of the UGC allocation in the context of the NPE 1986, no Visiting Committee was constituted. In connection with the Eighth Plan (1992-97), the UGC sent out Expert Committees to visit colleges to finalize proposals sent by them and for finalization of the Ninth Plan Proposals (1997-2002), a meeting of all State Secretaries was held in May 1996. Thus, the Visiting Committees as a mechanism for a tripartite dialogue have lost their importance. The latest thinking appears to be that the Visiting Committees are time-consuming and Five Year Plans may be finalized in discussions across the table. This is highly ironical, especially because Kothari Commission considered the Visiting Committees as a perfect substitute for statutory inspections to be conducted by the UGC (Kothari Report: 13.73).

Deconcentration: Regional Offices of the UGC

Decentralization of a Central organization can take two forms, devolution or deconcentration, the former involving delegation of some powers to the regional formations. Deconcentration has been practised by the AICTE since its non-statutory Avatar in 1945 as pointed out by A.L. Mudaliar in 1960. Marina Pinto (1984) has pointed out that the idea was articulated in the minute of dissent to the Report of the Joint Select Committee on UGC Bill by Hiren Mukerji, MP as early as 1954. Unfortunately, there was consistent opposition to the idea of deconcentration of the UGC both within the Government as well as within the academic community. Here, the opposition of the Jha Committee is particularly notable. The Jha Committee Report (p. 85) felt that regional offices of the UGC would smack of 'regionalism'. The Committee, however, suggested that in order to look at the special needs of backward regions, high-level academic experts could be appointed in the UGC who can keep direct contact through visits with universities, colleges and State Governments and depending on need, field staff can be appointed to assist the academic experts. During the discussion of the UGC (Amendment) Bill, 1985 Lok Sabha MPs from Karnataka, Kerala and Tamil Nadu and Rajya Sabha MPs from West Bengal and Tamil Nadu complained that the UGC was a highly centralized body and the Government should start thinking of opening some regional offices. The Minister of State (Ms. Sushila Rohtagi) in her reply asserted that while any grievance about delays could be looked into, there is no question of setting up regional centres of the UGC (L.S. Debate, dated 17th December, 1985).

The National Policy on Education (NPE) 1986 and its Programme of Action (PoA) 1986 with their centralist ethos did not touch on the issue of decentralization. It was the Ramamurti Committee which set the stage for regional offices of the UGC by suggesting that the UGC should have regional offices for decentralized disposal of the problems relating to higher educational institutions in respective regions (Ramamurti Report 2.72). UGC, which till then, was opposed to the idea appears to have undergone a change of heart following the report of the Administrative Staff College of India (ASCI), Hyderabad on the administrative reorganization of the UGC and the Gnanam Committee, which being helped by an Additional Secretary of the UGC, was aware of the latest thinking. The Janardhan Reddy Report, while noting that the UGC has accepted the need for some regional offices strongly recommended that regional offices of the UGC should be set up at the earliest, with adequate authority and functions (J. Reddy Report: 13.11). The CABE Committee (Soneri Committee) reportedly endorsed the Gnanam Committee recommendation that four to five regional offices of the UGC should be set up and some of the UGC programmes be transferred to the Collegiate Councils. It is thus clear that it was the conjuncture of (a) Ramamurti/Janardhan Reddy Committees with (b) ASCI Report on UGC's reorganization, and (c) Gnanam/CABE Reports that tilted the scales in favour of regional offices of the UGC which, as an organization, had opposed this idea right from 1956 till 1989!

The regional offices of the UGC came up in the year 1993-94 and thereafter and they are referred to, for the first time, in the Annual Report of UGC for the year 1994-95 (UGC: AR: 7-8). These regional offices are located at Pune, Hyderabad, Bangalore, Kolkata, Guwahati and Bhopal. A Bureau for Northern Office functions from the UGC Headquarters. It is stated that the UGC, pursuant to the NPE 1986, which should really mean NPE 1986 as modified in 1992, decentralized its working by opening six regional offices. It was decided that the regional offices would initially deal with selected programmes and schemes pertaining to colleges in the Eighth Plan, namely development of Colleges, College Development Council, COSIP and COHSSIP, Minor Research Projects, and autonomous colleges. Unfortunately data regarding activities of Regional Offices of the UGC are not available except in the Annual Report 1996-97 when the Plan grants paid to colleges were Rs. 6916.39 lakhs, indicating that roughly 4/7th of the Plan assistance for colleges was routed through Regional Offices (Annual Report, 1996-97: 177-187). Recent Annual Reports of the UGC merely list them in an appendix (*vide* Annual Report 2006-07 Appendix XIII) and UGC's official history gives them a summary treatment (Kavita Sharma, 2003: 236). It is clear that regional offices have a lot of potential if they could have advisory bodies of academics of the region attached to them. Marina Pinto suggested that these advisory bodies could consist of some Vice-Chancellors of Universities, representatives of State Education departments of the region, educationists and experts. They could assess the needs of institution in the area and submit the total financial requirements to the Centre (1984, pp. 183-184). But such interaction and participation would go against the grain of centralization and the UGC appears to regard these offices merely as its regional outposts!

Experiments with Mini-UGC at State level

The Radhakrishnan Commission was clearly in favour of a State level grants body (Para 13.62). The Model Act Committee chaired by Dr. D.S. Kothari, however, opposed the idea on the ground that such a body would undermine the autonomy and initiative of the universities. It left the issue open, stating that the question should be examined in consultation with the UGC (Model Act Committee Report: 31). Education Commission agreed with the Standing Committee of the IUB (which had opposed the idea suggesting that any State government requiring advice, should consult the UGC). It was believed that it may lead to confusion if the responsibility for co-ordinating standards was distributed amongst a number of bodies such as the Central UGC and the State UGCs and that it would also hinder the existing direct relationship between the UGC and the State universities (Kothari Report: 13.62). This argument was self-evidently fallacious because the State UGCs would implement rather than duplicate UGC's regulations on standards and the myth of direct relationship between the UGC and State universities ignored the realities of the Indian federalism where State universities are creatures of State legislation and are maintained by the State governments.

State Boards of VCs/CDCs

The Gajendragadkar Committee, recognizing the need for co-ordination suggested two bodies: (1) Coordinating Committee of Vice-Chancellors of Universities in the States which would be an advisory body, evidently to be presided over by the Chancellor. (2) Collegiate Education Committee in states where the number of colleges are large, which would be an advisory committee with representation of State Government officers, universities, UGC etc. (Gajendragadkar Report: 82-83; 34). The Jha Report was prescient because, while, in principle, opposed to any organization called State-level UGC, its conception of a co-ordinating body headed by the Chancellor was broader, consisting of all Vice-Chancellors, selected college principals, some independent academicians and also the representatives of the State Government as well as the UGC (Jha Report: 30-31). In the meanwhile, some State governments went ahead and established UGC-type bodies at the State level. Marina Pinto observes that States like UP and Bihar did set up State UGCs, but they did not last long because of inadequacy of funds and friction between state Secretariat, the Commission and the Universities. She also refers to the experiment in Kerala where three committees were set up respectively for consultation, for fixation of grants and for inter-University co-ordination (Pinto, 1984: 178-79; 182-83). The Madhya Pradesh Uchcha Shiksha Anudan Ayog, set up in 1973, did not last long (D.D. Kolhatkar, 1974).

The Gajendragadkar Committee's idea of co-ordination committee of Vice-Chancellors received official recognition when the UGC advised all universities to constitute Inter-University Coordination Boards in 1974-75 (UGC AR 1974-75: 33). It is notable that by this time Kothari was succeeded as Chairman by George Jacob. Its idea of a collegiate education committee received concrete shape with the UGC launching a scheme for College Development Council (CDC) within an individual university in the Sixth Five Year Plan (1980-85). The functions of the CDCs were manifold, the main being that of co-ordination between colleges and various agencies like the University, UGC and the State Government. One commentator does not find the CDCs to be very successful organizations (J. Indiresan, 1993: 309-333).

State Councils of Higher Education (SCHE)

By 1986, the idea of State-level co-ordinating body had become academically acceptable. The nomenclature of State Councils of Higher education was proposed by the NPE 1986, apparently building on the experience of previous experiments at co-ordination, namely (a) State level grant bodies, (2) Inter-University board of Vice-Chancellors, and (3) College Development Councils of individual universities. The NPE 1986 suggested setting up of Councils of Higher Education for State level planning and co-ordination of higher education (NPE 1986: 5.30), which in conjunction with the UGC would develop co-ordinative methods to keep a watch on standards. The PoA 1986 developed the idea further, expecting the Council to prepare a consolidated programme of higher education in each State to scrutinize the development programmes of universities and colleges, promote the UGC scheme of autonomous colleges and assist and advise the UGC generally in respect of maintenance of Standards. The Council was to assist State Governments in determining block grants and setting up new institutions (PoA 1986: 5.22). UGC was tasked to draw up model provisions for the composition and functions of these Councils. A 15 member representative committee appointed by the UGC in 1986 with five State Education Secretaries* as Members, reported in July 1987. As in many other matters, Andhra Pradesh tried to be the first State but its legislation for the purpose was rather hastily drafted. Teachers' Union challenged it and the Supreme Court upheld the challenge and quashed the Andhra Pradesh Commissionerate of Higher Education Act, 1986 (which defined powers of what was in effect a State Council on Higher Education), as unconstitutional, holding that the Act usurped the powers of the Central Government under entry 66/Central List/Schedule VII of the Constitution of India (Osmania University Teachers' case 1987). In the light of the SC judgment, the UGC modified the Guidelines for the SCHE and forwarded them to the Central Government for necessary action. The 'objectives' paragraph of the Guidelines states that the SCHEs, which would be statutory bodies, would enable the UGC to fulfil its own statutory responsibility, would act as a link between the universities and colleges and the State Governments and work closely with the UGC. Their fourfold functions were—Planning and Coordination, Academic, Advisory and Administrative (UGC 1986). The matter was taken up by the 66th Report of the Estimates

---

* The present author, in his capacity as Education Secretary, Maharashtra, was a Member of this Committee.

Committee (1989). The Ministry of Education's response in 1990, raised hopes that the SCHEs would become functional in most of the states during the Eighth Plan period then assumed to run for the period 1990-95 (Action Taken Report: 7th August, 1990). However, the Review of NPE 1986 ordered by the National Front Government in 1989 upset this schedule. While the Ramamurti Committee was not too enthusiastic about the SCHE, apparently because of the opposition of the Planning Commission on the basis that maintenance of standards should be left to the UGC, it did not oppose the proposal to set up State Councils of Higher Education. Rather, it opposed the proposal to set up a Central Council of Rural Institutes on the ground that the State Council of Higher Education together with the UGC can perform the function of the Central Council (Ramamurti Report: 230). The Gnanam Committee backed up SCHE whole-heartedly but there was a sting in its tail. Hence its relevant recommendations No. 26 and 27 bear full quotation:

> "(26). SCHEs should be constituted by the Act of the State Legislatures in every State to plan, monitor and ço-ordinate the functioning of universities and other institutions of higher education within the State. However, such a body should not infringe upon the autonomy of the universities. The composition of the Council should be predominantly academic with a provision for a nominee of the UGC. The Council should not degenerate into an additional hurdle to be overcome or a mere grant-transmitting agency. *The Committee of Vice-Chancellors of the state should perform this role as far as possible till such time the Council is set up.*
>
> (27). The Government of India may circulate model Bill on SCHE to all State Governments indicating the composition, functions, powers and other issues concerned with the state Councils for the purpose of uniformity" (Gnanam Report: 82-83).

The trouble was with the portion in italics in the recommendation at No. 26, extending support to the *status quo* in the interim period. The second source of problem was that the recommendation No. 27 was reportedly rejected by the CABE report which had however reportedly supported recommendation No. 26.

Allhough Janardan Reddy Report supported SCHEs (J. Reddy Report: 13.3), the PoA 1992, aware of the ambivalence of CABE (Soneri) report, which was perhaps at the draft stage at that time, noted the lack of consensus on the suggestion regarding establishment of SCHEs (PoA 1992: 11.3.3).

In practical terms, the Supreme Court judgment on AP legislation queered the pitch for SCHEs. The same coupled with reported lack of unqualified support for the SCHEs by the CABE Committee, appeared to have disheartened the State Governments. Hence, the States appear to have preferred to maintain the *status quo*. Successive Annual Reports of the UGC (1992-1996) do not make any reference to the State Councils at all. The Ninth Plan Working Group Report for Higher Education (1996: 1.14) revived the idea, but regretted that State Governments had departed from the UGC model and involved the Ministers and the bureaucracy in key roles. It noted that seven councils, i.e. four regular Councils in Andhra Pradesh, Tamil Nadu, Uttar Pradesh and West Bengal and three Advisory Councils in Himachal Pradesh, Arunachal Pradesh and Tripura had come into existence by 1995-96. (There was no clarification regarding why Councils in Bihar, Madhya Pradesh and Orissa reported in connection with it, to the Estimates Committee by the Ministry, as being in an advanced stage of legislation had stalled). Regarding future action, the Report suggested greater inter-action among the State Department of Education, the universities in the State and the UGC and periodic meetings of the UGC with the Chancellor and the State Department of Education, to discuss policy issues. The odd man out in this scenario was the Governor who rightly did not have any role in the model guidelines. UGC's Annual Report (1997-98: 14) under the heading "Improvement in Management of Education" refers to the scheme of State Councils as a new scheme. Since then, however, the scheme of State Councils appears to have vanished from the radar of the UGC. The Draft Tenth Plan proposals of UGC initially included the scheme but the final draft dropped it. The CABE Report on "Autonomy to Higher Education

Institutions" (June 2005, p. 12) refers to SCHE in its overview but there is no change in situation on the ground (4 SCHEs and 3 Advisory boards). There is no specific recommendation in CABE Autonomy Report regarding SCHEs. The Draft 11th Plan proposals of the UGC also do not refer to SCHEs.

Why has such a crucial body like SCHE not made much headway? The theoretical reason is the ill-fated combination of three circumstances, viz. (a) SC judgement of 1987, (b) Absence of support by PoA 1992 which was finalized when the CABE Report on Gnanam Report was not available, (c) the CABE Report reportedly rejecting the Model Bill for SCHE. A more practical explanation is in terms of the dynamics of power [Amrik Singh, 2004(a): 88-91]. Those actors whose powers would be taken away by the SCHEs are opposing it, i.e. State Secretaries and State Ministers of Education, university hierarchy and unions of university teachers and the Chancellor-Governor. The final point is that self-financing professional colleges run by the rural elite in States like Karnataka, Maharashtra, Andhra Pradesh and Tamil Nadu would not welcome any independent regulatory body working under the supervision of the UGC while the deemed universities would claim immunity from any control by any such State body.

Evolving Trend of Funding between Central and State Institutions

The Jha Committee had noted that in 1973-74, Central universities and Delhi colleges covering 3.8 per cent of enrolment got 52.6 per cent share of the UGC grants. Since then the number of Central Universities for which UGC is responsible has increased to 18, of Delhi Colleges to 53, and maintained deemed universities to 12 and, in addition, there are now three national facility centres, fifty-seven Academic Staff Colleges and six inter-university centres set up in terms of the 1984 amendment which are to be given both maintenance and development grants by the UGC. The number of State Universities has also gone up to 256 in 2007-08 of which 162 are eligible for the UGC assistance. Given ahead is a tabular statement (6.3) of the Plan and Non-Plan grants released by the UGC to various State and Central universities, including their colleges, Deemed universities and the

I-U Centres at four points of time, viz. 1984-85, 1991-92, 2003-04 and 2006-2007. The choice of years is dictated by the fact that data were available for the first time in 1984-85 and regularly from 1991-92, 2006-07 being the latest year for which the data are available. Table 6.3 shows that UGC's funding, for State institutions has gone down from 47.4 per cent in 1973-74 to 26.62 per cent in 1984-85 and to 22.17 per cent in 1991-92. It had marginally improved to 31.62 per cent in 2003-04, but has gone down to 30 per cent in 2006-07. No doubt, it is an improvement over the lowest level reached in 1991-92 but it is still way below the figure in 1973-74, the base year of Jha Committee Report.

Table 6.3: Statement of Grants paid by UGC to Universities and Colleges under Plan and Non-Plan

(Rs. in crore)

Items	*1984-85*	*1991-92*	*2003-04*	*2006-07*
Plan Expenditure				
1. Central Universities	23.86	48.18	197.18	480.60
2. Deemed Universities	6.73	10.62	29.25	24.82
3. Colleges of Central Univ.	1.47	2.57	4.67	17.92
4. Inter-University Centres/Misc.	0.91	13.52	4.80	47.56
Total Plan (Central)	**32.97**	**74.89**	**235.90**	**550.90**
Non-Plan Expenditure				
1. Central Universities	76.47	161.24	705.42	1029.61
2. Deemed Universities	13.16	34.74	70.31	100.04
3. Colleges of Central Univ.	25.47	57.32	272.54	356.14
4. Inter-Univ. Centres	—	0.30	15.92	25.29
5. INIs	—	—	—	0.63
Total Non-Plan	**114.63**	**253.20**	**1069.19**	**1411.71**
Total Plan & Non-Plan (Central)	**147.60**	**328.09**	**1300.09**	**1962.61**
State Institutions				
1. State Universities (Plan)	27.19	72.08	441.13	294.17
2. State Univ.(Non-Plan)	3.41	7.19	Nil	70.91
3. State Colleges (Plan)	20.85	20.55	160.32	383.83
4. State Colleges (Non-Plan	0.32	0.37	Nil	5.79
Total State Institutions	**53.24**	**93.44**	**601.45**	**754.70**
Grand Total (Central+States)	**200.84**	**421.53**	**1901.54**	**2717.31**

Source: 1. UGC Annual Report 1984-85, Appendix XXII-XXIII, (2) UGC Annual Report 1991-92, Appendix XI (3) UGC Annual Report 2003-04, Appendix XIX-XX, and (4) UGC Annual Report, 2006-07, Appendices XIX and XX.

Thus, the cumulative impact of (a) the increase in Central Institutions plus (b) creation of Inter-University Centres/National facility centres/ maintained Academic Staff Colleges, many of them cost-intensive, over a number of years, is to create what might be called an *in-House Institutional drag* on the UGC, so that its capacity to finance State institutions and colleges is very severely affected. *The UGC, from being a federal institution assisting Centre and the States equitably has been converted into a virtual Central Government institution which gives only peripheral funding to the States*. By way of a remedy, it may be suggested, firstly that, the recommendation of the Jha Report (p. 63), that maintenance grants to Central universities should be treated as the agency function of the UGC to be separately budgeted and reported upon be implemented and secondly, the recommendation of the Punnayya Committee (1994), to be dealt with subsequently, to set up Delhi and BHU Colleges Funding Councils totally disconnected from the UGC be acted upon.

Activities of UGC (1980-86)

In the remaining part of the chapter, the activities of the UGC would be reviewed with reference to Five Year Plans (Sixth to Tenth). It is convenient to consider Sixth and Seventh Plans and Two Annual Plans (1990-92) together because they were characterized by important developments, some of which tended to pit the UGC and the Ministry of Education against each other. It was not a period of total confrontation because there was always a *modus vivendi* but there was an underlying current of tension based on bonafide differences either of approach or of perception.

At the outset, based on content analysis of UGC's Annual Reports, some highlights are mentioned.

From the Annual Report 1978-79 (which forms a part of the earlier period), UGC began to include a section on—"Higher Education and Women" in its Annual Reports (*vide* pp. 130-132, AR 1978-79). It is stated in the context of the recommendations made by the Committee on the Status of Women that the Ministry has intimated that a separate allocation for women be made in the Development Plans and be separately monitored. This formal addition of a section to the Annual Reports of the earlier period ties up with a new Women's Studies Programme initiated by the UGC to which a reference for the first time occurs in the Annual Report of the UGC for 1985-86 (pp. 202-204). It is stated there that with a view to bring greater awareness about problems regarding women and to strengthen database for better analysis, the UGC agreed to assist universities for undertaking well-defined projects for research on women's studies as also for development of curriculum and relevant extension activities. A Ford Foundation grant for library collections on the subject in a few centres also came in handy. The Standing Committee on the subject had chalked out an ambitious project which included development of at least ten regionally based resource centres responsible for curricular development, teacher development and development of teaching-learning materials during the Seventh Plan.

From the year 1980-81, UGC, in view of the recommendations of the report of the Committee of the Seventh Lok Sabha on 'Papers laid on the Table' began to include in its Annual Report a section devoted to 'deemed universities'. This recommendation was made in the light of UGC's reply that annual audit reports of institutions deemed to be universities are not proposed to be laid before the Parliament (*vide* Annual Report, 1980-81, p. 49). A perusal of UGC Reports since then shows that the material on deemed universities, which is incorporated in the Annual Report is not in a uniform format or length, but simply reproduces whatever is sent by the respective deemed universities. It is high time the UGC prescribes a format and edits the material.

The Annual Report 1982-83 (pp. 54-55) shows that a new scheme for special assistance for development of backward districts was started for which the UGC adopted a well-considered definition of backward districts different from that of the Planning Commission (which was meant for school education), viz. those districts in which higher education enrolment is 50 per cent or less than the average higher education enrolment in that State (average enrolment = enrolment per 1000 population).

On the following points, differences were either reported or latent between the Ministry and the UGC in the period 1980-85:

(1) The appointment of a Review Committee for Central Universities by the UGC (January 1982 to November 1983).

(2) The introduction of Merit promotion scheme by the UGC with effect from 1st March, 1983.

(3) The circumstances leading to the amendment of section 6 of UGC Act with effect from 20-12-1985 which specifically related to the age of retirement of the Chairman and the Vice-Chairman.

(1) Report of the Committee to Enquire into the Working of the Central Universities

This Committee was appointed by the UGC under the Chairmanship of the then Chairman UGC in January 1982 with the following terms of reference:

(1) To examine whether the Central Universities fulfil the objectives set for them in their Acts and Statutes,

(2) To examine the general state of discipline in the Central universities,

(3) Grievance redressal machinery for students, teachers and administrative staff of the universities,

(4) Possible code of conduct for political parties limiting their involvement in university affairs, and

(5) To suggest other measures of reforms for efficient functioning of the universities.

Prima facie, the Ministry would not be happy that the UGC should have set up such a committee. The administration of the Central universities is within the purview of the Ministry, which advises the President of India in his capacity as the Visitor of all Central Universities in all matters including the approval of statutes, examination of whether any action of the Vice-Chancellors of the Central Universities is in accordance with the Act, statutes and regulations, the appointment of the Vice-Chancellor, the appointment of Visitor's nominees, the appointment of a Committee of enquiry in terms of visitorial powers etc. The UGC's role is confined to determination and release of grants to Central Universities and to Delhi and BHU colleges. In a sense, this is an agency function of the

UGC. UGC is concerned with all the universities and colleges in India including State universities and its main role, constitutionally recognized, is co-ordination and determination of standards. The Chairman, UGC being the Chairman of the Committee also raised protocol problems *vis-à-vis* the Education Secretary. The tension in the matter is not only latent or imagined but *also patent on the face of* the record. When the UGC requested the Ministry to send a note indicating their perception of the problems besetting the Central universities, the Ministry tersely replied as below:

> "We have carefully considered the matter. The terms of reference of the Committee are clear and specific. These terms of reference do not indicate that the Committee has to consider any problem that the Central Government faces *vis-à-vis* the Central Universities. We are, therefore, not sure of the scope and nature of the note sought by the Committee. We are of the view that while the Committee is free to seek any information on specific points from various sources including Government, which the Committee may require in connection with its deliberations and arrive at their own conclusions on the basis of such information, it may not be appropriate for the Government to identify a set of problems and refer it to the Committee for consideration, in view of the specific nature of its Terms of Reference" (pp. VII/VIII of the Report).
>
> The tension between the Ministry and the UGC is self evident. The Ministry, however, could not maintain this stand-offishness for long. When the Public Accounts Committee wanted the Ministry's view on various matters relating to the JNU, including a demand for visitorial enquiry, Ministry did refer the same to the Committee (p. 151 of the Report).

The recommendations of the Committee are no doubt valuable and some have been cited in higher education literature, especially in connection with the Code of Conduct for the Teachers (para 2.64 to 2.71 of Report). But some recommendations at least were questionable. From the Ministry's point of view, the Commission could be said to have over-reached itself by recommending that the Ministry consult the UGC before any advice to the Visitor in various matters regarding Central Universities (paras 5.49 and 5.50) of Report. For this recommendation, the Committee could not cite any authority except the recommendation of a BHU enquiry committee (1969) chaired by Justice P.B. Gajendragadkar which recommendation was incidentally *obiter dictum*, because it was outside the scope of its Terms of Reference. Incidentally, the fact that the Member-Secretary of the Committee (R.K. Chabra) was also Member-Secretary of the BHU Enquiry Committee (1969) was conveniently not mentioned by the Central Universities Committee. It is not necessary to go into the content and merits of the various recommendations of the Committee.

(2) The Merit Promotion Scheme

The merit promotion scheme for teachers was originally part of the package of pay revision of university and college teachers in 1973 in terms of the Sen Committee recommendations. As is pointed out in Mehrotra Committee Report (p. 21), the scale approved by the Central Government for lecturer in affiliated colleges was: Rs. 700-40-1100-50-1300—Assessment—50-1600. By Assessment, the Sen Committee (1974) meant: "A Lecturer/Reader who had completed six years of service and claimed that he had done outstanding work and fulfilled the minimum prescribed qualifications for Reader/Professor could offer himself for assessment by a duly constituted Selection Committee of the University".

The Finance Ministry had not agreed to the Assessment Scheme and therefore, the lecturers were not able to go beyond the limit of Rs. 1300. As was well-known at that time, Group I Officers' pay scale in the Central Government was Rs. 700-1300 and the lecturers especially the unionized teachers in the Delhi Colleges wanted to force the hand of the Government. For this purpose, the *Delhi University Teachers Association.(DUTA)* organized a strike in 1992-93 which lasted for 110 days. The strike ended after the matter had gone to the Delhi High Court where a Memorandum of Settlement was agreed. It is the general understanding in academic circles *vide* Amrik Singh (1989: 91-131), that in spite of UGC's advice to the contrary, the Ministry gave in to the teachers' demands. The facts were as below: The demand of DUTA was for extension of assessment scheme, (which they called the merit promotion scheme, and which was basically meant for the university teachers), to the lecturers in the affiliated colleges. The UGC was apprehensive that the extension of merit promotion to teachers in the affiliated colleges would, in effect, amount to the introduction of a time-bound promotion scheme, thus allowing sub-standard teachers to get, first, the Reader's scale and, then, the Professor's scale. The Report of Teachers' Commission II observes in this regard: "It was really unfortunate that the recommendations of the Sen Committee were put in cold storage for a considerable time; and as a consequence, there was a large-scale stagnation in the careers of faculty members spread over a considerable period of time. Not having conceded at the right time that which was due to the meritorious, a situation has arisen wherein the system succumbed to populist pressures for automatic promotion, irrespective of merit." UGC's order in this regard reproduced in its 1982-83 and 1983-84 Annual Report talks of lecturers who have completed 8 years of service being considered for merit promotion with a ceiling on the number of promoted teachers being 1/5th of total number of permanent posts in the college.

Amrik Singh (1989-97) states: "It must be said to the credit of the UGC that on its own, it did not wish to cave in but the Ministry of Education thought differently and pressurized everyone into accepting the demands of strikers." Later on he says: "Owing to weak leadership and inadequate understanding of academic issues, the Ministry of Education surrendered when it need not have" (p. 98, *Ibid.*). At that time, Serla Grewal with a high repitition was the Secretary of the Ministry and there was no question of a weak leadership of the Ministry or any lack of understanding by the Ministry of the issues involved. The UGC was well aware of why the Ministry resiled from the original stand. This would become clear when official records of the period are made public. It suited the UGC, however, when the Ministry was blamed. It is to be inferred that the things were not quite smooth between the Ministry and the UGC which inference is also strengthened by what is stated in the next paragraph.

(3) Amendment of the UGC Act in connecion with the Tenure of Chairman, UGC

The UGC compilation shows that section 6 of the UGC Act was substituted by Act 70 of 1995 for sub-section (1) of section 6 with effect from 20-12-1985, to provide for term of office of Chairman/Vice-Chairman being subject to the rider "until he/she attains the age of 65 year whichever is earlier". Since an amendment of the UGC Act is rare, it must be presumed that the amendment was meant to deal with an urgent contemporary issue. Rules regarding Chairman/Vice-Chairman are in the public domain and they did provide for retirement of Chairman after attaining the age of 65. It is reliably understood that the then Chairman took the stand that since he/she was appointed for 5 years, he/she would like to retire only after completion of tenure though he/she had attained 65 years earlier. Ministry received legal advice that Chairman's stand was correct since the Act did not specifically provide for 65 years as age of retirement. The Government therefore had to affect the amendment.

Let the facts as ascertained from the UGC Annual Reports and other published accounts speak for themselves [all data pertain to the then Chairman, UGC]. Date of assumption of charge—5th February, 1981. Date of Birth—13th December, 1919 [*vide* Suresh Dalal (1985). Date of completion of 65 years—12th December, 1984. (*NB*: Chairman did not retire on this date]. Actual date of retirement—4th February, 1986.

This episode is disquieting for two reasons. First of all, a very distinguished academic took a stand on personal legal rights rather than on the propriety and subjected the organization to latent conflict with the Government of the day. Secondly, since the Chairman was advised by the UGC Secretariat, the episode raises the delicate issue of conflict between the loyalty of the Secretariat to the incumbent of the Office on the one hand and the duty of Secretariat on the other to alert the Ministry in advance about the ambiguity of the Act on the other which then was required to be amended.

NPE 1986

Annual Reports for three years of 1986-87, 1987-88 and 1988-89 include a separate chapter on implementation of the new NPE 1986.

Thanks to this follow-up, UGC appears to have taken action to finalize guidelines for institutionalization of significant schemes like (1) State Councils for Higher Education, (2) Accreditation and Assessment Councils, (3) National Qualifying Test for recruitment of teachers, and (4) Academic Staff Colleges. No such chapter appears in the Annual Reports of 1990-91 onwards because by that date NPE had come under review. From the year 1987-88, there is a separate section on 'inter-university centres' for the setting up of which the UGC was empowered by the amendment of the UGC Act *vide* Section 12(ccc) which came into effect from 1-10-1984. In this latter period, there could have been differences between the Ministry and the UGC but they apparently hinged less on personal perceptions than on the policies or their consequences. It is to be noted that the Chairman was a distinguished space scientist and not given to controversies. The differences, apparently, were more to do with the approach of the Secretariat of the UGC, than with the Chairman. Moreover, these differences might have been accentuated by the change of the political scenario in 1989 leading to the NPE review, which put the Ministry in an awkward position. The issues were four as listed below:

(1) Establishment of the IGNOU (1985) and its consequences.
(2) The Proliferation of the Inter-University Centres in the S & T areas and the implications of such a proliferation.
(3) Action, or lack thereof, on the amendment relating to curbing of capitation fee colleges.
(4) Pay Revision in terms of the Mehrotra Committee Report.

Establishment of the IGNOU

In 1985, Indira Gandhi National Open University (IGNOU) for open/distance education was established. The problems arose apparently because the IGNOU was kept out of the purview of the UGC by the Ministry, which might have done this on the analogy of the Open University in UK, but the UGC may not have been happy about the departure from past policy.

The Annual Reports of the UGC for 1985-91 are eloquent for their studied silence on the role of IGNOU and how it fits in with the UGC's ongoing programme on Distance Education and

Correspondence Courses. Annual Report, 1985-86 does not even take note of the existence of IGNOU as a Central University in the Appendix I. The IGNOU is referred to, for the first time, in the Annual Report of 1986-87. Thereafter, four Annual Reports of 1987-88, 1988-89, 1989-90 and 1990-91 list the number of universities offering correspondence courses, which increased progressively from 35 to 38 to 39 (1990-91). Yashpal retired as Chairman UGC in February 1991. The year 1991-92 was a year of transition. Dr. Manmohan Singh was Chairman for a short 3-month period. It is only after his successor (Prof. Ram Reddy) took over as Chairman UGC, that there is a reference to the IGNOU, in the Annual Report (1991-92) though brief, as below: "On the recommendation of the UGC, IGNOU has set up a Distance Education Council as a statutory authority u/s 16 of IGNOU Act which will be responsible for determination and maintenance of standards in the field of distance education. During the year, proposals received from 9 universities to introduce/strengthen ongoing distance education programmes were referred by the UGC to the DEC for consideration."

The inside story of what was cooking can be gathered in the CABE report on Distance Education (February 1994). In June 1987, CABE recommended establishment of Co-ordination Council of all Open Universities in the country [at that time, there were Open Universities (OUs) in 2 States—AP (1982) and Kota (1987), apart from IGNOU at the national level], and it was duly set up but did not function effectively (apparently because of aloofness of the UGC). Rules for 'Fitness for Grant for OUs' were not notified till 1989 and UGC was apparently unwilling to cede control over the correspondence courses of conventional universities. So a mutual understanding was arrived at between the UGC and IGNOU that IGNOU would provide assistance to OUs, but, for the time being the UGC would continue to provide assistance to institutes of correspondence studies attached to conventional universities. In October 1990, UGC appointed a High Power Committee under the Chairmanship of Secretary, Education with Vice-Chairman, UGC and Vice-Chancellor, IGNOU as Members. The Committee recommended that: (1) the IGNOU should establish Distance Education Council as a statutory authority under the IGNOU Act, and (2) DEC should be assigned the responsibility for promoting coordination and maintenance of standards in the OUs (CABE Report on Distance Education, 1994: 33-34). That is how Annual Report 1991-92 refers to IGNOU for the first time. There is no doubt that Dr. Ram Reddy's being Chairman of UGC (Dr. Ram Reddy had chaired a committee in Andhra Pradesh which led to the establishment of AP-OU and was also its first Vice-Chancellor) helped UGC to get reconciled to the existence of a separate body for standardization in the OUs. The development of the OU stream is dealt with in a separate chapter.

Inter-University Centres (IUCs)

Under Prof. Yashpal's leadership, UGC set up a large number of Inter-University Centres mainly in the area of Science and Technology in the period 1986-91. This may be seen from the Table 6.4.

Table 6.4: Inter-University Centres

Sl. No.	*Name of IUC*	*Year of Establishment*	*Objectives*
1.	Nuclear Science Centre (JNU), New Delhi	1984	Accelerater Oriented Research
2.	Inter-University Centre for Astronomy & Astrophysics, Pune	1988	State of the Art astronomical instrumentation for research in astronomy and astrophysics
3.	Inter-University Consortium for DAE facilities, Indore	1989	Use of Facilities of Department of Atomic Energy
4.	Information & Library Network, Ahmedabad	1991	Networking of Libraries through electronic media

Note: In addition, several centres which led to the establishment of Consortium for Education Communication (CEC) were set up during the period. The CEC was formally established in 1993 as an I-UC.

There is no doubt that there was provision for these IUCs in the UGC Act and there could be formulations in the NPE 1986 which could be used to justify their quick establishment, but the issues involved were:

(1) Balance between hard science and social sciences/ humanities,

(2) Heavy capital cost and the recurring cost on development and maintenance and its effect on availability of resources for other heads including for state universities and colleges, and

(3) The effect of IUCs on UGC's work on determination, maintenance and enhancement of standards.

In the year 1991-92, plan and non-plan grants paid to the IUCs were Rs. 13.82 crore. In 2006-07, the financial allocations had risen to Rs. 72.67 crore—made up of Rs. 25.11 crore (Non-Plan) + Rs. 47.56 crore (Plan), of which only Rs. 7.65 crore were meant for NAAC—a quality enhancing IUC. The rest of the allocations for IUCs were for centres in hard sciences. The increase in the allocation in 15 years was fivefold. It is true that the UGC has set up no further IUCs, but that would appear to be precisely the point because apparently earlier centres have served as a constraint. The discretion of the UGC on the type of IUCs to be set up appears to be unguided. Section 26(1)(h) provides for the UGC framing regulations about establishment of IUCs but these regulations which are not available in the compilation of Rules/Regulations (of 2000) reportedly provide for only a project report to be submitted to the UGC for approval. In what areas are such IUCs to be set up is nowhere defined. The IUCs in the nature of education and communication in the areas of science (at IISc., Bangalore) and centres for social science education and communication at the SNDT University, Mumbai and M.S. University Baroda appear to have been discontinued with effect from the Tenth Plan. The recommendation of Amrik Singh Committee (1992) for setting up an IUC on Higher Education Research and Training also has made no progress.

Action on the Curbing of the Phenomenon of Capitation Fee Colleges

UGC was quick to take action in terms of the amendment to S.12(ccc) about Inter-University Centres as noted above. But there was another amendment to the UGC Act, effected side by side, to curb the capitation fee college phenomenon. This was the amendment to

Section 12(A) for regulation of fees and prohibition of donations in certain cases. The amendment specifically stated that UGC was to make regulations to ensure that no candidate secures admission to a course of study by reason of economic power and, thereby, prevent a more meritorious candidate from securing admission to a course of study. The amendment was generally worded but, at that time, the capitation fee college phenomenon was rampant in professional courses like medicine, dentistry, engineering, etc. The UGC was empowered to fix a scale of fees and no college could levy fees in excess thereof or for purposes other than those specified therein. The UGC was also empowered to ban the colleges from sending students for examinations and could disaffiliate them for three years, subject to the previous approval of the Central Government.

These were very drastic powers and showed the keenness of the Central Government in the matter. The UGC appointed a committee to draft regulations that may be notified and the scales of fees in accordance with which fees were to be charged by the colleges. Since the Medical Council of India was reportedly seized of the matter in relation to the medical courses, the Committee confined itself to first degree courses in engineering, technology, architecture and pharmacy only. The Committee reported in June 1986 of thereabouts. The report examined the capitation fees phenomenon in its historical context and after analyzing the various issues, proposed draft regulations. The timing of the report is significant viz. at about the time NPE was promulgated, which in its para 6.20 stated that in the interest of maintaining standards and for several other valid reasons, the commercialization of technical and professional education will be curbed. In 1987 the AICTE was given statutory status and in its Section 10(n) prescribed "taking all necessary steps to prevent commercialization of technical education" as one of the functions of the AICTE. For the First Five Years (1987-92), the Minister (Education) himself was the Chairman of the AICTE and therefore, time was opportune to take action to notify the regulations and implement them. If this had been done, subsequent court directions in *Mohini Jain case* (1992) and *Unnikrishnan case* would not have been necessary. Apparently, pro-commercialization political forces prevailed. The UGC's Annual Reports in the relevant period are silent in the matter.

Pay Revision in Terms of Mehrotra Committee Report (1986)

The recommendations of the Mehrotra Committee Report on pay-scales for university and college teachers were apparently designed to correct merit promotion anomalies after the 1982 DUTA strike. It recommended a multiplicity of scales. It also tried to downplay Ph.D. degree as a pre-condition for appointment as a Lecturer because of the impracticability and instead proposed that a Lecturer should at least have M.Phil in order to earn his promotion to the second stage of lecturership (computed as 8 years of service) and instead of a blind reliance on Ph.D., suggested that professional growth be ensured by participation in training programmes to be organized extensively in which the IGNOU was to play an important role. By now, trade unionism had seeped into the rank of teachers in all States and this time AIFUCTO (All India Federation of University and College Teachers Organization) organized an all-India strike to oppose various proposals including the multiplicity of scales. The strike lasted for about a month. The fall-out was a reduction in the number of scales and extension of merit promotion scheme which was earlier implemented in Delhi University and colleges to all States of India. While AIFUCTO called off the strike after a month, DUTA continued it for another 50 days. As a result of the strike, teachers were able to extract the concession of revision of scale of professor to go beyond that of Jonit. Secretary to Government of India and peg it at the starting salary of the Additional Secretary to Government of India. *As in the case of 1982 strike, there were differences between the UGC and the Government* which received a lot of criticism for having increased the number of scales especially for Readers (Amrik Singh, 1989: 102). This account relies on academic writings. Unfortunately, UGC's Annual Reports for 1987-88 or 1988-89 do not say anything about the revision of pay scales.

The Eighth Plan Period (1992-97): Review of Developments

During this period, the UGC saw two Chairmen,—G. Ram Reddy and Armaity Desai (w.e.f 9th February, 1995). Both were renowned scholars and constructive administrators. The appointment of Dr. G.D. Sharma as Secretary UGC (July 1996 to August 1998) also appears to have been helpful. The financial allocations for UGC were as below:

	VII Plan	*VIII Plan (Rupees in Lakh)*
Plan	575.00	1030.46
Non-Plan	845.00	1906.45
Total	**1420.00**	**2937.41**

The Financial allocations for the Eighth Plan were double the Seventh Plan allocation though in real terms it may not have maintained a high growth rate. During this period, the Ministry was focused on implementation of the World Bank assisted DPEP (District Programme Education Projects). There were not many areas of conflict and this may be considered to be one of the more creative periods of the UGC in recent times. The achievements of the UGC may be itemized as below:

(1) Reconciliation with the role of the IGNOU in the matter of co-ordination and development of standards in the ODL system.

(2) Decentralization of UGC structure through the opening of Regional Offices of the UGC. The regional offices were established in the following chronological sequence—

Southern (since named Southeastern) at Hyderabad	:	28-9-1994
Western at Poona (now Pune)	:	01-11-1994
Central—at Bhopal	:	01-12-1994
Northern—at Gaziabad	:	31-12-1994
North-Eastern at Guwahati	:	01-04-1995
Eastern at Calcutta (Now Kolkata)	:	03-09-1996
South-eastern at Bangalore (now Bengaluru)	:	25-04-1999

(As is known, the Northern office at Gaziabad is since closed and located in the UGC office.

3. Appointment and follow-up of the Punnayya Committee on funding of Central Institutions. As a follow-up, UGC began

to give 25 per cent of mobilized resources as incentive grants to the universities.

4. Establishment of the National Accreditation and Assessment Council at (NAAC) Bangalore (1994).
5. *Revision of Curriculum*—the UGC reconstituted subject panels to update and modernize courses—9 panels in Science subjects and 19 panels in Humanities and Social Sciences were set up.
6. UGC introduced a new scheme from 1994-95 for career orientation to education at the first degree level. 31 universities and 698 colleges were assisted, to introduce one to three such courses in 35 subjects identified by the core committee. Training programmes and Seminars for Principals were also organized. The scheme was expanded in successive plans and subsequently the UGC had apparently unsuccessfully approached the World Bank with a Project Proposal for achieving the target of bringing *one-fourth* of the under-graduate enrolment under the fold of the programme (UGC, Annual Report, 2001-2002).
7. *Pay Revision*: In the context of the Fifth Central Pay Commission, the UGC appointed in 1994 a Committee to review and revise structure of emoluments and conditions of service of university and college teachers (Chairman: Prof. Rastogi). The Committee submitted its Report in May 1997. The Ministry was consulted and revised emoluments were communicated by the Ministry between July and November 1998. The same were notified by the UGC on 24th December, 1998. Side by side a Professional Code of Ethics was also circulated, but without any specific directions about implementation (UGC: AR 1997-98: 6 and AR 1998-99: 7-8).
8. *Fee Regulations*: It was earlier noted that the Report of the Committee on fee regulations submitted in or about June 1986 was in a limbo. The same was activated consequent on the Supreme Court judgement in the Unnikrishnan case and draft regulations were sent to the Government of India (Ministry of Education). The Ministry, in turn, issued a policy paper on fee regulations on 18th March, 1997. The UGC

redrafted its regulations which were gazetted on 16th may 1998. Under the regulations which bind all the universities, there is a provision to form State level committee for State universities and UGC committees for Deemed Universities to determine the fees to be charged in respect of courses conducted by private unaided universities (UGC: AR, 1997-98: 8).

9. *Follow-up on Amrik Singh Committee Report*: Education Ministry had appointed a Committee under the Chairmanship of Prof. Amrik Singh in 1992, in connection with training and research facilities in higher education. The Report of the Committee was initially accepted in principle by the UGC and it was decided that a nodai institute should be set up under Section 13(ccc) of the UGC Act. However, there was a rethinking subsequently and it was felt that in a large university system with lakhs of teachers, a single institution at the national level would not suffice. A planning committee was set up which intended to seek collaboration with foreign agencies (Higher Education Funding Council for England, Fulbright Foundation and Shastri-Indo-Canadian Institute, N. Delhi). The Annual Report of the UGC (1998-99: 1) refers to a task force having been set up by the UGC which held a workshop in March 1999. Subsequent Annual Reports are silent on the issue. Maybe, the issue had got linked up with a new Building for the UGC for which foundation stone was laid in 2003. The fact needs to be noted that till 2010 no training/research institute has come up under the UGC.

Ninth Five Year Plan (1997-2002)

A statement showing the Ninth Plan Development Schemes to be implemented by the UGC is annexed at Annexure 6.1. It indicates that guidelines of continuing schemes were to be revised, some schemes were to be dropped (Research Associates and Research Scientists) and some new schemes were to be introduced. Among the notable new schemes were:

(1) Incentive schemes for implementing reforms.

(2) Value Education.
(3) Modernization of Teaching (audio-visual aids etc.).
(4) Several schemes for improving access of weaker sections like—women (day care centres etc.); SC/ST (coaching for NET) and facilities for the disabled persons. This latter scheme was under two heads—TEPSE (Teachers' Preparation in Special Education) and HEPSN (Higher Education for Persons with Special Needs).
(5) Training of Administrators.
(6) State Councils of Higher Education.
(7) Setting up of a Planning and Development Division in the UGC.

Apparently, the three last mentioned schemes were non-starters. On the other hand, there were some new schemes, not in the original Ninth Plan, but introduced by the new NDA Government which could be stated to be steps in the direction of privatization and cultural turn to the Right.

It is likely that many new schemes could not be started because of financial stringency. The Ninth Plan allocations indicated as minimum requirement by the UGC was Rs. 4600 crore as against which Rs. 2000 crore were received (UGC: AR, 1998-99: 11).

Privatization

In August 1995, the Government introduced in the Rajya Sabha 'The Private Universities (Establishment and Regulation Bill) 1995'. The statement of objects and reasons of the Bill stated: "Of late, considerable interest has been generated in establishment of self-financing universities not requiring any financial support from the Government. It was hoped particularly that in the emerging areas of S & T, these universities may provide useful instructional inputs." The then Congress Government appears to have developed cold feet consequent on the leftist inspired criticism of the Bill which had envisaged a permanent endowment fund of Rs. 10 crore to be maintained by the sponsoring body of the private university. However, since education is a subject on the Concurrent List, since 1977, some

States appear to have taken inspiration from the Bill to set up private universities in their States as a money-making proposition. In any case this was done by the then entrepreneurial Chief Minister of Chhattisgarh who by the end of the period had passed "Chhattisgarh Niji Kshetra Vishwa Vidyalaya (Sthapana Aur Viniyaman) Adhiniyam, 2002", which enabled the State Government simply to notify private universities on the basis of project reports. This raised the question of the regulatory role of the UGC. The matter went to the Supreme Court and its outcome in 2005 would be dealt with in the next section on the Tenth Plan.

However, during the period under review, privatization took a sinister form, viz. notification of *de novo* institutions as deemed universities. It has been noted earlier that there was a lack of clarity about the nature of institutions to be so declared, but about one point there was perfect clarity, viz. that they must be pre-existing and doing work of a high standard in a specific area. In 1999-2000, the Central Government appears to have directed amendments to be carried out to the UGC guidelines so as to grant deemed university status to quality institutions on a fast-track basis. This appears to have been a short hand for altogether new institutions. The ostensible purpose was to promote participation of the private sector (UGC AR, 1999-2000: VIII). This amendment has opened floodgates for proliferation of deemed universities whose suitability is not transparent. The apprehensions expressed by the Kothari Commission on this count appear to have come true. Yashpal Committee has noted that between the year 2000 to 2005, 26 private sponsored institutions got the DU status and the number had increased to 108 by 2009.

Cultural Turn to the Right

A few schemes started by the UGC, some of them apparently under written directions, of the Ministry betray a cultural turn to the Right. They are listed below:

1. The UGC observed 1999-2000, as a year of Sanskrit on the specific direction of the Government of India. The reasons for the selection of the particular year are not clear. The UGC also sponsored a new programme, viz. UGC Sanskrit Award,

'to promote quality teaching/research in Sanskrit and to identify and recognize outstanding teachers' (UGC: AR 1999-2000: viii). Later on, a scheme for setting up "Simple Sanskrit Teaching Centres" was started (UGC: AR, 2001-02: 6).

2. UGC had since long been assisting Centres of Gandhian/ Nehru/Ambedkar studies to acquaint teachers and students with the thoughts and ideas of these social thinkers. During this period, new thinkers were added to this list, viz. Swami Vivekanand, Rabindranath Tagore, Dr. Zakir Husain, Dr. S. Radhakrishnan and more significantly Pandit Madan Mohan Malaviya (UGC: AR, 2000-01: 5). Later on, the name of Sardar Vallabhbhai Patel was also added (UGC: AR, 2002-03: 11).
3. There was a programme for promotion of Yoga Education and Practice in the universities since 1994. An expert committee decided on a new programme for creating independent departments of Human Consciousness and Yogic Science for which 10 universities were assisted (UGC: AR, 2000-01: 15).
4. UGC reportedly wanted to rejuvenate the subject of Vedic Astrology and paid an assistance of Rs. 271.00 lakhs to 16 universities for setting up departments of Jyotir Vigyan and providing teaching and training in the subject leading to UG, PG and Ph.D. degrees (UGC: AR, 2001-02: 6). The decision of the UGC, apparently under directions of the then Union Education Minister, became quite controversial and leading scientists like Jayant Narlikar wrote against it in *EPW* and *Times of India* as a move which goes against the constitutional mandate to promote scientific temper. The above stricture however would not apply to the UGC courses on human rights and duties noted below.
5. The Western liberal political traditions recognized the importance of human rights. However, the emphasis on duties is regarded as the special feature of the ancient Indian tradition. Apparently, on the basis of the recommendations of the Justice Varma Committee on 'operationalization of the suggestion to teach Fundamental Duties to the citizens of the country', the scheme was designated as Human Rights and Duties Education (UGC AR, 1999-2000: 110).

Subsequently, Justice Malimath Committee framed a syllabus for the subject which has been commended to the universities.

Judicial Activism—Inspired Scheme

6. It was reported in the UGC Annual Report 1999-2000 that as per the Supreme Court directions, the guidelines for the combat of the menace of ragging in universities were circulated to all the universities for strict compliance (UGC AR, 1999-2000: viii).

NAAC Assessment becomes Mandatory

7. The NAAC which was started in 1994 and was equipped to assess and accredit a large number of colleges of universities was not eliciting a good response. The Annual Report 1999-2000 reports that it was decided to make accreditation and assessment by NAAC mandatory for all universities in India.
8. In 1999-2000, reservation of 3 per cent was made for the physically handicapped candidates for the post of lecturer in University/Colleges (UGC: AR, 1999-2000: viii).

The Tenth Plan Period 2002-2007

The general objective of the Tenth Plan is stated to be: "To achieve a profound transformation of higher education so that it effectively promotes sustainable human development and at the same time, improve relevance with closer links with the world of work and ensure quality in teaching, research and business and community extension functions including life-long learning". Some new schemes/programmes planned to be implemented during the Tenth Plan are:

1. Special Development grants for universities and colleges in backward areas (apparently, the scheme of universities with potential for excellence started in 2001-02 is to be continued).
2. Special development grants for young universities and colleges.
3. Colleges with potential for excellence.

4. UGC infonet.
5. Promotion of export of higher education.
6. Digital Depository of Research and Training Materials.
[In view of the above scheme, National Information Centres (at Bangalore, SNDT and M.S. University, Baroda) set up during the Ninth Plan are to be closed down.]

The Tenth Plan period is required to be perceived in two parts—some of the NDA Government's schemes and priorities during the first two years (2002-03 and 2003-04) were altered in the subsequent three years (2004-07). In the first two years, the UGC appeared to be preoccupied with the celebrations of its Golden Jubilee Function taking 28th December, 1953 as the foundation-day of the UGC*. On this occasion, apart from issuing some publications, the first Inter-University Centre in Humanities and Social Sciences for SAARC Region was inaugurated.

UGC as an Instrument to Implement the NCMP of UPA-I

After the UPA-I Government came to power in May 2004, it provided additional earmarked funds to the UGC for implementation of the National Common Minimum Programme (NCMP). It is reported that in 2004-05, 11 Central Universities were provided assistance to the tune of Rs. 103.05 crore for items like infrastructure development, networking, procurement of major equipment, the setting up of faculties of engineering and management, etc. Moreover, although the IGNOU is directly funded by the Ministry, Rs. 7 crore were released to it by the UGC under the direction of the Ministry. In 2005-06, three State universities were provided assistance to the tune of Rs. 50.00 crore and 11 Central Universities Rs. 86.91 crore under the special package of the Prime Minister. An amount of Rs. 5 crore was paid to HP University (UGC AR: 2004-05: 3, AR 2005-06: 4). Such assistance, *prima facie*, would be against the budgetary norms and the autonomy of the UGC, which is expected to decide on *inter se* allocation and the purposes of grants.

---

* It has been conclusively demonstrated in chapter 4 *vide* p. 83 that the correct year of establishment of the UGC is not 1953 but 1956.

The role of the UGC as a mere instrumentality of the Ministry is also underlined by the Ministry indicating the universities where the Rajiv Gandhi Chairs for Contemporary Studies are to be set up (three Central and six State universities including Mumbai University) (UGC AR: 2004-05: Executive Summary).

Other highlights of the recent years (2004-07)

1. The scheme for support for Infrastructure in S&T (COSIST) has been renamed as ASIST and a new scheme for similar support to Humanities and Social Sciences (ASIHSS) has been started, the maximum assistance for the former being Rs. 1 crore and for the latter Rs. 60 lakh.
2. The UGC assisted a National Institute of Studies in Sri Guru Granth Sahib at Guru Nanak Dev University, Amritsar.
3. Travel Grant Scheme appears to have been extended to the UGC Members [this would be, *prima facie*, improper as raising issue of conflict of interest].
4. New Fellowships for SC/ST students (for Ph.D., post-Doctoral and professional courses) and new schemes for minority students have been introduced (UGC : AR 2005-06: Executive Summary).

Privatization

During the Tenth Plan period, pseudo-privatization in the form of bogus private universities received a set back with the Supreme Court upholding the challenge made by the former Chairman UGC (Prof. Yashpal) in his private capacity, to the legality of the relevant Act of Chhattisgarh State (2005). But the Chhattisgarh episode also exposed the weakness of the UGC's surveillance. From the judgment, it is evident that the UGC had conducted an enquiry into the malpractices, but the report was not finalized till the judgement day (11th February 2005). UGC had also issued "UGC (Establishment and Maintenance of Standards in Private Universities) Regulation 2003" on 27th December, 2003, i.e. almost 2 years after the Chhattisgarh Act was passed. The State Government appears to have taken steps to amend the Act to lay down some standards but the Supreme Court was not impressed.

Globalization

With the opening up of the educational services through the World Trade Organization's General Agreement for Trade in Services (GATS), the regulatory burden on the UGC is expected to increase. Unfortunately, although the UGC, in co-operation with the AIU, appointed a Working Group, spelling out the modalities and the competing countries like the UK, Australia and Canada have a robust regulatory network in place, Central Government has dragged its feet perhaps because of the Leftist opposition. "Foreign Education Providers (Regulation of Entry and Operations)" Bill 2006 was introduced in the Rajya Sabha in December 2006 but there was no further movement to take up the Bill and pass it. The Bill was revised and reintroduced by the UPA-I Government in May 2010.

The UGC has also been working at the opposite end, viz. for the promotion of export of Indian education abroad for which a scheme has been drawn up on the basis of the report of an expert committee (January 2003). Unfortunately, beyond stating that the UGC officers have been attending international conventions on the subject and also attending education fairs abroad, the progress on the ground by way of increased export of education is not known.

Diminution of UGC's Role as Clearing House of Information

During this period, UGC's role as a Clearing House of information for Higher Education has diminished. UGC stopped bringing out its Annual Statistical Publication called—'Higher Education in India' containing data regarding colleges and universities from the year 1985-86. The National Commission on Statistics (1999) desired the UGC to streamline its system and also to bring out a Quinquennial survey of higher education on the pattern of NCERT on School Education. No action is in sight because the UGC Annual Reports do not refer to the matter. This grave lacuna was highlighted by the *CABE* Report on financing of higher and technical education (2005), which states: "The database on higher education in the country is very weak. The Ministry of Human Resource Development used to publish earlier reasonably good amount of data on higher education in their annual publication "Education in India". But it ceased to cover higher education since the mid-1980s and as a result, a huge vacuum exists on data on various aspects of higher education. It is important that M/HRD and the UGC launch a programme on a priority basis, of building up a strong database on higher education" (NIEPA, 2005: 51).

In the 1970s, the UGC used to bring out a quarterly Bulletin on higher education which was information-rich and also three issues a year of the '*Journal of Higher Education*' which was research based. Both have ceased publication in 2000 apparently because of audit objections. The Bulletin was replaced by "*UGC News*" in 2003, but its recent issues (2005 onwards) are not available in the Mumbai University Library. The UGC has a full-fledged publication branch and the number of publications are listed, i.e. numbered in the Annual Reports (24 items in 2006-07), but these appear to be confined to pamphlets on "Guidelines" for various UGC schemes which are revised at five or ten yearly intervals. Apart from a publication after 40 years edited by R.P. Singh and Golden Jubilee Publications, no other publications are issued. Surprisingly, the Rashtrabhasha cell of the UGC is quite regular in bringing out various journals for promotion of Hindi as official language in the UGC office.

UGC's Draft Eleventh Plan (2007-2012)

A perusal of the Draft Elevanth Plan of the UGC shows that the Planning Commission has, by and large, advised an expansionist thrust. The Plan wants quantitative expansion coupled with qualitative improvement and inclusive education for which setting up of "an Equal Opportunity Office" in all the universities is contemplated. Thirty new Central Universities would be set up of which 14 would be of world-class standards (WCU). In the States, apart from 16 new universities in un-served States, about 6,000 colleges and 150 universities with focus on under-serviced areas would be set up. 160 State universities and 5625 colleges already assisted would be provided one time assistance at the rate of Rs. 1 crore (for college) and Rs. 5 crore (universities) on the basis of Detailed Project Reports. In the State of Bihar, MP and Orissa where the GER is very low, a new Centrally Sponsored Scheme with Centre-State Funding pattern of 1 : 2 is proposed to be introduced. For achieving inclusive growth, financial assistance would be provided to the States on the basis of specific projects, submitted for SCs/STs/OBCs and Minorities. About 2,000 hostels for girl students @ Rs. 1 crore per hostel would be set up. A high level Committee was to be set up to suggest reform agenda for an apex regulatory institution and the appointment of the Yashpal Committee in February 2008 might be a sequel to this mandate.

Over-all Conclusion (1980-2007)

Diminution of Space

The sad conclusion has to be that over the 27 years (1980-2007), the UGC has become a bureaucratic organization which has lost both its autonomy and its soul, and occupies a diminished space in the field of higher education. This is due to a variety of reasons:

(1) Opening of new regulatory bodies like the AICTE/NCTE/NCRI, etc.
(2) Establishment of more Central universities, not funded by the UGC.
(3) Expansion of activities of various Bureaus of the Ministry like Language, Cultural Exchange, etc.
(4) Diminution of the authority of the UGC as manifested by the UGC promoting courses in astrology under directions of NDA Government and acting as an instrument to implement the National Common Minimum Programme (NCMP) of the UPA-I Government.

At the end of 2010, survival of the UGC in the second decade of 21st Century was doubtful.

ANNEXURE 6.1

Ninth Plan Development Schemes

(Vide page 159)

During the Ninth Plan period, the University Grants Commission launched many new schemes and revised the guidelines for most of the schemes under the broad sectors of: (a) Relevance and Quality, (b) Access and Equity; (c) Role of universities in promoting social change and (d) Management of Education and Resource Mobilization. The new schemes proposed and the revised schemes to be introduced in the Ninth Plan are given below:

1. Development of Universities and Colleges

(i) One time grant to Universities for books and equipment (universities which have not been covered so far) (Continuing Scheme).
(ii) Autonomous colleges (Continuing Scheme).
(iii) College Development Councils (Continuing Scheme).
(iv) Assistance to colleges for development during the Ninth Plan period (Guidelines revised).
(v) Development assistance to central, deemed and state universities during the Ninth Plan (Guidelines revised).
(vi) Construction of building in colleges under the scheme of development assistance to colleges (Guidelines revised).

2. Promotion of Relevance

(i) Incentive schemes for implementing reforms (New Scheme).
(ii) Value Education (New Scheme).
(iii) Development of sports infrastructure in universities and colleges (Guidelines revised).

(iv) Promotion of adventure sports in universities and colleges (Guidelines revised).

(v) Promotion of Yoga education and practice in universities (Guidelines revised).

(vi) Ninth Plan approach to promotion of human rights education (HRE) in universities and colleges (guidelines revised).

(vii) Scheme of epoch-making social thinkers of India: Buddha, Gandhi, Nehru and Ambedkar (Guidelines revised).

(viii) Guidelines for submission of proposals for introduction of vocational subjects at the first degree level in colleges and universities from 1999-2000 (Guidelines revised).

(ix) Reimbursement of expenditure on Gandhian Literature (Scheme dropped).

(x) Seminar on 125th Birth Anniversary of Mahatma Gandhi (Scheme dropped).

3. Promotion of Excellence and Quality

(i) Networking of Universities and Colleges (New Scheme).

(ii) Modernization of teaching (Audio-visual aids etc.) to universities and colleges (New Scheme).

(iii) Financial support for major and minor research projects (Guidelines revised).

(iv) College Humanities and Social Science Improvement Programme (COHSSIP) (Guidelines revised).

(v) Unassigned Grants (Guidelines revised).

(vi) Organization of seminars/conferences by colleges (Guidelines revised).

(vii) Junior Research Fellowship (JRF) and Research Associateships (RA)—foreign nationals (Guidelines revised).

(viii) Award of Junior Research Fellowships in Science and Humanities and in Social Sciences (Guidelines revised).

(ix) Teacher fellowship scheme—college faculty development programme (Guidelines revised).

(x) Appointment of Visiting Professors/Visiting Fellows (Guidelines revised).

(xi) Research Award Scheme (Guidelines revised).

(xii) Research Associates (Scheme dropped).
(xiii) Research Scientists (Scheme dropped).

4. Inter-University Resources for Promotion of Quality

(i) UGC-CSIR Inter University Programme (Scheme dropped).
(ii) Science Education Centre, Madurai Kamraj University (Scheme dropped).
(iii) Science Education Centre, Delhi University (Scheme dropped).
(iv) Science Education centre, Rajasthan University (Scheme dropped).
(v) Centre for Advanced Studies in Physics, Punjab University (Scheme dropped).

5. Enhancing Access and Equity

(i) Day Care Centres (New Scheme).
(ii) Infrastructure for women students/teachers (New Scheme).
(iii) Scholarships for women in professional courses (New Scheme).
(iv) Gender sensitivity programmes in colleges and universities (New Scheme).
(v) Data bases on women (New Scheme).
(vi) Remedial coaching for SC/ST and disadvantaged groups (Scheme revised).
(vii) Coaching for NET to SC/ST (New Scheme).
(viii) Coaching classes for disadvantaged groups for entry in service (Continuing scheme).
(ix) Facilities for disabled persons (New Scheme).
(x) Colleges in backward districts (New Scheme).
(xi) Bharat Bhavan Hostel complexes (New Scheme).
(xii) Counseling centres (New Scheme).
(xiii) Development of Women's studies in Indian Universities and Colleges (Guidelines revised).
(xiv) Introduction of remedial coaching for Scheduled Castes and Scheduled Tribes in Universities and Colleges (Guidelines revised).

(xv) Adult Education, Continuing Education and Extension Work and Field Outreach (Guidelines revised).

(xvi) Establishment of Special Cell for Scheduled Castes and Scheduled Tribes for universities and deemed to be universities (Guidelines revised).

6. Improvement In Management of Education

(i) Training of administrators (New Scheme).

(ii) State Councils of Higher education (New Scheme).

7. Strengthening of UGC Administration

(i) Setting up a Planning and Development Division (New Scheme).

8. Pogramme to Strengthen Scientific Research (SACC)

(i) Financial support for major and minor research projects (Guidelines revised).

(ii) College Science Improvement Programme (COSIP) (Guidelines revised).

(iii) Strengthening of Infrastructure in Science and Technology (COSIST) (Guidelines revised).

(iv) Special Assistance Progrramme (SAP) (CAS/DSA/DRS) (Guidelines revised).

9. Engineering and Technology

(i) Technical courses for women (New Scheme).

(ii) Assistance for providing computers to colleges (Guidelines revised).

7

Allied Organizations of the UGC

Introduction

In this chapter, author would deal with four organizations allied to the UGC, viz. : (1) National Assessment and Accreditation Council (NAAC), Bangalore, (2) Distance Education Council (DEC), New Delhi, (3) Association of Indian Universities (AIU) formerly called Inter University Board (IUB), and (4) National University of Educational Planning and Administration (NUEPA), formerly called National Institute of Educational Planning and Administration (NIEPA). NAAC is a quality enhancing Inter-University Centre under the UGC, DEC is the co-ordinating and standards arm of the IGNOU, not supported by the UGC but closely allied to the Distance Education Institutes (DEIs) of the conventional universities under the UGC. AIU supplements UGC's work, *inter alia,* in the role of clearing house of information and is a 'foil' of the UGC bringing to it the considered views of the academic community in the form of the VCs and NUEPA is involved in training and research in higher education with special reference to educational planning and administration.

The NAAC: A New Approach to Quality Assessment and Accreditation

In the 1970s and 1980s, there was general disillusionment with the capacity of higher education sector to deliver on national development and there was a clamour for accountability which required quantified performance indicators. The Jha Committee's reference (1977:

5.14-5.16), therefore, to the American system of assessment and accreditation of higher education institutions came just in time. The Committee, after referring, first to the academic systemic evaluation arrangements in France, Russia and the UK observed: "In the US, there is a very elaborate system of accreditation (of which the) basic purpose ... is to encourage institutions to improve their programmes by providing for them standards or criteria established by competent bodies... It is necessary in the interest of maintenance of standards that in India also, the university departments and colleges whose standards vary sharply from institution to institution are subjected to a system of accreditation and grading" (By grading, they meant what is now termed assessment). Jha Committee's highlighting the need for American type accreditation is quite credit-worthy. Both Radhakrishnan Commission and Kothari Commission had American experts associated with them and although there had been no dearth of delegations of academics which visited the USA in the 1950s and 1960s at the cost of the UGC for study of a variety of problems including the study of "general education", "examination reforms" etc. none of them caught on to the significance of the American system of assessment and accreditation which goes back to the end of the 19th Century.

Evolution of the NAAC

Unfortunately, in the political transition from the Congress Government to the Janata Government (1977-79) and back to the Congress Government (1980ff), this recommendation got sidetracked till it was revived by the PoA 1986 of NPE 1986 which noted that excellence of institutions is a function of many aspects of which self-evaluation and self-improvement are important and that there should be self-assessment by institutions followed by assessment and accreditation by a Council, which would be an autonomous body (PoA 1986: 5.27). The UGC prepared in 1987 a concept paper for discussion. The follow-up action was delayed by the Ramamurti review of the NPE 1986. PoA 1992 simply stated (para XI. 13.4) that in March 1992, UGC resolved to set up a National Accreditation and Assessment Council (NAAC) as an autonomous body for the achievement of the objectives envisaged in the NPE. NAAC eventually came into existence with headquarters in Bangalore (now

Bangalore (Now Bengaluru) in September 1994 as a quality-promoting Inter-University Centre [(IUC) u/s 12(ccc)] of the UGC Act. Since the NAAC is a clone of the UGC, it is not surprising that it is centralist in design, though in practice, more proactive than the UGC. The format of the IUC makes it difficult to gather adequate data for the evaluation of NAAC from a perusal of Annual Reports of the UGC which in recent years has stopped giving any information about NAAC's activities.

The NAAC: Structure and Functions

NAAC is a registered society with a General Council, Executive Committee and Finance Committee. Chairman UGC is *ex-officio* President of the General Council, but autonomy is ensured by having a separate academician as the Chairman of its Executive Committee. Four Vice-Chancellors are members of whom two are from the State Universities. Four Principals of affiliated/autonomous colleges are also members. The Executive Committee includes nominees of the UGC who would be generally academics, i.e. V-Cs, Principals, educationists, etc. (S.N. Pathan, 2005: 49-54). Neither the General Council nor the Executive Committee of NAAC have any representative from State Governments, although they are vital stake-holders, the main clientele of the NAAC being State Universities and colleges. This reflects, as noted, the centralist approach of the UGC. As part of its expansion, NAAC was reported to be planning in 2005 to set up four regional offices, but the latest information is that there are to be no regional offices and the work is to be looked after from the Headquarters itself through the officer-in-charge of Zones.

NAAC functions as a mechanism, accepted the world over, for External Quality Assurance (EQA), which has replaced the traditional regulatory methods of ensuring quality through recognition/affiliation and control through inspection. NAAC assessment is based on seven major criteria of: (1) Curricular aspects, (2) Teaching and learning-evaluation, (3) Research consultancy and extension, (4) Infrastructure and Learning Resources, (5) Student support and progression, (6) Governance and Leadership, and (7) Healthy and innovative practices. The assessment is based on a process of self-study and peer review. The assessment and accreditation by the NAAC was initially voluntary but made mandatory from 2002 for UGC-assisted higher education institutions. Any statutory/deemed university or recognized college can approach NAAC for assessment. A grading once granted is valid for 5 years when the institution is required to undergo post-accreditation assessment. NAAC promotes the establishment of Internal Quality Assurance Cell (IQAC) in the institutions, i.e. colleges and universities. The first accreditations were done by NAAC in 1998-99 (21 institutions). As in the middle of September 2008, NAAC had accredited 142 universities and 3,721 colleges including 30 re-assessed and 163 reaccredited institutions (Communication from NAAC, dated 2-1-2009). The data are shown in Tables 7.1 and 7.2 below:

Table 7.1: State-wise Universities Accredited by NAAC
(As on September 16, 2008)

State/Union Territory	*Nos.*	*State/Union Territory*	*Nos.*
Andhra Pradesh	12	Madhya Pradesh	7
Arunachal Pradesh	1	Manipur	1
Assam	4	Meghalaya	1
Bihar	3	Nagaland	1
Chhattisgarh	2	New Delhi	4
Goa	1	Orissa	3
Gujarat	7	Pondicherry	1
Haryana	3	Punjab	4
Himachal Pradesh	1	Rajasthan	8
Jammu and Kashmir	2	Tamil Nadu	19
Jharkhand	1	Tripura	1
Karnataka	8	Uttaranchal (now Uttarakhand)	4
Kerala	4	Uttar Pradesh	15
Maharashtra	17	West Bengal	7
Total Number of Universities			**142**

Table 7.2: State-wise Colleges Accredited by NAAC
(As on September 16, 2008)

State/Union Territory	*Nos.*	*State/Union Territory*	*Nos.*
Andhra Pradesh	257	Madhya Pradesh	126
Arunachal Pradesh	5	Manipur	7
Assam	192	Meghalaya	9
Bihar	37	Nagaland	12
Chhattisgarh	33	New Delhi	1
Goa	15	Orissa	165
Gujarat	218	Pondicherry	06
Haryana	150	Punjab	114

(Contd.)

(*Contd.*)

State/Union Territory	*Nos.*	*State/Union Territory*	*Nos.*
Himachal Pradesh	20	Rajasthan	100
Jammu and Kashmir	26	Tamil Nadu	254
Jharkhand	19	Tripura	4
Karnataka	476	Uttaranchal (now Uttarakhand)	27
Kerala	157	Uttar Pradesh	108
Maharashtra	952	West Bengal	229
Total Number of Colleges			**3,721**

Source: Communication from NAAC, dated 2-1-2009

NAAC and the States

Roughly up to 2005, NAAC had been fairly active in organizing awareness seminars and workshops, involving, *inter alia*, Education Secretaries of States and Directors of Collegiate Education. As a result, Karnataka and Maharashtra in the Southern and Western region respectively had shown considerable progress in the matter of assessment and accreditation. However, the progress was very slow in the northern and especially in the eastern region. It is estimated that 25 per cent of institutions accredited by NAAC were in Maharashtra. NAAC has a scheme for establishment of 'State-level Quality Assurance Coordination Committee' (SLQACC) with financial assistance of Rs. 80,000 (non-recurring) and Rs. 1.20 lakhs (recurring) per year for 5 years (NAAC, 2004), but as happens in such cases, when the financial assistance ceases, the staffing of the cell may suffer and interest in the subject flags off as appears to have happened in Maharashtra where an officer-in-charge of NCC was concurrently looking after the work of the QA Cell of NAAC (information as in December 2008). The guidelines envisage the Minister Higher Education to be the Chairman and Secretary Higher Education (HE) Department to be the Vice-Chairman with Director, Higher Education as convener of the Co-ordination Committee. The State level cell is to work as information and resource centre and to publish literature on assessment and accreditation in the regional language. Maharashtra was the first State to establish such a Committee in 2001. However, its composition showed it to be top-heavy (S.N. Pathan, 2005). In Karnataka which enjoys the advantage of having the Headquarters of the NAAC at Bangalore (now Bangaluru), such a State level committee was set up with provision for State Resource Group and District level lead college by means of an MoU between the NAAC and the State in November 2002, thanks to the interest taken by a particular officer who was dedicated to the movement for Total Quality Management (TQM) (NAAC, 2003).

Till 2010, the NAAC had not achieved its target of universal coverage for which the original date was March 2007. It was over-optimistic on the part of the NAAC to have expected that merely by establishment of State-level-Co-ordination Committees, the target of covering all institutions by the end of Tenth Plan could be achieved in addition to the load of re-accreditation work which falls due five years after initial accreditation. The annual rate of even 1000 institutions per year may not be maintained since the NAAC has to tackle hard cases of institutions in the northern and eastern State Governments. There would appear to be an urgent need to associate State governments as partners in the process. This can be done by having an Assessment and Accreditation Council (SAAC) in each state which can be jointly promoted by the State Councils of Higher Education already part of the NPE and State Chapters of AIU (which are proposed in the next section). About 50 per cent of universities and colleges in general education stream have switched over to regional languages as a medium of instruction. The preparation of the list of evaluators has, therefore, to be from those who have experience of teaching through the regional language, of the particular State and this makes a State-centred approach all the more necessary.

The problem of co-ordination between the NAAC and other professional bodies has been identified in the UGC Annual Report as an urgent one (UGC: AR, 2003-04: 110-14). Recent UGC Reports (2005-2006/2006-07) do not give any data about NAAC. Earlier reports indicated that, NAAC has been able to secure co-operation of DEC (IGNOU), the Bar Council of India and the NCTE with which it has entered into an MoU, but the progress on the ground is unclear. Co-operation from other agencies like—AICTE/NAB, the ICAR/NAC and the MCI is yet to materialize. The issue of co-ordination with the AICTE/NAB and MCI is perhaps the most important in the context of the rampant growth of unaided engineering and medical colleges in the country. In the case of professional colleges, moreover, there is a risk that there would be assessment by multiple agencies and the process could be perceived as intrusive. The fact that professional bodies like the AICTE/NAB accredit programmes and not institutions as is done by the NAAC is also relevant. As for medical institutions, NAAC appears to be having a dialogue with State level Health Universities (NAAC Annual Report 2002-03: 23), but without involvement of the MCI, substantial progress is not practicable.

The Future of the NAAC

Yashpal Committee on the UGC/AICTE has suggested a single window for accreditation. This puts a question mark over NAAC's survival as a separate agency. Press Reports (*Economic Times*, 25-11-2010) indicate that National Accreditation Regulatory Authority for Higher Education Bill has been introduced in Parliament. It seeks to make accreditation mandatory for higher educational institutions, certification of their programme and infrastructure by independent agencies and provides for establishing an independent statutory authority for the same.

The DEC: Co-ordination of Open and Distance Learning (ODL) System of Higher Education

Unlike the NAAC, which had a slow but surer start, the Distance Education Council, as a co-ordinating body both for correspondence Course Institutes (CCIs) of the conventional universities and of the free-standing Open Universities (OUs), in other words, for the ODL system, has been hobbled by problems which are partly historical but partly rooted in the lack of policy coherence. As a result, the cause of increasing the access to higher education, an important objective of the Eleventh Plan has suffered.

Distance education courses in the Western countries began as correspondence courses depending on print materials with emphasis on imparting information/knowledge. In 1961, the CABE appointed a Committee under the Chairmanship of Dr. D.S. Kothari and on the basis of his report, the correspondence courses came to be introduced first in Delhi University in 1961 to tackle the problem of students remaining without admission. Here, the Delhi-centricity of the UGC appears to have come in the way. The problem was common to all big cities and the scheme ought to have been introduced quickly in all metropolitan cities like Mumbai, Calcutta (Now Kolkata), Madras (Now Chennai), Hyderabad, Bangalore (now Bengaluru) etc. In Delhi, the scheme was targetted at students who wanted to have a less expensive method or who were denied admission to regular colleges or for employed persons/housewives, etc. The Kothari Commission did take a positive attitude and wanted one third of the total enrolment in higher education to be provided through the system of correspondence courses as a long term goal. It was, of course, recognized that these courses would be restricted to higher education branches not requiring laboratory classes or practical work (e.g. science, engineering, medicine, teaching, etc.). However, partly due to the inferiority of the correspondence course materials (for which universities were squarely to blame, because they treated these courses as cash cows), the correspondence education came to be tainted as a second class system of education. The UK Open University (OU) experiment (1969) was an eye-opener in this regard. The standard of its print materials was so high that students even of conventional universities began to use them as textbooks. Initial enthusiasm for going in for a similar initiative in India could not be sustained because of adverse political environment in the terms of Bangladesh war, inflationary pressures and political unrest leading to the declaration of Emergency in June 1975. In the same year the Prime Minister appointed a Committee under the Chairmanship of G. Parthasarathy, then Vice-Chancellor of Jawaharlal Nehru University, which recommended establishment of a National Open University on the model of the Open University of UK (V.C. Kulandai Swamy: 1991, 100-103). However, it was not a priority either for the Emergency regime (1975-77) or for the Janata regime (1977-79).

After Indira Gandhi returned to power in 1980, her priority was to amend the Vishvabharati and the AMU Acts, which were perceived to pay political dividends. Preparatory work was going on, however, and in 1985 the Indira Gandhi National Open University (IGNOU) came to be established, which made use of multi-media in addition to printed materials. *The IGNOU was directly assisted by the Ministry, being kept out side the purview of the UGC*. In the meanwhile, correspondence courses had been introduced in other conventional universities apart from Delhi. The progress in the first ten years was slow, but the number of universities with such correspondence course institutes (CCIs) rose in 1983-84 to 35. As noted above, there was a delay of 15 years from the time a national open university was thought of (shortly after 1969) and till the IGNOU came up (M.S. Yadav, 1999: 12-17). In the meanwhile, thanks to the enthusiasm of the then Education Minister in Andhra Pradesh, A.P. State Open University, came up in 1982 (CABE Committee Report on Distance Education: 8). In due course, open universities have come up in twelve more States including Rajasthan and Bihar (1987), Maharashtra (1990), Madhya Pradesh (1993), Gujarat (1994), Karnataka (1996), West Bengal (1998), Uttar Pradesh (1999), Chhattisgarh (2002) and Tamil Nadu (2005).

The IGNOU is much more than a Central University—it is in fact a national resource centre in distance education plus a locus for co-ordination for open and distance education. Within a short time, it has grown into what John D. Daniel, a former V-C of UK OU, terms as a *mega-university* with enrolment exceeding 1 lakh active students (Daniel, 1996: 28-45). In this study, its significance is as the locus of the Distance Education Council (DEC).

The Open and Distance Learning (ODL) system received a fillip as a result of the NPE 1986 as modified in 1992. The original NPE 1986 contained the formulation that the IGNOU will be strengthened and this powerful instrument would be developed with care and extended with caution (NPE 1986: 5.35 and PoA 1986: 47-48). This appears to reflect a certain reservation, on the part of the UGC, about the potential of ODL. Moreover, there was some lack of clarity regarding the relative roles of the UGC and the DEC in the whole matter and some resultant tension between the UGC and the IGNOU. It was after the report of a high-powered committee of CABE consisting of Secretary Education, V-C, UGC and V-C, IGNOU that the following *modus vivendi* was arrived at:

(1) The IGNOU should establish a Distance Education Council (DEC) as a statutory authority under the IGNOU Act.
(2) The DEC should be assigned the responsibility for promotion, co-ordination and maintenance of standards in the open universities and the DE system.

(3) The composition of the DEC should be broadly comparable to that of the UGC.

The UGC endorsed these recommendations in February 1991 (Government of India, 1994: 35). The NPE 1986/92 no longer talks in terms of extension of OU with caution but with confidence as a means to augment the opportunities for higher education in which the IGNOU would provide support for the establishment of open universities in the States and, therefore, would need strengthening itself (NPE 1986/92: 5.35 and PoA 1992: 47-48).

The IGNOU Act 1985 defines "Distance Education System" to mean the system of imparting education through any means of communication, such as broadcasting, telecasting, correspondence courses, seminars, contact programmes or the combination of any two or more of such means. In practical terms, this system includes State open universities of which there are 13 now and correspondence course institutes of traditional universities of which there are 130 now. The Act further lays down that it is the duty of the University to take all such steps as it may deem fit for the promotion of the open university and distance education system and for the determination of standards of teaching, evaluation and research in such a system and to allocate and disburse grants [IGNOU Act 1985, Section 2(3) and Section 5(2)].

The Statute 28 of IGNOU dealing with Distance Education Council came into effect on 16-9-1991 and the DEC was constituted in 1992. It is chaired by the Vice-Chancellor of IGNOU and includes two Vice-Chancellors of State Open Universities and two heads of institutions of correspondence education/distance education from conventional universities. There is no provision for representation of any State Government. Statute 4(a)(i) specifically contains a reference to State Government, which states: "DEC is to develop a network of OUs/DEIs, *inter alia* in consultation with State Governments". DEC, presided over by the V-C, IGNOU, as a body is subordinate to the Board of Management of the IGNOU. This detracts from the autonomy of the DEC. A committee which formulated guidelines for the support to SOUs and CCIs for the Ninth Plan suggested that the DEC should be restructured to provide it with an independent status, that it should not be perceived as a sub-structure of IGNOU and that this should be done through appropriate statutes [DEC (1999) Guidelines: 38], issued by an Act of parliament). This implies that the DEC's relationship with IGNOU could, at the least, be similar to that of NAAC with UGC. While V-C, IGNOU could continue as the President of the General Body, there could be a separate Chairman of the Executive Committee of the DEC who could be responsible for day-to-day operations. The DEC as such needs to be outside the purview of the Board of Management of IGNOU.

The DEC had devised its own guidelines in July 1996 and suggested replacement of the UGC rules on OUs of 1988 by the Guidelines of DEC. The Correspondence Course Institutions (CCIs) of the conventional universities were to be converted to the DE mode. None of this has happened, apparently because universities are reluctant to make the necessary investments; they still treat DEIs as 'cash cows'. The DEC has reportedly developed collaboration with sister agencies like NCERT, NCTE, AICTE and most significantly, with the NAAC. It has been decided that NAAC should do accreditation of the distance education institutions (OUs and CCIs) on the basis of jointly developed format but there is no progress.

Recently, the DEC has come in for considerable criticism from veteran experts who have pointed out weaknesses in the working of the DEC and have suggested that the DEC be made into an independent body or it be merged with the UGC [Amrik Singh, 2004(b): 127-148]. In particular, the proliferation of franchising centres by the conventional universities, and the failure of the DEC to check the growth has been adversely commented upon. As regards the latter, UGC has promulgated norms for "Franchising of Higher Education through off-campus study centres" (*UGC News*, January 2004: 38-44). But several important suggestions regarding: (1) autonomy of the DEC and (2) the setting up of an independent accreditation mechanism for ODL remain unimplemented (Government of India, 1994: 35). It was envisaged that the DEC should prepare a Master Plan for development of Distance Education in the country and the centres set up by the conventional universities should be in accordance with the Master Plan, and that the Chairman, DEC should arrange inspection of each University conducting ODL courses once in three years. The projected expansion of the ODL system in a desirable direction has not come about. The growth of the new SOUs has been slow, but DEIs have proliferated (from 106 in 2004 to 130 in 2007). The IGNOU has apparently progressed by leaps and bounds, but has not been able to nurture State OUs, nor has it been able to shape the DEC as a co-ordinating and standards body. It tends to compete with the State OUs and has no rapport with conventional universities, which are on an expansion spree of CCIs for their own financial gains. Nor has the IGNOU the same concern as the UGC with the quality of education. The eminent proposal to give a co-ordinating role to the projected Andhra Pradesh State OU in relation to other universities which was made by the founding State level committee chaired by G. Ram Reddy was not accepted in Andhra Pradesh in 1982 and may not be accepted in other States also owing to vested interest of conventional universities. Quality has suffered and expansion without quality is giving a bad name to the ODL system in India.

Prospects for ODL

Press reports in February 2009 indicated that the Government has decided to separate the DEC from the IGNOU and to develop it into an independent statutory Distance Education Council which proposal, however, had reportedly been opposed by a sister Ministry (Commerce Ministry), may be, because it has already promoted a rival Quality Council of India. UPA II Government was focused on other issues. One no more hears about the statutory DEC. By all accounts, ODL system and, therefore, the DEC also should be under the umbrella of the newly proposed NCHER, but there appears to be a lack of clarity on the issue.

IUB/AIU

IUB was established in 1925 and can claim to have played the co-ordinating role in relation to Higher Education in India till the establishment of interim UGC in December 1953 (to eventuate in the Statutory UGC in November 1956). It was an association of heads of universities and its achievements till 1947, according to the judgement of Radhakrishnan Commission (1949: 15) were: (1) acting as a forum for discussion of university problems, (2) bringing out many informative publications about universities in India, the most important being '*Handbook of Universities*' brought out biannually, the main source of information about Indian universities, (3) the organizing of quinquennial conferences of Indian universities in which some of the most controversial issues of higher education were taken up for careful consideration by representatives of the universities. Radhakrishnan Commission opined that IUB's influence as an advisory body had not been as potent as might have been because the universities, its members, had not always been inclined to follow its advice. A Lakshmanswami Mudaliar, a staunch supporter of IUB as an organization, appeared however to think that IUB's weakness was its lack of statutory recognition and absence of stable leadership due to frequent change of Vice-Chancellors, which became common in post-Independence India (Mudaliar, A.L., 1960: 33).

The IUB suffered from some additional administrative problems. Till 1947, it had no full-time Secretary. Its address was also uncertain. In 1954, it had been operative from Delhi, but between 1954 to 1959, it was headquartered at Madras (Now Chennai), at the instance of A. Lakshmanswami Mudaliar, then Chairman of the Board. It shifted back to Delhi in 1959, though there was also a view that it should be cited elsewhere (Bhandarkar, S.S., 1975: 28-31). It had also some structural problem. Its Presidentship changed annually. It was only in 1945 that a Standing Committee was constituted to decide all questions of procedure, preparation of agenda for meetings of the Board and annual conferences, budget, etc.

As the forum of the universities in India, IUB enjoyed consultative status with the CABE, which was revived in 1935 and this gave a sense of self-importance to the IUB, which tended to enter into argument with the Government of India. Thus when John Sargent was Adviser to the Government of India, it took umbrage at two instances of Government not having consulted IUB and protested at "serious encroachment on the functions of the IUB". Sargent replied that one of the issues pertained to routine administration (Air Force Scheme) and another involved diplomacy with China. He concluded by saying: "I have sometimes found the IUB is inclined to postpone consideration of matters which are likely to be difficult or controversial, e.g. remuneration of university lecturers or welfare of Indian students overseas" (Bhandarkar, S.S.

1975: 169-70). This may be another reason why the IUB tended to lose influence.

The IUB was initially set up: (1) as a bureau of information, and (2) as an agency (a) to facilitate exchange of professors, (b) for obtaining recognition for Indian degrees abroad, and (c) to nominate delegates for international conferences. Subsequently in 1930, it expanded the scope of its work to become a co-ordinating and standard setting body for Indian universities. The original function of serving as an authorized channel of communication and facilitating co-ordination of university work was expanded to include the function of co-ordinating the courses of study among the universities, co-operating with other universities or bodies in the matter of common interest and acting as a liaison between the universities and the Government of India and between the universities and the Grants Commission and other bodies as may be established (Bhandarkar, S.S., 1975: 5).

The specific reference to Grants Commission was quite significant because establishment of such a body was in the air. The IUB gave its views on the Sargent Plan and was vehement in its opposition to the Government of India proposal to pass a Universities (Regulation of Standards) Bill in 1953. In effect its argument was that when the IUB was there, a co-ordinating body was not required; only a grant-giving body would suffice. It also ensured that the Vice-Chancellors of universities were well represented on the Commission when set up. As it happened, it had a sympathetic channel to the Commission because its former Secretary became the First Secretary of the UGC. Subsequently, goaded by conservative members like A.L. Mudaliar, IUB took its stand on opposing admission to its Membership of single-faculty universities like Roorkee Engineering University in UP, Agricultural Universities under ICAR and institutions of national importance like IITs. The Sapru Committee's (1964) recommendation for excluding VCs' from membership of UGC and the passing of an amendment to this effect in 1970 marked a set-back to the IUB. Fortunately for the IUB, that particular amendment was not brought into force. The 1972 UGC Amendment Act did not completely exclude Vice-Chancellors from the Membership of the UGC, but it certainly marked a turning point in the fortunes of the IUB because a Vice-Chancellor may or may not be a member of the UGC unlike in the 1956 dispension, where three seats were guaranteed to the V-Cs.

The Education Commission was given a memorandum by the IUB that there should be frequent points of contact between the UGC and IUB, e.g. UGC can meet Standing Committee at stated intervals of a few months to discuss pending important issues (Bhandarkar, S.S., 1975: 124-125). Kothari Commission, apparently, did not react to this suggestion. It, however, tried to redefine the role of the IUB, which it considered as one of the two agencies (the other being the UGC) charged with the overall promotion and co-ordination in Indian Higher Education. It said: "The Board has helped to enforce some standards and code of conduct among the universities. It is a useful channel through which the Government and the UGC can ascertain the opinion of the universities on important problems. It plays the important role of representing university to the Government and the public and in this regard was comparable to the CVCP (Committee of Vice-Chancellors and Principals) in the UK." Education Commission's suggestions were: (1) Its membership should be made automatic to include all statutory universities and all institutions deemed to be universities. (2) It saw no real justification for the self-assumed function of the Board, of assisting Indian universities in obtaining recognition for their degrees, diplomas and examinations in other universities. (3) It wanted its responsibilities in the matter of acting as a clearing house of information on university affairs and as the central agency for organizing inter-university sports to be expanded. It wanted the IUB to deliver certain advisory research and service functions for and on behalf of universities, for which it should be strengthened financially and enabled to maintain an adequate secretariat. Kothari Commission agreed with the IUB on issues like State level UGCs (no need) and reproduced its resolution on university autonomy as a supplement to its Chapter 13.

It was also in 1966, the year of publication of Kothari Report, that Dr. V.K.R.V. Rao, who was then Member Planning Commission, in his inaugural address at the 43rd annual meeting of the Board went so far as to state as below:

> "IUB (being a democratic and representative body of all the universities) was the supreme body for the consideration of problems of university education and should be treated as such by government and by the UGC; that a convention

should be established by which the annual reports of the UGC should be placed for discussion not only before Parliament but also before the annual meeting of the IUB" (Bhandarkar, S.S. 1975: 201-204).

Dr. Rao hastened to add that the Parliament remains the acknowledged and authentic spokesman of the nation. The exaggerated claims of Dr. Rao have to be understood in the context of the tendency in the UGC circles to devalue IUB and the studied silence of the Kothari Report on IUB's request to be part of the inner consultative circle of the UGC, a status enjoyed by CVCP in relation to UGC in UK.

In the meanwhile, the IUB came be registered in 1967 under the Societies Registration Act and in 1973 changed its nomenclature to that of Association of Indian Universities (AIU), to reflect the fact that it primarily represented Indian Universities, Pakistan and Bangladesh universities having disassociated since 1947 and 1971 and Sri Lanka and Burma having ceased to be members. AIU appeared to have drifted apart from the UGC, its funding being drawn from membership fees and research grants from the Ministry of Education. UGC and the Ministry called Conferences of the Vice-Chancellors as per need (e.g. when NPE 1986/92 was evolved), but the AIU as such was not involved. This was not a desirable scenario. In UK, e.g. till the UGC was abolished (1989), it formally and informally consulted with CVCP (later on renamed as the "Universities UK"). One has to surmise that the AIU leadership worked behind the scenes, for the 66th Report of Estimates Committee of the Lok Sabha (1989) noted that no formal mechanism has been evolved to maintain co-ordination between the UGC and the Ministry on the one hand and AIU on the other. The Committee appears to have been impressed by the ancestry of the AIU (estd. in 1925), being older than either the Ministry or the UGC, its representative character and its capacity to understand the problems of university education, association with which would strengthen the effectiveness of the UGC. Government realized that the Estimates Committee meant business. Its recommendations were promptly accepted and the Government intimated to the Lok Sabha Secretariat the following steps being taken in compliance:

(1) Revival of the practice of holding at least one joint meeting between the Standing Committee of the AIU and the UGC in a year.
(2) The Constitution of a Co-ordination Committee consisting of the Chairman of UGC/Members of UGC and the President of AIU/Members of AIU's Standing Committee.
(3) The practice of holding a Conference of V-Cs during the annual meeting of the AIU at which Chairman UGC and members of the Commission may also participate.

These steps were implemented w.e.f. October 1989 (66th Report of the Estimates Committee (1989).

Thus AIU, from being an ineffective advisory body as judged by Radhakrishnan Commission in 1949, became an eloquent advocate of its role as a rival of the UGC and was quite strong till 1964. After a transitional period lasting till 1971, it lost favour with the UGC and with the Government in the period from 1972 to 1989, but re-asserted itself by getting consultative status with the UGC in that year, thanks to the intervention of a Parliamentary Committee.

The IUB/AIU with its ups and downs has endured as a professional body with considerable research output to its credit. It has been a source of information relating to educational facilities available in various universities through its: (a) Biennial handbook of Indian Universities (of which 31st edition was published in 2006), (b) Bibliographies of Doctoral Dissertations in Indian Universities going back to 1857 and since 1975-76 being published annually in two series: Natural and Applied Sciences and Social Sciences and Humanities, (c) Thematic handbooks on medical, engineering, management, distance and computer education and its Directory of Distance Education Institutes, (d) 13 publications on examination reforms and question-banks in 20 subjects which have resulted from its research programmes assisted by the Ministry, (e) Weekly periodical "*University News*" which is widely read, though its quality could be improved, (f) It had earlier brought out valuable monographs in the area of economics of education, but of late, the research programme appears to have weakened. The credit for the success of AIU in its publication and research programme must go to some of its distinguished Secretary-Generals including Amrik Singh and S.K.

Agrawala. In 1992, a symposium was organized by AIU on the well-known Supreme Court Judgement in *Mohini Jain's case*, which contributed to generating public opinion in favour of an amendment of the Constitution to make universalization of elementary education (UEE) as a Fundamental Right.

IUB's achievements for the first sixty years (1925-1985) have been ably summarized by S.S. Bhandarkar (1975, 1985). Its achievements for the next 15 years have been narrated by K.K. Vashishtha (2002). In this account, AIU's role in countering what is called the 'crisis of autonomy' has been described. AIU has also brought out a monograph in this regard (AIU 1991). AIU felt vindicated by the Supreme Court judgment in Civil Appeal No. 2056 of 1999, which held that the clause 10(k) of AICTE Act did not apply to the universities. Prof. Vashistha's book is quite informative though not as analytical as Bhandarkar's account.

However, there are some basic issues regarding the approach of the AIU which need to be underlined:

(1) The AIU appears to have interpreted university autonomy in a very narrow sense. The Education Commission had appended IUB's resolution on university autonomy as a supplementary note to its Chapter 13. However, IUB appear to be overmuch concerned with the security of tenure of Vice-Chancellors and it is not known to have protested on curbs on fundamental rights including fundamental right to freedom of expression during the Emergency (1975-77).

(2) AIU is selective in its criticism of Governments. It has criticized State legislations or State universities, but is not known to have criticized Central legislation relating to Central universities. It has criticized CMs/State Education Ministers/Governors of States but has not criticized PMs/ Union Education Ministers/Presidents of India for their action or default. India is a functioning federalism which involves co-operation between the Centre and the States. In this scenario, AIU has firmly aligned itself with the centralizing Union Government.

(3) It functions regionally in terms of Zones corresponding to Zonal Councils set up under the State Reorganization Act, 1956.

The AIU could do well to set up State Chapters. It also needs to upgrade its research output. It should make its journal into a referee-ed journal or alternatively split it up into a newsletter and a learned journal, the latter carrying quality articles duly referee-ed. This appears to be necessary especially because the UGC has stopped its *Quarterly Journal on Higher Education*. AIU needs to professionalize the contents of its Memoranda submitted to the Government. It has criticized Finance Ministry for treating Higher Education as a 'non-merit Good'. It could have enlisted the services of professional economists and submitted a technical memorandum. Lastly, the judiciary of late has felt compelled to intervene in certain issues of Higher Education, like ragging of junior students by senior students, the elections to student councils, etc. The Supreme Court appointed Committees in this regard (Raghavan Committee on ragging; Lingdoh Committee on university elections), which have evolved guidelines, which are circulated by the UGC for strict compliance. These are really matters of improvement of internal management of universities and AIU would do well to take initiative in such matters and serve as an effective self-governing supplement to the UGC.

National University of Educational Planning and Administration (NUEPA)

NUEPA began in 1962 as a UNESCO Regional Centre for the training of educational planners, administrators and supervisors in 14 Asian countries as part of implementation of the Asian Plan for universal primary education drawn up at Karachi in 1959. It was one of the five such regional institutions. Thus, in its conception, NUEPA is an organization in the school sub-sector although its thematic focus makes it janus-faced, having interest in the areas of planning, administration, research and training in higher education, especially because the NCERT gradually shed its interest in these areas. In 1972, after the expiry of stipulated 10 year-period, it was taken over by the National Staff College for Educational Planning and Administration, which was earlier set up in 1970. In 1979, it was renamed as NIEPA with an amended Memorandum of Association. Since then, it has emerged as a small but reputed establishment in its chosen field with academic linkage with the Paris-based International Institute of Educational Planning (IIEP) maintained by the UNESCO (G.D. Sharma, 1989: 506-562). In August 2007, it was notified as a deemed university and since then known as NUEPA.

The relationship of NUEPA with higher education sub-sector has been somewhat tenuous. In 1975-76, the training of higher education functionaries like College Principals, Finance Officers and Registrars was, for the first time, included in the ambit of its functions. The Jha Committee on the UGC which recommended the establishment of a Research, Planning and Evaluation Organization as a limb of the UGC opined that it would be desirable to have a close linkage with the training programmes in the area of higher education run by institutions like the National Staff College (as NUEPA was then known) and the research activities done on behalf of the UGC (Jha Report, 1977: 5.4). With the coming up of the Academic Staff Colleges under the auspices of the UGC, higher education sub-sector has its own training resource for its academic staff, but the lacuna in regard to the training of higher education administration remained which NIEPA continued to fill in its own modest manner.

Kavita Sharma, the official historian of UGC reports that the Government of India had appointed a nine-member committee to review the status of the existing training facilities for educational administration and identifying their needs and suggesting measures to augment facilities for their professional development. The Committee chaired by (Late) Dr. Amrik Singh submitted its report to the Government in September 1992. It recommended that a nodal training institute at the national level to be called the National Institute for Training and Research in Higher Education (NITRHE) be established. It was to be set up as an inter-university centre to formulate the training policy, to promote common training facilities, and to promote research and management of higher education. The Institute would also identify needs and provide the training, share information and expertise in the field and work out the feasibility of establishing community colleges. The report was placed before the Commission which accepted it in principle (Kavita Sharma, 2003: 203-204). The Annual Report of the UGC for 1997-98 states (pp. 9-10) that the approval in principle to a central training institution was followed by re-thinking on two or three counts: Firstly, of course, there was the problem of resource constraint which made it difficult for a capital intensive project like this to be taken up immediately. Secondly, it was thought that India has lakhs of teachers especially in affiliated colleges. Their training requirements could not be handled by a single training institution. It is also the surmise of the author that the project has been made part of the bigger project of construction of a building for the UGC in the 20-acre plot on the JNU campus for which ground-breaking function was performed in December 2003 at the time of the so-called Golden Jubilee of the UGC. The fact remains that in 2010 there is no such institution on the ground.

Structure and Functions of NIEPA

The objectives of the NIEPA include: (i) organization of training programmes in the areas of educational planning and administration (EPA) for (a) senior educational officers of the Central and State Governments, (b) teacher-educators and university and college administrators, (c) legislators; (ii) undertaking of research in the EPA area; (iii) offering of consultancy services to the State Governments and other educational institutions; (iv) acting as a clearing-house of ideas and information and collaboration with the UGC, universities and management institutions (Government of India, 1989: 68-73). Its authorities include the Council, the Executive Committee and the Finance Committee. Minister HRD is the *ex-officio* President of the Council. Its units are partly thematic (financing, planning), partly related to the educational level (including higher education) and partly spatial (sub-national systems unit). The general body of the NIEPA called the 'Council' consists of education Secretaries of five States and Education Secretary of one UT by rotation plus 6 Directors of Education. The Executive Committee of the NIEPA consists of 7 persons among whom there is one State Education Secretary nominated by the Minister HRD. The Finance Committee has no representation from any State. As compared with the NCERT, the presence of a State representative on the Executive Committee of NIEPA as a progressive pro-federalism step showing that the NIEPA has adopted a more participatory approach but the absence of all States on the Council makes it less representative than it could otherwise have been.

The sub-national systems unit of NIEPA deals with States and District Policies and Programmes. Its functions include getting and sharing information regarding educational developments and innovations in various regions and States of India, helping State, District and Block level units in development of monitoring and evaluating systems, providing training and consultation to States in the EPA area and carrying out research studies on educational needs and problems of States and districts. However, a perusal of the Review Report of the NIEPA (cited above) shows that the consultancy output of this unit was meager and that the only major States which consulted the then NIEPA were Haryana and Rajasthan, the rest being smaller States (J&K/Sikkim) or Union Territories like Dadra/Nagar Haveli, Pondichery etc.

During the Seventh Plan it is understood that the NIEPA unsuccessfully tried to have a centrally sponsored scheme for the establishment of State Institutes of Educational Planning and Administration (SIEPAs). This would have provided the then NIEPA with its counterpart institutions comparable to the NCERT in the form of SIEs/SCERTs. Subsequently, the World Bank provided assistance as part of the District Primary Education Projects (DPEPs) to set up SIEPAs where DPEP was in operation. However, only two States, Maharashtra and U.P., have established institutions called Maharashtra Institute of EPA (MIEPA) at Aurangabad and State Institute of Educational Management and Training (SIEMAT) at Allahabad (Srilekha Majumdar, 2000: 229-243) respectively, with Assam making a beginning. Thus, the State level capacity in the area of educational planning and administration remains severely limited.

The conduct of the training programmes takes up 75 per cent of NIEPA faculty time, the two main training programmes being National Diploma Programme for District Education Officers (DEOs) and International Diploma Programme for countries in West Asia, Africa and South East Asia, in addition to the orientation and training programmes for principals of District Institute of Education and Training (DIETs), functionaries of District Primary Education Programme (DPEP), Principals of colleges, Senior education administrators, university administrators etc. There is a feeling that NIEPA should concentrate on training of trainers and key functionaries. The research output of NIEPA is considerable, much of it being supported by international organizations or the Ministry (e.g. the work of the NIEPA on NPE 1986/PoA 1992 and earlier, the National Commission on Teachers No. II (Higher Education). More recently, NIEPA has concentrated on topics like financing of higher education, internationalization of higher education, GATS (General Agreement on Trade in Services), the role of secondary education in the 21st Century etc. Thus, in 2004-2005 it served as secretariat for CABE Committee on Financing of Higher and Secondary Education (CABE Committee, 2005). It has conducted two surveys of State Administration. It publishes a quarterly journal of Educational Planning and Administration, which enjoys a high academic reputation. The journals of the UGC and of the Indian Institute of Education, Pune having closed, JEPA appears to have developed autocratic academic gate-keeping tendencies in a virtual monopolistic market. NIEPA brings out occasional papers on various themes and Best Practices series. NIEPA appeared to suffer from an absence of a critical mass of academic manpower having only 49 academic and 13 academic support staff in 2005-06 (NIEPA Annual Report). It needs to be strengthened organizationally and financially, so that it can actively help State level organizations (SIEPAs) to come up. It also needs to build a capacity in the area of District Planning and Administration and to have an institutional survey and research strategy. Thus it can fix a 5-yearly periodicity for surveys of State Administration and can also periodically bring out yearbooks in EPA area focusing on State and District Planning and Administration. It can ascertain the UGC's future plans for research in higher education and training of higher education administrators and enter into an MoU with it.

Recent Developments: From NIEPA to NUEPA

The NIEPA's work was earlier reviewed in 1989. Subsequently, in terms of the National Commission on Expenditure's recommendation it was further reviewed in 2003-04 by a Committee chaired by Dr. Subhash C. Kashyap. The report of the Committee is not available, but it reportedly endorsed the view of the 1989 Review Committee that NIEPA has done extremely well in terms of fulfilling the objectives for which it was set up. It suggested capacity building at State level in the form of SIEPAs or as part of SCERTs. It also wanted NIEPA to devote more resources to higher education sector as compared with school education. The institution of a Diploma in Planning and Administration at university education was suggested. The Committee referred to the opinion expressed that NIEPA could be given a deemed university status, but made no definite recommendation in this regard. NIEPA, however became NUEPA, a deemed university in August 2007. Apart from other programmes, NUEPA has instituted M.Phil. and Ph.D. (MoA of NUEPA: 5.10). The course outlines of its M.Phil. papers would indicate the priority areas—

Compulsory papers

- Education and Development
- Research Methodology and Statistics
- Educational Policy and Planning
- Educational Administration

Optional papers

- Contemporary Issues in School Education
- Contemporary Issues in Higher Education
- Sociology of Education
- History of Education
- Comparative Education
- Financing of Education
- Inclusive Education
- Early Childhood Care and Education

The University has now following Ten Departments:

(1) Educational Planning,
(2) Educational Administration,
(3) Educational Policy,
(4) School and Non-formal Education,
(5) Higher and Professional Education,

(6) Educational Financing,
(7) *Comparative Education* and International Cooperation,
(8) *Inclusive Education,*
(9) Educational Management and Information System, and
(10) *Foundation of Education.* [*Note*: The portions in italics indicate new areas].

The MoA of the NUEPA is an adaptation of the original MoA. The Union Education Minister is the President of Council of NUEPA. There is a post of Chancellor as in most Central Universities (which is generally honorary). The Council has five representatives of States by rotation (the number five corresponds to the number of Zones). Unfortunately, there is no representative of any State on the Board of Management. In other words, NUEPA has become much more Centralized than NIEPA, it is no longer a federal body but a Centrally supported deemed university.

The higher education scenario in the country is in a state of flux and it needs to be seen how NUEPA shapes *vis-à-vis* the newly emerging co-ordinating bodies for higher education. One possibility is to take NUEPA under the umbrella of the proposed National Council for Higher Education & Research (NCHER).

8

The Role of Research Councils in Higher Education

Introduction

According to common understanding, the functions of the university are threefold: teaching, research and extension. But the question is: teaching of what? Research in what? The simple answer is—in a particular discipline. The disciplinary specialization has proceeded apace in the second half of the twentieth century and there is a view that a university now is really an umbrella for housing a host of disciplines which were traditionally divided into two types: Science and Technology and the Arts and Humanities. A theoretical underpinning for such a division has been provided by C.P. Snow (1959, 1965) in his well-known thesis of two cultures: a scientific culture and a literary culture, which, after industrial revolution, had developed in isolation of each other and lacked intercommunication.

When C.P. Snow wrote, it was pointed out that he failed to factor in social sciences. There is ample literature on how this division arose and how the scientific revolution and the rise of the nation state played a causative role. The social sciences staked a claim to separate existence in the nineteenth century, as a concomitant to the rise of the nation states, which wanted to know more about their territory, their population, their revenues etc. So the basic binary division came to be amplified into the following threefold division:

(1) Science and Technology,

(2) Arts and Humanities (which include literature, languages, history and philosophy), and
(3) Social Sciences.

In the UK, the Labour Party grew *inter alia* out of the exertions of the Fabian Society of the nineteenth century. It began to talk of the need for central planning àla Soviet Union in the context of the Great Depression and after Second World War, the Labour Party became committed to the Welfare State. The Congress Party had its socialist wing in the 1930s. Although Jawaharlal Nehru and Subhas Chandra Bose did not formally belong to this group, they became great votaries of Planning for Development. During the years of provincial autonomy, while the second rung leadership was busy ruling the provinces, a National Planning Committee under the guidance of these leaders produced a series of sectoral reports. The vision of these leaders but especially Nehru led in two directions. Firstly, the setting up of a chain of scientific laboratories which were to promote industrialization by engaging in research relevant for rapid industrialization of the country. The umbrella for these laboratories was provided by the Council of Scientific and Industrial Research (CSIR) set up in war-time in 1942, which in its turn, took as its model the British Department of Scientific and Industrial Research set up in 1916. The second direction was the establishment of the Planning Commission in 1950 for formulating and implementing plans for socio-economic development. These plans required inputs from social sciences for survey, evaluation, etc. The genesis of ICSSR lies in a committee appointed by the Planning Commission as noted below. As would be seen, there is a British precedent for ICSSR as well.

Research Councils in Social Sciences and Humanities

The successive Annual Reports of the Ministry of Education (2002—2005) refer to five research councils functioning outside the university system, namely Indian Council of Social Science Research (ICSSR), Indian Council of Historical Research (ICHR), Indian Council of Philosophical Research (ICPR), Indian Institute of Advanced Studies (IIAS), Shimla and National Council of Rural Institutes (NRI)

(Annual Reports: 2002-03: 2; 2003-04: 12 and 2004-05: 14). This is not strictly correct. The last two mentioned are not research councils at all, the former being an advanced centre of research modelled on the Institute of Advanced Studies, Princeton USA/All Souls' College, Oxford,UK about which more is said later, and the latter is an incipient co-ordinating body for rural higher education. Before considering the three Research Councils and the Shimla Institute, one basic issue needs to be addressed: why have separate research councils at all if the primary funding agency for the universities, viz. the UGC does in fact support research and can as well earmark funds for research?

The Dual Support System

The reply is that the UGC is designed to support universities as such and while they are no doubt multi-functional with the triad of teaching, research and extension, universities give high priority to teaching. The general university funds support infrastructure like laboratories and computers and administrative and secretarial staff which are necessary both for teaching and research. The UGC, however, is not equipped to decide what research areas to support, though it may earmark a proportion of funding for research generally. As pointed out by a Report of the Advisory Board for Research Councils (ABRC) in UK (1982), this necessitates the Dual Support System (i.e. both UGC and Research Councils supporting research). The essence of the dual support system is that by the joint support of research by the UGC, the Universities functioning thereunder and the Research Councils, *fundamental research whose results are unpredictable is helped along in a way which otherwise would not be possible*. A leading example is the discovery of penicillin. The support from general university funds enables academic staff to keep in touch with the frontiers of their subject and this contact feeds back beneficially into the liveliness and quality of their teaching and the atmosphere of the university. It provides a continuity of research which is protected to some extent from the disruptive influences of an uncertain flow of external income. Support from external specific funds enables the most promising lines of research being supported selectively after independent review.

The Rothschild Report in UK (1982) has schematically defined prime functions of a Research Council as:

(a) to identify the best research which may be done in its field defined by its charter,
(b) to identify the best way of getting it done, and then
(c) to provide the means by which it may be done.

In this background are studied three Research Councils in India, viz. (1) Indian Council of Social Science Research (ICSSR) (estd. 1967), (2) Indian Council for Historical Research (ICHR) (estd. 1973), and (3) Indian Council for Philosophical Research (ICPR) (estd. 1980).

ICSSR

A social science research council was set up in UK four years prior to the setting up of ICSSR and two years prior to the setting up of the V.K.R.V. Rao Committee (1967) on whose recommendations ICSSR was set up. The Heyworth Committee in UK (1963) gave following reasons for setting up a Social Science Research Council (SSRC) in UK at that stage:

> "We have noted the great increase in the social science in the universities and corresponding developments outside... The social sciences are ready to move to a new level of performance and for this, they need funds for research on a larger scale ... there should be resources to finance research which is needed but which the universities or users cannot find the means to support" (as quoted in Rothschild Report: 22).

In India, the initiative for social studies came from the Planning Commission which in order to meet its own need for socio-economic research, had set up a Research Programme Committee to fund research, as early as 1953. In August 1967 it set up a Committee on Social Science Research under the Chairmanship of Dr. V.K.R.V. Rao, Member (Education). Its terms of reference were: (1) to survey the current situation in relation to research in social sciences in the country, and (2) to make recommendations regarding its future line of development as also the organizational and other terms necessary. The Committee harked back to the Science Policy Resolution of 1958, which had emphasized the role of science in the progress of the nation. The Committee recommended establishment of ICSSR which was expected to supplement UGC's structural role (development of departments) by providing facilities like documentation, data library, promotional facilities for seminars, workshops and conferences. In regard to the organizational pattern, the specific model of the CSIR was commended. The CSIR gave maintenance grants to research laboratories and the Committee did include the following function in its list: "to give both development and maintenance grants to research institutions in social sciences that do not constitute either affiliated or constituent institutes of statutory universities in India". This function, however, was omitted by the Government from the MoA of ICSSR, as notified. The Council was set up in December, 1968 its composition was approved in April 1969 and the first meeting held in May 1969 which was inaugurated by Dr. V.K.R.V. Rao who had, by then, become Minister (Education), Government of India. Dr. Rao in his address also mentioned the need for Regional Centres for ICSSR (A.R.: ICSSR, 1969-70). D.R. Gadgil was the first Chairman of the ICSSR.

The primary objective of the ICSSR is to promote research in social sciences and to facilitate its utilization. For this purpose, it may review progress of research, sponsor research programmes and projects, and finance seminars. Special emphasis is placed on promotion of research in universities, especially by young social scientists and on international co-operation. It may also support documentation/data services. It may advise the Government of India but no specific reference is made to the State Governments. Neither reference is made to maintenance of Research Institutions or regional centres in its Memorandum of Association.

The Governing Body of the Council is 25 members and Chairman (Honorary) and Member-Secretary (full-time) as well as Members of the Governing Body are appointed by the Central Government. There are 18 social scientists and six persons to represent the Government. They mandatorily include three secretaries of the Departments of Finance, Education and Social Welfare (which was then under Home Ministry). As a matter of convention, three other Government Officers are included, viz. Secretary, Planning Commission, Registrar-General of Census and Director-General Anthropological Survey of India. A representative of the UGC and representatives of other research councils are special invitees.

The ICSSR completed 40 years of its existence in 2009. Although more limited in scope than the UGC and with very limited funding as compared with the former, it is a crucial institution in making sense of the emerging global society which is full of conflicts and contradictions. The Annual Report of the Ministry for 2007-08 broadly devotes three columns to each of the three Research Councils which would appear to under-estimate the leading role of the ICSSR. An overall review of its functioning is therefore called for. Unfortunately, the material for this is not readily forthcoming although ICSSR itself had appointed Review Committees in 1970, 1978 and 1986 and more recently in 2004-05. In 2002, Social Science Research Council of New York reviewed its work under the title of "Social Science Research Capacity in South Asia". In all the latest reviews, a sense of disappointment with its performance is voiced. It may be worthwhile to have a look at its achievements as assessed in a mid-term review by its former Member-Secretary (Iqbal Narain, 1989), and then look at findings of various reviews mentioned above to get a sense of what ICSSR has achieved, what might have gone wrong and what needs to be done.

In 1989, the Council had six regional centres at Bombay (Now Mumbai), Culcutta (Kolkata), Chandigarh, Hyderabad, New Delhi and Shillong. The establishment of the regional centre at Shillong, headquarter, of NEHU, a Central University, was part of the policy of helping less developed regions. (Now this policy also embraces the mandate of devoting 10 per cent of gross budgetary support to the North-Eastern Region).

The Council had taken over Regional Research Institutes started by the Central Government and thereafter created more such institutions, whose number went up from 9 in 1974 to 25 in 1987-88. The role of these institutes is crucial in (i) improving quality of social science research, (ii) promoting an interdisciplinary perspectives, and (iii) in building up research capacities in different regions of the country. In the period 1984-88, i.e. during a period of 4 years, the institutes completed 626 research projects and 1274 were ongoing. They brought out 242 books, 1670 working papers and 327 monographs. The Council also undertakes periodical reviews of the work of the Institutes. In recent times, however, as a perverse side effect of the UGC pay scales, the institutes suffered and there was reported to be a sense of frustration that the Indian system rewards teaching rather than research and that too, inferior teaching in affiliated colleges as against superior research in ICSSR institutes.

The work of surveys of research in different disciplines, however, had not progressed as planned. Surveys in some disciplines had forged ahead (e.g. in 1988, work on the Third Survey of Public Administration had started but the work on the Second Survey of Economics had also started in the same year which shows a lag in that discipline). The Council had a well-developed Documentation Centre which was named as National Social Science Documentation Centre (NASSDOC) in 1986. The Council's scheme of Data Archives had, however, not made adequate progress for which an expert group had made recommendations in 1986 which were to be implemented in the Eighth Plan. The Council had also brought out a National Register of Social Scientists in India.

The Council has been implementing the Social Science component of the Cultural Exchange Programme (CEP) of the Government of India. It has networked with regional and international associations for social science research. Social science community in India benefited considerably from Indo-Dutch Programme on Alternatives in Development (IDPAD), which was initiated during the Chairmanship of Prof. Sukhamoy Chakravarty.

The Council, of course, implements a substantial programme of Fellowships and funds project research. It also funds a large number of seminars and journals of various social science associations.

Apart from the ICSSR, which is a government body, there are some NGOs which purport to promote social science research. It is well-known that the post-Emergency Janata Regime which gave a sense of liberation to latent social forces also gave a fillip to such NGOs. Typically, these NGOs emphasized development from below. In the field of social science research, an Indian Association of Social Science Institutions (IASSI) was set up in March 1979, with which, *inter alia*, (late) *Tarlok Singh*, former-Member, Planning Commission was associated. The IASSI emphasized the need for helping research in affiliated colleges in rural areas. The IASSI membership, however, was eclectic ranging from universities through national social science associations to State Government institutions and public authorities (Tarlok Singh, 1978). It approached the ICSSR for an annual financial grant. Initially the ICSSR was not responsive, but later on relented. This episode is mentioned to underline the image of the ICSSR as an elite metropolitan institution out of touch with the grassroots reality of India, and also its ethos of centralization. This point may be further illustrated by reference to ICSSR's attitude to State Governments which are the basic building blocks of the federal polity of India.

The Neglect of the Role of State Governments

In social science research and allied fields, States/Regions can have much more interest academically than in the fields of natural science and technology. The Report of V.K.R.V. Rao Committee shows that wide-ranging consultations were held with academicians and learned associations all over the country at different places, e.g. Varanasi, Allahabad, Bangalore (now Bangaluru) and Bombay (Now Mumbai). The Committee also considered that 'promoting a co-ordinated and balanced distribution of research over different disciplines, different regions and different categories of research' was one of the tasks to be performed for putting social science discipline on the path of sound development. The ICSSR adopted a Policy Statement on its role in October 1971. A paper was placed before the ICSSR (on the basis of which the Policy Statement was adopted) in which reference was made to the report on 'Social Science Research in India' submitted by Mr. Shonfield and Prof. Cherns making some important suggestions in regard to close relations with State Governments. Shonfield-Cherns Report (1971: 74 and 75) stated:

> "The relationship of the Council with the State Governments is of especial importance. Not only are some State Governments major sponsors of social science research, all are potential users and many of the results of research invite interest and action more within the ambit of State Governments than of the Central Government. Although

ICSSR receives its funds from the Federal Government, it should avoid being seen by State Governments as an exclusive servant of the Centre. It must be recognized, however, that the social science policy is not something which is best determined at State level; every aspect of it transcends State boundaries and State responsibilities. Thus, the ICSSR needs to be seen by the State as a resource, a source of help and advice, as the voice of social science community as a whole, but not as an embodiment of superior power."

Unfortunately, the ICSSR's final decision treated State Governments as 'Other Agencies' and simply stated that the Council would also have to develop relations with State Governments who had begun to take greater interest in social science research and especially in relation to the regional social science documentation centres. Since then, the devaluation and derogation of States has continued apace and the ICSSR, as feared by Shonfield and Cherns, is perceived by the States as purely a Central agency.

Successive review committees have referred to regional bias in the selection and funding of the ICSSR projects given their concentration in the North, within the North, in Delhi and within Delhi in JNU. The region-wise break up of projects of ICSSR as available to the First Review Committee showed that out of 235 research proposals sanctioned by the Council the highest number was from Delhi (42), followed by U.P. (39) and Maharashtra (Vol. II of Report, p. 67). The percentage of ICSSR's resources going to various States showed a similar pattern (Vol. I, *Ibid.*, p. 26). Gujarat and Maharashtra accounting for 10-15 per cent of resources, U.P. 15-20 per cent and Delhi above 20 per cent. The State-wise distribution of 323 Doctoral Fellowships given by the Second Review Committee shows 48.9 per cent going to Delhi and 10.8 per cent going to U.P. Within Delhi, JNU accounted for the bulk of Fellowships (Report of Second Review Committee, p. 30). The Third Review Committee's data showed that this concentration continued though with some moderation, in the period 1980-81 to 1985-86, Delhi accounting for 23 per cent of research grants, UP 15 per cent Maharashtra 11 per cent and West Bengal 8 per cent (Third Review Committee Report, p. 14). The Committee observed that there is little hope of remedying this bias as long as there is a thin spread of research across the country (*Ibid.*, p. 17).

Decentralization: Regional Centres

In the context of V.K.R.V. Rao's early suggestions, ICSSR's attempt at decentralization may be noted. The First Review Committee recommended that ICSSR should accept as a long term objective, the principle of decentralization in the structure and techniques of functioning which would involve setting up of a State Social Science Research Centre in each State and decentralizing to it the powers and responsibilities for promotion, liaison and project formulation and project approval in fellowship awards and documentation and library services. As a beginning, it wanted six Regional Centres to be set up in the North, North-West, East, West and the South (two Centres) with an advisory committee consisting of one person from each of the universities and research institutions in the region and a few officials of the (State) governments (First Review Report Vol. I: 137-139). Accordingly, Western [Bombay (Now Mumbai)], Southern (Hyderabad) and Eastern (Kolkata) regional centres were created in 1975, followed in the period 1975-77 by the Northern (New Delhi at JNU), the North-Eastern (Shillong) and the North-Western (Chandigarh) Centres. However, no State Centres could be set up. The Second Review Committee while supporting the proposal for Regional and State Centres also recommended establishment of ICSSR Information Centres in each of the universities of the country (Second Review Report: 47-50). Observing that the idea of State Centres has not taken off because of budget constraint, the Third Review Committee suggested that Research Institutes could also undertake some of the functions of regional centres. The ICSSR bureaucracy, however, opposed the proposal.

Among other things, the Regional Centres are to be responsible for promoting the policies and programmes of the ICSSR in the region, assist in the organization of its programmes within the region, assist it in identifying young social scientists in the region, maintain documentation and bibliographical services especially in the modern Indian languages, operate the programmes of study grants and fellowships assigned to them and collect, preserve, and make available research materials about the region (and in the regional languages) to all social scientists in the country. The work of the Regional Centres has been reviewed by various Committees in 1980, 1988, 1998 and 2002 (ICSSR Newsletter, 2004). However, none of them led to any major changes or revitalization. In 2001, the Council decided to make the Regional Centres an integral part of the ICSSR and granted its employees the status of ICSSR employees which really meant deconcentration and not devolution.

Regional Research Institutes—A second aspect of decentralization, originally envisaged by the V.K.R.V. Rao Committee, was Regional Research Institutes that do not constitute either affiliated or constituent institutions of statutory universities and that are entitled both to maintenance and development grants from the ICSSR. The Ministry initiated a scheme of its own in 1969 (in the Fourth Plan), but transferred it to the ICSSR in the Fifth Plan when there were nine such institutes including two in Delhi (ICSSR, 1974). These Institutions are referred to as Regional Research Institutions not only because they were either started/assisted by the respective State governments but also because the focus of their research was on the regional problems of the State in which they were located. The Third Review Committee noted that beginning with nine institutes in 1974-75, their number was expected to rise to 25 in the Seventh Plan period (1985-90), and that they accounted for 42 per cent of Sixth Plan expenditure of the Council. The Annual Report of the ICSSR for 2002-03 shows that there were then 27 such research institutes and that State governments paid them grants totalling Rs. 747 lakh as against Rs. 1152 lakhs paid as grants by the ICSSR. A detailed statement for one year (2002-03) may be seen in Table 8.1.

Five of the Institutes were located in Delhi, being effectively Central institutions and they got Rs. 525 lakhs as grants. In States like AP and Karnataka where there are multiple institutions, state governments funded only one institution. Maharashtra had one, but the State government did not fund it. State governments, of course, are in greater financial difficulties and their grants have tended to remain static over a period but there appears to be a lack of a dialogue between the ICSSR and State governments. The Third Review Committee noted the dysfunctional role of some State governments in the following terms:

Table 8.1: Tabular Statement showing State & ICSSR Grants to ICSSR Institutes in 2002-03

(Rupees in Lakh)

No.	*Name of the Institute*	*Grant by State Govt.*	*Grant by ICSSR*
1	Institute of Social and Economic Change (ISEC), Bangalore, (Karnataka)	102.46	141.00
2	Centre for Development Studies (CDS), Trivandrum (Kerala)	89.90	128.00
3	Centre for Study of Social Sciences (CSSS), Calcutta (West Bengal)	66.74	78.30
4	Gandhian Institute of Studies (GIS) Varanasi (U.P.)	—	—
5	ANISS, Patna (Bihar)	50.00	70.00
6	IPE, Hyderabad (A.P.)	—	41.00
7	CSS, Surat (Gujarat)	46.00	46.00
8	MIDS, Chennai (Tamil Nadu)	24.05	70.00
9	IIE, Pune (Maharashtra)	—	37.00
10	GIDS, Lucknow (U.P.)	57.52	67.00
11	SPIESR, Ahmedabad (Gujarat)	39.25	86.00
12	GBPSSI, Allahabad (U.P.)	54.07	62.00
13	IDS, Jaipur (Rajasthan)	18.00	56.00
14	CRRID, Chandigarh (Haryana)	51.00	52.00
15	CESS, Hyderabad (A.P.)	15.00	51.00
16	NKCCDS, Bhubaneswar (Orissa)	101.00	50.00
17	GIDR, Ahmedabad (Gujarat)	19.00	38.00
18	OK DISC&D, Guwahati (Assam)	10.00	78.00
19	CMDR, Dharvad (Karnataka)	—	48.00
20	BANISS, Mhow	310.00	13.00
21	MPISSR, Ujjain	10.00	40.00

Source: Annual Report of ICSSR, 2002-03, pp. 122-123, and passim.

> "When the Institutes were established, ICSSR together with the 'founder' attempted to establish close links with the State governments. The expectation was that institutes stood to gain financially and academically from this linkage. In some cases, this expectation has tended to be misplaced. There are instances of State governments wanting to thrust their nominees as Director or postponing decisions for a long time

> to the detriment of the Institute. The nominees (of the Council) on the Governing Body can play an effective role in persuading the State governments and the institutes to take necessary decisions expeditiously."

The same Committee, however, rightly emphasized the regional role of the Institutes, stating: "They have played a significant role in expanding and raising the quality of research and in strengthening the research capability in regions away from Delhi. Their close links with the State Governments, planning bodies and public sector organizations have led to greater consciousness about the use of research to help policy makers."

Policy for Social Science Research

At this stage, two general issues, one of which was specifically articulated by V.K.R.V. Rao and the other one which was implicit may be considered. The first related to a policy for Social Science Research—para 98 of the recommendations of Rao Committee reproduced in appendix of ICSSR: Annual Report 1969-70 states:

> "The scientific policy resolution of March 1958 declares its faith in scientific and technological research. What is needed is an extension of this declaration to social science research with similar emphasis and expression of Government attitude."

The first Chairman and Member-Secretary who perhaps did not share the exuberance of Prof. V.K.R.V. Rao, do not appear to have pursued this aspect.

The UGC came up for the first time in 1978 with a policy framework for higher education in which, however, there is no reference to the role of social sciences within the arena of the UGC. The UGC is represented on all Social Science Councils but not the other way around. The NPE 1986 does not make any reference to social sciences. In the period 2002-04, ICSSR talked about the need for a 'National Social Science Policy' (*ICSSR Newsletter*, October-December, 2002) which, among other things would emphasize proper institutional linkages between ICSSR, ICPR, ICHR and CSIR, co-ordinate with the UGC in the matter of social science teaching and research and increase funding for social science research. This is followed up below. The S & T Policy Statement (2003) announced during the NDA Regime says that closer interaction of those involved in the natural sciences and technology, social sciences, humanities and other scholarly pursuits will be facilitated to bring about mutual reinforcement, added value and impact.

In view of above the matter of enunciating a social science policy was revived. The IASSI appears to have taken a lead in this matter. While a detailed presentation of the contents of the policy is out of the scope of present survey, it may be said that they consider the basic objective of the National Social Science Policy to be to restructure social science education at the school and higher level of education so as to make it relevant to the Indian social realities. Apparently, the focus is on making social science education vocation-oriented and the administrative agenda is to have a National Social Science Council on which *inter alia*, IASSI and other professional societies would be represented. IASSI organized a series of discussions, one of which was held in Tata Institute of Social Sciences, Mumbai in March 2003, which was reported in *Economic and Political Weekly (EPW)* (Ritambara Hebbar, 2003).

For some time, ICSSR also engaged in public discussion in this matter, but the matter became politicized, i.e. it was identified as an agenda of the right-wing intellectuals within the NDA and, therefore, after May 2004, the issue fell by the way side.

Funding Target for Social Science Research

The other important issue which arises out of V.K.R.V. Rao's comparison with S & T is that of funding and specifically whether social science research in India should get a fixed percentage of public investment as a proportion of National Income. Such debates have become common since the Kothari Report, which fixed a target ratio of 6 per cent for education, which includes higher education and research including social science research. It may be noted that for higher education as a whole, a ratio of 1.5 per cent of National Income has been projected by the CABE Report on Financing of Higher and Technical Education (CABE, 2005).

In relation to social science research, in the founding Conference of the Association of Social Science Research Councils of Asia (ASREC) held at Shimla in May 1973, Malcolm Adisheshiah (1974) enunciated a goal of 5 per cent of total investment in S & T to be available as minimum allocation for social sciences in any given year. Since investment in S & T was Rs.17,660.21 crore in 2000-01, in the social science field, it should have been Rs. 883 crore as per this norm. Actually it was in the region of Rs. 40 crore (Rs. 31.50 crore by Research Councils and Rs. 8 crores under UGC). The Research Council-wise break up was:

- ICSSR—Rs. 25.50 crore,
- ICHR—Rs. 3.86 crore, and
- ICPR—Rs. 2.14 crore.

Unfortunately, the lead of Adisheshiah, who was a distinguished economist as well as a former UNESCO bureaucrat with exposure to such global issues, has not been followed up subsequently either by the ICSSR or by any NGO.

Vaidyanathan Review Committee suggested allocation of 0.1 per cent of public sector plan outlay be earmarked for social science research. This leaves non-plan component hanging in the mid-air. Moreover, the basis for suggesting such a ratio is unclear (Vaidyanathan, 2008).

ICSSR on the Decline?

An international review (2002) has deplored perception of the decline of the role of the ICSSR as an apex body of the social sciences research since the latter half of 1980s, the two symptoms of decline being: (1) physical expansion of the administrative apparatus that consumed an ever-increasing share of resources, and (2) a perception of delays, hassles and unimaginative routinization of the ICSSR's procedures for awards, grants and fellowships.

After 1986 which is generally considered to mark the turning point when the decline of the ICSSR began, there was no internal review of the Research Council. It was reported that the Council Body considered that since there was no formal provision for review in its MoA, there was no need. As noted, ICSSR continued to review its Regional Centres and Research Institutes periodically. Apparently, the last act of the outgoing Chairman, Andre Beteille was to appoint a Review Committee, but the Review might have been arranged in terms of the Expenditure Commission's recommendation rather than from any urge at periodical self-assessment. The Report has not been disseminated in hard form, but the EPW of 2nd February 2008 has given a summary of the same.

Briefly, the Fourth Review Committee, after noting the achievements of the Council till date (support to 27 national institutes, funding of 3000 research projects, award of 400 research fellowships and 860 doctoral fellowships and provision of services like documentation, training in research methodology and use of computers) is blunt in underlining the disappointing performance of the Council as below: (1) Commercialization of social research in that it is driven by the interests and concerns of the sponsors as distinct from public interest, (2) Decline in the supply of teachers in higher education, (3) Decline both in intent in and competence of academics for rigorous research on societal trends: survey of research articles in select social science journals showed that 40 per cent of authors were located in research institutes and only a one-third in universities, (4) External constraints in the form of governmental domination of decision-making, (5) Internal weaknesses in the form of ad-hocism in promotions and recruitment. The Committee recommends: (i) functional and financial autonomy to the Council (it suggests that the reconstituted body be called Indian Academy of Social Sciences), (ii) Expansion in the scope of its activities as also 0.1 per cent of public sector plan outlay being earmarked for social science research, (iii) Changing strategy of funding—a substantial part of its resources should be devoted to selected broad areas/themes, (iv) Block grants to existing Institutions to be frozen, Institutions being required to seek Council funding for individual projects, (v) Simplification of monitoring of funding system and (vi) Autonomy in personnel matters.

The basic proposal for devoting the bulk of funding for selected broad themes is reminiscent of the old strategy of planned social research. The essence of research process is the freedom of the researcher to choose his topic. This needs to be honoured. Moreover, there is lack of clarity relating to the source for meeting non-plan expenditure of the Council. It needs to be noted that reducing Government representation on the Board of Governors may not reduce politicization of the Council which began with the appointment by Indira Gandhi of G. Parthasarathi (a journalist-diplomat) as Chairman. After all, the Government representatives were appointed as users or producers of research and if present at all, could not have dictated priorities in any substantial manner. Where is the guarantee that a Member-Secretary may not be approached by Minister's office for a particular course of action contrary to the Council's academic policy, and be made to face the consequences for non-compliance? Politicization eroded the Council's authority further during the NDA Government. This was apparently due to an inappropriate choice of the Chairman. The ICSSR became as politicized as the ICHR. But a Chairman may adversely affect the functioning of the Council not only because he does not know the limits of propriety but because he may be cliquey. The point of the change of nomenclature of the Council to Academy is not clear. (Margaret Thatcher renamed SSRC in UK to ESRC because of her allergy for the term 'society' but this made no difference to the functioning of the Council).

Lastly, the Review Committee's approach to the point of involvement of the States in the working of the Council is not clear. Would the number of 27 institutes be frozen? There are multiple Institutions in Delhi and also Karnataka. The Council needs to go beyond the conventional wisdom about developed States not being eligible for any more institutions. Take the case of Maharashtra which has no ICSSR institution worth the name. The Pune-based Indian Institute of Education is narrow in focus and, by all accounts, its functioning could be improved. The Gokhale Institute also at Pune having opted for the Deemed University status with a focus on Economics, there is a dire need for a well-funded ICSSR institute in Maharashtra, which can devote itself to research on socio-economic problems of Maharashtra. It is not clear if the Review Committee's approach would allow this.

Other Research Councils: General

The discussion relating to the remaining Councils devoted to historical and philosophical research respectively has to be necessarily brief, partly because of their smaller compass and limited funding, but mainly due to paucity of documentation. A word may be said about the choice of these particular disciplines which are basically humanistic. History appears to have claimed priority partly because of interest of powerful personalities (Nurul Hasan as Minister of State for Education being a historian of the Aligarh School) and partly because of the coincidence of the British Government's "Transfer of Power" volumes on the end of the Raj having appeared at about the time and the clamour for Indian side of the historical source material being published for which an organization was required. Philosophy was perhaps prioritized because of the interest of a Minister close to Indira Gandhi (Prof. D.P. Chattopadhyay). It was also considered as an area in which India was perceived to have made a unique contribution in the past and because, in the face of the increasingly vocational bias in the choice of subjects (Commerce, Information Technology, etc.), it was considered as an area requiring special government patronage.

In the matter of projects financed and the level of funding, the Indian Council of Historical Research (ICHR) and the Indian Council of Philosophical Research (ICPR) have always been junior partners of the ICSSR. Their funding is about one-fourth or less than that of ICSSR. The comparative financial allocation for a single year for which comparable data are available (2002-03) is as below:

Name of the Council	*Final Outlay (Rs. in crore)*
ICSSR	33.61
ICHR	07.31
ICPR	04.37

Indian Council of Historical Research (ICHR)

The ICHR was set up because it was felt that "there was a need to promote historical research to strengthen national consciousness and identity, to promote application of historical method to the study of social sciences and to enunciate and implement a national policy of historical research" (ICHR Review Committee, 1982). A working group was set up in December 1971 by the Ministry of Education to work out the details of such a body, its objectives, functions and organizational set-up. The Council was inaugurated on 27th March, 1972. The ICHR's 'objects' contain a specific reference to State Governments, i.e. about entering into arrangements with Government of India, State Governments and other public or private organizations for furtherance of its objectives. There is no indication however, that it has acted in terms of this object. In addition to Chairman and eighteen historians nominated by the Government of India, there are three representatives of Government, viz. Department of Education, Culture and Finance on its Council. Representatives of the UGC and other Councils are special invitees. Director-General (DG), Archaeological Survey of India and D-G National Archives are *ex-officio* members.

Review Committees for ICHR were reportedly appointed in 1982, 1999 and 2004 but these were not disseminated as was done by the ICSSR. ICHR has no regional institutions, but it has regional centres at Bangalore and at Guwahati. Unlike ICSSR which was comparatively free from political controversies till recently, ICHR has been hobbled by controversies from the times of the Janata Rule (1977-79). The axis of controversy has been about the control of that institution by scholars of a particular ideology. Thus, it was perceived that till 1977, it was controlled by historians of the leftist-secular ideology. In June-July 1998, it was alleged by leftists that the then NDA Government was trying to alter the aims and objectives of the Council and pack the Council with historians of rightist—communalist perspective. The well-known journalist Arun Shourie wrote a polemical tract on this subject (1998). The gist of what he argued was that there was no substance in allegations regarding the change of aims and objects of ICHR during the NDA regime, but that eminent historians from JNU, AMU and from Delhi University made statements which were not factually based and had benefited personally from their earlier control of the ICHR from which they had drawn substantial advances which were not accounted for properly. Arun Shourie, may be considered to be an interested party but some of the factual material marshalled by him was compelling and does not appeared to have been refuted. After the arrival on the scene of the UPAI Government from May 2004 onwards, the tide has turned. The ICHR, along with the school sector institution NCERT, were charged with having implemented during the NDA regime a 'saffronizatien agenda' in their textbooks and projects respectively which trend was sought to be reversed. The point to note is the political struggle for capture of cultural institutions *à la Gramsci* which raises the issue of feasibility of insulation of such institutions from political influences, when they depend almost cent-per-cent for their funding on the Government.

Indian Council of Philosophical Research (ICPR)

There was a time gap between registration of ICPR in March 1977 and its activation in July 1981. Fresh elections had been called in 1977 and the Janata Government (1977-79) had no interest in the new institution. It appears that in the mid-seventies a team of scholars made a careful study of the whole question relating to the revitalization of the Indian tradition of philosophizing and suggested that in addition to other efforts, the Government of India should come forward to establish an Indian Council of Philosophical Research (ICPR). Its first Chairman was Prof. D.P. Chattopadhyaya. The Government of India nominates 12 members to the ICPR Council and the Council has the power to co-opt four philosophers as well as a representative of Indian Philosophical Congress. *It is to be noted that ICSSR and ICHR do not have an analogous power*. In addition to representatives of the UGC and the two research councils (social science/history), there is a representative of the Indian National Science Academy (INSA) and two representatives of the Government of India (Education Ministry/Finance Ministry). ICPR has an academic centre at Butler Palace, Lucknow and hence some linkage with the Uttar Pradesh Government, but otherwise it has no regional/state institutions/branches (ICPR, 2002).

A Council for Art and Humanities?

There is one organizational lacuna in the research scene of Indian higher education, namely the absence of a council for promotion of arts and humanities. In UK, which has served as a model for India in regard to the setting up of Social Science Research Council, there was a Research Board for Arts and Humanities recently converted into a regular Council (THES: issues for 2005). What is clear is that for any Arts and Humanities Council, we have to begin with in India Sahitya Akademi as a core institution. It gives awards for best books in various Indian languages every year, but does not promote research in literature and languages, which remains confined to the universities. Haksar Committee reportedly reviewed the working of all Akademies and its Report should be a starting point for any Arts and Humanities Research Council in India.

In UK, there is also a post of D-G Research Councils to co-ordinate activities of all such councils. One alternative is to have the ICSSR, which is the senior Council, to assume the role of a co-ordinator as well as regional facilitator on behalf of the two remaining Councils. But this requires Inter-Council co-ordination, which is lacking. A heartening step was taken recently by the UGC which constituted a committee involving the academic heads not only of ICSSR, ICHR and ICPR but also the Sahitya Akademi and the first meeting was held under the Chairmanship of the then Vice-Chairman of the UGC in July 2003 (*UGC News*, 2003 issue). But this was an isolated initiative without any continuity.

Indian Institute of Advanced Studies, Shimla

The Report of the Ministry for 2007-08 states (pp. 140-142) that IIAS was set up in 1965 and housed in Rashtrapati Niwas, Shimla. (This was at the personal initiative of S. Radhakrishnan who was then the President of India). The objects of the Institute are stated to be: free and creative enquiry into the fundamental themes and problems of life and thought. For this, the Institute promotes advanced research in humanities, social sciences, S & T and Development, maintenance of a library and documentation facilities. It gives financial assistance for advanced study for teachers. The Institute organizes national seminars. Recently, IIAS has been made into an "Inter-University Centre" (IUC) of the UGC as part of which 40 university and college teachers visited IIAS, Shimla. The latest UGC Reports indicate that this arrangement has been terminated and future UGC assistance would be on project basis.

Initially the IIAS had eminent scholars as Directors, e.g. Prof. S.C. Dube, Prof. V.K. Gokak, etc. They organized seminars on important subjects which became standard reference material, but there has been a progressive deterioration in the quality of research and publications. The basic problem about the Institute appears to be its location on a hill-station, as a result of which it is not able to work the year round, being closed for three winter months. In 1982-84, there was some exploratory thinking to shift the Institute to the plains, but there was no consensus about any alternative location. Subsequently, a committee was appointed which plumped for retention of the existing location and all talk of shifting ceased. Another stir was caused when there was a court case about conservation of the Rashtrapati Nivas but it apparently subsided. The Institute which was modelled on the Centre for Advanced Studies Princeton/All Souls College, Oxford has not been able to attain similar eminence.

Private Sector Initiative

A charity of the Tatas has recently set up a National Institute for Advanced Studies (NIAS) in Bangalore (now Bengaluru) along the lines similar to the IIAS. Naturally, there can be comparison between the Shimla and Bangalore Institutes. But time is not ripe to judge definitively about superiority of either. In a vast country like India, there is scope not for two, but at least for five such advanced centres corresponding to the Zones of the country identified in the Zonal Councils Act set up consequent on the States Reorganization in 1956.

Part II
Higher Technical and Professional Education and Research

9

Technical (Engineering and Management) Education

Introduction

In this chapter, author will deal with the development of technical education in India with special reference to various apex bodies and also the IITs and IIMs.

Technical Education is tripartite, consisting of: (a) craftsmen level education imparted in the Industrial Training Institutions (ITIs), (historically ITIs have been handled by the Labour Ministry), (b) diploma level education imparted in polytechnics, and (c) degree level education imparted in engineering colleges and other degree awarding Technical Education Institutions (TEIs). These latter two comprise higher technical education under the Education Ministry. On the eve of Independence, India had 39 degree level and 53 diploma level TEI's with an intake capacity of 2940 and 3670 respectively, and the facilities for post-graduate degree courses in engineering and technology were non-existent (Mathew, 1990: 97).

Organization

The Sargent Plan envisaged the establishment of an all-India body to stimulate, co-ordinate and control the policy and provision of higher technical education facilities which would be needed for substantial industrial development in the post-war period, and since the

Association of Principals of Technical Institutions in India (APTI), set up in 1943, could not play the role of such an all-India body, it recommended the establishment of a National Council for Technical Education to control policy and to deal with all higher technical institutions except the technological departments of the universities. The Sargent Plan conceived of higher technical education as a national rather than a provincial subject, *inter alia*, on the following grounds: (a) locations of higher technical institutions should logically be determined by location of connected industries, (b) admissions must be on merit to exclude provincial pressure for admission on the basis of domicile, (c) provinces would not be able to maintain a strong staff component for performing the functions of inspection and advice in regard to technical institutions of the first rank. As a corollary, the whole cost of higher technical institutions was to be borne by the Central Government (Sargent Plan, 1944: V. 14).

Advisory AICTE as an Apex Body

The Government of India, however, established by its Resolution dated 30th November, 1945, what was called not a national but an All-India Council for Technical Education (AICTE) which was specifically mandated to be an advisory body. The functions of the proposed advisory body were: survey of the field, consideration of the immediate projects and conduct of preliminary investigations. The Government stated that grant of executive, administrative or controlling functions to the proposed body would take some time, as it required discussions with and agreement with various authorities, thus reflecting uncertainty on the constitutional front at that time.

The advisory body had more than 100 members, including representatives of the UGC, the IUB, industry, labour, etc. but care was taken to make it (federally) representative, i.e. each of the States (having an engineering college/polytechnic) was represented. The Union Minister for Education was its Chairman and the Bureau of Technical Education of the Ministry worked as its Secretariat. Its functioning was decentralized with four regional offices. The AICTE continued to be advisory instead of being converted into a national body with substantive powers apparently because the CABE had not approved its conversion into a statutory body. It was assisted by a co-ordinating committee, regional committees and all-India Boards of Technical Education.*

Incidentally, there appeared to be a disconnect between the thinking of the Sargent Plan and of the Radhakrishnan Commission (1949) whose mandate covered technical education also. The Commission was aware of the existence of the AICTE because it has referred to the information furnished by the AICTE regarding progress of the setting up of four Higher Technical Institutes (*ibid.*, pp. 162-163), but it deals with the financial assistance to higher technical education, without taking note of AICTE's functions. Thus, it suggests in Chapter VII. 42 that the distribution of government funds should be done through the UGC which will be assisted by an Advisory Panel of Engineers and Technologists which would advise the Commission: (a) on the needs of the country for technical and engineering personnel by periodic surveys of industry and other institutions, (b) on the initiation of post-graduate training and research at different centres. This recommendation is repeated in Chapter XIII.16 also.

The Education Commission (1966) is somewhat critical of the AICTE, calling it an unwieldy body meeting hardly once a year, whose Boards of Studies do the work which normally should be done by universities through their Board of Studies. While conceding that it performs a useful function as a high level policy formulating agency, it wanted it to be replaced by a UGC-type body to be specially set up for engineering education (Kothari Report: 15.85). The author feels that the Education Communiohas underestimated the performance of the AICTE in its formative years. The assessment of the valuable work performed by the AICTE is set out in the paragraphs which follow *vide* pp. 223-227.

The National Policy on Education (NPE) 1968, altogether skirted the issue of a UGC-type body to replace advisory AICTE. Regarding technical education it contented itself with the following bland statements: [para 8(6)].

> "In technical education, practical training in industry should form an integral part of such education. Technical education

* Some of the material in this chapter is drawn from the Ninth Report of the Estimates Committee (1977-78) on Higher Technical Education (New Delhi, Lok Sabha Secretariat, January 1977).

and research should be related closely to industry, encouraging the flow of personnel both ways and providing for continuous co-operation in the provision, design and periodical review of training programme and facilities."

Reorganization of Advisory AICTE

Till 1974, the AICTE was served by the multiplicity of Boards of Studies as mentioned below:

1. Board of Post-graduate Engineering and Research.
2. All-India Board of Technical Studies in Management.
3. All-India Board of Technician (i.e. Polytechnic) Education.
4. All-India Board of Technical Studies in Engineering and Metallurgy.
5. All-India Board of Architecture and Regional Planning.
6. All-India Board of Applied Arts.
7. All-India Board of Chemical Engineering and Technology.
8. All-India Board of Textile Technology.
9. All-India Board of Commerce.
10. Pharmaceutical Education Committee.

The AICTE in its meeting of 17th May, 1974 authorized the Chairman to reorganize these Boards and redefine their functions. Accordingly, from May 1976, the ten Boards were consolidated into the following four Boards (*vide* Ninth Report of the Estimates Committee, January 1977: 238-253, 283-287):

(1) The All-India Board of Post-Graduate Engineering Studies and Research.
(2) The All-India Board of Under Graduate Studies in Engineering and Technology.
(3) The All-India Board of Management Studies.
(4) The All-India Board of Technician Education.

The logic of the organization was to consolidate all the various Boards for under-graduate education including pharmaceutical education into one single Board on the analogy of the Post-Graduate Board, the identity of Technician Board (for polytechnics) and

Management education being kept intact. The functions of the Boards included not only to identify and approve new institutions and courses but also to lay down minimum standards and norms, to promote research and development and collaboration between technical education institutions on the one hand and the national laboratories on the other.

Achievements of Advisory AICTE

Expansion and Diversification of Technical Education

The main achievement of the Advisory AICTE was the tremendous expansion and diversification it brought about in the technical education streams and courses and the role performed by it as a federal body. At the time of the adoption of the National Policy on Education 1986, the number of engineering colleges and technical institutions at the degree level had increased from 39 in 1947 to 150 with an admission capacity of 30,000 and the number of polytechnics had increased from 53 in 1947 to 450, with annual admission capacity of 70,000 students. The number of institutions offering Post-graduate courses in engineering and technology had increased from nil in 1947 to 80 with an annual intake capacity of more than 6,000 students. At central level, high quality institutions like five Indian Institutes of Technology (IITs) had come up—IIT, Kharagpur 1951; IIT, Bombay (Now Mumbai) 1958; IIT, Madras (Now Chennai) 1959; IIT, Kanpur 1960 and IIT, Delhi 1961. In addition, on the recommendations of the Engineering Personnel Committee (1955) of the Planning Commission, eight Regional Colleges of Engineering were set up in early sixties (two in each region—East, West, North and South), whose number went up to 17. The four Indian Institutes of Management [Ahmedabad and Culcutta (Kolkata) in 1961, Bangalore in 1973 and Lucknow in 1984] imparted management education at the highest level. Apart from this, MBA was offered in 45 universities. Other Central Institutions were: National Institution of Training in Industrial Engineering (NITIE) at Bombay (Now Mumbai); National Institute of Foundry and Forge Technology (NIFFT) at Ranchi and the School of Planning and Architecture in New Delhi. Other courses available were: computer education and hotel management and catering technology (PoA 1986: Chapter VIII).

Its role as a Federal Body

AICTE had no doubt a dual role—planning for the country as a whole and implementation of Plans in relation to the Centre. In sharp contrast to the approach of the UGC, however, AICTE involved State Governments, i.e. State Ministers and State Secretaries and Directors of Technical Education closely in its decision-making. The interface between the AICTE and the States may be considered under five broad heads: Representation and Participation, Decentralization in the shape of deconcentration, State level Capacity Building, creation of National Resource Institutions and creation of Regional Engineering Colleges (RECs) embodying Centre-State co-operation.

(i) Representation and Participation

All the State Governments were represented on the general body of the AICTE. There was a co-ordinating committee equivalent to an executive committee consisting of 26 members whose decisions relating to the opening of new institutions and expansion of existing institutions were required to be implemented by the State Governments, which received financial assistance from the Planning Commission (Estimates Committee Report 1977: 240). In the first twenty years or so, the quadrangular relationship between the Ministry, the AICTE, the Planning Commission and State Governments worked comparatively smoothly. The meetings of the AICTE were initially held regularly, i.e. at least once a year and State Governments were fully involved when important systemic decisions were required to be taken, as when in February 1968 intake capacity of engineering colleges and polytechnics was cut back due to the economic recession. This unpleasant decision was required to be taken because the target of the Third Plan (1961-66) to have admission capacity of 25,000 degree holders in engineering courses was nearly achieved in 1966-67. When in 1967, reports started coming in from several parts of the country about increasing unemployment among engineering graduates and diploma holders due to recession in industry, Ministry advised State Governments in February 1968, to reduce admissions to technical institutions on a selective basis. As a result, admissions to the degree courses were cut back from 24,000 earlier to 15,400 and to diploma courses from 48,000 to 38,000 in the year 1968-69 (A. Mathew, 1990: 103, Estimates Committee, 1977: 13).

(ii) Decentralization through Deconcentration

While the UGC, for long, resisted the idea of setting up of regional offices on the ground that such a step smacked of "regionalism" and was against national integration, AICTE took a pragmatic view and, *ab initio*, worked through four Regional Committees located at Bombay (Now Mumbai), Culcutta (now Kolkata), Kanpur and Madras (Now Chennai). The functions of the Regional Committees included surveying facilities in technical education and making recommendations as to the development of existing institutions, the introducing of new courses and establishing of new institutions, promoting liaison between the technical institutions and technical research establishments, reviewing the academic aspects of training in collaboration with the respective State Boards of Technical Education and rendering advice and guidance to technical institutions. These Regional Committees which were fully representative of State Governments, technical institutions and the industry in the region were served by a secretariat drawn from the Ministry. The State Governments in the region submitted their proposals for expansion and development of technical education to the Regional Committees, which examined the same with the assistance of Visiting Committees. The Regional Committees made recommendations regarding both the first-degree institutions and the diploma-level institutions for consideration of the AICTE, the latter in consultation with the State Boards of Technical Education (Estimates Committee, 1977: 241).

(iii) Capacity Building at the State Level

The administration of technical institutions was a divided responsibility between different departments in most States partly due to the legacy of the Dyarchy when it was common for the State Industries Departments to deal with technical education. The AICTE ensured that each State established a Directorate of Technical Education and a separate State Board of Technical Education for diploma education. The State Board was composed of representatives from industry and commerce, universities, technical institutions and other interests concerned, as well as departmental officers. It was competent to prescribe courses of study for institutions not affiliated to universities, especially polytechnics, hold examinations and award diplomas and certificates. Thus, States were equipped to manage as well as ensure quality and standards of technician education including work relating to apprenticeship training in industries. In the 21st meeting of the AICTE (1972) it was decided to prepare a Model Act for the establishment of State Boards of Technical Education as statutory bodies and most State Governments had set up such boards to manage polytechnic education (Mathew, 1990: 93-94).

(iv) Creation of National Resource Institutions for States and UTs

The setting up of the Technical Teachers' Training Institutes (TTTIs) at Bhopal, Culcutta (Kolkata), Chandigarh and Madras (Now Chennai) in 1967 by the AICTE in a way represents establishment of National Resource Institutions at diploma level technical education, comparable to the NCERT in school education. The TTTIs organized training of polytechnic teachers and curriculum development work for the States, involving development of instructional material. They also offered continuing education programmes through the Distance mode (AICTE, 1999: 127-129). To bring the story up-to-date, a review committee (2000) [Chairman—P.V. Indiresan] reviewed the work of the TTTIs and recommended that they be renamed as "National Institutes of Technical Education & Research" with the enlarged scope of co-ordinating training programmes for degree level institutions not only in engineering, but in architecture and management, with corresponding enhanced financial allocation (Annual Report of Ministry, 2004-2005: 216).

(v) Centre-State Co-operation through the RECs

The 17 Regional Engineering Colleges, roughly one REC per major State which came up in the period 1959 to 1987 are examples of Centre-State Cooperation in degree-level engineering education. The State Governments provided developed land free of cost, bore 50 per cent of recurring expenditure on UG courses and had parity of representation on the Board of Governors of the REC with the Chairman being appointed in consultation with the State Government.

Jai Krishna Committee (1974), which reviewed their work specifically identified following as an important aim of an REC: "to act as important link in the interaction between the Central and State institutions of technical education." Their under-graduate intake capacity as assessed in 1978 was 5182 and 14 RECs had facilities for post-graduate education also. They were to serve as pace-setters for State engineering colleges—State Government's Brand IITs, so to say. Admissions were made through a common entrance test conducted at the State level and 50 per cent of seats were filled from within the State (AICTE, 1979: 85, 87, 118-125). The fact that consequent on a high-powered review committee's recommendations (Report of the REC's, 1998), they have been converted into National Institutes of Technology (NITs) does not detract from the initial achievement of the Advisory AICTE.

The Delay in Making the AICTE Statutory

The advisory AICTE pre-dated the UGC by at least a decade. Before giving financial assistance to the university departments of engineering and technology for teaching and research, the UGC turned to the AICTE whose visiting committees examined and assessed the requirements of the universities/institutions within the broad policies laid down by the AICTE for development of engineering and technology (Report of the Estimates Committee, 1977: 248-249). The engineering colleges and polytechnics were directly assisted by the AICTE, i.e. in effect, by the Ministry. The Radhakrishnan Report idea of the Panel of Technologists and Engineers for the UGC had not worked out. The Kothari Commission had criticized the AICTE as an unwieldy body and suggested creation of a UGC-type body for technical education as noted earlier. However, the Technical Education Bureau of the Department was not inclined to let go of its powers and wanted *status quo* to be continued. The Estimates Committee (1977) was not convinced with Government's reasoning for not acting in time on the recommendations of the Kothari Commission for having a joint committee between the AICTE and the UGC to review technical education at under-graduate level. Ironically a decision was taken about this in 1972, but such a committee was set up only in 1974 which was likely to complete its work in 1980. It noted that many of the AICTE's important decisions (like those relating to the abolition of domiciliary restrictions, abolition of capitation fees in private engineering colleges, fixation of norms for recurring expenditure, etc.) were ignored by State governments, apparently because the Council could not take penal action for violation of its decisions/directions. What is more, even the Technical Education Bureau ignored or delayed action on AICTE decisions (e.g. a professional unit for Quality Improvement Programme, assessment of manpower requirement, etc.). Generally, AICTE had failed to perform monitoring and evaluation functions, and there was fragmentation of powers and functions as between the AICTE and the UGC. Moreover, AICTE while it used to meet yearly in the initial years, it had met only 6 times in the 10 years (1966-1976) which gave an impression that bureaucrats ruled the roost. The Estimates Committee, therefore, categorically recommended a single body with suitable administrative, executive and financial powers for development of technical education in the country at the earliest (Report of the Estimates Committee, 1977: 238-264).

This had the desired effect. In the 25th meeting of the AICTE held in 1981 it was decided by the AICTE that in order to ensure its effective functioning, the Council should be conferred statutory status (A. Mathew, 1990: 112). The AICTE Act was, however, passed only in 1987. It would be useful to consider the policy environment which led to this delay.

Policy Environment of the Functioning of the Statutory AICTE

As noted, NPE 1968 did not give any lead in the matter of technical education. After the Prime Minister Rajiv Gandhi had assumed office in November 1984, and after he had announced in January 1985 to revise the NPE 1968, 'The Challenge of Education Document' issued in August 1985 had a lot to say about technical education. After acknowledging the significant contribution made by technical education to India's economic development, it noted following weaknesses in the system: obsolescence of machinery and equipment, outdated curricula, weakness of polytechnic (i.e. technician) education, shortage of teachers (estimated in 1985 at 20-30 per cent), institutional dualism (IITs/RECs on the one hand and Sate institutions on the other). It significantly referred to the Technology Policy

Statement issued in January 1983 which emphasized the need for modernization, action in respect of newly emerging technological areas, expansion of management education for public sector and other underserved sectors (agriculture, rural development, education, health, social welfare) (para 3.41 to 3.48 of Technology Policy Statement). NPE 1986/92 devoted one whole part (VI) to Technical and Management Education. Its policy recommendation related to statutory status for the AICTE (para 6.19) and a stance against commercialization of technical education (para 6.20). Its thrust areas were: Development of technician education, diversification of U-G courses, special attention to P-G education, strengthening and expansion of technical teacher education and training, provision of facilities for continuing and distance education, women's education and interaction networks. The specific measures suggested by it are: improvement of laboratories, provision of libraries, provision of building amenities, creation of national technical manpower information system (NT-MIS), autonomy for institutions, entrepreneurship development, curriculum development, technical education for women, distance learning, community polytechnics, linkages with industries and R & D organization, modernization and removal of obsolescence. AICTE Act was, no doubt, passed in 1987 but in the meanwhile NPE came under review. Ramamurthy Committee's specific thrust was on Technology for the Poor, strengthening of Regional Offices and regulatory powers to close down non-standard and sub-standard institutions. J. Reddy Committee while agreeing with the first two suggestions stated about the third suggestion that it had opposed such regulatory powers for the UGC and that AICTE should not be more regulatory than the UGC. Moreover, it suggested that the State Education Ministers should head the Regional Offices of the AICTE by rotation. This last suggestion amounted to the take-over by the backdoor of the AICTE by the lobby of self-financing capitation fee colleges. The NPE 1986 when it was amended in 1992 did not accept this suggestion of J. Reddy Committee. In the NPE 1992, the relevant para of NPE 1986 has been amplified to read that "the Council will be strengthened and will function in a decentralized manner with greater involvement of State Governments and technical institutions of good quality" (NPE 1992: 6.19).

AICTE as a Statutory Body

The AICTE Act was passed in 1987 and came into force in 1988. As per S.3(5) of the Act, for the first five years; the Minister HRD was to be the *ex-officio* Chairman and Education Adviser (Technical) of the Central Government, the *ex-officio* Member-Secretary. It is not clear why there should have been a five year delay in the start of the functioning of the AICTE as a statutory body, especially when the recommendation about the statutory AICTE was as old as 1966. Obviously, the Minister HRD was loath to part with power.

The preamble of the AICTE Act lays down the objectives of the AICTE to be (a) proper planning and co-ordinated development of the technical education system throughout the country, (b) promotion of qualitative improvement of such education in relation to planned quantitative growth, and (c) regulation and proper maintenance of norms and standards in the technical education system.

The powers and functions of the Council as laid down in S.10(a) to S.10(u) are correspondingly wide and include: survey, coordination, fund giving, promotion of innovations, R & D, formulation of schemes for weaker sections, training of teachers, norms and standards for courses and curricula, etc., guidelines for tuition and other fees, conduct of inspection of technical institutions and universities, norms for grant of autonomy, steps to be taken to prevent commercialization of technical education, student admission guidelines, inspection, withholding or discontinuance of grants, advice on deemed university status and lastly, setting up of a National Board of Accreditation to periodically conduct evaluation of technical institutions and make recommendations regarding recognition or de-recognition. S.10(k) provides for "granting of approval, for starting of new technical institutions and for introduction of new courses or programmes".

The Council comprises Chairman and Vice-Chairman and Member-Secretary appointed by the Central Government and thirteen officers representing Central Government departments and organizations. Besides, there are on the Council the Chairmen of the Regional Committees, Chairmen of various Boards of Studies, three MPs, four members representing industry and commerce, four members representing professional bodies in the field of technical and management education, and representatives of seven consultative or professional bodies namely CABE, AIU, ISTE, Council of IITs, Pharmacy Council, Council of Architects, and the National Productivity Council. However, there are only eight representatives of the States/UTs appointed by the Central Government in alphabetical order by rotation, although the Council of the advisory AICTE had given representation to all States and UTs having engineering colleges. Not only is the number of state representatives in a 52 strong body of the statutory AICTE very small, the bracketing of States with the UTs for rotational representation would appear to be unfair to the States, because the UTs are basically Centrally administered areas.

The Executive Committee, which is 21 strong, includes four representatives of State Governments. Originally, there were five All-India Boards for Vocational Education, for Technician Education, for under-graduate studies, for Post-graduate education and for Management Studies (*vide* S.13), which number has subsequently been increased to nine. In addition, it has four Advisory Boards. The original Act provided for four regional committees at Kanpur, Madras (Now Chennai), Bombay (Now Mumbai) and Calcutta (Kolkata) but more Regional Committees have been set up at Bangalore (now Bangaluru), Bhopal and Chandigarh and a new one is coming up at Hyderabad (Annual Report of Ministry, 2007-08: 161). There is a provision (S.20) for Central Government giving written directions on questions of policy, but a reference to 'national purposes' (which occurs in the UGC Act, S.20) is absent. S.21 provides for the contingency of the Central Government superseding the Council in case the Council defaults in performance of its duties. It is notable that there is no such provision in the UGC Act. Clearly, the statutory AICTE was designed to be less autonomous than the UGC.

Unfortunately, in spite of Central Government's unhappy experience with a toothless UGC unable to perform its constitutional responsibility of co-ordination and determination of standards, AICTE Act lacks adequate penal provisions. Apart from S.10(g) (withholding or discontinuance of grants in respect of course programmes to such TEIs which fail to comply with the Council's directions) and S.10(u) (which talks of making recommendation regarding de-recognition of institution or programmes), there are no powers with the Council which would hurt self-financed institutions enough to enforce compliance with the Council's directions.

AICTE has been fairly active in regard to formulation of norms and standards for courses and institutions of technical education. It is perhaps the only academic co-ordinating body in India, which, as early as 2003, spelt out detailed regulations for entry and operation of foreign universities/institutions wanting to establish operation in India for imparting technical education. These include mandatory registration with the AICTE, valid accreditation of the institution in its parent country, degrees/diplomas being on par with corresponding degrees in the parent country etc. (Review Committee Report of AICTE, 2003).

A National Board of Accreditation was first set up in 1989 but since it was found to be oversized, its constitution was revised and a 15 member Board started functioning from 1994. Thus the statutory NBA started functioning in the same year as the non-statutory NAAC under the UGC. The NBA, unlike NAAC, accredits not institutions as a whole but programmes. The purpose of the accreditation exercise is to identify those programmes, which meet and exceed current norms and standards as well as other criteria specified by the AICTE, viz. organization and governance, financial resources, allocation and utilization, physical resources, human resources, teaching-learning processes etc. As in December 2003, only 879 programmes from 256 institutions had been accredited as against a total of about 28,000 programmes in 3,589 accreditable institutions. By January 2005, this number had increased to 2,235 programmes from 793 institutions. While about 1/3 of engineering programmes have been accredited, in other areas the proportion is 10 per cent or less (Annual Report of Ministry, 2007-08: 161).

The AICTE Report for 2000-01(p. 12) shows that it has signed an MoU with the Distance Education Council of the IGNOU and that a joint committee had been formed to look into various aspects of technical education imparted in Distance mode in general and for management education and information technology in particular.

Statutory AICTE: A Critique

However, the statutory AICTE has not lived up to the expectations with which it was set up. Part of the blame must be shared by the Ministry of Education which has retained with itself management and funding of major institutions like the IITs, the RECs (now NITs) and several deemed universities in the areas of mining, architecture and town planning and information technology. AICTE cannot conceivably ensure co-ordinated development of technical education all over the country when major institutions remain outside its purview and its main work is confined to sanctioning new institutions and programmes of State Governments and private trusts in the field of technical education, coupled with release of grants for a few development programmes!

Secondly, the drafting of the Act leaves much to be desired. Universities have been claiming that they are outside the purview of the AICTE in terms of S.10(k) of the Act (*vide* p. 230 *ante*) and this stand was upheld by the Supreme Court in the *Bharatidasan University case* (2001). This judgment of the Supreme Court does appear to affect the powers of the AICTE adversely so far as integrated development of technical education is concerned. Certainly, the effect of starting a programme by the university in an area with an over-supply of manpower cannot be said to be desirable. The Supreme Court judgment underlines the need for having a fresh look at the AICTE legislation.

Thirdly, there is inadequate co-ordination with the UGC. While the Chairman UGC is represented on various bodies of the AICTE, Chairman AICTE is not represented on the UGC or its Committees. This creates a lacuna. A related issue is the regulation of deemed universities, AICTE, apparently, does not have any role once any technical institution is declared as such. After 2000, Central Government notified several self-financing institutions as deemed universities most of which were technical or management institutions. The UGC, while making its recommendation about the deemed universities in technical education area, to the Central Government, is required to consult the AICTE, but there was confusion about the post-notification role of the AICTE. Press Reports (*Times of India*, 15th April, 2006) indicate that on 7th April, 2006, Central Government issued a notification under which deemed universities are not required to obtain approval of the AICTE to start any programme in technical or management education. However, they are required to maintain minimum standards prescribed by the AICTE. Since the UGC is not required to ensure compliance with AICTE's minimum standards, the deemed universities appear to have been left scot-free. In the matter of assessment and accreditation there is no co-ordination between the NAAC of the UGC and NAB of the AICTE. Apparently, NAB would require clearance of UGC before accreditation of a university's engineering faculty, but whether NAAC would require co-ordination with the AICTE before accreditation of technical institutions is not clear. There is also confusion regarding academic programmes in hotel management and catering technology. The AICTE norms require a 4-year programme but the universities have been affiliating institutions with 3-year programmes, which are supposed to be under the UGC (AICTE Review Committee Report 2003). There is need for an AICTE-UGC forum to sort out such issues.

Fourthly, AICTE's approach in the matter of rampant expansion of technical educational institutions has not at all been effective. There is the well-known phenomenon of what were originally called 'capitation fee' engineering colleges and what are now euphemistically called as "self-financing". The NPE 1986 enunciated the policy of the Government of India to curb commercialization of technical education and professional education in the interest, inter alia, of maintaining standards (NPE: 6.19). It was included as one of the objects of the AICTE Act [S.10(o)]. The final power of approval vests in the AICTE and not in the Government of India, this being a vital difference between the AICTE and the MCI. The AICTE, however, has failed in curbing commercialization of technical and professional education implying *politicization* of its top leadership. According to the AICTE Review Report 2003, the total number of engineering degree colleges practically doubled in the decade 1980-1990 from around 158 institutions to over 337 and during the decade 1990-2000, it more than doubled, from 337 to over 776, three quarters of which were self-financed. As on 31st August, 2007, their number stood at 1668 colleges with an annual intake of 6.53 lakh students. Such an increase would imply stultification of anti-commercialization stance of the official policy. The commercialization, no doubt, appears to have deep roots in the socio-political reality. According to Rekha Kaul's study relating to development of professional education in Karnataka, which state appears to have started it all, the rich peasants and landlords belonging to the dominant intermediate castes in the State, initially Lingayats, but subsequently also Vokkaligas, in addition to linguistic/ religious minority institutions, exercised their political influence reinforced by constitutional protection to set up and get recognition for "capitation fee" medical and engineering colleges (Rekha Kaul, 1993: 241 ff). Maharashtra, Andhra Pradesh and Tamil Nadu have followed suit. The scholarly contributions to the *EPW* in the period 2000-2004 show that the phenomenon has spread to northern States like Uttar Pradesh and Bihar and that corruption has spread its tentacles to the AICTE, its Visiting Committees which recommend recognition, Universities which grant affiliation and State Governments which recommend affiliation/ recognition (J.V. Deshpande, 2000; T.H. Chaudhary, 2001; B.K. Jha, 2004). Granted that the "capitation fee" college phenomenon has deep socio-political roots, AICTE as a statutory/regulatory body should have shown minimum rectitude, probity and energy in exercising its statutory powers bonafide for curbing the evil but not only did it utterly fail to do so but was not even energetic in the implementation of the Supreme Court directions in its Unnikrishnan judgment of 1993.

The AICTE's statutory power to fix norms and guidelines for charging tuition and other fees [vide S.10(j)] were not exercised till 1988 when the UGC issued its regulations. Thereafter a larger bench of the Supreme Court reversed its stand in the *Unnikrishnan case* in the *TMA Pai case* of 2002. After the Supreme Court interpreted its TMA Pai judgment in *Islamic Academy* case in August 2003, the AICTE followed suit by issuing a policy pronouncement whereby the powers of fee determination were to be exercised by State level committees pending decision of a high-level committee to be set up by the AICTE/MHRD Government of India (*vide* E 37/3—Legal 2003, downloaded from the AICTE website). Since *P.A. Inamdar's case*, Government has changed track and the AICTE is left to engage in damage control exercises. The unplanned expansion of engineering and similar colleges worsened the pre-existing faculty crunch. Recent press reports indicate that the AICTE has reduced 22,722 engineering seats for the academic year 2006-07 in respect of 409 colleges where they lacked more than 25 per cent of the teaching staff as per norms (*Times of India*, 6th May, 2006). This appears to be mere window-dressing and would only underline a clear lack of supervision on the part of the AICTE which allowed under-staffed institutes to come up in the first instance.

Fifthly, the AICTE has shown utter disregard of its function to serve as a clearing house of information in regard to technical education in terms of Section 10(a) of the AICTE Act, which talks of undertaking surveys in the various fields of technical education, collecting data on all related matters and making forecast of the needed growth and development in technical education. No doubt, AICTE implements a scheme called National Technical Manpower Information System (NTMIS) through the Institute of Applied Manpower Research (IAMR), New Delhi for estimation of short-term and long-term demand and supply of technical manpower. But the data are not published, there is no indication that the Council uses the same in its decision-making processes about sanction of institutions and their intake, but above all, this is a very limited area. The Commission issues no publications other than its Annual Report. The National Commission on Statistics (2001) noted that the AICTE had yet to install statistical machinery for data collection on technical education. Although IAMR developed a NTMIS database, it is not serving the purpose of providing the essential statistics on technical education annually for all States on a regular basis. The National Commission recommended that the AICTE should create a central statistical unit with a required back up and that States should develop a database on technical education specially in areas of new and emerging technologies.

Sixthly, while there is an enormous quantitative expansion, the expansion is accompanied by severe regional imbalances and this shows that AICTE has not lived up to the mandate of ensuring co-ordinated development of technical education.

The data relating to regional distribution shows that 52 per cent of the institutions are located in the South (i.e.Tamil Nadu, Andhra Pradesh, Karnataka and Kerala) and the South-West (i.e. Maharashtra) and the East and the North account for 7 per cent and 10 per cent institutions. Likewise 43 per cent of MBA institutions and 59 per cent of MCA institutions with an intake of respectively 35 per cent and 57 per cent of students in the above disciplines are in the South and the South-West. Similar is the case with Pharmacy and Architecture. In Hotel Management, the regional inequity is so great that 50 per cent of the institutions and intake are in the South (mainly in Karnataka).

Table 9.1 below gives data relating to Degree and Diploma level institutes and their intake as on 31st August, 2007.

Table 9.1: Number of AICTE approved Technical Education Institutions and their Annual Intake (as on 31-08-2007)

Sl. No.	*Programme*	*Degree Institutions*	*Annual Intake*	*Diploma Institutions*	*Annual Intake*
1.	Engineering	1668	6.53 lakh	1414	3.54 lakh
2.	Architecture	0116	4,543	05	120
3.	MCA	1017	0.71 lakh	—	—
4.	Pharmacy	0854	0.52 lakh	583	0.35 lakh
5.	Applied Arts & Crafts	0009	650	08	1,010
6.	Management	1149	1.22 lakh	—	—
7.	Hotel Management	0081	5,272	92	4890
	Total	4894	9.08 lakh	2102	3.95 lakh
Institutions (Grand Total)			6,996		
Intake (Grand Total)			13.03 lakh		

Source: Report of the Union Department of Higher Education (2007-08), Ministry of HRD, New Delhi, p. 160.

Some Recent Developments

The Role of Regional Committees vis-à-vis State Governments

The AICTE Act has made Regional Committees statutory bodies and their number has been increased from four in 1988 to eight in 2007. It is to be noted that the AICTE, unlike the NCTE, is not required to obtain prior permission of the Central Government before increasing the number of its Regional Committees. The Report of the Ministry (2004-05: 205-207) indicates that for involving various State Governments actively in monitoring technical education in the country, the Council has delegated all powers relating to approval of new institutions, starting of new courses and variations in the capacity at diploma-level technical institutions to the concerned State Governments. Also, the recommendations of the concerned State Governments are given due weight by the Council while considering the proposals for establishment of new degree-level institutions. Recent press reports, however, suggest that apparently, under pressure from the private unaided institutions, the AICTE has decided to dispense with No-Objection Certificate (NOC) from State Government in respect of new unaided engineering colleges (*Times of India*, 26th Nov., 2005), which clearly is a retrograde step, education is a concurrent subject and in a federal set up, State Governments have a vital role to play in the regionally oriented development of technical education institutions.

The topic of the role of State Governments in the approval of new engineering colleges was considered important enough by the Law Commission by taking note of the Supreme Court Judgment in the *State of Tamil Nadu* v. *Adhiyaman Education and Research Institute case* (1995), and by suggesting *suo motu* amendment to S.10(k). In the Adhiyaman case, the Supreme Court held that provisions of AICTE Act superceded the provisions of Tamil Nadu (Private Colleges) Regulation Act, 1976 as well as the Madras University Act, 1923. The Law Commission pointed out that the Supreme Court had not given due weight to the duty of the AICTE to consult the agencies concerned in terms of S.10(k) which necessarily included State Government. It also took notice of the provisions contained in S.10-A to 10-C of the Medical Council of India Act and the Regulations made thereunder which confer the power to grant approval for establishment of a medical college upon the Central Government in consultation with the concerned State Governments which were necessary parties. It proposed appropriate amendments, which had also incorporated the proper sequence of steps and safeguards (Law Commission Report, 1998). Unfortunately, the Central Government appears to have ignored the recommendation in this regard which shows its scant regard for the need for involving the States in the process of recognition of new engineering colleges, in derogation of the spirit of Centre-State partnership in technical education.

State Level Technical Universities

The Thomason College, Roorkee (in UP, now in Uttarakhand) was the first engineering college in the country (1847) and after completion of its centenary, it was converted into a unitary State university. Thanks to substantial foreign assistance in the form of visits of foreign experts, training of faculty abroad and establishment of a Water Resources Development Training Centre, the University made rapid progress until it was declared as an IIT in 2001. Examples of unitary State level technical universities on the analogy of Roorkee were Andhra Pradesh Technological University 1972, Bengal Engineering College (estd. 1856) notified as a deemed university in 1992, and since made a statutory State university, and Dr. Babasaheb Ambedkar Technological University, Lonare (estd. 1989) in Maharashtra. However, the increase in the number of engineering colleges, especially self-financed, in various States necessitated a mechanism to provide academic support to these technical institutions, which the traditional universities were not in a position to provide. As a result, the Andhra Pradesh Technological University became an affiliating university in 1995-96 and various States established such affiliating universities in rapid succession: Punjab (1997), Madhya Pradesh and Karnataka (1998), Uttar Pradesh (2000) and West Bengal (2001). The irony is that the AICTE Act does not refer to these universities, that they continue under the UGC and the "fitness rules" for such universities have apparently not been framed by the UGC. The AICTE Review Committee (2003) suggested that the technical universities should provide support to private colleges by organizing digital libraries and experimental facilities on the lines of Regional Sophisticated Instrumentation Centres of the Department of Science & Technology. It had suggested that their financial needs should be assessed and they should be accredited jointly by the UGC and the AICTE. There is no indication regarding any follow-up action.

Funding by the AICTE: Central v. State Institutions

The Ministry has transferred implementation of various development schemes in technical education like modernization, thrust areas, research and institutional development, staff development and industry-institute interaction to the AICTE. The Annual Budget of the Council in 2002-03 was of Rs. 120 crore. However, unlike in the case of the UGC, no systematic analysis of the institutions to which the plan grants are released is available. A quick scan shows that a substantial chunk might have been released in favour of Central Institutions like the IITs/NITs etc. Out of 37 emeritus fellowships in one year, 14 were in favour of IISc/IITs. Only 9 out of 26 Quality Improvement Programme (QIP) cells in engineering were located at State institutes (Annual Report of AICTE, 2004-05: 30 and 116).

Other Professional Bodies in the Technical Education Field

The AICTE is unique in its management structure in having to deal with two statutory professional bodies (Pharmacy Council and the Council of Architects) and one non-statutory Council (National Council of Hotel Management and Catering Technology). The statutory bodies maintain a Register of persons entitled to practise the profession and they lay down a professional code of conduct and enforce it. But they also have a role in education to the extent that they are authorized to frame educational regulations which are binding on the universities.

The Pharmacy Council

The Pharmacy Act, 1948 which is designed to regulate the profession and education of pharmacy was amended in 1987 to provide for representation of the UGC, the AICTE and State Pharmacy Councils. The Central Council has been empowered to frame Education Regulations (S.10) and they were duly framed in 1991. The Central Council is required to circulate draft Education Regulations to State Governments and take their comments into consideration before finalizing the same [S.10(3)]. The State governments are required to be consulted before withdrawal of recognition of a course (S.13) and are also sent a copy of inspection report for comments (S.16). State Pharmacy Councils do not appear to have any role in pharmaceutical education.

The Council of Architects

The Architects Act, 1972 gives power to the Council to prescribe minimum standard of architectural education and the Council framed the same in 1983. The Council has powers to call for information (S.18), make inspection (S.19) etc. The power of withdrawal of recognition of sub-standard courses is that of the Central Government. The role of the State Governments is recognized in two ways. Firstly, an architect from each State nominated by the Government of that State sits on the Council [S.3(3)f] and secondly, the State Government is required to be consulted before withdrawal of recognition of a particular course of any institution (S.20).

National Council for Hotel Management and Catering

The subject of hotel management falls under the domain of the Ministry of Tourism to which it was transferred in 1982 from the Ministry of Food and Agriculture. The Tourism Ministry inherited four institutions of hotel management, catering technology and applied nutrition which had been set up at New Delhi, Mumbai, Chennai and Culcutta (Kolkata) between 1962 and 1964. The Ministry has set up an advisory body called "National Council for Hotel Management and Catering Technology" in 1984 with the following objectives: to advise the Government on co-ordinated development of hotel management and catering education; to keep abreast of all international developments in this area and to serve as a technical store house for use in framing suitable programmes; to affiliate institutions and prescribe courses of study and instructions leading to examinations conducted by it; to standardize courses and infrastructure requirements; to give certification and accreditation at the national level (Annual Report of Ministry of Tourism, 1997-98: 135-145). It is evident that the Council is a purely advisory body and not a statutory regulatory body but its existence enables the Ministry effectively to co-ordinate the functioning of a multiplicity of institutions. The Council has obviously to comply with the norms and standards of the AICTE.

Indian Institute of Technologies (IITs)

The foundations for India's edge in knowledge economy can be said to have been laid by the establishment of the five IITs in India at Kharagpur, Bombay (Now Mumbai), Madras (Now Chennai), Kanpur and Delhi (1951-61) during the hey day of planning. Their model was the MIT in the USA and their establishment was recommended by the Sarkar Committee on technological education as far back as 1944. With their small teacher-pupil ratio, semester system, modern equipment and above all a scrupulous selection process by means of Joint Entrance Test, they were expected to help India meet manpower needs of its industrialization. Initially, their alumni contributed to the brain-drain. They were considered as elite institutions till the policy shift in 1991. Now, in retrospect, they are regarded as a valuable asset. Incidentally, the number of IITs was raised to 7 by 2001, (Shillong established in 1995 and Roorkee re-classified in 2001). They account for the highest number of Ph.Ds., research papers and patents within academic institutions in India. However, they suffer from Faculty shortage and need to be upgraded further before they can be said to attain global standards. This was well brought out by McKinsey Report submitted to the Prime Minister of India in December 2000 entitled "Shaping the Knowledge Economy in India: The Need to set up a national mission for technology education". Unfortunately, the Government of India appears to be focused on equity rather than excellence. Hence reservation for the SCs/STs was introduced in 1973 and in 2007 reservation was extended to cover the OBCs for which a special legislation was brought forward whose validity was upheld by the Supreme Court in the well-known judgment of *Ashok Kumar Thakur* v. *Union of India* (April 2008). In spite of the faculty crunch faced by the existing IITs, the Government has already set up 8 new IITs, whose admissions were completed in August 2008.

Indian Institutes of Management (IIMs)

Two Indian Institutes of Management were set up in 1964 at Ahmedabad and Bangalore. Four more followed in 1974 (Bangalore now Bengaluru), Lucknow (1985), Kozikode (1997) and Indore (1998). In the context of the fact that commerce education in India failed to produce managers for business, IIMs, modelled on American graduate schools in management have emerged as institutes of excellence, imparting high quality management education and training, conducting research and providing consultancy services. They have, however, failed to address problems of under-served sectors like agriculture, health, education etc. They have tended to serve rather as finishing schools for IIT graduates (since IIT graduates account for a large intake). Unlike the IITs which are statutory institutions of national importance, IIMs are run by registered societies. Their Boards of Management are headed by distinguished industrialists or technocrats. Their problems are similar to the IITs. i.e. under-funding, faculty shortage, and Government interference in management. The Government is focused on reservations and expansion. (There is a plan to start seven more IIMs of which one at Shillong has already been set up).

Other Institutions of National Importance (INIs) in Technical Education Field

IITs are governed by Institutes of Technology Act 1961 which declares IITs to be INIs. IIMs, though not so-called, are also effectively INIs. It may be noted that the Central Government, while diversifying technical education has started two new types of INIs in (a) information technology and (b) science education. They are noted below:

Indian Institutes of Information Technology (IIITs)

As is well known, India has made a big name in the information technology, thanks to the various spin-offs from the Electronics Commission, later on converted into Electronics Department and now renamed Ministry of Information Technology. In the late eighties the need for dedicated IIT-type institutions for IT began to be emphasized by the scientists who felt that the existing facilities like bachelor or master in computer applications (BCA/MCA) was not adequate. Hence, an Indian Institute of Information Technology was set up at Allahabad in 2000 and another one at Gwalior in Madhya Pradesh. One more Institute which combines Design and Manufacturing with the IT came up at Jabalpur. The Eleventh Plan has the ambitious target of setting up 20 more IIITs, making their number 23. Their number will exceed the number of IITs (since the Eleventh Plan envisages only eight more IITs, making a total of 15). This, no doubt, highlights India's ambition to emerge as an IT Superpower.

Indian Institutions of Science Education and Research (IISERs)

The Scientific Advisory Council to the Prime Minister (SAC—PM) chaired by Prof. C.N.R. Rao recommended, in 2006, creation of five new institutions devoted to science education and research to be named "Indian Institute of Science Education & Research" broadly on the lines of the Indian Institute of Science, Bangalore (est. 1909). Three such institutions have already been established at Kolkata (on the Kolkata campus of IIT, Kharagapur), Pune (on the Campus of the National Chemical Laboratory near Pune) and at Mohali (Chandigarh). Government has also approved the setting up of two more Indian Institutes of Science Education and Research (IISER) at Bhopal and Thiruvananthapuram. Three more IISERs are to be set up in the Eleventh Plan. This initiative is part of making India a leading nation in the emerging Knowledge Economy scenario.

Conclusion

Technical Education is crucial to India's emergence as a knowledge power, not to talk of knowledge super-power. The AICTE has, however, not proved equal to the task. In terms of Yashpal Committee Report 2009, the Government is set to establish a National Commission for Higher Education and Research which would cover the AICTE as well as the UGC. This puts a question mark on the survival of the AICTE. It would appear, however, that some organization for higher technical education may need to be maintained in the context of India's aspirations to be a significant 'Knowledge Power'.

10

Teacher Education

Introduction

Teacher education is required to be considered in a survey of higher education for the following reasons:

(1) Teachers of secondary and higher secondary education streams have generally been trained by B.Ed. colleges which are post-graduate degree institutions under the Universities. (Incidentally, the Government of Maharashtra was reportedly considering in March 2009 making D.Ed. a P-G Diploma).

(2) Even elementary school teachers, merely because they are awarded a diploma regulated by the School Directorates of respective States, may not be considered to be in any way inferior to B.Ed. teachers. The work they do might conceivably require greater skills and grounding in psychological, philosophical and sociological foundations of education. In fact, the Kothari Commission, perhaps with this aspect in view, had recommended (pp. 124-158) upgradation of all training institutions for primary and pre-primary teachers to the University level in phases by establishment of comprehensive colleges which would prepare teachers for several stages of education and/or for a number of special fields (e.g. education for the differently abled). In the 1990s, the Delhi University started a Bachelor in Elementary Education Degree which appears to have received a good response.

(3) There are (a) teachers in the general higher education stage called lecturers, readers and professors in Arts, Commerce and Science Colleges and the University departments, (b) teachers in the professional branches of education like technical (engineering and management), medical, legal, agricultural etc. In general, these are teachers who have specialization in various 'disciplines'.

(4) An additional reason for considering 'teacher education' under the rubric of higher education has to do with teaching as a profession (for which the European Continental term is "pedagogy" which is not too common in the Anglo-American usage) and with education as an inter-disciplinary knowledge area. The ICSSR, since the time of J.P. Naik, as its founder Member-Secretary (1969-78) has always recognized "education" as a social science area eligible for assistance from the ICSSR.

(5) Lastly, as so felicitously put by the Sadler Commission: The intellectual vigour of the university is prepared by the quality of teaching given in the secondary schools and the tone of the school influences the university not only in the sphere of teaching and study but even more intimately in the temper of its corporate life. This is the classic argument based on the importance of secondary and higher secondary teaching as the very foundation of higher education.

The fact remains that teaching as a profession is socially regarded as one of the weakest professions considered from various points of view like social function, knowledge base, practitioner autonomy, collective autonomy and ethical values. In the teaching arena, therefore, the regulator or the governments encounter trade unions rather than professional organizations unlike in the case of traditional learned professions like the medical, veterinary, legal, etc.

The Position of Teacher Education at the time of Independence

Radhakrishnan Commission's criticism (pp. 140-144) of the existing teacher education institutions in 1947, may be noted because it is still relevant:

(1) Too little time was given to school practice.
(2) Teacher educators had little school experience.
(3) Courses in methods of Psychology and in Principles of Education were deficient and not adapted to local conditions.
(4) There was not much systematic research in education going on in the universities and the original work by professors and lecturers suffered from isolation and lack of inter-university planning.

In quantitative terms, there were in 1947, 34 secondary training colleges with 2,493 trainees and 937 primary training schools with 33,947 trainees. Since then there has been an immense expansion and diversification of the teacher training programmes. As on 1st January, 2007, 7,461 teacher training institutions offering 3,045 courses were recognized by the regulatory body (NCTE), with an approved intake of 7,27,155 teacher trainees. Types of courses available at present can be classified as below (Ministry of HRD, AR, 2006-07: 54):

1. Elementary for entrant teachers
2. Elementary for working teachers
3. Secondary/Higher Secondary for entrant teachers on full time/part time basis
4. Secondary/Higher Secondary for working teachers through (a) correspondence courses conducted by Directorates of Correspondence Education of traditional universities, (b) Distance education courses conducted by National/State Open Universities
5. Special education for the handicapped
6. Physical education
7. Non-formal or Adult education.

This diversification can be seen at a glance from Table 10.1.

Since Lord Curzon's Education Policy Resolution (1905), training of primary teachers is regarded as a prerequisite for employment of teachers. The quality dimension of the century-long programme of Universalization of Elementary Education (UEE) as well as the more recent programme of universalization of school education is greatly

Table 10.1: The Network of Teacher Education Institutions in India

Level	*Clientele*	*Nature*	*Institutions*	*Modes*	*Duration*
Elementary	Entrant teachers	Full time certificate/diploma/ degree	Elementary TEIs, TTIs, STCs, BTCs, DIETs MACESE, DU	Face-to-face Face-to-face	Two Years Four Years
Elementary	Working Teacher	Full time by deputation	DIETs, NCERT	Face-to-face	Short-term Programme Specific
Secondary/ Higher Secondary	Entrant teachers	Full time/Part time degree	College of Education College of T.E.(CTEs) IASEs University Departments of Education RIEs	Face-to-face -do- -do- -do-	One Year
Secondary/ Higher Secondary	Working Teachers Working teachers	Own time degree Own time degree Full time by deputation	Directorates of Correspondence Edn. Offer first degree in TE to untrained working teachers with at least 2 years experience State Open Universities in Andhra Pradesh, Gujarat and Rajasthan offer this programme; IGNOU has it on the anvil CTEs, IASEs, SCERTS, NCERT, CCRT, NIEPA	Correspondence-cum-contact Distance Education Modes Face-to-face	One-Two Years Two Years Short to Medium term Programme Specific

Elementary/ Secondary	Entrant teacher of distinct groups (handi-capped, language, Edn. Guidance physical Edn. Technical Edn. Music Edn).	Full time; certificate/ diploma/degree	Institutions with special focus on distinct areas, e.g. National institutes for Handicapped, ELT Institutes, CIEFL, RIEs, CIIL, Lakshmibai National Institute of Physical Education, Gwalior TTIs Bairagadh University	Face-to-face	One-four years

Source: NCTE (1998), Policy Perspectives on Teacher Education: Critique and Documentation, (New Delhi, p. 40).

affected by whether the teacher is trained or not. In 1946-47, the percentage of teachers trained was 61.5 per cent (PoE Report, 1948: 131). It is, therefore, deplorable to note that at the start of the 21st century, not only in the North-Eastern States but in States like Madhya Pradesh and Kerala, the percentage of untrained teachers at primary level was quite high; it was also quite high in secondary/higher secondary school systems in States like West Bengal. This may be seen from Table 10.2.

Notable Developments since Independence

The recommendations of various relevant Commissions and Committees since the British times, bearing on Teacher Education can be gathered from the NCTE (1998). The changes which took place on the ground are listed chronologically:

(1) Establishment of the Central Institute of Education (affiliated to Delhi University) in 1945, about which Radhakrishnan Commission had great hopes. It continues as the Faculty of Education under the Delhi University. Its envisaged role has been taken over by the NCERT [Sr. No. 3 (*Infra*)].

(2) Establishment of a professional organization viz. Conference of Principals of Teacher Training Colleges in 1950 (now renamed as Indian Association of Teacher Educators).

(3) Establishment of NCERT in 1963 under the Ministry of Education, Government of India by consolidation of all school related research and training activities. Since then till 1995 NCERT has remained a source of all important initiatives and innovations in teacher education through its five Regional Colleges of Education (now called Regional Institutes of Education) located respectively at Ajmer, Bhubaneswar, Bhopal, Mysore and Shillong and two constituent units, viz. Central Institute of Educational Technology (CIET) and Central Institute of Vocational Education (at Bhopal). NCERT started a 4-year integrated (integrated in the sense of integration of pedagogy and subject matter) course in teacher education at its RECs. The University College of Education, Kurukshetra and the

Sardar Patel University, Gujarat started similar integrated courses.

Table 10.2: Percentage of Untrained Teachers in Schools as on 30 September, 1996

Sl. No.	*States/Union Territories*	*Primary*	*Upper primary*	*Secondary*	*Higher Secondary*
1	Andhra Pradesh	03	08	04	03
2	Arunachal Pradesh	54	57	47	33
3	Assam	32	64	70	70
4	Bihar	17	10	08	15
5	Goa	04	03	05	23
6	Gujarat	07	05	01	01
7	Haryana	03	08	04	03
8	Himachal Pradesh	14	01	02	00
9	Jammu & Kashmir	39	47	33	21
10	Karnataka	00	00	00	00
11	Kerala	33	05	01	00
12	Madhya Pradesh	40	33	32	24
13	Maharashtra	06	05	04	10
14	Manipur	50	71	68	54
15	Meghalaya	55	63	64	12
16	Mizoram	22	26	53	100
17	Nagaland	78	71	70	75
18	Orissa	01	02	01	00
19	Punjab	01	03	01	07
20	Rajasthan	02	03	03	02
21	Sikkim	60	53	49	40
22	Tamil Nadu	00	00	01	02
23	Tripura	68	70	65	47
24	Uttar Pradesh	02	02	03	03
25	West Bengal	—	—	27	28
26	A & N Islands	05	03	03	01
27	Chandigarh	00	00	00	00
28	D & N Haveli	00	01	00	01
29	Daman & Diu	03	00	05	00
30	Delhi	00	00	00	00
31	Lakshadweep	00	00	00	00
32	Pondicherry	05	05	02	00

Source: Selected Educational Statistics, MHRD, Government of India.

(4) The NCERT inspired the establishment in 1963-64 of State Institutes of Education which became in 1980s State Councils of Educational Research and Training (SCERT) and were its instrumentality for changes in teacher education at the State level. NCERT was initially very active in in-service training of teachers and even collaborated with the UGC for improving science education in secondary/higher secondary schools through the organization of summer courses in science subjects for secondary teachers. NCERT was also active on the curriculum front. It developed a Curriculum Framework for Teacher Education for the first time in 1978 which was revised in 1988.

(5) On the University front, apart from the Central Institute of Education under the Delhi University, a centre for Advanced Study in Education was started at the M.S. University, Baroda (now Vadodara) in 1966 and Zakir Husain Centre for Educational Studies at Jawaharlal Nehru University New Delhi in 1972.

(6) Establishment in 1973 of the NCTE as an advisory body under the NCERT.

(7) Teachers' Commission I: Report (1985).

(8) Establishment of the NCTE as a statutory body in 1995.

Kothari Commission on Teacher Education

The Kothari Commission envisaged first of all, the establishment of a State Board of Teacher Education which would consist of representatives of Universities, State Departments of Education, Principals of training institutions, National Association of Teacher Educators and teachers' organizations, in close association with the SIE but with no role for the Education Department. The functions of the State Board were those in the nature of academic regulation relating to standards, curricula and textbooks, study programmes, examinations, conditions for the recognition of training institutions including periodical inspection, and preparing plans for development of teacher education. Secondly, it recommended at the national level the establishment by the UGC, in collaboration with the NCERT, of a Joint Standing Committee on Teacher Education empowered to develop and establish standards for training institutions and university departments, co-ordinate and improve standards of teacher education at all levels, grant funds to teachers' colleges, departments and schools of education in the universities and arrange for periodical inspection of training institutions and university departments of education (Kothari Report: 124-158).

A comparison of the functions and powers of the National Standing Committee with those of the State Boards of Teacher Education would show that the latter are far wider, dealing with university departments and covering the powers of the purse (grant-giving). While the emphasis of the Kothari Commission on State Boards is notable for the insight that this is an area where States are required to be involved much more than in the case of other sectors of education, its recommendations were "University"-centric, and failed to note that universities had not distinguished themselves in their stewardship of teachers' training colleges, and that since the pre-Independence period, teacher training as a subject was dealt with by the State Education Departments which looked up in the post-Independence period to the Ministry of Education and the NCERT. Naturally, the follow-up action to set up a national level body was taken not by the UGC but by the NCERT under direct control of the Ministry.

NCTE as an Advisory Body

National Council for Teacher Education as part of the NCERT was set up by a resolution dated 21st May, 1973, with the functions of advising the Government of India and the State Governments on all matters concerning teacher education including maintenance of standards. NCTE was conceived not merely as a central body but as an All-India body, which could review and advise on plan schemes of State Government. Its composition provided representation to all the State Governments. It functioned through Standing Committees relating to various stages and developed, as noted earlier, a Framework for Curriculum of Teacher Education (1978), with emphasis on skill aspects of teaching subsequently replaced by a revised framework in 1988. NCTE guidelines for revision of Teacher Education curriculum were adopted by all the States at the elementary level and by some universities. State Boards of Teacher Education had been formed in 16 States. One of the regular activities of the NCTE was to hold annual conferences of Directors of SIEs/SCERTs in States/UTs and of State Boards of Teacher Education. In 1982, the conference took a stand against B.Ed. degree through correspondence education and this became official policy with the formulation of NPE 1986, *vide* Annual Report of NCERT, 1982-83, p. 76.

It was the National Commission on Teacher-I set up by the Government of India in February 1983 which recommended giving a statutory status to the NCTE because, according to it, the impact of the advisory body had been marginal (NCT-I: para 10.47). The POA! 1986, not only endorsed this recommendation but also suggested (para XXIII.17), a one-time matching grant for the SCERTs. The Annual Report of NCERT for 1988-89 shows that a draft bill for according statutory status to the NCTE was being developed and discussed (NCERT, AR 1988-89: 18) but it was delayed because of the Ramamurti Review. The Ramamurti Committee (pp. 300-315) suggested an internship model for teachers of elementary education and a licensing system for teachers, which did not find favour with the Janardhan Reddy Committee (pp. 63-68). The POA 1992 spelt out objectives and functions of the proposed NCTE (para 22.2).

The advisory NCTE was in existence for 21 years from 1973 to 1994. The period from 1989 onwards was one of transition to a statutory body. In its short lived existence, it served as a co-ordinating body for teacher education in the country, initiating and co-ordinating the work of the State Boards of Teacher Education, functioning as a standard-setting body, framing draft teacher education curricula and serving as a clearing house of information. It was able to do this, firstly, because it had the resources of the NCERT at its command, not only in the form of its Teacher Education Department but also the whole National Institute of Education and the four Regional Colleges of Education and secondly, because it worked closely with the State governments especially State Teacher Education Boards. It could also back up its precepts with financial resources through various schemes of NCERT implemented through the RECs, like the Centres of Continuing Education (CECs), etc. In later years, it took a firm stand against the correspondence courses and distances education B.Ed. programmes of some universities like Kurukshetra and Madurai Kamraj which were out to make money at the cost of quality (NCTE, 1998: 87-96).

NCTE: Statutory

Structure and Functions: In terms of the NPE 1986/92, the National Council for Teacher Education Act, 1993 came into force from 17th August, 1995. The General Body of the Council consists of about 40 members, including the Chairman, the Vice-Chairman and Member-Secretary appointed by the Central Government, and four Chairmen of Regional Committees nominated by the Council. There are only nine members who represent the States/UTs. The Council is a general supervisory body, meeting only once a year; the Executive Committee (which is provided for in section 19 of the Act), has four State representatives on it. Each of the State Government/UTs within the region is represented on the regional committee. Thus, in design NCTE follows the model of the statutory AICTE, which is inadequately representative of the States at the apex but fully representative at the regional level. During discussions on the NCTE Bill in the Rajya Sabha in December 1993, it was suggested that all States/UTs should be represented on the Council, which should meet twice a year instead of once a year, but the Central Government ignored the suggestion (Rajya Sabha Debates, 7th December, 1993).

The functions of the Council include planned and co-ordinated development of teacher education, and determination and maintenance of standards of teacher education. In particular, the NCTE is empowered to lay down minimum qualifications for teachers, norms for courses of training including minimum eligibility criteria for admission, guidelines for physical and infrastructural facilities, staffing pattern and staff qualifications, examination standards, guidelines regarding tuition fees and devising suitable performance appraisal systems and mechanisms for enforcing accountability. The NCTE can undertake surveys and studies, give advice to Central and State Governments and universities, promote and co-ordinate innovation and research and is enjoined to take all necessary steps to prevent commercialization of teacher education. The weakness of the AICTE Act caused by the definition of an institution to exclude "university" has been avoided. Moreover, an affiliating body can grant affiliation only after recognition or permission by the Council and a valid qualification is made a prerequisite for employment under Central/State Government/University etc. (NCTE Act S.16/17).

As in the case of the AICTE, the NCTE functions through regional committees (Section 20). The Act provides for the Eastern, Western, Northern and Southern Regional Committees. NCERT has four regional committees at Bhubaneswar, Jaipur, Bhopal and Bangalore, with various States attached to them. The locations of the regional committees significantly mirror regional college locations under NCERT with the difference that in Rajasthan, the Centre is located at Jaipur rather than Ajmer. The proposal for setting up a fifth Regional Committee for NE States (where there is a large number of untrained teachers) first made in 1997-98 does not appear to have materialized. The composition of the Committee comprises: (1) one member nominated by the Council, (2) one representative from each of the States and UTs, and (3) six experts nominated by the Chairman of the Council of whom one is designated as Chairman. The scheme of the Act is such that all the original work of the Council like approval (recognition) of new institutions, permission to existing institutions to start new courses and action against institutions for contravention of conditions of recognition, etc. is entrusted to the Regional Committee. Its action is final subject to appeal to the Head Office of the Council (s.18). However, it has been seen that the NCTE has been involved in considerable litigation. Apparently, all dissatisfied parties approach not only the Head Office but almost invariably also the Court of Law if the appeal is not granted. The data of statutory appeals disposed of by the Head Office of the Council in successive years is as below: 152 (2000-01), 154 (2001-02), 137 (2002-03) and 259 (2003-04) (Annual Reports of the NCTE).

The introduction of a regulatory regime in teacher education especially for teachers of elementary education was an altogether new experiment since even after Independence the States had continued to control standards of Diploma in Elementary Education, simply called D.Ed. Therefore, the teething trouble of NCTE (statutory) *vis-à-vis* State Governments in relation to courses in Elementary Education were of a serious nature.

The Functioning of NCTE: An Assessment

Since NCTE started functioning in August 1995 it has been subjected to a lot of criticism. In particular, universities and their representative body, the AIU have been highly critical of it. Such criticism has become strident since newspapers in July/August 2007 carried reports that two high level committees called Anand Sarup Committee and Sujit Banerjee Committee had suggested the winding up of the NCTE because its regional committees and the Central Office had become a den of corruption. Similar criticisms about commercialization of technical and medical education have been common but they have been subdued, because it is known that commercialization in those areas cannot flourish without blessings of the high ministerial level.

It is, therefore, necessary to maintain a perspective in this matter and to attempt an objective assessment of the achievements and deficiencies of the NCTE. This may be done under three headings—

(1) Action of the NCTE in relation to B.Ed. course by correspondence run by some universities (Rohtak, Kurukshetra, Madurai, Kamraj, Annamalai) as profit making activities.
(2) Achievements of the NCTE in its initial phase of 1995-99.
(3) Progress of the NCTE after the year 2000.

B.Ed. by Correspondence

Since the British times, it was axiomatic that teacher education involved practice lessons and was to be conducted only in the face-to-face mode. However, the perception changed after a visit by 3 UGC delegations to the ex-USSR in 1967-69 to study the system of correspondence courses and to suggest the suitability of this channel for India. These delegations made a positive recommendation and included teacher training as one of the areas in which courses through the Correspondence mode could be offered to begin with. Many universities instituted such courses in the seventies, apparently without consulting the NCERT or the advisory NCTE. In the 1980s, such courses assumed a form of a racket. In 1988-89, Maharshi Dayanand University, Rohtak enrolled 33,000 students in the very first year of its inception which exceeded total enrolment of all teacher education institutions elsewhere put together. This flew in the face of the NCTE resolution of 1985 that the first degree in the professional programme of a secondary school teacher should be obtained only through formal and regular institutionalized course of studies and practical work. This was also emphasized by the National Commission on Teachers-I. A high level delegation met the Chairman, UGC in 1987 and the matter reached the Ministry. Unfortunately, the matter dragged on through numerous committees [Ramlal Parekh Committee of UGC, Kenna Lyngdoh Committee of UGC, Das Committee of NCTE and Takavale Committee of UGC/IGNOU/NCTE]. It was only in 1996 that an end was put to the racket of B.Ed. by correspondence by traditional universities (about 24 universities were running such courses). The decision arrived at was as below: B.Ed. correspondence mode be confined to serving teachers only; maximum admission in any single university in an academic year would be 500 and the duration would be 24 months. There would be 10 core faculty and 10 part-time faculty members. This can be said to be a major achievement of the NCTE in its year of foundation [*vide* NCTE (1998)].

NCTE (1995-99)

(a) The Council during its formative years declared and notified in the form of regulations, norms and standards following 10 teacher education programmes: (i) Pre-primary, (ii) Elementary, (iii) Secondary, (iv) B.Ed. (Distance education including correspondence), (v) M.Ed. (face-to-face), (vi) M.Ed. (Distance education including correspondence), (vii) C.P.Ed., (viii) P-G Diploma, B.P.Ed., (ix) M.P.E., and (x) Bachelor of Elementary Education.

(b) It released a "Curriculum on framework for quality teacher education" (August 1998).

(c) It published 12 State level reports on teacher education.

(d) It brought out monographs on leading educators of India, viz. Mahatma Gandhi, Zakir Hussain, Sir Aurobindo and others.

(e) It started a professional journal entitled 'Indian Journal of Teacher Education.'

These achievements are sought to be overlooked by certain critics apparently to serve their own agenda.

NCTE 2000 onwards

Eleventh Five Year Plan document, Vol. II says about NCTE that:

> "NCTE is a statutory body vested with the responsibility of maintaining quality standards in teacher education institutions. Performing this task is obviously linked to regulating the establishment of Teacher Training Institutions (TTIs) in accordance with specified norms and matching the need for qualified teachers. Uncontrolled growth in the number of private TTIs in recent years has led to unevenness in the quality of TTIs. There has been a mushroom growth of low quality private institutions. While the NCTE is very active in Southern States and in Maharashtra, it is virtually dormant in the Eastern States. The existing mechanism for regular monitoring has proved inadequate" (Eleventh Five Year Plan: Vol. II: 20).

This is as severe an indictment as an official document can make. What appears to have happened is*:

(1) Inappropriate composition of Visiting Committees with disproportionate representation to private institutions.
(2) Sanction of new TTIs without considering the manpower needs, availability of teacher educators, capacity of the applicants to implement the projects.
(3) Over-burdening of the Council with litigation especially by private TTIs.
(4) Absence of strong legal cells at the Central Office and at the Regional offices.
(5) Frequent change of norms.
(6) Absence of a vision of a teacher education scenario in the next 10-15 years.

---

* *Vide* several issues of University News of 2007 and 2008.

(7) Some wrong policy advice by the Ministry [It has been pointed out that dispensing with NOC from State Governments was decided by the Central Government itself when the Supreme Court had given an interpretation in favour of the need for NOC from the states even in the absence of specific legal provision].

Clearly, there is need to clean the augean stables of the NCTE. But abolition of the NCTE or wholesale condemnation of the NCTE as a corporate body is not the solution. It may also be useful to replace regional committees by State level committees (except for small States).

According to Press Reports in August 2011, the existing body of the NCTE was superseded and its administration entrusted to an administrator appointed by the Ministry of Education, Government of India.

The Future of the NCTE

Irrespective of the recommendations of the earlier committees, the survival of the NCTE as a separate entity is in doubt in the context of the recommendations of the Yashpal Committee Report to set up a National Commission for Higher Education and Research as an umbrella organization of various apex organizations in the field including NCTE. "A Bill in this regard was introduced in the Parliament in May 2010".

11

Legal Education

Introduction

The significance of Legal Education and profession in modern India is partly due to sheer numbers, India having the second largest number of advocates (with the minimum qualification of LL.B. which is a post-graduate degree) next only to the United States. In the U.S. the number of lawyers was 6,50,000 in 2002 as compared with the Indian number of 4,92,000 (rounded) advocates on the roll with the data relating to State Bar Councils as in December 1994, i.e. 8 years earlier (*Indian Bar Review* 2002).

Secondly, Legal Education is subject to a dichotomy of Control, viz. Bar Council of India, the regulatory body of the legal profession on the one hand and the universities and University Grants Commission, being the academic regulatory bodies on the other. One of the functions of the Bar Council of India, set up under Advocates Act, 1961 is "to promote legal education and to lay down standards of such education in consultation with the universities in India imparting such education and the State Bar Councils" [Section 7(1)(h) of the Act]. While the section does not distinguish between under-graduate and post-graduate education, Bar Council's regulations deal only with under-graduate education. Therefore, academic authors like S.K. Agrawala (1973) have taken the view that the universities are solely concerned with post-Graduate education and research. In the British tradition which India has partly inherited, the Bench is drawn from the Bar and traditionally, the Bench especially the Chief Justices of High Courts, used to have significant supervisory powers over the selection and disciplining of the personnel of the Bar. Even under s.38 of Advocates Act, 1961, the appellate powers over the disciplinary decisions of Bar Council of India have remained with the supreme judiciary). As a result, the Bar tends to play a subsidiary role *vis-à-vis* the Bench. We see concrete examples of this in the interventions made by the Supreme Court on its administrative side in the matter of reorganization of Legal education by way of Ahmadi Report (1994) [*Indian Bar Review* (4) 1995: 7-34]. No doubt, the recommendations were well meaning, but objectively speaking, they do smack of a tendency to arrogate powers to the superior judiciary which statutorily did not belong to it (This is apart from the adjucatory role of the Supreme Court).

Constitutional Position of Legal Education: Legal Education a Central Subject

At the outset, a reference may be made to the Constitutional position of legal education. It may be assumed that in common with other species of education, legal education was a State subject (*vide* entry 11 of the State list of Schedule VII of the Constitution of India) till the 42nd Amendment of the Constitution (i.e. till 3rd January, 1977) and thereafter it became a concurrent subject *vide* entry 25 of Concurrent List of the Constitution. Legal profession has been a subject on the Concurrent List (entry 26) throughout. However, this is not so since 1968 *vide* the judgment of the Supreme Court in the *Mahendru case* (1968). In that case, the Supreme Court held that the Advocates Act, 1961 which basically governs legal profession but incidentally also legal education, has been passed by the Parliament by virtue of its powers under entries 77 and 78 of the List I of the VIIth Schedule (these entries relate to persons entitled to practise in the Supreme Court and the High Courts). These entries, it is held carve out the areas relating to the above subjects out of the legislative powers of the States in entries 25 and 26 of List III of the Constitution.

The practical consequences of this interpretation is that both the legal education and legal profession have been bifurcated into (1) legal education of advocates who practise before the High Courts (HCs) and the Supreme Court (SC), and (2) legal education of advocates other than (1) above. Similarly, in respect of legal profession. This interpretation is clearly a forced one, in the face of the fact that entries 77 and 78 relate to the SC and HCs and not education/profession. The Law Commission in its 184th Report (2002/2007), had a great difficulty in reconciling the role of the Bar Council of India and the UGC in regard to the final authority for standards of legal education since entry 66 of the List I of the Constitution clearly gives the supreme role in regard to standards to the UGC. In spite of the wording of Section 7(1)(h) of the Advocates Act, there is no warrant to hold that the UGC's role is in any way taken away. Surprisingly, the Ahmadi Committee almost took away the role of the academic community from legal education. As against the then prevalent composition of the Legal Education Committee of the Bar Council of India, which gave parity to the Bar Council and the academic community (5 members of Bar Council and 5 legal academicians), Ahmadi Committee suggested *only* one academician, the remaining four members being—2 judges, Secretary, UGC and Secretary, Ministry of Law.

The Law Commission (184th Report) had to concede that the criticism of the Ahmadi Committee to the extent it recommended only one member of the faculty to be on the Legal Education Committee was justified. It is not necessary, at this stage, to go into other recommendations of the Law Commission, which proceeds on the basis of correctness of Mahendru Judgment. It is submitted that Mahendru judgment needs to be reviewed because it is against the Constitutional scheme of education as a State subject till 3rd January, 1977 and as a concurrent subject, thereafter, with the UGC having the decisive role in the matter of standards of all education including professional legal education.

Legal Education Before the Advocates Act, 1961

In this background, the progress in legal education may be reviewed with reference to a few landmarks. The main actors are: The Bar, the Bench, the Central and State Governments, and the academic community of law teachers.

In the first decade after Independence, a formative role was played by a few canonical reports, viz. Radhakrishnan Report (1949), and

Setalvad Report on Legal Administration (1958). Radhakrishnan Report deplored the poor state of law education in India and emphasized the need for uniformity in various aspects of the degree course, and introduction of P-G course and research. The only false note it struck was its advocacy for retention of Roman law as a subject in the curriculum. The Setalvad Report (Chapter 25 on Legal Education) remains required reading even today. It observed that the main purpose of the University Legal Education seems hitherto to have been not the teaching of law as a science or as a branch of learning but merely imparting to students knowledge of certain principles and provisions of law to enable them to enter the legal profession. Its various recommendations like: (a) law being taught in full-time institutions by full-time teachers to full-time students selected through stringent tests, (b) being a 3-year course, including one year's practical training, preceded by a degree course, and as its emphasis on a variety of methods of teaching are relevant even today. If only they had been followed in letter and spirit, legal education would have been in a healthier condition in India. Its conservatism, however, prevented it from making a dispassionate study of the proposal to have a Council of Legal Education as recommended by Dr. B.R. Ambedkar as early as 1936. There was a third report, viz. Report of All-India Bar Committee (1953) which is said to be the foundation of the Advocates Act, 1961 (Unfortunately author could not have access to this Report).

Secondly, some new institutions were established with a lot of hope. Not all lived up to their promise for want of proper leadership. There was a cluster of institutions related to legal studies and research, viz. *the Indian Law Institute, the Law Commission of India (LCI), the Indian Institute of Constitutional and Parliamentary Studies, and the Indian Institute of International Law*, of which the first two were notable. The Law Commission, first set up in 1956, is an advisory research body which helps in the task of law reforms and to keep law up-to-date. In 1958, a general objective was added, viz. "to suggest a general policy in revising the laws". The Commission is periodically reconstituted with a retired judge of the Supreme Court as its Chairman. It has somehow not associated law teachers with its work (with the exception of Prof. P.K. Tripathi of the Delhi law faculty). Till 2010 it had produced about 200 Reports. As observed by

Rajkumari Agrawala (2001), factual evidence of acceptance of the Commission's recommendations or even consideration of its recommendations does not stand established. In the concluding part of this chapter, the author has considered the foray of LCI in the field of Legal Education.

The establishment of the Indian Law Institute in 1956 on the lines of the American Law Institute, though with broader objectives, was a landmark. Its three main objectives are: (1) and (2) Promotion and development of legal research/education, and (3) Improvement in administration of justice. The American Law Institute was primarily meant for research, especially with a view to codify American law on subjects like evidence and commercial law etc., in the face of diverse State laws on the subject. In India, this task was not required to be performed. What was required was creation of India-wide forum for scholarly writing. The ILI did this by starting its quarterly journal of Indian Law Institute (ILI), the Annual Survey of Indian Law and related publications which provided impetus to a new generation of scholarly writing. Its seminars and other fora facilitated interaction between legal academics and leading judges and advocates. It also started one-year Diploma programme in legal education in about 10 areas including administrative law. The ILI is managed by the leading Supreme Court judges including CJI and initially it proved to be advantageous. Upendra Baxi (1996) has pointed out that in late 1980s, ILI fell on evil days. While membership and resources rose, academic activities stagnated. Staff positions fell to an abysmal low; at one time, there was no full-time Director or any Professor or a full-time Librarian on the rolls of the Institute. It was looked after by a group of seven sub-professorial academics, acquisition of books and journals did not grow and no workshops or seminars for teachers were held. Evidently, Supreme Court judges were not able to devote sufficient time for the management of the affairs of the Institute (1996). Perhaps, it was as a way out of this sorry state of affairs that in 2004, the ILI was given the status of a deemed university. The impact of this new status on the role of the ILI as a unique all-India forum for legal education, studies, research and reform needs to be watched.

The Indian Institute of Constitutional and Parliamentary Studies did not live up to expectations. Its role of active research is being taken over by some NGOs, e.g. PRS Legislative Research, New Delhi.

The third important development in the first decade after Independence was the facelift received by the infrastructure of legal education through an alliance between Sir Maunce Gwyer, the then Vice-Chancellor of Delhi University and Dr. R.U. Singh, who was Dean of Law Faculty, first at Delhi and then at Lucknow. The crucial change was replacement of part-time practising lawyer-teachers by qualified full-timers. Post-graduate instruction was regularized and course content, both at graduate and post-graduate level was modernized. Archaic subjects (like Roman law) were deleted and courses such as legislative principles were instituted, thus constituting the first step in the direction of sociology of law. Fresh full-time law teachers were sent to the American Law Schools for research and doctoral work and they became the first band of academic law teachers in the country. The experiment spread to other law faculties in the vicinity. This changed environment encouraged legal research and above all, the profession of academic law teacher was established (Baxi, U., 1996 and R. Agrawala, 2001). The modernization of legal education in North India was helped by the UGC which without in any way being hampered by the Bar Council Regulations, was in a position to financially assist Law Faculties for their post-graduate programmes.

The role played by the Bar Council of India and the State Bar Councils in the promotion of under-graduate legal education is considered below:

The Bar Council of India (BCI)

Under the Advocates Act, 1961, there is a Bar Council of India (BCI) entrusted with the function of "promoting legal education" and "laying down standards" of such education in consultation with the Universities in India imparting such education and the State Bar Councils. An allied function is "to recognize universities whose degree in law shall be qualification for enrolment as an advocate and, for that purpose, to visit and inspect universities." Along with the State Bar Councils, it is also expected to promote and support law reforms. The Bar Council consists of 18 members. The Attorney General and Solicitor General are *ex-officio* members and there are 16 members representing 16 State Bar Councils (Bar Council of India, Annual

Report 2001-02). The Act provides for the constitution of a Standing Committee of the BCI called, "Legal Education Committee" consisting of ten members of whom five are members of the BCI and the remaining five are co-opted members. The BCI has framed rules, called "Standards of Legal Education and Recognition of Degrees in Law for admission as Advocate Rules." One of the criticisms of the Legal Education Committee has been that it meets only periodically and is not in a position to exercise regular and continuous supervision over legal education throughout the country. Hence, it has been suggested that the body must act in close co-operation with the Law Panel of the UGC, that one or two members of the Bar Council Legal Education Committee could be co-opted in the UGC law panel to establish this liaison and that the UGC Committee must have wide powers to suggest and carry out such reform in legal education as may be found necessary. These suggestions appeared to imply transfer of control of under-graduate legal education from the BCI to the UGC to which a member of the BCI (Shri Ram Jethmalani) reacted strongly but constructively, stating that the Bar Council would not cease to control admission to the bar but that mutual adjustment and constant consultation was necessary, with the representation of the law teachers in the Legal Education Committee being raised to 50 per cent (S.K. Agrawala, 1973). The composition of the Legal Education Committee of the Bar Council of India has since been sought to be further modified at the instance of the Judges' Committee on Reforms of Legal Education as noted earlier.

Apparently, because of the conservatism of the legal profession, various reform initiatives of the BCI did not have a smooth run.

Soon after its inception, the BCI decided to have a law course of three years' duration including practical training, and enforced it from March 1967. This reform elicited considerable opposition on the ground of the length of the course. Hence, practical elements were built into the three year course and the Advocates Act, 1961 was amended with effect from 31st January, 1974 (quoted in V. Sudeer's case, 1987). Thereafter, the BCI after prolonged consultation with the universities and the State Bar Councils, extending over the period 1977-1982, introduced from June 1982 the five year law course after 10 + 2, the idea being to give the students a sound grounding in social sciences, followed by the teaching of law subjects. Here again, there was opposition from the lawyers and not only was the introduction of the five-year course delayed till 1985-86 but the existing three-year law course was allowed to co-exist.

State Bar Councils (SBCs)

The Advocates Act also provides for the setting up of State Bar Councils of which there are 16 at present, there being a common Bar Council for the North-Eastern States and also for the Punjab, Haryana and Chandigarh with some other States/UTs also being attached to neighbouring States. There are 15, 20 or 25 elected members depending on the strength of the electorate with the State Advocate-General as an *ex-officio* member. The powers of the State Bar Council are substantial. Apart from professional disciplinary matters, they are expected to promote and support law reforms and they have a right to be consulted by the BCI in its function of promoting legal education and laying down standards. Between 1961 to 1973, they had some role in pre-enrolment training, but this power, contained in S.28(2)(b) was, however, deleted by the Amended Act of 1973 with effect from 31st January, 1974. The object of the amended Act was to have built-in practical elements in the 3-year law programme for which law colleges were to be responsible.

The SBCs dating back to 1926 by dint of pre-Independence legislation are older than the Bar Council of India (1961). Being dominated by District level bars and being mainly concerned with narrow vocational issues they appear to be plagued by mismanagement and petty politicking. As a result, five yearly elections are not held regularly. The incumbent bodies try to remain in power as long as possible by adopting delaying tactics. Thus, the Supreme Court was compelled to appoint a committee to look after the affairs of the Bar Council of Maharashtra and Goa as the body, even after completion of its 5-year term and further extension of six months had not initiated action to prepare electoral rolls of eligible voters so as to hold elections in time (*Indian Express*, 17th September, 2003). This is a problem common to periodical re-constitution of elected bodies of the State and National level professional bodies like BCI/SBCs in legal education field and MCI/SMCs in medical education field. The way out may be to conduct these elections through the respective State Election Commission for which, of course, an amendment of the Advocates Act may be required.

The Role of the UGC

The Advocates Act implicitly left the post-graduate legal education to the UGC, whose activities have included the holding of some important workshops under the auspices of its Law Panel whose reports dealing with the status, problems and perspectives and social relevance of legal education have become landmark publications (S.K. Agrawala, 1973 and 1981; Upendra Baxi, 1977).

The arrangements for the post-graduate legal education, however, remain varied following a regional pattern. As pointed out by S.P. Sathe (1973), the universities in North India have unitary law faculties, combining under-graduate and post-graduate teaching. The universities in the rest of India, particularly Bombay (Now Mumbai), Poona, Nagpur, Madras and Kerala have federal law faculties where the LL.B. teaching is done by the affiliated colleges and the post-LL.B. teaching is done entirely by the university departments.

In the 1980s, the UGC set up Curriculum Development Centres (CDCs) for various subjects. The CDC for law was set up in 1986 at the University of Delhi under the Chairmanship of Prof. Upendra Baxi, which reported in 1990. It had proposed reform of the curriculum and issued detailed syllabi for 31 LL.B. courses, 31 LL.B. (Hons.) courses and 59 LL.M. courses. It is understood that as a result of the interaction between the UGC and the BCI, the latter conveyed in 1997, to all colleges/universities a list of 21 compulsory papers to be taught in an LL.B. course. However, the details (contents of programmes and bibliography) were left out. This lacuna was filled in by the UGC which circulated a model curriculum for LL.B. (three-year programme after graduation), LL.B. Hons. (one year course after LL.B.) and LL.M. [two-year P-G course after LL.B./LL.B. (Hons.)]. However, the UGC has been criticized for not having prescribed the syllabus for the Five-year integrated LL.B. programme (Dr. A.K. Awasthi, 2002/2004).

It may be added that a fresh UGC model curriculum was prepared in the year 2001 by the CDC constituted by UGC in 2000. Another interesting development was that the National Law School of India University held the first National Consultative Conference of Heads of Legal Education Institutions at Bangalore (now Bangaluru) in August, 2002 and its report incorporating "issues and recommendations" was finalized in November, 2002 (Law Commission of India, 2007).

Reforms in Legal Education

In 1980s and 1990s there have been two policy initiatives for reforms of legal education, taken by (i) the Bar Council of India Trust and (ii) Judges' Committee on Reforms of Legal Education and Entry into Legal Profession which are referred to below.

(i) Bar Council of India Trust

The Bar Council of India Trust (BCI Trust) was set up in 1974 specifically to establish, maintain and run a model law college at a central place in India and other regional law colleges in various places in India where education of a high standard may be provided so that these colleges may act as model law colleges in India (Annual Report of BCI, 2001-02: 13). The Trust has subsidiary objectives like publishing a journal, books and reports. The first National Law School was set up in Bangalore (Now Bengaluru) under a Karnataka State Act 1986, with the object of (a) advocating and disseminating learning and knowledge of law and legal processes and their role in national development and (b) developing in the student-scholars, a sense of responsibility to serve society in the field of Law. The National Law School, Bangalore has all-India jurisdiction. The Chief Justice of India is its *ex-officio* Chancellor. It runs a five-year law course. Within ten years the school had become the premier centre of legal studies and acknowledged as the best in India and comparable to the best any where else in the world. An International panel of Experts appointed by the Chancellor to review the working of the University in 1995 opined: "the National Law School of India has fully met the objectives of being the centre of excellence that serves as a pace-setter for Indian Legal Education and a testing ground for bold experiments", *vide* Convocation Address of N.R. Madhav Menon at Jadavpur University 2001, reported in *University News*, 40(3), January 21, 2002.

More recently (September 2011) there has been a 'worm in the paradise' in the form of press reports about deterioration in some areas of the University.

Other State Governments were, however, slow to follow suit. It took the intervention of the Supreme Court Judges' Committee (1994) and a Resolution of the Law Ministers' Conference (1995) (as is noted in succeeding paragraphs) to give them a push. In the result, the four States of Madhya Pradesh (Bhopal, 1997), Andhra Pradesh (Hyderabad, 1998), West Bengal (Kolkata, 1999) and Rajasthan (Jodhpur, 1999) started multidisciplinary 5-year law programmes in succession (*vide* AIU Universities Handbook, 2004). Gujarat and Chhattisgarh States have reportedly followed suit. Reports in the Press (March 2009) indicate that the NCT Administration has since established its own Law University. Thus, in a desert of a very large number of poorly equipped and poorly run 400+ law colleges affiliated to different universities in India, we have seven to eight oases of elite legal education, which are comparable in standards to the IITs in the engineering education, IIMs in management education, AIIMS and PGIMER in medical education and SAUs at Pant Nagar and Ludhiana in agricultural education. Unfortunately, the alumni of these universities appear to prefer corporate jobs so that the mainstream legal profession has remained unaffected by this new enterprise.

(ii) Judges' Committee on Reforms of Legal Education

Pursuant to a 'resolution' of the Chief Justices' Conference in December 1993, the Chief Justice of India constituted a committee with Justice A.M. Ahmadi as Chairman and Justices B.M. Kirpal and M. Jagannatha Rao as Members to make suggestions regarding admission to law colleges, syllabus, training, period of practice at different levels of courts etc. This Committee submitted its report in 1994. Its major recommendations included: (i) restructuring of the Legal Education Committee of the BCI so as to involve the judiciary, the UGC and the Law Ministry, with the BCI being required to act strictly in accordance with the recommendations of the Committee, (ii) review of existing law colleges by a special review committee, (iii) introduction of an additional year of apprenticeship prior to enrolment to the bar, (iv) one sitting High Court Judge being made in-charge of legal education in each State, and (v) the establishment of the National Law School-type universities in each State [*Indian Bar Review*, 1995 (4): 7-34].

These recommendations of the Judges' Committee though well meaning did not respect the autonomy of the stakeholders, namely the Law Ministry, the UGC, the Bar Council of India, the State Governments, and the State Bar Councils. They assumed omnipotence based on presumed omniscience of the higher judiciary. In the circumstances, however, the law Ministry was compelled to call a Law Ministers' Conference in Bhubaneswar in September 1995. The Law Ministers considered the Ahmadi Report along with other relevant reports, and issued what is called the Bhubaneswar Statement.

A perusal of the Bhubaneswar statement indicates that the thrust of the recommendations of the Ahmadi Report was accepted but there were major departures in some respects [*Indian Bar Review* 1995 (4): 7-34]. Thus, instead of leaving the review of colleges already affiliated to a special review committee as suggested by the Ahmadi Committee, it was recommended that the Bar Council should consider using the services of NAAC set up by the UGC. It was suggested that the Bar Council should obtain the comments of State Governments in the matter of affiliation and dis-affiliation of law colleges because the latter gave maintenance grants to the law colleges and that a representative of the Union Ministry of Law should also be included in the Legal Education Committee of the BCI. The suggestion to have a National Law School-type university in each State was accepted.

Thanks to the BCI Trust's first National Law School in Bangalore (now Bangaluru), the labours of the Curriculum Development Centre in law of the UGC, the Ahmadi Report and the Bhubaneswar Statement of Law Ministers' Conference, a movement for reform of Legal Education can be said to have started at least in the States where such Law Universities have come up and done well. The reconstitution of Legal Education Committee of the BCI to include two representatives of the Judiciary, of the Law Ministry and of the UGC has effectively crowded out law teachers which cannot be said to be desirable on academic grounds. The matter needs review.

In concrete terms, it is reported that during the period 1994-98, the BCI has turned down about 60 applications for establishment of law colleges and refused extension of approval to 50 law colleges. In the years 2000-2001 and 2001-2002 respectively, the BCI carried out inspection of 80 and 89 law colleges (Annual Report of BCI, 2001-02: 9-10). However, the BCI does not appear to have done much about Continuing Legal Education or on matters of assessment and accreditation or on distance education in law. The BCI has reportedly turned down requests of Madurai Kamraj, Annamalai and J & K universities to conduct LL.B. course in a distance mode, but has not explored the possibility of having the law courses cast in the distance education mode in collaboration with the DEC of the IGNOU. Though the Bhubaneswar Statement referred to the role of the NAAC apart from organizing stray conferences, the BCI has to take action on all these fronts in consultation with the UGC, the Indian Law Institute and the National Law Universities.

The Supreme Court in its judicial capacity has felt compelled to strike down several rules of the BCI on the ground of being unconstitutional, e.g. (i) setting age limit for enrolment (1991), (ii) Pre-enrolment training and apprenticeship (2001), and (iii) Banning morning and evening classes (1997). This has led one scholar to conclude that BCI is powerless to improve standards (Dr. Awasthi: 2002/2004, *op cit.*).

Finally, the Supreme Court's judgment in the "Legal Education" case upholding Bombay High Court order directing the State of Maharashtra to give grants-in-aid to affiliated private colleges may be noted for the innovation that whereas the Bombay High Court relied on discrimination as between Arts and Law Colleges for its decision, the Supreme Court also invoked the Directive Principle of Art. 39 A, relating to equal justice and free legal aid (M.P. Vashi case, 1995).

Law Commission of India's Report on Legal Education

The 184th report of the LCI which is a comprehensive report based on the perusal of previous reports and other relevant record, makes recommendations to amend Advocates Act, 1961 and the UGC Act, 1956 with a view to bring about co-ordination between the Bar Council of India and the UGC in the matter of legal education. It also proposes inclusion of ADR (Alternative Dispute Resolution) as a subject in the curriculum of under-graduate law colleges; introduction of problem method in law examination to the extent of 75 per cent, with theory being confined to 25 per cent, introduction of a system of accreditation of law colleges, starting of four colleges by the Central Government for providing professional training to law teachers etc. Apparently, it covers all perceived gaps in the legal education except Distance or Open Education. However, the recommendations regarding amendment of UGC Act appear to the author to be unrealistic because they do not show acquaintance with the scheme of the Act. Moreover, the blanket recommendations regarding ADR and problem method appear to need further examination. The report does not show acquaintance with the existence of the NACC under the UGC for assessment and accreditation. It only talks of accreditation. There is no reason why the NAAC should not be involved with the whole process. In general, the report, though it tries to be balanced, does appear to favour the Bar and the Bench and in other respects needs further examination before implementation. The Report, however, needs to be disseminated among all stakeholders (it was submitted to Government in 2002 and printed commercially in 2007) and its recommendations need to be debated.

Legal Education: The Way Ahead

As seen from the Bhubaneswar Statement, the Central Government, i.e. Law Ministry has not acted until goaded by the higher judiciary. The 184th Report of the Law Commission of India though valuable, is loaded in favour of the higher judiciary and its interpretation of legal education as practice before HC/SC. The BCI is concerned only with undergraduate education and apart from the initiative in respect of the Bangalore (now Bangaluru) Law School, has not shown any fresh initiative in the matter of legal education and has generally been unable to function effectively as an apex autonomous organization for legal education. The Indian Law Institute (ILI) has no active State Chapters apparently because they depend on the High Court Chief Justices to act. Its effectiveness as a deemed university remains to be judged. State Law Commissions, law faculties in State universities, law colleges and the new Bangalore type law schools are all under State Governments but States and the State Bar Councils play a negligible role in the promotion of excellence in legal education, research and law reform. There is a 'failure' of the executive wing of Government and in this vacuum the higher judiciary has stepped in. The Supreme Court obviously acts on the principle going back to the colonial times that lawyers are Law Officers bound to help the Court and relying on the ratio of the Mahendru Judgment, feels that not only their discipline but also their training are within its purview. However, the Supreme Court has its limitations when it assumes the role of a regulator for legal education. Firstly, the judges of the Supreme Court being drawn from the ranks of the legal profession have their class bias. Secondly, the Supreme Court is an institution of governance and not an academic body and is liable to trip up when it tries to enter the academic terrain. Thirdly, it has its blind spots. As pointed out by Upendra Baxi, the Ahmadi Report entirely ignored the work of the curriculum development centre for legal education set up by the UGC. It also tended to underplay the role of law as a social science discipline, which has been recognized by the ICSSR since its inception in 1969. Fourthly, neither the Supreme Court nor its individual judges have spare time on their hands to manage academic institutions as is noted by Upendra Baxi in the example of decline of the ILI in mid-1980s.

The solution to the problem of upgradation of legal education might well be an All India Council of Legal Education and Research first suggested by Dr. Babasaheb Ambedkar in 1936, in a rudimentary form (Magazine of the Government Law College, January 1936: 6-17). According to the Setalvad Report, such a body was also suggested by the Bombay and Rajasthan Legal Education Committees. However, the Bombay Committee was focused on unification of Bars at State level and Rajasthan Committee's details are not available. Hence the originality of Dr. Ambedkar's proposal stands out. In the author's view such an all-India body could regulate legal education both at under-graduate and post-graduate levels and promote research and interact with the NAAC and the DEC. Its structure could be similar to the AICTE with the Chairman of the Bar Council of India being *ex-officio* Chairman of the Board of Under-graduate Legal Education, leaving the matter of professional regulation and ethics to the Bar Council of India as a purely professional body. Its Board of Post-Graduate Studies would be analogous in composition to the Law Panel of the UGC and its Board of Research would have the ILI and the ICSSR associated with it. The Bangalore Model Law Universities could be appropriately associated with the various bodies.

No doubt, the Setalvad Report (1958: 544, 595) opposed such a body. But this opposition apparently stemmed from the fact that the Report had certain expectations regarding autonomous functioning of the Bar Council of India as and when established which have not been fulfilled. Further, while the Committee might have been aware of the establishment in 1956 of the UGC, it had not seen its functioning. It argued against State level Councils for legal education but did not appreciate the spirit of Dr. Ambedkar's proposal which had rightly distrusted the vested interests of the legal profession. Under the circumstances, the case for establishment of an *All-India Council for Legal Education* remains strong.

Conclusion

In terms of Yashpal Committee report the Bar Council of India/UGC would shed their powers relating to legal education if not legal profession, when the National Commission for Higher Education and Research is set up. The NCHER legislation does not exclude legal education. The present indications are that the Law Ministry is, however, not reconciled to the NCHER taking over legal education. One can only wait and watch!

12

Medical Education

Introduction

Medical Education differs from other types of education in some respects. The promotive, preventive, curative and rehabilitative health services provided by its practitioners have a bearing on the life and death of mankind. Hence, the practitioners of medical profession for which medical education is a preparatory stage, are in great demand. Secondly, medical education is cost-intensive in capital terms because the availability of abundant clinical material in the form of about 1000-bedded, well-equipped hospital is a prerequisite for a medical college with an intake of 100 students on the basis of a bed-student ratio of 10 : 1. It is in the public hospitals that such rich and varied clinical material is available, and therefore, medical colleges were more advantageously set up in the public sector and most medical colleges at the time of independence were public. Thirdly, the modern "scientific" medicine, formerly called allopathic, but now denoted as "bio-medicine', is a foreign plant, fostered by colonial rulers who considered traditional systems of Indian medicine (Ayurveda, Siddha and Unani) and the naturalised Homoeopathic system to have been based on 'false' doctrine and treated them as, at best, refined forms of quackery. This received official sanction through the Indian Medical Degrees Act, 1916 (which is still on the statute book) seeking to regulate the grant of title (e.g. 'doctor') implying qualifications only in Western medical science. This dualist system of medicine comprising modern and traditional sub-systems implies in India absence of a unified national system of medical education and research. There is logically a multiplicity of medical councils partly to take care of the traditional sub-systems and partly to deal with separate branches of bio-medicine like dentistry and the paramedical professions like nursing, pharmacy, physiotherapy, rehabilitation, etc. Fourthly, various medical councils are not academic regulatory bodies like the NCTE and the AICTE but professional bodies with substantial elective element as in the case of the Bar Council of India with the mandate to look after registration and ethics of the profession in addition to education. Fifthly, there are State Medical Councils but unlike the State Bar Councils, their role is confined to the areas of registration and enforcement of the professional code of ethics without any role in the educational aspects. The co-ordination of medical education and research at the State level is, therefore done, in most States, by the administrative directorates of medical education and research, but in some States by the Health Universities where they exist and are empowered (They exist in Tamil Nadu, Andhra Pradesh, Karnataka, Maharashtra, Punjab and Chhattisgarh). Sixthly, the integration between teaching, research and extension which is the publicly proclaimed characteristic of agricultural education from the 1960s and of the higher general education from 1978, when the UGC in its policy frame recognised it as the third dimension of education is rarely present in the area of medical education. Seventhly, the quality-consciousness implicit in the setting up of mechanisms of assessment and accreditation and off staff development and the concern for expansion of access entailed in the development of ODL system are not in evidence in this arena. Generally then, the field of medical education and research has been characterized by a hyper-centralising ethos of a particularly conservative kind.

The Radhakrishnan Commission (1949: 178-186) in its review of professional medical education was fairly critical of the Medical Council of India (established in 1933) and also of the Central and Provincial Governments for their inability to enforce standards. It particularly criticised the failure of various Governments to give adequate financial assistance to the colleges to come up to the minimum standard of efficiency. Unfortunately, the Commission omits to acknowledge the work of the Bhore Committee (1946) which has been noted by the author in the historical section. The Commission commented on the neglect of post-graduate training by the Medical Council and endorsed the recommendations of a Conference held in January 1949 in Madras (Now Chennai), to constitute an All-India Council of Post-Graduate Medical Education expected to function surprisingly under the Inter-University Board without any linkage with the Medical Council of India. However, it did not notice that the Bhore Committee had much earlier, recommended a central Committee for Post-Graduate Education with representation given not only to the central government and universities but also to provinces. The review of medical education by Radhakrishnan Commission was followed by several reviews (1961, 1975, 1983, 1987, 1989 and 1996) only a few of which are readily available, but thanks to the conservative orientation of the medical establishment, no substantial changes followed.

Medical Council of India: Structure and Functions

After Independence, the Indian Medical Council was reconstituted under the Indian Medical Council Act, 1956. The reconstituted IMC provides for the inclusion of licentiates to the membership of the Council and brings post-graduate medical education under the purview of the MCI Act, by constituting *a* Post-Graduate Medical Education Committee. This Committee, however, is distinct from the MCI; it is constituted by the Central Government with six Central Government nominees and three elected members of the MCI). If the MCI differs from the Committee in any matter the same is brought to the notice of the Central Government (S.20). Apart from these changes, the basic structure of the old Act was retained. The constitution of the Council, apart from the elective element, clearly shows the dominance of the Central Government. It consists of: (a) one member from each State to be nominated by the Central Government in consultation with the State Government concerned, (b) one member from each University, to be elected from amongst the members of the medical faculty of the university by members of the senate of the university, (c) one member from each State in which a State Medical Register is maintained, to be elected from amongst themselves by persons enrolled on such register, (d) seven members to be elected from amongst themselves by persons enrolled on any of the State Medical Registers who qualify to be elected in terms of Part I of the Schedule of the Act, and (e) eight members to be nominated by the Central Government. The President and Vice-President of the Council are to be elected by the members of the Council from amongst themselves. The Council is a large body which consisted of 117 members in 2002-03 of whom only 36, i.e. 32.5 per cent were nominated, the rest elected (The Calendar of MCI, 2002-03). The Council transacts its functions through two statutory committees: the Executive Committee and through any special or general-purpose committees appointed by it. Prior to the amendment of S.10 in 1993 referred to below, the powers of the Council included power to require information as to courses of study and examinations, inspection of examinations by medical inspectors appointed by the Executive Committee, visitation of examination by the visitors appointed by the Council and withdrawal of recognition (Section 19). The Council may prescribe the minimum standards of undergraduate medical education. The Supreme Court has held in the Preeti Srivastava case (1999) that these regulations are mandatory and not merely recommendatory.

During the Sixth and Seventh Plan periods, (1980-1990) the policy of the Government of India was to discourage the opening of new medical colleges in the country, as the existing medical colleges were considered to be sufficient to meet the medical manpower needs of the country. This policy was replaced in the 1990s by one of controlled growth. To reflect the policy changes, the President of India promulgated an Ordinance to amend the Indian Medical Council Act, on 27th August, 1992, which became law on 2nd April, 1993. According to its S.10A, prior permission of the Central Government is required before: (1) establishing an institution imparting education in medical sciences, (2) increasing the intake of students, or (3) introducing a new or higher course of study.

The Medical Council of India also works as the nodal agency along with the National Academy of Medical Sciences and other professional bodies to co-ordinate the Continuing Medical Education (CME) programme, for which a CME Cell was created in its office in December 1985 (Annual Report of MCI, 2002-03). There is a proposal to make CME at five yearly intervals compulsory for doctors. It is also intended to take the help of the open universities, for larger coverage of CME (National Education Policy in Health Sciences, May 1989). All these things are talked about but little action is in evidence. A National Accreditation Board for Hospitals and Health Care Providers has reportedly been set up under the Quality Council of India in February 2006 (*Hindustan Times*, 30th January 2006), but there is no proposal for an Accreditation Board for medical colleges and universities.

Some powers and functions of the Medical Council appear to represent archaic colonial attitudes. Thus, the executive committee may appoint medical inspectors to inspect a medical institution (*vide* section 17) and the President of the Medical Council may appoint visitors for the same purpose (Section 18) but the report of the visitor is treated as confidential except when otherwise directed, though a copy of the same may be sent to the Central Government. *Since visitors' reports are classified as 'confidential'*, a tendency appears to have developed in the medical bureaucracy to treat all information generated by these Councils including their Annual Reports as confidential. This contrasts sharply with specific provisions of the legal inspection of various corporate or collegial bodies under the Education and Agriculture Ministries, which direct Annual Reports of these bodies to be placed before the Parliament (e.g. S.18 of the UGC Act and S.18 of AICTE Act).

In most Academic Regulatory Acts, like the UGC, AICTE and NCTE, there is a provision for the Central Government to issue directions to the Councils on matters of policy (S.20, UGC Act; S.20, AICTE Act; S. 29, NCTE Act), and in the AICTE and the NCTE Acts there is also a provision enabling the Government to supersede the body (S.2 of AICTE act and S.30 of NCTE Act). The Medical Council of India Act (and its allied Councils) has no corresponding provisions, though there is a provision for appointment of a Commission of Enquiry and the Central Government requiring the Council to adopt its report (MCI Act, S.30). These powers are rather limited and hence, the Central Government has been trying to amend the MCI Act, which amendments according to press reports, *inter alia* provide for: (1) Four *ex-officio* members representing the Central Government, namely Director-General, Health Services, Director-General, Armed Forces Medical Services, Director, All-India Institute of Medical Sciences and President, National Board of Examinations, (2) Restriction on the tenure of President/Vice President to two terms, (3) Power with the Central Government (a) to remove a member of the Council, (b) to issue directions to the Council, and (c) to make regulations and direct Council to amend or revoke regulations, if the Council does not comply. The Bill has been criticized by the Indian Medical Association for curtailing the autonomy of the MCI (*Freedom First*, October-December, 2005: 25-26), but some such powers or at least supervisory authority appear to be necessary, considering the allegations of corruption referred to below.

The assessment of the functioning of the Medical Council of India is difficult because of absence of authentic data, except Annual Reports of the Health Ministry. It appear from the Presidential Addresses of the Council for 3 years 1956-59, which are available in printed form (Medical Council of India, 1961) that the medical profession was not happy with the way the MCI was reconstituted in 1956 with very large powers vested in the Central Government. The Scheme of the new sections added in 1993 amendment also shows that the final powers for permission for establishment of a new medical college or a new course of study vest not in the autonomous professional body but in the Central Government. The centralist design of the Act is evidently deliberate, allowing the process of opening a new medical college, increasing intake capacity, and starting new programmes to be "politicised".

However, the professional body cannot be said to have acquitted itself creditably judging from press reports from 1999 onwards indicating that the MCI was seen to be riddled with groupism, the misuse of the electoral process and corruption. The Delhi High Court in a proceeding before it, called it a den of corruption, removed Dr. Ketan Desai, the then Chairman of the Council and appointed an ex-Military Officer as an administrator to 'clean-up' the mess, though subsequently in an appeal, the Supreme Court directed the Vice-Chairman of the Council to act in place of the Chairman, pending disposal of the enquiry into corruption charges against Dr. Ketan Desai (Report, in *Indian Express*, 1999-2002) which apparently was infructuous. The administrator, however, remained undisturbed.

The sequel is interesting. Press reports in 2010 (*Indian Express*, 26th April, 2010) indicated that Dr. Ketan Desai managed to get re-elected as the Chairman of MCI for a second time. He was, however, arrested by the CBI in April 2010 in the act of taking a bribe of Rs. 2 crore to grant recognition to a Medical College in Punjab. Central Government, thereafter, took the extreme step superseding the body of the MCI as then constituted and replaced it by an *ad-hoc* Board of Governors. These facts about the apex body of medical education highlight the reality that the electoral processes of professional bodies like the MCI have been corrupted. Hence, the credibility of the professional bodies is suspect. Drastic steps are, therefore, required to be taken by the Government of India to reorganize professional bodies like the MCI and to rid them of corruption.

Lastly, reference may be made to the current medical education scene, which has been transformed since the 1980s by the phenomenon of the rise of unaided private medical colleges as in the case of engineering colleges. The number of medical colleges has increased from about 30 in 1947 to 229 in 2005, the socio-political roots of the proliferation being the same as in the case of engineering colleges, viz. the use by rural capitalists from dominant castes of a region who find in medical colleges a profitable investment opportunity or alternatively, establishment by the minority communities to avail of Constitutional protection. These colleges are expectedly concentrated in the States of Karnataka, Maharashtra, Tamil Nadu and Andhra Pradesh. There is faculty shortage in every discipline, varying from 42.50 per cent in Ayurveda, 27 per cent in Homoeopathy, 20.50 per cent in MMBS courses and 10 per cent in Dentistry courses (Ravi Bapat, May 2005).

The Role of State Governments in Medical Education

The limited role of the State Governments in medical education may be glimpsed from the following analysis. Firstly, the Medical Council Act [Section 3(1)(a)] relating to composition of the Council does provide for a nominee from each State, a provision for consultation with State Government prior to nomination having been added by the Rajya Sabha to give some voice to the States. Secondly, draft regulations regarding Standards of Medical Education in the under-graduate medical education are required to be sent by the Council to the States and can be finalized only after taking into consideration the comments of the State Governments (Section 19 A). Thirdly, the regulations made under the new Sections 10-A, 10-B and 10-C provide for an essentiality certificate from the State Governments as a prerequisite before the Council can consider application for a new college, course, etc. This requirement has been challenged by private institutions, as lacking any authority in the Act, but the Supreme Court has upheld the validity of these regulations holding that the State Governments are in the best position to give advice not only about location but also about the need for a new institute in the context of the need for additional medical manpower (Dental Council case, 2004). It may be noted that the State Governments have no role at all in the matter of regulations for standards of post-graduate medical education. It is understood that the Central Health Council's recommendation of incorporating the State Government's "essentiality certificate" for degree colleges in the text of the Act itself remains unimplemented.

State Medical Councils

State Medical Councils are a remnant of the inter-war legislation for registration of medical practitioners and for professional ethics in individual provinces and such Councils exist in all States other than Himachal Pradesh, Jammu & Kashmir and North-Eastern States except Assam. The Medical Council of India Act 1956 maintains an integral link with the State Councils for their representation. State Medical Councils have, however no role in education (*vide* Maharashtra Medical Council Act, 1965), nor is the MCI required to consult them before deciding on educational matters. There have been complaints regarding the proper and timely reconstitution of the State Medical Councils. Hence, as in the case of State Bar Council elections, interposition of the State Election Commission may be advisable by requisite legislative amendment.

State Universities of Health Sciences

An important State level formation for which initiative has come from the States themselves is the State University of Health Sciences. The aim is to create a physical and academic environment where all faculties of health science can inter-act with each other and provide a model for the educations and training of health care teams through multiprofessional and inter-professional education. The University would affiliate all medical colleges, dental colleges and para-professional colleges including nursing colleges imparting graduate level education in the State and ensure uniformity in admission criteria, curriculum and evaluation system and co-ordinate activities aimed at improving the quality of education. So far, only six States (Tamil Nadu, Andhra Pradesh, Karnataka, Maharashtra, Punjab and Chhattisgarh) have set up such universities. The Tenth Plan document suggested to all the remaining States to establish a University of Health Sciences (Tenth Plan, Vol. 2: 101). The Eleventh Plan document, however, is less enthusiastic and has suggested evaluation of experience of medical colleges to be considered first (Eleventh Plan, Vol. 2: 96).

Quality Medical Education Institutions at Regional Level: The Missing Dimension

There has always been dissatisfaction regarding the quality of Post-graduate medical education. The Bhore Committee recommended the establishment of All-India Medical Institute, on the lines of the British (Royal) Post-Graduate Medical School, Hammer Smith London or on the lines of the well-known American John Hopkins School of Medicine at Baltimore MD which would bring together, in one place, educational facilities of the highest order and not only provide post-graduate education of a desired nature but also promote research. Accordingly, the All-India Institute of Medical Sciences (AIIMS) was set up in New Delhi in 1956 as an Institution of National Importance. Other INIs in the area are: (i) the Post-Graduate Institute of Medical Education and Research (PGIMER) at Chandigarh estd. in 1965, (ii) The Shree Chitra Tirunel Institute of Medical Science and Technology at Thiruvanthapuram funded by the CSIR, (iii) National Institute of Pharmaceutical Education & Research (NIPER), Chandigarh funded by the Union Department of Pharmaceuticals. Incidentally, the Chandigarh and Thiruvananthapuram Institutions started as State level bodies. Unfortunately, though both Bhore Committee (p. 431) and the Mudaliar Committee (p. 146) had contemplated a chain of such institutions all over India, there are no such regional/State institutions of the like type elsewhere. The Mid-Term Appraisal of the Tenth

Plan indicates the intention of setting up tertiary level institutions on the lines of the AIIMS in the six backward States of Bihar, MP, Orissa, Rajasthan, Chhattisgarh and Uttarakhand and of upgrading one prominent medical institute in Uttar Pradesh, Tamil Nadu, J&K, Jharkhand, West Bengal and Andhra Pradesh to the level of AIIMS, and also to upgrade Shri Venkateswar Institute of Medical Sciences with 50 per cent expenditure to be borne by the Tirupati Trust (Mid-Term Appraisal of Tenth Plan, 2005: 100). Eleventh Plan document does not appear to refer to this aspect at all. Thus unlike technical education, the medical education sector is characterized by centralization and absence of regionalization in post-graduate education and research.

UGC-Type Body for Medical Education and Health Sector

The biggest lacuna in the field of health education is, however, that of an academic regulation-cum-grants body. The Kothari Commission recommendation (13.70), that UGC-type organization should be set up for dealing with, *inter alia*, medical education received the attention of the Ministry of Health only in 1975. The idea of setting up a Medical and Health Education Commission was mooted by the Group on Medical Education and Support Manpower (chaired by Dr. Srivastava, the then D.G. of Health Services) (Compendium 1985: 290-291). It envisaged that the Commission should have about 15 members, one-third representing the Central and State Governments and the Universities, one-third representing the National Councils and one-third consisting of leading persons in the field of health and medical education and services. Thus, all-India professional councils, viz. the Medical Council of India, the Dental Council of India, the Nursing Council of India etc. were incorporated in the structure of the proposed Commission. Each Council was to have an education panel, with the Medical and Health Education Commission functioning as an apex co-ordinating organization. Unfortunately, nothing came out of this proposal. The idea was revived, without acknowledgement to the Srivastava Group, by the Bajaj Committee (1987: 33-34), which called the body as the Education Commission for Health Sciences (ECHS), and which envisaged the Health Sciences Universities in the country as its implementing arm. The Bajaj Committee also went into related aspects like the relationship of the Commission with other systems of medicine like Ayurveda, Siddha, Yunani-Tibb and Homoeopathy, but was not as categorical about the integration of the Councils as was the Srivastava Group.

The Tenth Plan Working Group Report on Human Resources for Health (2001: 29) considered the proposal for establishment of the ECHS but decided to keep the proposal in abeyance partly due to lack of funds but mainly because it felt that most of the functions envisaged for the ECHS were already being performed by existing Statutory Councils. However, it was not averse to a Medical Grants Commission on the pattern of the UGC with the limited function of providing financial assistance for development of infrastructural facilities and uniform pay scales for medical teachers in the cash-starved medical colleges many of which were sub-standard. The National Health Policy 2002, repeated the suggestion (4.8.1). Apparently, the Health Ministry is averse to an autonomous UGC-type body combining the functions of grants and standards and would like to continue the existing arrangement under which various Councils are effectively subordinate offices of the Ministry which is the final authority in the matter of new institutions and new programmes and directly controls post-graduate medical education.

Indian Council of Medical Research (ICMR)

The development of research is a concern of the Indian Council of Medical Research (ICMR), which began life as noted in historical chapter, as the Indian Research Fund Association (IRFA) (estd. 1911). The IRFA was renamed in 1950 as the ICMR whose mandate is to support research in medical colleges, universities, laboratories and research institutes throughout the country. The control and management of the Council are vested in the Governing Body of which the Union Minister of Health is the President. It consists of administrative officers of the government as well as experts. The governing body is assisted by a Scientific Advisory Board and a number of advisory committees. ICMR has made continuous progress in successive plans. By the year 2003-04 the ICMR had expanded considerably with a network of 21 permanent institutes and 6 regional medical research centres spread all over the country. It also continues to give grants-in-aid to projects in the non-ICMR institutes (Annual Report of Health Ministry, 2003-04: 77-78). It publishes the Indian Journal of Medical Research' and has established a centre for bio-medical information, which provides relevant information to medical colleges even in remote areas. The data about the extent of involvement of under-graduate medical colleges in research, however, are not available.

Other Professional Councils in Scientific Medicine

In the following paragraphs the structure and functioning of the professional councils other than the MCI would be examined briefly to make the picture of scientific medical education complete, also underlining the extent of specialization consequent on modernization giving rise to new professions necessitating regulation of the same.

Dental Education

*The Dental Council of India**

There were only three Dental Colleges in India at the time of independence, viz. Nair Hospital Dental College, Bombay (Now Mumbai), the CEM Dental College, Bombay (Now Mumbai) (which later on became Government Dental College) and Culcutta (Kolkata) Dental College, Culcutta (Kolkata) of which only the Government Dental College in Bombay (Now Mumbai) was affiliated to the University of Bombay (Now Mumbai) for 4 years' BDS Course, the remaining colleges awarding only licentiate qualifications called L.D.Sc./L.D.S.

Bhore Committee's conclusions leading to the recommendation for establishment of a Dental Council of India were as below:

(1) Dentistry has unfortunately been one of the neglected subjects of study in 'practically all' Indian universities. There is an acute shortage of adequately trained dental surgeons.

(2) The vast majority of practising dental surgeons treats only the wealthy. For the poor, there is practically no provision at

* The account below draws on the Silver Jubilee Volume (1972) of the Dental Council of India.

all and dentists are employed only to a very limited extent in the State hospitals.

(3) The profession of dentistry is almost totally unorganised in India and there is no law to regulate the same (except in Bengal, where a Provincial Dental Act was in force since 1937).

(4) Provision be made for three types of dental personnel, viz. (a) Dental surgeons, (b) Dental hygienists (who scale, clean or polish teeth), and (c) Dental mechanics (who make or repair dentures).

(5) 25 Dental colleges should be established with 100 admissions at each, MDS courses should be started and Degree and Master's courses should be standardized.

(6) Satisfactory results from the above steps would not obtained unless the State undertakes establishment of a comprehensive dental service to meet the urgent needs of the population.

(7) Central and Provincial Dental Councils should be created to recognise training institutions and qualifications and maintenance of Dentists' Registers with disciplinary regulations for the profession.

In the troubled times leading to Independence, the fledgling dental profession rose to the occasion and formed an all-India Dental Association with its Headquarter at Delhi in 1946, and its leaders comprising Dr. S.K. Majumdar *et al.* prepared a Draft Dentists Act which was passed by the Constituent Assembly on 26th February, 1948. The Dental Council was founded on 12th April, 1948 and functioned as a wholly nominated body for the first 5 years. The Dentists Act, 1948 provides for a largely elected Dental Council (except for six members nominated by the Central Government) with a term of 5 years. The Executive Council consists of Director-General Health Services, *ex-officio* as a Member. This contrasts with the MCI whose Executive Council has no such nominee. The functions of the Dental Council include laying down of minimum standards of dental training, recognition of dental colleges and withdrawal of the same, conduct of inspections, obtaining information, etc. The 1948 Act vested the power of recognition of dental qualifications in the Dental Council but by an amendment in 1972 these powers were vested in the Central Government, which was however, required to consult the Dental Council. By the same amendment, the Council was empowered to appoint visitors (as distinguished from inspectors) who would report to the President and whose report, unlike that of an Inspector is treated as confidential. Whereas the inspector's report is sent to the Institution and Central and State governments in the normal course, the visitor's report can be submitted only to the Central Government on a requisition. In order to bring about uniformity, Central Dental Council was also empowered to prescribe standards of professional conduct, etiquette and code of ethics. Unlike in the case of the Medical Council of India, there is a built-in provision in the Dentists Act for constitution of the State Dental Councils. As in the case of the Medical Council of India, the Dentists Act was amended in August 1992 by an ordinance which was converted into an Act in April 1993 under which new Dental Colleges, or new higher courses could be established/ instituted and intake capacity of existing Dental Colleges could be increased only after prior permission of the Government of India which, of course, would consult the Dental Council.

The number of Dental Colleges in India in 2001 was 192 with an intake capacity of 8900. The number of Dental Colleges with post-graduate education facilities was 37 with an intake capacity of 427 seats. As in the case of medical colleges, there is a regional (South/ West *v.* North/East) imbalance, Karnataka having 42 Dental Colleges, Maharashtra 18 and UP 1. Also, as in the case of Medical Colleges, the expansion since 1980s has come about through privatization (113 out of the 143 recognised BDS colleges were private as in 2001), with its attendant evils of inadequate infrastructure, deficiency in clinical materials, faculty shortage (which Ravi Bapat has estimated to be 14 per cent in terms of senior staff and 7 per cent in terms of junior staff in Maharashtra), and the consequent wastage and low quality of the out-turn (i.e. the number of dental surgeons passing out each year).

While the structure of the Dentists Act shows a slight improvement over the structure of the Medical Council Act (to the extent of uniformity of Constitution of State Dental Councils, provision of Government nominee in the Executive Council etc.), the spirit is that of a closed system. The Act, therefore, needs to be modernized, made more open and the conduct of elections needs to be entrusted to the State Election Commission.

Nursing Education

*Nursing Council of India**

Bhore Committee had recommended the establishment of Nursing Council of India to ensure uniform standard of nursing training in India. The Constituent Assembly of India passed the Indian Nursing Council Act towards the end of 1947. Nurses are regarded as para-professional staff and it was the first para-professional council to be set up in India, the other such council being the Pharmacy Council.

The Nursing Council started functioning in 1948. Its priority was to develop a composite General Nursing and Midwifery (GNM) syllabus, which it did in 1951. In 1954, the subject of public health was integrated with the curriculum. In 1957, the Act was amended to provide for maintenance of Indian Nurses Register as a mandatory requirement. General nursing was distinguished from auxiliary nursing and the ANM syllabus and the syllabus for health workers were revised in 1977. In 1980, the permission of State Government was made mandatory for opening new schools/colleges of nursing. In 1981, the syllabus of B.Sc. (Nursing) was revised. In 1986, General Nursing and Midwifery (GNM) syllabus was revised providing for a mandatory duration of 3 years. The Council has also developed a syllabus for M.Sc. (Nursing).

The Council is a large body comprising elected registered nurses (State-wise), elected Heads of Institutions in nursing education institutions, Heads of Institutions elected from Health Visitor Institutions, and nominated officers of the Central Government and State Governments (by rotation in two groups). Interestingly, not only MCI, but also the Indian Medical Association and the Trained Nurses Association are represented.

The Council faced financial difficulties in 1994-95. Thereafter, it revised the fees for inspection and its financial situation stabilized. The Council's felt difficulties are: lack of response from State Nursing

---

* The account below draws on the Silver [Golden?] Jubilee Volume of Nursing Council of India (2000).

Councils (there are 18 of them: Andhra Pradesh, Assam, Bihar, Gujarat, Haryana, Himachal Pradesh, Kerala, Karnataka, Maharashtra, Madhya Pradesh, Orissa, Punjab, Rajasthan, Tamil Nadu, Tripura, Uttar Pradesh and West Bengal) the NE states other than Tripura are in the process of setting up their councils). The Council faces difficulties because of delay by the State Councils in sending up-to-date data regarding registered nurses.

There are at present 654 General Nursing/Midwives training schools in the country of which 456 are run by private/voluntary organizations/missionary institutions. As in other professional institutions, there is acute shortage of teachers. Around 20,000 nurses become available annually. It is difficult to arrive at the figure of nurses required, because of different norms, e.g. nurse : population; nurse : doctor or nurse : bed. Bhore Committee suggested a norm of one nurse per 500 population, which was brought down by Mudaliar Committee to 1 : 1000 to be attained by the year 1991. Bajaj Committee on Health Manpower (1987) had estimated a shortfall of 7 lakh nurses by the year 2000. The problem appears to be to have reliable data of practising, i.e. active trained nurses because only 40 per cent of trained manpower is estimated to be active. In practice, the tendency to utilise student nurses in hospitals shows that there is a real shortage, apart from the theoretical consideration that in India, the nurse:doctor ratio of 1 : 2 is stated to be contrary to global trend of having five nurses per doctor. It is in this background that one needs to consider the recommendation of a high power committee on "Nursing and Nursing Profession" (1989) to make provision for independent practice by nurses and to amend the INC Act for that purpose (Nursing Council of India, 2000).

Pharmacy Education

The position of pharmacy education in India is ambiguous. While as a discipline, it is allied to Medicine, the subject of pharmacy education is dealt officially with, not by the Ministry of Health but by the AICTE, which functions under the Ministry of HRD (Department of Higher Education). Administratively, however, the Pharmacy Council functions under the Ministry of Health. Its composition also reflects this as the Director-General of Central Government Health Services is an *ex-officio* Member of the Council.

Historically, pharmaceutical education dates back to pre-Independence period, the first institution having been started by the BHU in 1932. However, the need for regulation of training and profession arose because of practical difficulties caused by existence of unauthorized practitioners. The Pharmacy Act was passed by the Constituent Assembly at the same time as the Dentists Act was passed (in 1948); it received the President's assent on 4th March 1948. The practical difficulties were serious in that persons having no education in related disciplines were wrongly compounding, mixing or dispensing medicine and the system was causing a great havoc to the health of people. The Central Council consists of six experts elected by the UGC, six experts nominated by the Central Government, one member elected by the MCI, D-GHS, Drug Controller of India, Director, Central Drugs Laboratory, a representative of the UGC, a representative of the AICTE, Members elected from State Pharmacy Councils, and members nominated by State Governments (Pharmacy Act, 1948). It is seen that there is a large element of nominated members. The Council is empowered to frame Pharmacy Education Regulations, improve courses of study, withdraw approval, conduct inspections and maintain a Central Register. There is no provision for appointment of visitors/inspectors. There is a built-in provision for State Pharmacy Councils, which have to maintain State Registers. There is a provision for appointment of a Commission of Enquiry by the Central Government. A significant point about the Council is that *it is more autonomous than the MCI or the DCI, because it can finally approve the colleges to be recognised.*

Till 1987, the UGC, the AICTE and the State Pharmacy Councils were not represented on the Central Council when the Act was amended for that purpose. The Pharmacy Education Regulations appear to have been framed only in 1991 when the trend towards proliferation of pharmacy education institutions granting diplomas and degrees gathered momentum. State Governments are given a stake inasmuch as the Central Council is required to circulate draft Education Regulations among the States and take their comments into consideration before finalizing the Regulations. The State Governments are required to be consulted before withdrawal of recognition of a course and are also sent a copy of inspection report for comments.

The growth of pharmacy education was initially moderate. There were only 29 pharmacy colleges until 1980; however, in the recent past there has been a sudden upsurge in the number of Pharmacy Colleges at all three levels—Diploma, bachelor and M.Sc. no doubt partly due to the demand from the Pharma Industry, but also as part of the trend towards commercialization. In the year 2005-06, the number of colleges is reported to be 625 with an intake capacity of 53,000 students (Eleventh Plan Working Group Report on Technical Education, 2007).

It may be noted that a centre of excellence in pharmacy education has been established in the form of the National Institute of Pharmaceutical Education and Research, Chandigarh which was declared as an Institute of National Importance (INI) in 1991. It works under the Union Department of Pharmaceuticals and is apparently pharmaceutical industry-oriented.

National Education Policy on Health Sciences

The National Health Policy 1982 had recommended the formulation of a 'National Education Policy on Health Sciences'. Such a policy was framed in May 1989. It largely followed the prescriptions of the Bajaj Committee (1987) on health manpower. It deplored the medical bias in the process of health system planning and the lopsided development of health manpower in which nurse doctor ratio is 1 : 2 which should at least be 2 : 1 and also over production of post-graduates and super-specialists. It emphasized the need for increase in the number of dentists and post-graduates in dentistry. It suggested the establishment of a medical library network in which the National Medical Library, New Delhi would perform a co-ordinator's role. Above all, it recommended the establishment of Education Council in Health Sciences with the State universities as its implementing arms. It wanted the manpower in the Indian systems of medicine to be utilised for specific tasks like health education, drug distribution and family welfare. The policy has been criticized as being too bland (Imrana Quadeer/K.K. Nayar, 2005).

Education in Traditional Systems of Medicine: Ayurveda, Unani, Siddha and Homoeopathy (AYUSH)

The policy scenario of the Indian Systems of Medicine has been characterized by shifts and turns. This has been partly due to internal divisions within the Ayurved-lobby which was divided between supporters of "Shuddha Ayurveda Education" on the one hand and the supporters of "Integrated Ayurvedic Education" on the other. Several committees were appointed. It may broadly be stated that the supporters of Shuddha Ayurveda prevailed mainly because the dominant bio-medical establishment was opposed to Ayurveda and could not countenance any form of integration; therefore, co-existence was the only form of *modus vivendi*. With this background Central Council of Indian Medicine Act, 1970 was passed.

Initially, the proposal was to have a common Council for Ayurveda and Homoeopathy but both the groups opposed it and the idea was dropped. At present, there are two separate Councils, namely (a) Central Council of Indian Medicine, which covers Ayurveda, Siddha and Unani, and (b) Central Council of Homoeopathy. These Councils regulate under-graduate and post-graduate education and research in their respective systems (Department of ISM&H, 1998).

The budgetary support for Ayurveda in the overall budget has varied from 1-3 per cent. During the Janata regime, when Raj Narain, was Health Minister, Siddha Branch of Ayurveda, predominant in Tamil Nadu was added. In 1995, a separate Department of Indian Systems of Medicine came into existence which was renamed as AYUSH in 2001. The Ministry also brought out a Draft National Policy on Indian Systems of Medicine in 2001. In this document, the need for improving the quality of training and research in Indian systems has been emphasized. In addition, the need to check the quality of indigenous medicines by enforcing hygienic production and batch manufacturing has been unambiguously stated; standardization of raw materials and formulas is a first requisite for such an endeavour. The Ministry has announced that from 2004 onwards, only firms adhering to good manufacturing practices in terms of hygiene, quality control and documentation would receive a licence for the production of Unani and Ayurvedic Medicine (Maartin Bode, 2007). Madhulika Banerjee (2002) has pointed out that the Draft Policy is the first indication of the

Central Government that it is prepared to promote pluralism and introduce strategies to mainstream the indigenous systems of medicines.

The Eleventh Plan Document reflects the changed approach of the Central Government. It presents the following picture of the education and research institutions at the end of the Tenth Plan (Eleventh Plan, 2008, Vol. 2: 110 *vide* Table 12.1).

The Eleventh Plan document is aware of the weaknesses of the education in the institutions of ISM and sets the following agenda to upgrade Ayush under-graduate and post-graduate educational institutions by better regulation and establishing a system of NET type testing of Ayush teachers and NACC type assessment and accreditation of Ayush UG/PG Colleges.

Research in Traditional Systems of Medicine

The Government of India had established the Central Institute of Research in indigenous system of medicine at Jamnagar in 1953 and set up there a Post-Graduate Training Centre in Ayurveda in 1956. All three were merged in the Ayurveda University, Jamnagar in 1965 under the State Government. Systematic research in Ayurveda under the auspices of Government of India started in 1969 with the establishment of the Central Council for Research on Indian Medicine and Homoeopathy (CCRIMH). In 1978, CCRIMH was split into four separate Councils one each for (a) Ayurveda and Siddha, (b) Unani medicine, (c) Yoga and Naturopathy, and (d) Homoeopathy. They are apex bodies for formulation, co-ordination, development and promotion of research in their respective systems, with a network of research institutes and centres functioning under them. They engage in activities relating to scientific communication and information. Conventionally research is conducted by respective universities and post-Graduate colleges under them, but so far as Ayurveda is concerned, research is conducted by the Ayurveda University Jamnagar as well as. Moreover, the Central Government has also set up separate Central institutions/laboratories for conducting research in the respective systems as below: for Ayurveda at Jaipur, for Siddha at Chennai, for Unani Medicine at Bangalore (now Bangaluru) for naturopathy at Urulikanchan (Maharashtra), for Homoeopathy at Culcutta (Kolkata), for Yoga at New Delhi in addition to Pharmacopoeia Laboratories at Ghaziabad.

Table 12.1: Details of AYUSH Educational Institutions and their capacity

Items	*Ayurveda*	*Siddha*	*Naturopathy*	*Unani*	*Homoeopathy*	*Total*
(1)	(2)	(3)	(4)	(5)	(6)	(7)
UG Colleges	240	07	10	39	83	479
Admission Capacity (UG)	11,225	350	385	1,750	13,425	27,135
Colleges with PG Courses	62	03	—	07	33	105
Admission Capacity	991	110	—	67	1,084	2,252
Exclusive PG Institutions	02	01	—	01	02	06
Admission Capacity (PG)	40	30	—	28	00	197
Total Institutions	242	08	10	40	185	485

Source: Department of AYUSH, Statistics as on 1-4-2007.

Unani Medicine—An NGO Initiative

A reference may be made here to a NGO initiative in Unani medical education in the form of Jamia Hamdard (JH) at Tughlaqabad in South Delhi. It is established by the Hamdard National Foundation (HNF). UGC has recognised it as a deemed university in 1992 and has been paying 25 per cent of the operational cost as annual grant. In that year, HNF donatd Rs. 2.5 crore to Jamia Hamdard, UGC gave Rs. 1 crore and the University itself contributed Rs. 0.5 crore. However, it may be noted that the JH is mainly devoted to modern medicine with a Faculty of Science, faculty of Pharmacy and Majeedia Hospital, a modern Hospital with a modest Unani wing. It does have a Unani College under its wing. It has, therefore, been judged to be an Islamic cultural façade for global bio-medicine (Maartin Bode, 2007: 111-112).

An Overview

In the introduction, it was noted that Medical Education has some special characteristics as a species of higher professional education. This chapter underlines the fact that it is withal a complex subject because several issues relating to India's traditions and the process of modernization are raised when one considers its course of evolution. There is no doubt that Medical Education requires a thorough reorganization including modernization of its complicated legal framework. In the first instance, it requires its Flexner-type Report preparatory to thorough going reforms, the reference being to the Report prepared by Abraham Flexner for the Carnegie Corporation for the Advancement of Teaching in Medical Education in the US and Canada. Published in 1908, it led to the revamping of medical education in the US consequent on closure of a large number of sub-standard medical colleges and similar results may be expected in India also.

Whither Medical Education

Yashpal Committee Report has recommended Medical Education to be covered under the umbrella organization of the National

Commission for Higher Education & Research. However, the Health Ministry has successfully resisted the recommendation relying on the fact that the Presidential Address to Parliament in 2009 had announced Government's intention to set up an organization for development of human resources in health and medicine.

13

Agricultural and Forestry Education

The Constitutional Position

Since Dyarchy (1919-1936), agriculture including animal husbandry, veterinary practice and fisheries and since Provincial Autonomy (1935-1947) forestry, have been "transferred" provincial subject. In the Constitution, there was no change in the position till the constitutional amendment of 1977. The common supposition that since 1977 Education as a whole is on the Concurrent List is not factual; agricultural, veterinary and fishery education and research which represent a substantial institutional spread, student enrollment and financial outlay of the educational sector have been State subjects continuously since 1919. However, since 1972, when the Central legislation was passed on the allied subject of wild life education and research vide entry 17B of the Concurrent List and since 1977, forestry education and research, *vide* entry 17A of the Concurrent List, are concurrent subjects.

Indian Council for Agricultural Research (ICAR) began in 1929 as a research organization funding individual schemes either from general funds or from the proceeds of agricultural produce cess, for which proposals were received by it. After Independence it entered the field of agricultural education during the First Plan. In 1960s and 1970s, it was reorganized in the context of the stellar role of agricultural research in the Green Revolution in the country. It can generally be said that agriculture and forestry are areas in which research has led education. This is due to the fact that both agriculture and forestry are concerned with the natural resource of land and the colonial as well as the post-colonial States have found it expedient to invest heavily in research to maximize State revenue. Higher education in these areas has followed as a corollary. It would be logical, therefore, to consider agricultural and veterinary research first followed by agricultural and veterinary education.

Agricultural Research: Indo-American Teams and Reorganisation

In the 1950s the ICAR was perceived as an ineffective organization without any grip over the agencies in which agricultural research was conducted. These agencies included the Central Commodity Committees and the Central Research Institutes apart from State Directorates. The majority of the Central Commodity Committees dated back to the pre-1947 period, viz. cotton, lac, jute, sugarcane, coconut, tobacco and oilseeds. The Arecanut Committee was created in 1949 and the Spices and Cashew Nut committees in 1967. Support for cotton, lac, oilseeds and coconut committees was provided through a cess and for the rest through an allocation by the Ministry of Agriculture. All these Committees had their own research stations.

Similarly, there were Central Research Institutions for Agricultural Research (IARI, Pusa—estd. 1906 shifted to Delhi in 1930), Veterinary Research (IVRI, Izatnagar—estd. in Poona in 1889), soil research, research in specific crops [Rice at Cuttack; Potato at Patna, subsequently shifted to Shimla, Sugarcane breeding at Coimbatore, vegetable breeding at Kulu, Dairy—first at Bangalore and subsequently shifted to Karnal], research in fisheries (inland at Barrackpur and marine at Mandapam). The conceptual basis of the bureaucratic organization was that the Agriculture Ministry proper was concerned with increase in production and agricultural research, for which ICAR was responsible, was a subservient function to the primary function of production. The Ministry was headed by a Secretary level officer and the ICAR, which was categorized as a subordinate organization, was headed by an officer of the rank of Additional Secretary, designated as Vice-President of the ICAR and (Research) Adviser to the Government. ICAR funded research schemes including those of the Central Research Institutions but the

Vice-President, ICAR had no direct control over them. Initially, the Vice-President of the ICAR was the President of most of the Central Commodity Committees but gradually in respect of some committees (e.g. lac and tobacco) Agricultural Commissioner to Government of India (a technical officer of the Agriculture Ministry) was put in-charge. All these organizations had their own decision-making channels, e.g. ICAR worked through Advisory Boards and Scientific Panels; the Central Commodity Committees were large bodies and worked through a number of committees. The administrative cost of their working was high. Their sanction for research project was for a short period and since they followed the matching principle for funding rigidly, some committees accumulated reserve funds (oilseeds committee during 1947-1955 had a reserve fund of Rs. 70 lakh). Commodity Committee approach led to the neglect of non-commodity problems in areas like soil management, agricultural engineering, etc.

In this scenario was appointed in November 1954 the first Joint Indo-American Team on Agricultural Research and Education (1954-55) under the Chairmanship of Shri K.R. Damle, ICS then the Vice-President of the ICAR. The Terms of Reference of the Team were wide, covering study and needs of Indian institutions engaged in agricultural research, extension or agricultural education at college level, to suggest methods for co-ordinating the work of such institutions functioning under the Centre, the States and the universities and for strengthening them and improving them. It was clarified that the term 'agriculture' was used in the broad sense to include animal husbandry, veterinary science and other allied subjects. The resolution setting up the Team specifically referred to the Land Grant College experience of the United States as a justification for the association of American experts. The Team endorsed the recommendations of Radhakrishnan Commission to set up a Rural University comprising a group of colleges of agriculture, veterinary, home science, technology and applied liberal arts and science and recommended the *encouragement of development of such universities by substantial grants-in-aid from the Centre*. The Committee noted plans under consideration for setting up such Universities at UP (Tarai), West Bengal (Haringhatta), Bihar (Patna), Orissa (Bhubaneswar), Travancore-Cochin and Bombay, Anand (now in Gujarat).

Regarding the ICAR, the Committee's recommendations are scattered but reading them together, they envisage nothing short of a reorganization of the ICAR. Firstly, the diagnosis regarding lack of the co-ordination, is contained in para 88 as below: "Aside from a limited measure of co-ordination of schemes supported by the ICAR, there is no real integration of the agricultural research efforts... The work of the Central Institutes is entirely independent of the ICAR ... The independent action of the commodity committees presents a further problem."

Hence, para 89 suggests that "ICAR should be suitably strengthened to function as an organization at the Centre with responsibilities for co-ordinating leadership and services that are recognized by the Central Institutions, by the States and by other research organizsations." Further recommendation is made for setting up under the ICAR a central cadre of scientific personnel of Class II and above, for Central institutions to deal directly with ICAR and, in fact, to work as the executive arms or the operating side of the ICAR. It was suggested that the Indian Council of Agricultural Education (under the ICAR) should propose minimum standards of agricultural education. The Team also recommended establishment of post-graduate colleges at IARI (New Delhi) and IVRI (Izatnagar). The Team submitted its report in September 1955. Unfortunately, the recommendations of this Team, though accepted in principle by the Central Government, could not be implemented as the Report was submitted after the Second Five Year Plan was formulated. However, IARI, New Delhi and IVRI, Izatnagar did initiate post-graduate training. Another fall-out was expansion of the Extension Section of the ICAR.

On the eve of the Third Five Year Plan (1961-1966), the second Joint Indo-American Team headed by Dr. Randhwa, the Vice Principal of the ICAR was appointed in September 1959 to evaluate the progress of work relating to Agricultural Education, Research and Extension (ERE), to develop supplementary recommendations in the context of the Third Plan and to review the sisterhood arrangements concluded in 1955 with five land-grant universities of the USA (These were Illinois, Ohio, Kansas, Missouri and Tennessee and they were paired with (1) MP, (2) Punjab and Rajasthan, (3) West Bengal, Orissa, Assam, (4) Bombay (Now Mumbai) and UP, (5) Madras (Now Chennai), Mysore and Kerala respectively).

This second Report was shorter but its recommendations more pointed. It suggested that no recognition should be given either to new agricultural colleges or to p-g courses unless they conform to the minimum requirements laid down by ICAR. The Committee noted that the first agricultural university had come up at Rudrapur in the then UP (now Uttarakhand). It noted that proposals for establishment of such universities in Punjab, West Bengal, Madras (Now Tamil Nadu), Bombay (Now Maharashtra), Bihar and AP were pending. It suggested the following pre-conditions for assistance for establishment of such universities: (i) autonomous status, (ii) location of agricultural/veterinary/animal husbandry/home science, science, technological and science colleges on the same campus, (iii) integration of education research and extension. It recommended strengthening of the ICAR on the education side. On the research side, it categorically recommended that all the Central Research Institutes and the Commodity Committees be brought under the full technical and administrative control of the ICAR and the technical staff of the ICAR strengthened for the same. It wanted the branch and regional stations of these two categories of research institutions to be integrated with State stations. It made recommendations on strengthening extension all along the line. It recommended continuance of inter-university contract programmes at least till the end of the Third Plan. Building on cooperation between the Central Institutions in the crops of cotton, oilseeds and millets under PIRROM programme (Project for Intensification of Regional Research in Cotton, Oilseds and Millets), and the First Team's idea of MoU between States and Centre, it suggested Centre-State cooperation in research on the basis of agro-climatic zones, an idea suggested by the Agricultural Administration Committee (Chairman: Raja of Nalgarh, 1958).

While the re-organization of the ICAR was in the air for 5-6 years (1954-1960), it came to a head after Agricultural Research Review Team under Dr. Parker, suggested an organizational model. The Government of India decisions came in 1965 which involved:

(1) Reconstitution of the Governing Body of the ICAR to make it pre-eminently a body of scientists headed by a scientist designated as Director-General.
(2) Bringing all agricultural research Institutions (including for crops, veterinary, dairy and fisheries) and also including those under the commodity committees under the reorganized ICAR.

(3) Re-designating IARI, IVRI and NDRI as National Institutions.
(4) Giving of financial assistance for research and education to State Agricultural Universities (SAUs).
(5) Making of arrangements for recruitment to scientific posts through ICAR's own selection committee.

The reorganized Governing Board headed by Dr. B.P. Pal, a biological scientist (with specialization in roses) came into existence in May 1965. He was assisted by four DDGs in the areas of (i) Crop Sciences, (ii) Soil Agronomy, Irrigation and Agricultural Engineering, (iii) Animal Sciences, and (iv) Agricultural Education. However, the ICAR continued to be a subordinate organization of the Ministry.

ICAR underwent a second reorganization on the basis of the Report of the ICAR Enquiry Committee chaired by Justice P.B. Gajendragadkar (June 1973). Though the immediate occasion for the appointment of the Committee was the suicide in May 1972 by a young agricultural scientist, who was apparently frustrated by denial of promotion to him. The Committee was basically asked to review recruitment and personnel policies of the ICAR and suggest measures for improvement. In the light of the Committee's recommendations, the second reorganization involved:

(1) Creation of a Department of Agricultural Research and Education (DARE) in the Ministry of Agriculture to provide the ICAR with the requisite linkages with the Central and State Government agencies.
(2) Initiating a recruitment procedure through a special Agricultural Scientists' Recruitment Board with an eminent agricultural scientist as a whole-time Chairman.
(3) Creation of a separate Agricultural Research Service (ARS).
(4) Management Committees for the Research Institutions.

Accordingly, DARE was established with effect from 15-12-1973. The composition of the Council was reduced in number. The Advisory Board was abolished as unnecessary. Standing Committees were abolished and replaced by Scientific Panels for various disciplines under (1) Agriculture, (2) Animal Sciences, and (3) Miscellaneous including

Agricultural Education. The entire country was divided into 8 agro-ecological regions and Regional Committees were set up for each of them. After the two-stage re-organization of the ICAR in the period 1965-73, ICAR now ranks with other scientific bodies like CSIR, AEC, ISRO, ICMR etc. with the difference that since it deals with standards of agricultural education, it is also comparable to the UGC.

Since 1973, there have been at least three major reviews of the working of the ICAR as below:

(1) G.V.K. Rao Committee (ICAR Review Committee), 1988.
(2) Hemendra Kumar Committee (2002) (Committee set up to review administrative structure of the ICAR headquarters and its linkages with institutions and SAUs).
(3) Mashelkar Committee (July 2005) (Report of the ICAR Reorganization Committee).

It is not necessary to consider the recommendations of these committees individually. The same will be referred to as the occasion demands.

Structure and Functions of the ICAR as a Corporate Body

Since 1929, ICAR has functioned as a registered society (*vide* MoA of the ICAR, August 2000). The object of the society has been to undertake, promote and co-ordinate agricultural and animal husbandry education, research and its application in practice, development and marketing in India. However, Rule 12 A added in 1975 clarifies that agro-forestry, fisheries and home science are also its concern, that the ICAR has to act as a clearing house of research and general information, provide, undertake and promote consultancy services and look into the problems relating to the broader areas of rural development. This definition is in line with the thinking in the ICAR since 1954. The reference to agro-forestry underlines the synergy between agricultural and forestry education/research and it may be noted that both were under a single Ministry of the Central Government till 1980. The model Act for Agricultural Universities has, *ab initio*, worked with a broad definition including therein forestry, farm forestry, forest management and silviculture as well as sericulture including mulberry culture.

The ICAR Society is a large body with the Union Minister for Agriculture as the President and with the Ministers of various States in-charge of Agriculture, Animal Husbandry and Fisheries as Members. After Agricultural Universities came to be established from 1960 onwards, four Vice-Chancellors of Agricultural Universities are to be nominated on the Society by the President of the Society. The recommendation of the G.V.K. Rao Committee to reduce the number of Ministers from almost 75 to 20 was not accepted by the Government. The powers of the Society as given in Rules 16 and 17 include the power to issue directions, to review the progress and performance of the constituent units and give policy directions to the Governing Body (GB) which is presided over by the D-G, and includes, *inter alia*, three Vice-Chancellors of Agricultural Universities named by the Union Agriculture Minister, *vide* rule 35.

The Hemendra Kumar Committee suggested revision of the composition of the GB to include representatives of two State governments, an eminently reasonable suggestion in the context of India's federal polity, but this was not accepted. The ICAR Reorganization Committee (July 2005) recommended appointment of the Prime Minister as the President of the Society to give agricultural research the focus it deserves. This would bring the ICAR on par with the CSIR. This recommendation has apparently not been accepted since Union Agriculture Minister continues to be the Chairman of the ICAR till 2010.

In the federal context, the evolution of the mechanism of the All-India Co-ordinated Research Projects (AICRPs) is the unique contribution of the ICAR. It involved building up of a nation-wide co-operative inter-disciplinary research network linking the ICAR research institutes with the SAUs to focus attention on commodities and species of national importance. The first projects in maize and agronomic trials go back to the mid-1960s and are ongoing. By pooling together national resources, some of the projects were able to effect a breakthrough in production by (i) generating an improved technology through inter-disciplinary research, and (ii) evaluating the suitability, adaptability and transferability of technology to different ecological regions. The Kothari Commission commended (14.20) AICRPs as below: "[They are] all-India (projects) with active Centre-State co-operation which are proving to be highly effective not only in making research activity more efficient, expeditious and productive but also in the development of valuable research potential in the country and in the creation of a cadre of able research leaders."

The ICAR research system in 2007 comprised 48 Central institutes including 4 National Institutes, 33 Institutes in the field of Agricultural Science, and 11 institutes in the field of Animal Sciences and Fisheries. In addition, there are 4 National Bureaux, 12 Project Directorates, 62 All-India Coordinated Research projects, and 32 National Research Centres. There are 158 Research Stations under the ICAR institutes. The ICAR also supports research in State Agricultural University and one Central University (at Manipur). The financial allocation for ICAR increased from Rs. 3.72 crore in 1958-59 to Rs. 131.09 crore in 1984-85 to Rs. 1253 crore in the year 2004-05 (Annual Report, DARE, 2004-05).

The Pathology of Agricultural Research

Over the years, however, there has been a massive centralization, failure to engage in fruitful co-operation with the SAUs and reluctance to take hard decisions. Thus the G.V.K. Rao Committee noted examples of duplication of work between commodity research institutes and related All-India Co-ordinated Research Projects and between Research Stations of the ICAR institutes and the SAUs. This proliferation of institutes and manpower and increase in expenditure have unfortunately been associated with a decline in agricultural productivity in the 1990s (2.3% as against 3.7% in 1980s). The Planning Commission in its Mid-Term Appraisal of the Ninth Plan had observed, "The proliferation of Institutions is pushing the establishment cost significantly, leaving very little for the R & D work. This also places scientists in watertight compartments leading to sub-optimal utilization of manpower and equipment. The results of research activities undertaken by the ICAR are not commensurate with the high infrastructure set up" (Planning Commission, October 2000: 73).

This assessment has been echoed, only more bluntly, by the Mid-Term Appraisal of the 10th Plan (June 2005; 214-216). It noted that the multiplicity of institutes with overlapping mandates has led to duplication of research work. It has urged redefining the mandate of the system's operating units and possible reduction in the number of institutions and work-force. It has suggested that there should be a better definition of research responsibilities as between the ICAR institutes and the SAUs, and also a greater synergy between the two sets of institutions, with the ICAR assuming the role of a mentor of the SAUs and back-strapping this role by larger financial assistance to the SAUs but based on a performance oriented award system, up to Rs. 10 crore.

The Eleventh Plan document (Vol. I, 2007: 10) suggests that a comprehensive view of the functioning of the agricultural research system should be taken so as to make systemic changes in the course of the Eleventh Plan. It deplores the tendency to concentrate on increasing the yield potential without attention to environmental impact and methods and practices for the efficient use of these inputs for sustainable agriculture.

It is clear that India has built up a strong manpower base in agricultural research and its utilization needs to be optimized by devising modalities for Centre-State Co-operation. Hemendra Kumar Committee recommended shifting of five out of eight DD-Gs at ICAR headquarters to make the five Regional Committees effective which recommendation was unfcrtunately not accepted. Mashelkar Committee had bluntly advocated abolition of existing posts of DD-Gs and AD-Gs but it also favoured revival of some of them by the device of renaming them. Since regions are conceptual entities without the benefit of embedded administrative structures, the best course according to the author would be to have State-wise committees of the ICAR for at least the major States.

The author now considers how agricultural education has evolved, partly in response to the needs of agricultural research and partly autonomously.

Agricultural Education (1947-1973)

Prior to Independence, the ICAR did not have a specific role in relation to agricultural education. CABE appointed a committee on Agricultural education in 1944, which observed in its report (1946:

62-78) that although agricultural education was logically a branch of technical education, it may, for the present, continue to be in the administrative charge of the Agricultural Departments, to enable them to bring together the research workers and the farmers, thus recognizing the symbiosis between research and education through extension. It recommended the setting up of an Indian Council of Agricultural Education (ICAE) within the ICAR, to ensure that the institutions concerned maintain proper standards of instruction, examination and training and bringing under the purview of the universities the examinations for bachelor and higher degrees in agriculture.

The Radhakrishnan Commission (1949: 136) after noting that at present there are 17 agricultural colleges in India with an intake of 1500 and that the report of the CABE Committee on Agricultural education suggests establishment of resident rural high schools in addition to pre-existing 19 agricultural schools, recommended that an agricultural education and research panel, attached to the UGC, along the lines proposed in the report for engineering education and research, be established for apportioning available resources for agricultural education and research. The Commission, however, recognized the ICAR's role as a clearing house and co-ordinating agency for all advanced agricultural research centres, as a source of publications and as a source for publicizing the results of research and wanted it to have an Institute of Agricultural Policy with international staff. The Commission envisaged that new agricultural colleges be associated with the Rural Universities proposed by it so that agricultural education may be supported and enriched by contact with other fields. Evidently, Radhakrishnan Commission conception of Rural Universities did not quite equate them with the American Land Grant Colleges as was done by the two joint Indo-American Teams. Thus, no role was envisaged by the Commission for the ICAR in agricultural education. The ICAE was duly set up under the ICAR during the First Plan and comprised representatives of State Agriculture and Veterinary Colleges and State Departments of Agriculture and Animal Husbandry.

Attached to this chapter is a Supplementary Note on Rural Higher Education of Mahatma Gandhi's conception which had struck a path different from agricultural universities (pp. 334 *et. seq.*).

State Agricultural Universities (SAUs): Regional Counterparts of the ICAR

Significantly, the process of reorganization of the ICAR (M.S. Randhawa, 1979) ran parallel to the process of establishment of State Agricultural Universities (SAUs), which can fittingly be called regional arms of the ICAR in respect of agricultural education, research and extension. The basic features of the SAUs have already been referred to in the context of the Report of the Second Joint I-A Team on AERE (1959). The feature of extension was meant to ensure that agricultural research contributed to enhancement of agricultural productivity on the farms and solve food problem at the national level. *ICAR can be said to have broken new ground in the educational scenario of the country by highlighting the role of 'extension' as the 'third dimension' as early as in 1960 to which UGC awoke only in 1977*, while enunciating its policy frame for higher education in India.

The evolution of agricultural universities has not been smooth but its course underlines the role of Indian agency and especially the role Pandit Govind Ballabh Pant, the then Chief Minister of U.P. and later, the Union Home Minister, initially played. Pandit Pant had given support to Major Harpal Singh Sandhu in the reclamation of Tarai. In 1950, Major Sandhu and Mr. A.N. Jha, ICS, the Chief Secretary of U.P. jointly visited the US and were impressed by the Land Grant Colleges and the contribution they had made in developing agriculture in that country. Pandit Pant accepted the advice of the duo that the establishment of such a university in the reclaimed area of Rudrapur in the Tarai would give an impetus to agriculture in the area (K.C. Naik, 1972). So the idea of agricultural universities pre-dates the report of the first Joint Indo-American Team on AER (1954-55). The State of U.P. took full advantage of the recommendations of the first team and well before the report of the second team was submitted, an MoU had been signed by the UP State with the University of Illinois in 1959, the UP Agricultural University Act having been passed by the State Legislature earlier in 1958.

In fairness, it has to be noted that Dean H.W. Hannah's blueprint of agricultural universities had been circulated by the ICAR to all the State Governments in 1956 itself and proposals of various State

Governments were pending with the Government of India. However, only the UP Agricultural University could come up in the Second Plan. It was inaugurated by the Prime Minister in November, 1960. The University of Kalyani in West Bengal too was established in 1960 but it did not strictly follow the model pattern. In the Third Plan, on the basis of the observations by the Cummins Committee (1962), Agricultural Universities came up at Ludhiana (Punjab), Udaipur, Jabalpur, Hyderabad, Bangalore (now Bangaluru) and Bhubaneswar.

There was, however, conservative opposition to the very idea of an Agricultural University on the ground of its being a single-faculty university which violated the traditional norm. Inter University Board in its meeting dated 3-2-1961 at Dharwar passed a resolution in this regard (*vide* K.C. Naik, 1972: 8). It is in this background that the support of Kothari Commission to the idea proved decisive. It diplomatically eschewed any reference to the twin reports of the Joint Indo-American Teams, but traced the origin of the idea to the Rural University concept of Radhakrishnan Commission. Apart from independently recommending the integration between research, training and extension, it spelt out scope of coverage of the academic and professional fields much more broadly than the ICAR (e.g. rural sociology, anthropology and law) (E.C., para 14.10). It deplored the tendency to restrict admission to p-g courses in agriculture to agricultural graduates. It supported the idea of one agricultural university per State. It wanted agricultural education outside the Agricultural Universities also to be looked after by the ICAR. It recommended a system of quinquennial inspection of all agricultural colleges jointly by the ICAR and the UGC, one objective being to disaffiliate colleges which did not come up to minimum requirements. The idea of Agricultural Polytechnics thrown up by it, was, however, not taken up by the Ministry of Agriculture/DARE.

By 1977, there were 27 Agricultural Universities in the country. The Government appears to have been concerned that these Agricultural universities were serving as a source of manpower for ICAR institutes and the Government agriculture departments and hardly any were seen going back to the rural areas and bring about improvement in agricultural productivity. Hence, in January 1977, a Review Committee on Agricultural Universities under the chairmanship of Dr. M.S. Randhwa was set up with the following Terms of Reference:

> "To assess how far agricultural universities are meeting the needs of trained manpower at different levels and producing *non-elite graduates* with motivation for self-employment in agriculture, with competence to identify and resolve practical problems and with an attitude to demonstrate to farmers even by working on them. The Committee to assess quality of education programmes, particular attention being given to orientation of home science education to suit conditions in rural areas."

The composition of the Committee was rather non-descript [Two of the members (Smt. Lilavati Munshi and Dr. N.K. Panikkar—a fisheries expert), had died before its report was submitted. Out of the remaining four, one was a linguist and three were laymen]. In spite of these limitations, the Committee was able to submit a good report by July 1978 by which time a new, i.e. Janata Government had come to power. On its main Term of Reference, it made several recommendations, one being that at least 25 per cent seats should be reserved for students who had their schooling in rural schools. As for home science, it wanted that agriculture should constitute one-third component in the home science programme. The Report certainly served as a useful mid-term review of the working of Agricultural Universities but unfortunately, such reviews have not been repeated.

As in 2007, the country has 41 State Agricultural Universities, five Deemed Universities and one Central Agricultural University (Manipur). Although each State was expected to have only one University, this norm had been violated early by Maharashtra and Uttar Pradesh on sub-regional considerations and also by Himachal Pradesh, which wanted to encourage forestry and horticulture. Moreover, the establishment of separate animal sciences universities in the four States of Tamil Nadu, West Bengal, Maharashtra and Karnataka goes against the basic tenet of integration of agriculture and animal husbandry.

The Co-ordinating Role of the ICAR

The ICAR co-ordinates formulation of uniform course curricula and course contents, provides guidelines for admission to various courses and nominates certain number of students both at the under-graduate and post-graduate levels for admission. ICAR has promoted quality education through establishment of Centres of Advanced Studies in specific areas. It assists the SAUs in taking up extension activities through district-level Krishi Vigyan Kendras (KVKs), and participates in the selection of teaching and related posts in the SAUs. The general division of labour is that SAUs would concentrate on under-graduate programmes, and the National Institutions on post-graduate programmes though there are exceptions as in the case of NDRI, Karnal which runs a highly regarded U-G course in Dairy Technology.

Governance Norms

On the basis of the report of the Agricultural Universities Committee chaired by Dr. Ralph W. Cummings (1962), ICAR developed a Model Act for the Agricultural Universities in India in 1966 which was further revised in 1984 and 1994. *This was an advance over the record of the UGC whose Gnanam Committee talked about the Model Act only in 1990*. Based on the recommendations of Agricultural Universities Review Committee in 1978, the ICAR took various steps to persuade the State Governments to adopt the provisions of the Model Act. The ICAR Review Committee emphasized the need for co-ordination among agricultural universities in States, with multiple agricultural universities like Maharashtra, U.P. etc. through the mechanism of State Councils for Agricultural Education and Research (SCAER). Maharashtra has such a State Council with headquarters at Pune. Unlike in the general education sector, such Councils have been readily accepted in the agricultural education sector, but their bane is that they are headed by retired politicians, although with some expertise in agriculture. The arrangement could work well when enlightened statesmen like A.P. Shinde, former Union Minister of State for Food worked as the Chairman of the Maharashtra—SCAER (Savita Bhave, 1994), but more often than not, it leads to 'politicization' of the body, making it ineffective.

Examination/Evaluation System

The State Agricultural Universities having followed the American model, have broken new ground by adopting trimester/semester system and a flexible course credit system, buttressed by continuous internal evaluation. While examination reforms were attempted and given up in the general education, agricultural education along with technical/management education in the IITs/IIMs can be credited with renovations in the examination system of the country.

Funding Norms

The Norms and Accreditation Committee (NAC), which replaced the original Standing Committee on Agricultural Education is the main body for prescribing funding norms and educational standards for agricultural education. The NAC tried to evolve norms for financial assistance for different kinds of institutions like (1) the SAUs, (2) the Deemed Universities, (3) Faculties of Central Universities, and (4) Affiliated agricultural colleges. During the Fourth, Fifth and Sixth Plans, ICAR used to provide for development and strengthening of the SAUs to the tune of 25-30 per cent of its funds. This declined to 9 per cent during the Eighth Plan and then rose to 11 per cent (Hemendra Kumar Committee: 35). Because several State Governments have established more than one SAU, the problem of evolving acceptable criteria had become difficult. Thus, in the Eighth Plan, a single agricultural university in a State got Rs. 3.25 crore as assistance, whereas an Agricultural University in a State like Maharashtra, which had 4 universities, got Rs. 2 crore each. The AMU, a Central University, was assisted to the tune of Rs. 2.60 crore, to set up an Institute of Agriculture in the Eighth Plan. The deemed universities, IARI, IVRI, NDRI and later the Central Institute for Fisheries Education (CIFE) were also under the purview of the NAC.

Agricultural education being a State subject, the States and the Centre together have to evolve an agreed strategy. The Hemendra Kumar Committee had suggested that up to 20 per cent of the funds available to the ICAR should be provided to the SAUs for supporting their education, research and extension activities including development and strengthening of infrastructure, but added a significant rider that the SAUs must reform themselves (by elimination of duplication, abolition and merger of some departments, management reforms etc.).

Accreditation Board

The Norms and Accreditation Committee referred to earlier which replaced the Standing Committee on Agricultural Education is also the main body for prescribing educational standards for State Agricultural Universities. In the course of time, it was involved with the work of academic assessment and accreditation of agricultural institutions comparable to the NAAC under the UGC (Darshan S. Padda and N.L. Maurya, 2000: 125-139). As it was felt necessary to establish and implement academic norms and standards in a more systematic manner, under Agricultural Human Resource Development (AHRD), a project financed by the World Bank, an Accreditation Board was established and the ICAR Rules amended in 1996 for that purpose to set, enforce and monitor compliance with the norms and standards for agricultural education in India comparable to NAAC under UGC. It appears that all deemed universities (four) and about 18 SAUs have been accredited till 2004-05 (Annual Report of DARE, 2004-05: xii).

Staff Development

ICAR was among the pioneers in thinking up and implementing the concept of staff development in higher education sector. A Central Staff College for Agriculture was set up in 1976 at Hyderabad, which has since been renamed as the National Academy of Agricultural Research Management (NAARM). Apart from conducting a very large number of training programmes for Central Agricultural Research Service (CARS) personnel, it undertakes a systematic review and study of management problems of agricultural research institutes, programmes and systems, and also assists the SAUs in developing regional centres of management to cater to the needs of various universities. It has 88 scientific/technical posts and serves as a think tank for the ICAR in staff development issues. It works in close co-operation with the International Service for National Agricultural Research (ISNAR) (S.N. Saha, 2000: 333-337).

Distance Education

Compared with general education, agricultural education sub-sector has not made much progress in distance education. The ICAR has entered into a dialogue with the IGNOU to develop distance education facilities in its area. The Task Group on Revamping Agricultural Research (Planning Commission, Feb. 2005:35) has suggested setting up of a National Virtual University for science in agriculture through the instrumentality of NAARM, Hyderabad and in collaboration with the IGNOU.

The Problem of Weak Agricultural Colleges

Forty-Seven agricultural colleges and one veterinary college, of which 24 are in UP, are outside the SAU system. Most of them are sub-standard. This point was noted by the Kothari Commission which suggested five-yearly inspections. This recommendation does not appear to have been followed up. The Randhawa Committee (1978, 12 : 15 : 3) suggested that they should be induced and assisted to discontinue their collegiate teaching programmes in agriculture and transform themselves into science colleges or farmer/technician training centres. Apparently, this was not done, but the ICAR in the Sixth Plan recognized and assisted 14 colleges for ongoing programmes. The G.V. K. Rao Committee, therefore, recommended (p. 106) that the ICAR, jointly with the UGC, may constitute a task force to look into the problems of poor standards of education in these colleges and advise them on improving the standards of education and that the UGC and the ICAR should sign an MoU to help the ICAR to discharge its role in agricultural education. This was not done. Since 1991, ICAR has stopped assisting these colleges.

ICAR—UGC Co-ordination

This incidentally raises the question of relationship between the UGC and ICAR, in respect of recognition of newly set-up institutions. Consequent on the amendment of the UGC Act in 1972, the "UGC (fitness of Agricultural Universities for Grants) Rules" 1975 were framed (UGC Compendium: 29-31), which stipulate that the UGC has to satisfy itself that the establishment of a new agricultural university is justified in terms of adequacy of facilities, integration between teaching, research and extension, co-ordination between the agricultural university and the concerned Department of State Government, and existence of an apex body at the State level. However, the UGC Rules ought to have referred to the Model Act for Agricultural Universities framed by ICAR as early as 1966, which would have enabled the UGC, through the agency of the ICAR, to ensure compliance by the State Governments with the Model Act. The ICAR has reportedly (ICAR 1998: 19) proposed an amendment of the UGC Rules, 1975 so as to incorporate a reference not only to the "Model Act" but also to the accreditation of the programmes by the Accreditation Board under the ICAR Rules. The UGC apparently has not acted so far.

Veterinary Education and Practice

The conventional wisdom in the agricultural sector has been that in the Indian situation, the problems of animal husbandry are integrally linked with those of agriculture. The subject of veterinary education, however, is being dealt with separately, though sequentially because of the existence of an all-India co-ordinating body for veterinary education and practice established in the 1980s. Since the Government of India Act, 1935, veterinary training and practice, unlike medical education, was a State subject but attempts at State level regulation were not successful. Thus the Bombay (Now Maharashtra) had its 'Bombay (Now Maharashtra) Veterinary Practitioners Act, 1953' and corresponding Rules 1955, but they were reportedly ineffective. The Indian Veterinary Council Act, 1984 was, therefore, passed by the Parliament providing for the constitution of a Veterinary Council of India (VCI). The 'preamble' to the Act states that, as the Act was for regulation of veterinary practice, a subject on the State list, accordingly it was extended to the States in terms of Art. 252 of the Constitution, which deals with the power of Parliament to legislate for two or more States by consent and adoption of such legislation by any other State.

The Act is a comprehensive one containing the constitution of the State Veterinary Councils, which however, have no role in 'education'. The VCI has 27 members including five State Directors of Veterinary Science and four heads of veterinary institutions nominated by the Central Government. There are 11 elected members. The structure of the Act is similar to that of the Dentists Act, 1948. The Council is to furnish reports and other information required by the Government (S.14). A Commission of Enquiry (S.63) may be appointed when the Council is not complying with any provisions of the Act and on the basis of the Report, the Central Government may order the Council to adopt the remedies recommended by the Commission and State Governments may take similar action in relation to State Councils. The VCI has been given powers in relation to minimum standards of under-graduate education *vide* S.22 of the Act because the Parliament wanted to regulate standards of veterinary practice through regulation of standards of veterinary education (P.N. Bhatt, 2000). The Council has ancillary powers relating to obtaining information, inspection of veterinary institutions and of examinations through appointment of visitors, withdrawal of recognition etc. The VCI was first constituted in 1989. It issued minimum standards of veterinary education in 1993.

At present, there are 32 veterinary colleges with an annual intake of 2700. The Randhawa Committee (1978) noted that unlike in the case of agricultural graduates, veterinary graduates have no problem in finding jobs. In fact, there is a shortage of graduates/p-graduates not only in the teachers' ranks but also generally. The post-graduate veterinary education continues to be the responsibility of the State Agricultural Universities under the ICAR except in the case of four States of Tamil Nadu, West Bengal, Maharashtra and Karnataka which have set up State Veterinary Universities.

As in most such pieces of legislation, the design of the VCI is centralized. However, there are wholesome provisions relating to consultation with State Governments and with ICAR at the crucial stages of prescribing regulations and withdrawing of recognition of the veterinary institutions. The Act and Regulations, however, are silent regarding the role of UGC. Some of the Veterinary Institutions (VIs) are outside the purview of the SAUs and are under the umbrella of the UGC The DARE/ICAR, therefore, need to consult the UGC in these two matters.

The first State to establish a separate university for veterinary and fisheries was the Tamil Nadu (1989) which established Tamil Nadu

Veterinary and Animal Sciences University at Chennai. West Bengal was the second State to have a separate Veterinary University (1995), a decision about which appears to have been taken on the occasion of the celebration of the centenary of the Bengal Veterinary College (estd. in 1893). Since it covers fishery sciences also it is named appropriately (C.P.B. Mallick, 2000: 296-99). Maharashtra, which had the first veterinary college in India at Parel, Bombay (Now Mumbai) (estd. 1867) has followed West Bengal in combining veterinary and fishery sciences university in one university which is located at Nagpur.

Fisheries Education

Fisheries Education is of recent origin. Although the ICAR, since 1954-55 has recognized fisheries education as part of agricultural education, the departmental authorities were reluctant to part control with fisheries education (as distinguished from training) institutions. Thus, the Central Institute of Fisheries Education (CIFE), Bombay (Now Mumbai) was set up in 1961, but was brought under the ICAR only in 1979, and was subsequently notified as a deemed university in 1989. The Agricultural University, Bangalore was the first one to start a separate college of fisheries (at Mangalore) in 1969. As a result of its success, other SAUs followed and at present there are 12 colleges of fisheries. Four Agricultural Universities have post-graduate programmes [Karnataka, Tamil Nadu (Tuticorin), Orissa (Behrampur) and Kerala (Kochi)]. IIT, Kharagpur has a programme in Aqua-culture Engineering (since 1994). Cochin University of Science & Technology has a p-g programme in industrial fisheries.

Forestry Education and Research

At the time of Independence, India had no tradition of academic forestry education programmes. The significance of the British policy of putting newly recruited IFS officers through a rigorous academic training, in the Universities of Oxford, Cambridge and Edinburgh was not appreciated by the forestry establishment of the newly independent India and the staff training programmes in Dehradun were not only continued but justified and extended. The National Forest Policy 1952 bluntly declared its stand against decentralization of forest education. It stated: "The States would be well advised to continue taking advantage of the facilities provided by the Central Government at Dehra Dun. Openings in the profession of forestry being limited, the decentralization of forest education will militate against economy and efficiency, encourage fissiparous tendencies, generate unemployment and render planned development of forest resources difficult." Nor did the Forestry Division of the Agriculture Ministry see eye to eye with the ICAR whose official doctrine considered forestry education to be an integral part of agricultural education *vide* the Model Act for Agricultural Universities. After Independence, important developments were: the creation of the Indian Forest Service in 1966, the report of the National Commission on Agriculture (1976), major reorganization of forestry training and research by way of converting Indian Forest College into a National Academy and the creation of the Indian Council of Forestry Research and Education (ICFRE) in 1987. All these developments culminated in the revised National Forest Policy, 1988. The National Forestry Action Programmes 2000 incorporates the latest official thinking.

Indian Forest Service (IFS)

The Indian Forest Service is the only new all-India service to be created in independent India, as a sequel to the Resolution adopted by the Rajya Sabha on 6th December, 1961, after the deliberations of the Chief Ministers' Conference held in 1961. It was formally created in 1966 and became operational in 1968 (V.P. Agarwal, 1985). The induction training of the IFS probationers was conducted at the Indian Forest College, Dehra Dun which was renamed as Indira Gandhi National Forest Academy (IGNFA) in 1987 without any change in the two-year training programme. The general perception is that the Academy programmes are strong in the field component, but they are weak in the research component. The most important consequence of the establishment of the Academy which functions directly under the Ministry is that there is a disconnect between the mainstream training on the one hand and research on the other, conducted at the Forest Research Institute (FRI), Dehra Dun and its allied research institutions (P.D. Dogra/R.C. Dhiman, 1994).

Impact of National Commission on Agriculture

Himachal Pradesh, had taken a lead in starting a separate teaching and research department in Forestry at Solan as part of H.P. University, as early as 1971. M.Sc. and Ph.D. programmes were started in 1976 and 1983 and a separate University of Horticulture and Forestry was established at Solan in 1985 (L.R. Varma *et al.*, 2000). However, it was the recommendation of the National Commission on Agriculture (1976) to start forestry education programme as part of the SAUs that picked up with the UNDP assistance and gave a big push to undergraduate forestry education programmes though there have been problems in inter-departmental co-ordination. In particular, SAUs have been criticized for greater emphasis on Agriculture than on Forestry and less emphasis on field programmes (Dogra/Dhiman, *Ibid.*). Secondly, institutions for training and research in specialized forestry programmes were established as indicated below: (a) the Indian Institute of Forestry Management, Bhopal (estd. 1982) conducts a master-level programme in forest management, (b) the Institute of Paper Technology, Sahranpur conducts degree level programmes in pulp and paper technology, and (c) the Indian Plywood Industries Research Institute, Bangalore conducts training programmes useful for the plywood industry. As a result, an educational and research base was created for the co-ordinating body for forestry education and research, which came to be set up in 1987.

National Forest Policy, 1988 emphasized that forestry should be recognized as a scientific discipline as well as a profession and that agricultural universities and institutions dedicated to the development of forestry education should formulate curricula and courses for imparting academic education and promoting post-graduate research and professional excellence. It also spelt out priorities in forestry research. Surprisingly it omits any reference to the role of the Indian Council of Forestry Research and Education (ICFRE) which was established only one year earlier.

Indian Council for Forestry Research and Education (ICFRE)

The objectives of the ICFRE, set up in 1987 are: to undertake, aid, promote and co-ordinate Forestry Education, Research and its application, to act as a clearing house for research and general information relating to forests and wild life, and to provide consultancy services in the field of forestry research, education and training and in allied sciences. The Council has under its aegis eight research institutes and three advanced research centres in various parts of the country, to cater to the research needs of different bio-geographical regions of the nation. The Forest Research Institute (FRI) was notified as a deemed university in 1991. It conducts three p-g diplomas plus three M.Sc. programmes. The ICFRE has a research core in the form of FRI and other research institutions, but does not appear to have an educational core if one excludes peripheral educational work of FRI. It has taken over from the ICAR the funding of the SAUs for their agro-forestry education programmes with effect from the Ninth Plan onwards (1997-2002). It is presided over by the Minister-in-charge of the portfolio of Forests, Government of India. The Council has 45 members including seven Secretaries of the Central Government, three Heads of Scientific Organizations and the Chairman, UGC as its members. There are only six representatives of State governments who are nominated by the Union Minister. The design of the Council is highly centralized and the State representation low. The financial assistance granted by the ICFRE to various universities imparting forestry education and conducting research in the year 2000-01 was to the tune of Rs. 104.94 lakh (ICFRE: Draft Annual Report). Since September 1994 it has been implementing Forestry Research Education and Extension (FREE) project with the involvement of the Ministry of Environment and Forest and the States of Himachal Pradesh and Tamil Nadu with a total estimated cost of Rs. 215 crore.

National Forestry Action Programme (NFAP), 2002

NFAP refers to the IGNFA Dehra Dun and other institutions providing professional training and observes that human resource development in the sector is inadequate. It further says that research is a neglected sector and it is hoped that the establishment of the ICFRE as an autonomous institution would help to improve the situation. It, however, does not refer to the role of the agricultural universities in forestry education.

The ICFRE in the Successive Plans

The following observations in the Mid-Term Appraisal of the Ninth-Five Year Plan (1997-2002) in regard to forestry programmes tell us a lot not only about the ICFRE but especially about the quality of work in this sector. In Forestry, important research positions in research institutes are occupied by Officers of the Indian Forest Service (IFS) who are frequently transferred and hence are not able to keep up with the rapid advances in science. This could also be a major reason why forestry research has lagged behind agricultural research in India (*ibid.*: 337).

> "The World Bank assisted Forestry Research, Education and Extension (FREE) project is being implemented by ICFRE. The implementation experience of the project has not been good. Effective co-ordination is lacking and there are overlaps and duplication in various projects being undertaken by different institutes. It brings out the isolation of scientists working in those institutes from other institutes in the country as well as international institutes" (Mid-term Appraisal, *Ibid.*).

The Mid-Term Appraisal of the Tenth Plan is rather dismissive of the ICFRE. It states: "The Council has established planting stock improvement programmes all over the country in close cooperation with State Governments. Other thrust areas are the utilization of forest produce, development of appropriate agro-forestry systems and their extension. As the forestry research programme predominantly caters to the Government Sector, budgetary support to ICFRE may have to be continued. However, the Institution should generate resources through consultancy and other technical services and progressively reduce dependence on Government grants" (*ibid.*: 436).

The Eleventh Five Year Plan, Vol. I (pp. 72-73) makes no specific reference to Forestry Education but has following to say regarding Forestry Research: It commends the role of the Indian Institute of Forestry Management (IIFM), Bhopal, which has emerged as a premier Forestry Institution and has contributed to development of criteria and indicators for sustainable forest management and participatory forest management processes. Based on an evaluation, it is stated, it would enlarge its educational and management development programme as well as policy-relevant research focused on forestry and its linkages with rural institutions. Regarding the ICFRE, it points out that it has to rise above the pre-1988 mandate of largely silviculture-based management systems. It suggests the setting up a Task Force, which would (a) propose a working mechanism including resource mobilization for its research and education components, and (b) deliberate on integrating wildlife, biodiversity, habitat/landscape ecological research concerns within the Council. For the Plan period, 50 per cent of the total grants-in-aid to the ICFRE would be earmarked exclusively for research and education. The ICFRE's institutes would be encouraged to collaborate with other institutions in the relevant fields including State Forest Research Institutes. Indian Plywood Industries Research and Training Institute is to be involved in the research and education programme of utilization of wood and wood products. Survey of medical and aromatic plants is to be launched. It is also advised to take into account concerns of climate change including carbon trade methodologies. This is a big agenda and it is to be hoped that leadership of the ICFRE would rise to the occasion.

The ICFRE: Looking Ahead

The ICFRE has no State counterparts other than the State Forestry Departments. ICFRE may need to gear itself to tackle the problems of forestry education and research in the areas of curriculum planning, evaluation, delivery through distance education, institutional assessment and accreditation, faculty development and continuing education. The bracketing of forestry with environment and wild life does not appear to have been conducive to the healthy development of forestry education and research. The possibility of retransfer of Forestry Education and Research to the Department of Agricultural Research and Education (DARE) could perhaps be seriously considered in the interest of synergistic development of agricultural and agro-forestry education.

Agricultural and Forestry Education and Research: Prospects

In terms of the logic of the Yashpal Committee Report, the agricultural and forestry education and research should be covered by the umbrella of the apex national organization but reportedly agricultural education is being excluded on the ground that it is a State subject. Forestry education was not even under the Committee's/Government's radar. It is forgotten that since forestry is a concurrent subject, it is on the same footing as general education.

Supplementary Note on Rural Higher Education

At present there is a National Council for Rural Institutes with headquarters at Hyderabad functioning since 1995. It was set up in terms of a mandate of the National Policy for Education 1986/92. As the Council has a chequered history, it would be useful to review the evolution of policy in the matter and link it up with the related topic of agricultural education.

Radhakrishnan Commission had recommended the establishment of rural universities by which they meant a ring of small under-graduate residential colleges with specialized university facilities at the centre. Later on, an international team of experts was constituted by the Government of India to visit foreign countries to survey the work of Danish Folk High Schools and Colleges and institutions of higher learning of similar type, to find out how best India could benefit by those ideas and experiences. On the submission of their report, a committee on Rural Higher Education under the Chairmanship of K.L. Srimali was constituted to undertake a comprehensive survey and appraisal of the previous ideas, institutions and experiments in the field of rural education and to recommend a possible pattern of education and evolve a sound and a reasonably uniform system of education suited to the needs and resources of the country. Srimali Committee did not go into Radhakrishnan Commission's ideas in the matter. It had perhaps intended to develop India's own model of Folk Colleges which it chose to call Rural Institutes which could give to the rural youth in India that training and skill which could make them effective leaders of the community. It aimed at one Rural Institute at least in each Revenue Division of the States. The RIs were expected to "help in breaking down economic and geographic barriers between the rural and urban population. They will also help in bridging the gulf between culture and work; between the humanities and technology and between the practical and the ideal."

Rural Institutes were planned to accept students who had completed their higher secondary education. Six types of curricula were recommended:

1. A three-year diploma course in Rural Services,
2. A one-year course in addition to above for Teaching Diploma,
3. A one-year course for a Teaching Certificate,
4. A two-year certificate course for Rural Health Work,
5. A two-year certificate course for Overseers,
6. A two-year certificate course in Agricultural Science.

The Rural Institutes were to cover all three aspects of higher education, viz. teaching, research and extension, and there was a National Council for Rural Higher Education (NCRHE) to assist them.

The attitude of the Report towards examinations is apparent from the declaration that "a definite shift in emphasis away from the stereotyped written examinations and towards depending for assessment on cumulative records of practical and social activities of students will be essential for the success of the Rural Institutes."

The March 1958 proceedings of the 4th meeting of NCRHE give the following list of Rural Institutes which were assisted at that time:

1. Gandhigram Rural Institute, Madurai, Madras (Now Tamil Nadu).
2. Jamia Rural Institute, Jamia Nagar, New Delhi.
3. Vidya Bhavan Rural Institute, Udaipur.
4. Rural Institute of Higher Studies, Sundarnagar, Birouli (Bihar).
5. Institute of Rural Higher Education, Sriniketan.
6. Balwant Vidyapeeth Rural Institute, Bichpur, Agra.
7. Ramakrishna Mission Vidyalaya, Coimbatore.
8. Lok Bharati, Sanosara (Bhavnagar Dist.), Gujarat.
9. Rural Institute, Amravati, Maharashtra (established by Punjabrao Deshmukh, former Union Minister for Agriculture).

10. Mouni Vidyapeeth Rural Institute, Gargoti, Kolhapur, Maharashtra (with which the educationist J.P. Naik was associated).

The first joint Indo-American Team had gone into the way the Rural Institutes had evolved and was of the view that they were a half-way house between the Rural University envisaged in the Radhakrishnan Report and the Manjri type vocational agricultural schools (in Maharashtra). Rural Institute appeared to chart a midway for economy reasons. The Team sounded a note of caution.

Since Rural Institutes had official support with K.L. Srimali becoming Union Minister of State for Education, after the death of Maulana Azad in 1958, Ford Foundation organized an exchange programme with Berea College (apparently a community college) in Kentucky, USA (Fourth Inter-State Seminar on Rural Higher Education, 1961: 9). However, the report of the second Joint Indo-American Team was rather blunt because what in its view was the sound advice of the first team was not heeded. It stated, "The Rural Institutes as presently organized are serving no useful purpose in the agricultural education programme. The Team recommends that the Ministry of Agriculture determine whether or not these Institutes could be organized as vocational agricultural schools or extension training centres, thereby becoming part of the agricultural education programme. The Team recommends that teaching of agriculture in Rural Institutes be discontinued."

Available literature shows that the Rural Institutes had great difficulty in convincing the IUB about the equivalence of Rural Services Diploma programme with a university degree. The States were equally lukewarm in recognizing the courses of the Rural Institutes for various jobs under the State Governments. Available accounts do not indicate the reasons but note the fact that in 1969 it was decided to discontinue the National Council. Various Rural Institutes were left to fund for themselves. Only one of them, viz. Gandhigram Rural Institute, Dindigul, became a Deemed University in 1976 (i.e. during the Emergency). Some other institutes were already part of universities (Jamia was a deemed university since 1962 and Vishwabharati of which Sriniketan was a part was a Central University since 1951). Some institutes (e.g. Sanosara in Gujarat) were being supported by the Central Government under a special scheme till as late as NPE 1986/92.

Interestingly, Kothari Commission makes no reference to Rural Institutes. Although there was no reference to the Rural University, in the preliminary "Challenge of Education" (1985) document, para 5.23 of the NPE 1986 states:

> "The new pattern of the Rural University will be consolidated and developed on the lines of Mahatma Gandhi's revolutionary ideas on education so as to take up the challenges of micro-planning at grassroots level for the transformation of rural areas. Institutes and programmes of Gandhian basic education will be supported."

The Government of India had reportedly appointed the Kudal Commission in 1982 apparently to investigate and then to take appropriate action in regard to the Gandhian institutions some of which had supported Jai Prakash Narain's ideology of 'Total Revolution' which led up to the agitations on the eve of the Emergency. It may be noted that Kudal Commission Report is not in the public domain but is referred to in literature about the NGOs which were sought to be regulated by the Guidelines for Voluntary Organisation (VOs) in the Sixth Plan Document. It may perhaps be speculated that the policy declaration of 1986 was meant as an assurance to the Gandhian Institutions which were still active. The Programme of Action: 1992 had suggested setting up a Central Council of Rural Institutes to formulate and implement well-co-ordinated programme as spelt out above. The Central Council was subsequently renamed as National Council*.

The MoA of the NCRI sets out various objectives in terms of the NPE including designing a variety of courses at tertiary level around emerging rural occupations, strengthening the content of rural

---

* Incidentally, the author of the chapter "Higher Technical and Professional Education" (pp.264-278) in the NIEPA Publication edited by K. Sudha Rao: "Eucational Policies in India: Analysis and Review of Finance and Performance" (2002, Paperback Edn. 2009) states blindly about Rural Uniersities/Institutes. While reviewing the policy initiative now in year 2000, "there is no progress made under the scheme so far any further comment is superfluous (p.168).

institutions with emphasis on science and technology, promoting research as a tool for social and rural development and advise Government of India on all matters pertaining to the rural institutes. These objectives, no doubt pertain to education, research and extension, but none of them pertains to standards. In other words, the Council has no role in relation to recognition of rural institutes which continues to be the function of the universities/UGC.

The Annual Report of the Ministry for 2007-08 states in relation to NCRI as below (p. 140):

> "The Council has sanctioned projects in the field of 'Nai Talim', skill development in rural areas, rural education and rural higher education."

A little probing shows that the activities of the Council have to do much more with rural development projects (e.g. 'water supply'). The Council has assisted Tripura University in starting a two-year P-G degree entitled Master of Social Work and M.A. (sustainable Rural Development) and P-G Diploma Course in Trade, Transport and Communication. Earlier, one Chairman of NCRI had floated the idea of starting a new institution called 'Indian Institute of Rural Technology', similar to the Indian Institute of Information Technology, during the NDA regime, but the proposal appears not to have taken off. In other words, the Council is partly duplicating the work of the UGC in giving grants to State Universities and of the Rural Development Ministry in regard to development works.

It is felt that it would be desirable to review the functions and powers of the Council to avoid duplication with activities of the UGC, Rural Development Ministry etc. Basically, education for practical purposes may be classified into urban/rural but academic norms as to education, research or extension do not vary as between urban and rural areas. Perhaps, the NCRI could carve out a niche for itself as a regulatory body for community polytechnics under the Bureau of Technical Education of Education Ministry, but polytechnics are normally dealt with by the State Boards of Technical Education. Hence a review appears to be urgent.

Part III
Some Issues and Conclusion

14

Some Common Problems of Higher and Technical/Professional Education

Introduction

In this chapter there will be focus on three common problems of higher education, viz. (1) Medium of education which is significant for the process of teaching-learning, (2) Financing which indicates the priority accorded to the sector, and (3) A super-regulator for higher education and research.

Medium of Education

The issue of the medium of education (covering both the instruction and examination) is important in multilingual India. Modern higher education made its beginning through English language, but at the time of independence the claims of regional languages in respective provinces and of Hindi as a medium for inter-provincial communication were insistent.

Radhakrishnan Commission reported before the linguistic settlement of the constitution envisaging Hindi as the official language to replace English after 15 years. However, the Commission devoted one whole chapter to discuss this issue (Chapter IX) and made valuable recommendations which have tended to be neglected. It is worthwhile, therefore to refer to them at length.

(1) That the federal language be developed through the assimilation of words from various sources.

(2) That international technical and scientific terminology be adopted.

(3) That for the medium of instruction for higher education, English be replaced as early as practicable by an Indian language.

(4) (i) That the pupils at the higher secondary and university stage be made conversant with three languages—the regional language, the federal language and English.

(ii) Higher education be imparted through the instrumentality of the regional language with the option to use the federal language for some or all subjects.

(5) That Devanagari script be employed for the federal language.

(6) That immediate steps be taken for developing the federal and regional languages:

(i) A Board consisting of scientists and linguists be appointed to prepare a scientific vocabulary of words which will be common to all Indian languages and also to arrange for preparation of books in different sciences to be rendered into all Indian languages.

(ii) Provincial Governments be required to take steps to introduce the teaching of the federal language in all classes of higher secondary schools, in degree colleges and in universities.

(7) That English be studied in high schools and in universities in order that we may keep in touch with the living stream of ever-growing knowledge.

Unfortunately, the sequence of events relating to higher education and official/regional languages listed below shows that the Government did not have a well-thought out policy for medium of instruction and capacity building for this purpose and precious time was lost till a policy was formulated almost 20 years after Radhakrishnan Commission reported.

Sequence of Events (1950s and 1960s)

(1) Advisory UGC established in 1953.

(2) Report of the Official Language Commission (Kher Commission) appointed in terms of Constitutional provisions became available (1956). The Kher Commission opined in favour of Hindi replacing English as the medium of instruction in spite of the known Southern opposition to Hindi.

(3) States Reorganization Commission favours linguistic reorganization (1956).

(4) The Commission on Scientific and Technical Terminology, constituted in October 1961 with functions, *inter alia*, of co-ordination and evolution of scientific and technical terminology in Hindi and other languages and preparation of standard scientific textbooks using the new terminology evolved or approved by it.

(5) As observed by S.S. Bhandarkar, historian of the AIU (1975-1985), throughout the 1950s there went on an undulating controversy as to whether the regional language or Hindi should be the university medium; whether English should be taught and what its place should be in higher education. Unfortunately, UGC failed to read the signs. As late as 1961, its Working Group on medium of instruction issue in the light of recent experience continued to plump for replacement of English by Hindi as the medium of instruction (Bhandarkar, 1975: 74). In the meanwhile, States in the North abolished English and replaced it wholesale by Hindi; Gujarat opted for Gujarati, but Southern States continued with English till replaced by respective regional languages.

(6) It was at this stage that the National Integration Council (June 1962) gave the lead and suggested a three-language formula for secondary schools and replacement of English by the regional language at higher education stage with an option to continue English and use Hindi. National Integration Council particularly noted that the switchover was important for development of latent talent in the country and establishing a rapport between the elite and the masses.

(7) Kothari Commission (1966) spelt out the academic rationale for NIC's decision as below:

(A) The medium at the university stage should enable

students to acquire knowledge with facility, express themselves with clarity and to think with precision and vigour. From this point of view, the claims of the mother tongue are pre-eminent.

(B) The medium of education at higher and school education stages should generally be the same.

The Kothari Commission also set out a practical agenda, which comprised UGC and universities to work out a feasible programme within a time horizon of 10 years. A large programme of producing the needed literature in the Indian languages would have to be undertaken and adequate arrangements would have to be made for the training and retraining of teachers. In its Chapter on University Education, the Kothari Commission deplored the tendency of some universities to conduct teaching in English and allow students the option of taking the examination in regional language [11.58(1)]. This only showed the apathy of teachers. It noted: "If the student can be expected to express himself in the regional language in his examination it should not normally be difficult for a teacher do the same in the class-room." It also emphasized use of English as a library language.

(8) The NPE 1968 based on the Kothari Report simply stated (4.3): "The regional languages are already in use as media of education at the primary and secondary stage; urgent steps should now be taken to adopt them as media of education at the university stage." The subsequent NPE 1986 (para 8.7) merely reiterated the 1968 policy formulation stating that its essential provisions can hardly be improved upon.

In terms of NPE 1968, the Government of India started a plan scheme in 1968-69 to be implemented through the CSTT. Under the scheme, the Central Government agreed to give 100 per cent Central assistance, subject to a maximum of Rs. 1 crore for expenses in connection with the scheme. The participating State governments were to set up University Textbook Boards (called Grantha Academies in Hindi Speaking States), managed by the universities in the State. Till 1977-78, grants totalling a little over Rs. 9 crore were released, and 4800 books in Indian languages were reportedly produced and another 3500 books were under production. Most of them related to under-graduate—arts and science courses. There was little work at post-graduate level or for professional courses.

The One-Crore Scheme has been reviewed successively by Suresh Dalal Committee in April 1987 and by M.R. Kolhatkar Committee* in May 1995. The Reports of these Committees are not in the public domain but the progress on the ground is reported to be poor.

The latest report of Ministry of Education (2007-08) devotes two pages to CSTT in which the following brief para appears: "Grants-in-aid was provided to the Granth Academies/Textbook Production Boards/University cells, etc. during the year 2007-08" (pp. 236-37). Unfortunately, no further details regarding the names of academies, amounts disbursed, and the number of textbooks produced, are available.

N. Jayaram (1993: 84-114), has reviewed this whole issue in the overall perspective of language question in higher education, and his conclusion based on research done by some scholars in Tamil Nadu as well as analysis of data in the Diamond Jubilee volume of the Universities Handbook brought out by the AIU in 1984-85 is as below:

1. English is still the predominant medium of instruction in all courses of higher education and the only medium in professional courses. Hindi comes a distant second, being available in 50 per cent of universities in arts and commerce courses, 41 per cent in law and 25 per cent in library science courses.
2. Regional languages are available as a medium of instruction at the under-graduate level, in over 40 per cent of the universities in arts and commerce courses, in over 30 per cent of the universities in education and in nearly 28 per cent in science courses.
3. While Hindi has made some headway at the p-g level, regional languages have not made any noticeable headway.
4. A complete switchover to regional language as media of instruction is not a possibility in the foreseeable future. *The only option that seems to be open is selective bilingualism.*

---

* The Committee was chaired by the author and there were two other members.

An Honest Solution: English as Sole P-G Medium

It is well to remember that Justice M.C. Chagla, the then Union Education Minister resigned on the issue of switchover to the regional language as medium of instruction in 1966 (M.C. Chagla, 1974). He took the stand on retention of English as a medium of instruction in the universities in the interest of national unity and to ensure free movement of teachers, students, writers, artists, and scientists from one part of India to another and from one educational institution to another, to ensure that we have all-India institutions and all-India elite.

In this connection, it is noted that Radhakrishnan Commission had laid particular emphasis on the Central responsibility for post-graduate education, suggesting to the Central Government to aim at the short-term goal of taking responsibility for an over-all total amounting to 50 per cent of the cost of p-g and research work (XIII. 14). This is an authority for making the distinction between U-G and P-G levels in Arts and Commerce faculties. More recently, the late Dr. Amrik Singh, the renowned scholar had invited attention to the fact that one reason for decline in educational standards is unplanned expansion of p-g education in affiliated colleges and suggested that there is considerable scope for consolidation and sharing of facilities in this area. He had also made some suggestions regarding upgrading the Ph.D. degree [Amrik Singh 2004(a),: 131-153 and 154-68]. The Kothari Commission observations on English as a library language are also relevant. The current tendency of introduction of English at the school stage even from the first standard onwards, is also notable. The National Curricular Framework 2005 (drafted under the guidance of Prof. Yashpal) states: "English in India is a global language in a multi-lingual country. A variety and range of English-teaching situations prevail here owing to the twin factors of teacher proficiency in English and pupils' exposure to English outside school. The level of introduction of English is now a matter of political response to people's aspirations rather than an academic or feasibility issue and people's choices about the level of its introduction in the curriculum will have to be respected." Such latitude in regard to English in the context of status of English as a global language cannot but have consequences for the role of English as a medium of instruction at the university level.

In this background, the author is of the view that English which is already the sole medium of instruction in all Science and Professional courses (Engineering, Medicine and Law) both at the UG and P-G courses and that at the P-G and Research level courses in the Arts, Commerce, Education and Library Science faculties of the universities should be declared to be the sole medium of education at these levels (viz. all professional and all p-g and research courses in Arts and Humanities faculties). This should be done in the interest of intellectual and cultural unity of the elite discourse in India for the reasons mentioned *inter alia* by M.C. Chagla and also in the interest of raising standards of higher education in India. In other words, regional language should be the medium of instruction only in Arts and Commerce faculties at the U-G level. The author would call it a policy not of selective bi-linguism but of advanced anglification. Thus, not so much restoration but rather continuance of English as an all-India medium of education at all levels of professional courses and P-G research courses in Arts and Humanities faculties would contribute to the final resolution of the problem of switchover of medium of instruction. It would not solve the problem of textbooks as such because the question of producing Indian language textbooks for U-G courses adapted to Indian conditions with Indian illustrations and reference at the under-graduate arts/science/commerce courses and English language in textbooks of p-g courses would still be with us. This really amounts to freezing of the *status quo* but its merit is that "it would be a conscious policy of advanced anglification rather than a (non-) policy of drift". Moreover, it has important implications regarding reintroduction of English at p-g level in arts, commerce and humanities faculties in Hindi speaking States. There is bound to be resistance but the problem has to be faced. Just as North Indian States have realized the importance of English as a global language at school stage, they would also realize the greater importance of English as a global language at p-g and research stage because they have also to share in the benefit of the emerging Knowledge Society, i.e. India.

Financing of Higher Education

A concise identification of the critical issues involved in financing of higher education with special reference to India is contained in J.B.G. Tilak (1993: 41-83). A few points are highlighted below and at some places, the author has added his own notes:

- Higher Education is a quasi-public good.
- Hence, public financing of higher education is justified to a limited extent.
- In India, with its federal polity, public financing includes both the Central Government and State governments; the share of local bodies in this sphere being limited (Author's *Note*—This however needs to be qualified to the extent that some municipal corporations do run higher education institutions, e.g. the Municipal Corporation of Greater Mumbai runs medical colleges, hence local sector funding may not be as limited as assumed).
- In the context of India's adoption of Central Planning as a strategy for development, higher education expenditure has to expand through additional provisions in successive plans. However, since non-plan element in higher education as in other sub-sectors is high, the scope for development becomes limited in the context of the finance constraint. Moreover, the share of States in the non-plan expenditure is also high. At the end of the First Plan, non-plan expenditure was as high as 71 per cent. [According to data given by Ramamurti Report, State Government share in non-plan was 86 per cent in the Second Plan and had risen to 94 per cent in the Seventh Plan].
- Sources of funding for higher education were computed only up to 1983-84. As compared with 1950-51, the position was as below:

Table 14.1: Sources of Funds for Higher Education (Per cent)

Year	*Government*	*Local Bodies*	*Fees*	*Other (endowments etc.)*	*Total*
1950-51	49.1	0.3	36.8	13.8	100
1983-84	79.6	1.1	13.8	05.4	100

Author's Note: These statistics indicate a need for increasing the share of non-Government sources including, particularly, fees and endowments.

- Non-Government sources which can be tapped include 'Graduate Taxes' (not recommended), student fees, student loans, voluntary contributions and various forms of privatization.
- There is also a scope for more effective utilization of resources used up in higher education since according to one study, somewhere around 20 per cent of the total educational expenditure in the country is 'wasted' in various forms of feather-bedding in teacher placement (Tilak, *Ibid.*: 77).
- Percentage share of expenditure on higher education in GNP had increased from 0.19 per cent in 1950-51 to 0.89 per cent in 1983-84.
- Considering that higher education comprises both higher general and higher technical education, it may be useful to consider expenditure on both together. On this basis, the highest plan outlay for higher general education was in the Fourth Plan (25 %), and for Technical Education in the Annual Plans (1966-69) (25 %).

In this general background, various issues relating to financing of higher and technical education in India may be considered.

As is well known, the NPE 1968 laid down the target ratio of public expenditure on Education of 6 per cent and the same was reiterated in the NPE 1986. In this target ratio, no disaggregated ratios for higher and technical education were contemplated. Allocations for higher education (which substantially meant allocations for the UGC) were initially cut in 1990-91 in the context of the Gulf War and although the cut was restored in 1991-92, it really amounted to a substantial reduction, because the usual increase in connection with the D.A. etc. were not permitted. In the 8th, 9th and 10th Plans, Higher educations allocation for Plan were also reduced. Table 14.2 shows the Five Year Plan allocations for Higher and Technical Education from the First Plan to the Ninth Plan.

The important post-NPE (1986) developments in regard to the financing of higher and technical education are as below:

Table 14.2: Allocation of Plan Expenditure on Higher and Technical Education in the Five Year Plans in India (Rs. In Crore)

Five Year Plan	*Higher*	*Technical*	*Total Education as % of Total Plan Outlay*
First	14 (9)	20 (13)	7.86
Second	48 (18)	49 (18)	3.83
Third	87 (15)	125 (21)	6.87
Annual Plans (3)	77 (24)	81 (25)	4.86
Fourth	195 (25)	106 (13)	5.04
Fifth	205 (22)	107 (12)	3.27
Sixth	530 (18)	324 (11)	2.70
Seventh	1201 (14)	1083 (12)	3.50
Annual Plans (2)	595 (11)	848 (16)	4.20
Eighth	1516 (7)	2786 (13)	4.90
Ninth Plan	4350 (8)	4778 (9)	6.20

Note: Figures in parenthesis are per cent to total.
Source: CABE Report on Financing of Higher & Technical Education (2005).

(1) Ramamurti Report (1990) and Janardan Reddy Report (1992) (Ministry of Education)
(2) Punnayya Committee Report (1993). (UGC)
(3) Swaminathan Report (1994). (AICTE)
(4) Mungekar Report (2005). (NIEPA on behalf of CABE)
(5) Approach paper for the Eleventh Five Year Plan (2006). (Planning Commission)
(6) Union Budget 2008-09 (28th February, 2008).(Finance Ministry)

The significance of the Ramamurti Report in regard to the funding of higher education is that it made the following stark statement about technical and professional education:

> "All technical and professional education should be made self-financing, education being viewed as involving the use of resources (inputs) that should be necessarily paid for by the beneficiaries as it confers on them greater employability (output)" (p. 346).

This highlighted the point that as distinguished from general higher education, professional education confers greater employability on the beneficiaries and private rates of return as compared with social rates of return are very high. Ramamurti Report also produced a Table displaying very low level of tuition fees charged in State and Central universities and stressed the need to raise those fees [as well as fees for examination and other specific purpose fees] (p. 363). Since, the issue of tuition fees is politically sensitive in India, this was a good lead. It listed out several other measures for catalyzing institutional finance, higher and technical education.

Janardan Reddy Committee broadly endorsed Ramamurti Committee recommendations and, in particular, the need for progressively making higher education and technical and management education largely self-financing by revising the fee structure with appropriate support to the needy students by way of student loans (pp. 74-75).

The *Punnayya Committee* was appointed by the UGC to suggest measures to overcome the resource crunch faced by the Higher Education Sector consequent on the Structural Adjustment Programme (SAP) undertaken by the Central Government to overcome the economic crisis of 1991. Its terms of reference included norms for expenditure, efficiency of resource use, measures for resource mobilization etc. Unfortunately, the Committee's report was confined to the Central institutions and thus a valuable opportunity of knowing something about the financial position of higher education institutions in the States in an authoritative manner was lost. (There could have been parallel high-power committees at State level whose reports could have fed into the Central Report). All the same, it made valuable recommendations which included the following:

- Additional resources generated by the universities not to be adjusted by the UGC against grants; rather, the UGC to provide matching grants as an incentive. (*NB*—This recommendation has been accepted.)
- There should be 100 per cent income tax concession on all endowments and contributions made to the universities.
- The State must continue to accept the major responsibility for funding the essential maintenance and development

requirements of the universities. (*NB*: This recommendation is to be read in conjunction with the further recommendation for upward revision of tuition fees, hostel fees, etc.)

- The unit cost system of calculation of eligibility for grant should replace the existing incremental system by the beginning of the Ninth Plan, i.e. from 1997-98.
- The subsidy element in the supply of electricity, transport, water etc. to the students, to professors and to the *karmacharis* of the universities should be substantially reduced.
- Development grants to universities should be linked to an academic audit system and performance indicators to be developed by each university and these should be monitored by the UGC. [*NB*: The Committee was influenced by the work done by CVCP in the UK in this regard. It eventually fed into the NAAC in India, just as in the UK it led to Quality Assurance Agency.]
- UGC should constitute a Standing Advisory Committee of experts on a long term basis for examining perspective plans drawn by the Central universities and monitoring them.
- UGC must develop a system of presenting annually a set of selected data on academic, administrative and financial parameters of institutions which should be utilized in decision-making processes.
- The relative proportions of academic, administrative and auxiliary service expenditures may approximate: 60-65 per cent, 10-12 per cent and 20-25 per cent. The student-teacher ratio should be 12:1, teaching to non-teaching staff ratio may be 1: 30.
- Tuition fees, fees for other services, hostel fees etc. should be revised upwards. There should be cost recovery of all municipal services. Universities should mobilize resources from various avenues (endowments, hire of infrastructure, consultancy, self-financing short-term courses). The resources generated by the universities should constitute at last 15 per cent of total recurring expenditure at the end of first five years and at least 25 per cent at the end of 10 years. [Author's Note: The significance of the term *at least* is that,

according to the Committee, these are floor values and not ceiling values, the ceiling would be 100 per cent because, in principle, fees should cover costs.]

- Alumni associations may be set up for mobilising resources from within the country and abroad.
- The institutions may build up a corpus fund into which may flow a significant proportion of internally generated resources and incentive grants from the UGC plus specific corpus fund grant from the UGC.
- The UGC may introduce a student scholarship scheme for p-g students studying in Central universities covering 20 per cent of total student enrolment.
- Government may eventually shift the funding of the universities to a system of student unit cost-based funding. [*Author's Note*: As distinguished from institutional funding as at present.]
- UGC is not the appropriate body to administer and provide grants to Delhi College. There should be a statutory *Delhi College Grants Council* to do the needful. There should be a similar arrangement for the BHU Colleges.

It would be seen that the Punnayya Committee made path-breaking recommendations about the future pattern of funding by the UGC. The suggestion for the unit cost system for calculation of grants was really radical. Unfortunately, UGC has not been able to implement many of them.

So far as the Swaminathan Committee in regard to higher technical education is concerned, its available report appears to suffer from the limitation that its recommendations are based on the background report of the Task Force under C.S. Jha set up in 1991 by AICTE, which perhaps contained the requisite data which have not been printed as Annexure to the Report. Hence the report does not make for a connected reading. However, its recommendations regarding enhancement of fees are more drastic (fees to cover at least 20 per cent of recurring cost as against Punnayya's 15 per cent floor for all resource generation measures for the first five years). Its novel recommendation is to set up an Educational Development Bank of India (EDBI). The proposal in short is as below:

- The EDBI is to be set up with a capital base of Rs. 3,000 crore with participation by Central Government, State Governments, financial institutions and international organizations. The EDBI may give soft loans for establishment and development of new institutions (all types—Government funded, Government aided, and Government un-aided) as well as for modernization, and also to assist students to meet their fee and living requirements.
- A National Loan Scholarship Scheme (NLSS) may be set up as a division of the EDBI. The scheme should be operated by the EDBI through associate banks in all States/UTs. The disbursement and repayment of loans should be through the associate Banks.

  (*Note*: It is evident that the idea of the EDBI is attractive, but it has not been thought through carefully. So far at least the Union Finance Ministry does not appear to have given its clearance. Incidentally, the past record of recovery of pre-existing national loan scholarship scheme has been in the region of 5 per cent)
- The Swaminathan Committee Report, also notices that the Union Finance Minister, in his budget speech for 1993-94 had proposed (perhaps in the light of the Punnayya Report) to raise the income tax deduction given to contributions to approved universities, institutes of technology, institutions of management and equivalent institutions from 50 per cent at present to 100 per cent. A weighted deduction of 125 per cent of the contribution out of income from business or profession for research programmes in approved national laboratories and institutions carrying out R & D in natural and applied science was also introduced (Swaminathan Report: 12).

Not much is known about implementation by the AICTE or by the Ministry of Swaminathan Report.

As is well known, the Central Advisory Board of Education was dormant for about eight years (1996-2003). It was revived and reconstituted in July 2004 with the advent of the UPA Government. The reconstituted CABE appointed several committees of which one was on Financing of Higher and Technical Education. The committee was chaired by Prof. Bhalchandra Munagekar, Member (Education) Planning Commission.* It submitted its report in June 2005.

The Committee emphasized the crucial role of the state financing of higher education. It noted that higher education is widely recognized as a public good and the Ministry of Finance (which in its 1997 paper on subsidies had called it a non-merit good) had revised its stand to classify post-elementary education as Merit 2 good (Elementary education being recognized as Merit 1 good). Moreover, the Gross Enrolment Rate (GER) in higher education in the relevant age group was 8-9 per cent as against a desired target ratio of 20 per cent in the Eleventh Plan. Higher education was also the solvent of social inequalities. In the background of the recent decline in state funding, a significant growth, the Committee said, was critically needed. The most important recommendations of the Committee were as below:

- There should be a target ratio of 1.5 per cent for Higher and Technical education in the overall target ratio of 6 per cent for public investment as a proportion of GNP.**
- There should be an upper limit of 20 per cent of recurring income on resource mobilization effort of an individual university/college. (*NB*: This may be contrasted with Punnayya Committee's stipulation of minimum 25 per cent of recurring income being the limit for resource mobilization. The reason for this revised stipulation is stated to be considerations of equity.)
- An 'Operation Blackboard'—like programme may be launched for provision of basic facilities to all universities and colleges in the country (NPE, 1986).

---

* The author was a Member of the Committee.

** This has been incorporated in the working out of data by the Tapas Majumdar Committee appointed by the UPA-I Government. This target ratio compares with 0.4 per cent of GNP spent on Higher Education and 0.1 per cent of GNP spent on Technical Education in 2005. Thus a threefold increase is contemplated to be achieved, perhaps by the end of the Eleventh Plan (2011).

- Allocations for quality-related inputs in higher education, particularly research, may be substantially increased.
- In financing higher education, a proper mix of block/ matching/earmarked maintenance/development grants may be deployed to promote excellence.
- Progressive taxation by the Government is the best means of State funding of higher education.
- Professional graduates may be required to take up employment in public sector in rural, tribal and remote areas for a minimum period as a method of cost recovery.
- Student Loan programmes may be implemented through Higher Education Finance Corporation.
- Growth of self-financing courses of distance education programme and of private higher education may be monitored and regulated.
- Proliferation of poor quality institutions should be curbed.
- MHRD and UGC may launch a programme, on a priority basis, for building up a strong database on higher education.

There is no indication regarding the status of the implementation of the CABE Report.

A Critique of CABE Report

While the CABE Report's justification for enhanced funding for higher education is well-meaning, and its concern for equity is understandable, some of the recommendations of the Committee appear to run counter to the known policies of the Planning Commission/Government, e.g. its stand against open education; stipulation about 20 per cent being the upper limit for measures for resource mobilization as against Punnayya Committee's 25 per cent being the minimum, its attitude towards privatization, etc. Thus, the Eleventh Plan Approach paper talks of internal resource generation by the universities by realistically raising the fees. It states that Open University system is an important instrument for expanding higher education and talks of a suitably facilitative environment of private sector in providing quality higher education.

The Approach to the Eleventh Plan (November 2006) (para 4.3.29 to 4.3.31)

The Approach paper for the Eleventh Plan which emphasizes inclusive growth is significant as highlighting UPA-I Government's stand as distinguished from the previous NDA Government which had finalized the Tenth Plan Document. It refers to the GER in higher education in many developing countries being in the region of 20 to 25 per cent as against India's 10 per cent. The UGC in its draft proposals for the Eleventh Plan works with a target of 15 per cent. The Planning Commission proposes to set up new colleges and universities and upgrading of at least 20 universities with potential of excellence. It also recognizes the difficulties faced by higher education institutions in attracting good faculty. Since all this requires resources, the Commission argues, for internal resource generation by realistically raising fees. The Commission proposes a wide merit-cum-means based loan and scholarship programmes through the banking system and other agencies. In the context of the faculty crunch, the Commission emphasizes the need for relying on the Open University system.

Higher Education in the Union Budget 2008-2009

The Government's policy of substantially increased fund allocations for higher education is clearly evident in the Union Budget 2008-09. Table 14.3 shows Plan and Non-Plan allocations for the previous year and for the year 2008-09 (J.B.G. Tilak, 2008).

Table 14.3 shows that as compared with revised estimates, the plan allocation for the department of higher education has been more than doubled (Rs. 7600 crore as against Rs. 3262 crore). The increase is mainly accounted for by increase in the allocation for the UGC from Rs. 1633 crore (RE) to Rs. 3095 crore (Budget 2008-09). There is a slight reduction in allocation for Technical Education. The increase in the UGC allocations may be in the context of the Plan to set up 16 new Central Universities in each of the States where there exists no Central University. A new scholarship scheme for college and university students was launched in 2007-08 with an allocation of Rs. 12.60 crore, which was raised to Rs. 45 crore in the current budget.

Table 14.3: Allocation to Selected Institutions/Programmes in Higher Education in the Union Budget

(Rs. Crore)

Agency	*Non-Plan*			*Non- Plan*			*Total*		
	2007-08 BE	*2007-08RE*	*2008-09BE*	*2007-08BE*	*2007-08RE*	*2008-09BE*	*2007-08BE*	*2007-08RE*	*2008-09BE*
UGC	2,124.8	1,633.1	3,095.5	1,638.8	1,948.9	2,009.4	3,763.5	3,581.9	5,104.9
IITs	1,111.7	0,335.3	1,020.7	422.0	490.0	525.0	1,553.7	0,825.3	1,545.7
New IITs	80.0	0.0	50.0	—	—	—	80.0	0.0	50.0
IIMs	103.0	43.0	88.0	41.0	42.2	27.0	144.0	85.2	115.0
IISc.	196.0	40.0	130.0	87.2	87.0	91.0	283.2	126.0	221.0
AICTE	892.0	297.4	718.0	234.1.	263.0	285.0	1,126.1	560.4	1,003.0
Total (Gen)	2,910.0	1,958.4	3,946.0	1,755.0	2,072.7	2,137.7	4,665.1	4,031.1	6,083.7
Total (Tech)	2,929.0	981.5	2,888.5	941.0	1,020.4	1,074.7	3,870.0	2,001.9	3,963.3
Grand Total (dept. of higher education	6,483.0	3,262.0	7,600.0	2,729.0	3,136.0	3,259.4	9,212.0	6,398.0	10359.4

Source: Union Budget 2008-09: Expenditure Budget, Vol. II.

The scheme aims at providing scholarships to at least 2 per cent of students passing out of schools every year for pursuing higher education.

It is reported that the Eleventh Plan raised the allocation for higher education by nine times to Rs. 85,000 crore. Press reports indicate, however, that the outlay has been cut to half in the recent mid-term review.

Conclusion

After a series of Plans in which Higher Education Plan Budgets saw a declining trend, higher education allocation has been increased substantially in the Eleventh Plan but the increase has not been sustained. The target ratio of public investment of 1.5 per cent of GNP in higher education is a significant development, but there is no indication that the Government is committed to it. The higher allocations moreover appear to be directed toward quantitative expansion. How they play out in terms of higher standards is a moot point.

A Super Regulator for Higher Education and Research

The third and the last problem to be dealt with in this Chapter is that of overall regulation in higher education including technical education and also research (Earlier one talked of co-ordination).

The problem was first identified by the Sadler Commission in 1919 which considered it in the context of "Government and the Universities" (*vide* Section 43.55 of Chapter L, Vol. 5 of the Commission's Report). It identified the aspects which required Central control into (1) visitation, (2) co-ordination (including avoidance of duplication among universities, technological and agricultural institutions), (3) stimulation and promotion of research, and (4) recruitment which in modern terms may be termed as the manpower function. Radhakrishnan Commission similarly dealt with the problem under the heading of Relation to Provincial and Central Governments. It identified four areas: (1) Finance, (2) Coordination of facilities in special subjects, (3) Liaison between universities and National Research Laboratories, scientific surveys, etc., (4) Adoption of the policies in areas like communal quotas, use of national or regional languages etc.

The Radhakrishnan Commission, for purposes of finance, recommended the setting up of the UGC and did not go into other aspects enumerated by it.

The Kothari Commission did not give much thought to the issue. It felt that overlapping membership and periodical meetings could do the trick (para 13.72). The Jha Committee (1977) had the merit that it pointed out the need for co-ordination not only among educational apex bodies but also apex bodies in research.

In the post-independence period, the problem of co-ordination has arisen in the form of multiplicity of apex regulatory bodies. Amrik Singh (2004) and Yashpal Committee (2009) have attempted enumeration of the bodies but the same are not comprehensive. The author have attempted the task. He classified them under three heads: (1) Academic bodies, (2) Professional-cum-Educational bodies, and (3) Research bodies. They number 22 as below:

(1) Academic Bodies

1. University Grants Commission
2. All India Council for Technical Education
3. National Council for Teacher Education
4. Indian Council for Forestry Education and Research
5. Distance Education Council

(2) Professional-cum-Educational Bodies

1. Bar Council of India
2. Medical Council of India
3. Dental Council of India
4. Nursing Council of India
5. Pharmacy Council
6. The Council of Architects
7. Veterinary Council of India
8. Central Council of Indian Medicine
9. Central Council of Homoeopathy
10. Rehabilitation Council of India

(3) Research Bodies

1. Indian Council for Agricultural Research
2. Council of Scientific and Industrial Research
3. Indian Council of Medical Research
4. Central Council for Research in Ayurveda and Siddha
5. Central Council for Research in Homoeopathy
6. Central Council for Research in Unani Medicine
7. Central Council for Research in Yoga and Naturopathy

NPE 1986/92 contains a clear cut formulation on the subject in its para 5.34 as below:

> "In the interest of greater co-ordination and consistency of policy, sharing of facilities and developing inter-disciplinary research, a national body covering higher education in general, agricultural, medical, technical, legal and other IT professional fields will be set up.

The POA 1986 states firstly that separate bodies would be set up for agriculture, medicine, engineering, distance learning etc. and secondly, that the major functions to be performed by the apex body as below:

(a) To advise government on policy,
(b) To co-ordinate activities of the other bodies in different fields,
(c) To encourage inter-disciplinary activities and promotion of interface among different areas,
(d) To allocate resources,
(e) Establishment and management of common infrastructures and institutions, and
(f) Co-ordination of policy concerning external academic relations.

The POA 1992 states that a proposal was prepared but a consensus on structure and functioning could not be reached (POA para 11.12.30). There is no indication in the published reports since 1992 about the progress in the matter.

The National Knowledge Commission in its Reports on higher education has recommended establishment of an Independent Regulatory Authority for Higher Education (IRAHE) with Standing Committees for different branches like teacher education, legal education, medical education, open and distance education. The proposals of the NKC followed by those of Yashpal Committee are dealt with in the next chapter.

The author is of the view that the solution suggested in the NPE 1986/92 as approved by the Estimates Committee of the Parliament is the optimum one in spite of Yashpal Committee's view to the contrary. The apex body may be called Super-co-ordinator or Super-regulator as per one's choice.

15

From the NKC (National Knowledge Commission) to the NCHER (National Commission for Higher Education and Research)

Introductory

In this chapter the author would consider the functioning of the National Knowledge Commission, its recommendations and how the same were sought to be rendered ineffective by their having been rejected by the influential CABE (Central Advisory Board of Education), the highest policy making forum in India on which both the Centre and the States are represented. Thereafter would be considered the recommendations of the report of the Yashpal Committee (February 2008 to May 2009) on renovation and rejuvenation of higher education. In terms of the Yashpal Committee Report, the Government have drafted and introduced in May 2010 a Bill for constituting a single apex institution called the National Commission for Higher Education and Research (NCHER).

The National Knowledge Commission (NKC)

The National Knowledge Commission (NKC) was constituted on 13th June 2005 as a high-level advisory body to the Prime Minister (Dr. Manmohan Singh). It had a tenure of 3½ years and ceased functioning at the end of December 2009.

The NKC—Functioning (2005-2008)

The last known composition of the NKC was as below:

Mr. Sam Pitroda, Chairman (Industrialist/former Adviser to Rajiv Gandhi in Telecom); Dr. Ashok Ganguly (Research Chemist), P. Balaram (Scientist, Director, Indian Institute of Science); Dr. Joyati Ghosh (Economist, JNU); Dr. Deepak Nayyar (Economist and former V-C, Delhi University); Mr. Nandan Nilekani and Dr. Sujatha Ramdorai (Mathematician).

In the context of Education Ministry's plan of reservation to the extent of 27 per cent of seats for OBCs in the IITs and IIMs, the NKC was required to give its views. Its support to reservation as proposed by Government was highly qualified (Reservations are essential but are only a part and one form of affirmative action; there is a need to address the multi-dimensionality of differences, e.g. "a deprivation index" to supplement a student's examination score etc.). Two members, Pratap Bhanu Mehta, a political scientist, and Andre Beteille, a sociologist, resigned apparently because they did not agree with the formulation of the NKC. Vice-Chairman, P.M. Bhargava, a microbiologist, who was pro-reservation also resigned because of differences with the Chairman. The NKC, therefore, was reconstituted as indicated.

The terms of reference of the NKC in so far as they related to higher education were: "Build excellence in the educational system to meet the knowledge challenges of the 21st century and increase India's competitive advantage in the world of knowledge".

A summary of the NKC's recommendations in the field of higher education, legal education, medical education, management education and Open and Distance Education is indicated in the Annexure 15.1.

At the outset, it may be noted that the general thrust of the NKC's recommendations on various areas of higher education is to have an umbrella body which it calls Independent Regulatory Authority for Higher Education (IRAHE), and to have Standing Committees on sub-fields of higher education like medical education, legal education, management education and ODE. In regard to professional bodies, it proposes to restrict the role of Medical Council and Bar Council of India to enforcement of professional ethics and issue of licences to practise. Management education which is under the AICTE is to be delinked from the same. Similarly, the ODE would be delinked from the IGNOU.

The IRAHE is to be set up by an Act of Parliament. It would be the only agency that would be authorized to accord degree-granting powers to higher education institutions. It would also be responsible for monitoring standards and settling disputes. It should also be thought of as an authority for licensing accreditation agencies. The Chairman and Members of the IRAHE would be appointed by the Prime Minister based on the recommendation of a Search Committee. The IRAHE would be considered by the author in the context of the recommendations for General Education (UGC). The recommendations of the NKC on sub-fields other than General Education are considered first.

Management Education

The separation of Management Education from the AICTE as proposed by the NKC as would be a welcome step. This is because management education is not a technical subject at all, but an interdisciplinary subject in the broad field of social sciences. Its yoking to the AICTE was illogical and its separation from the AICTE was long overdue. Most of the recommendations of the NKC on management education are well-taken. However, there may have to be a State level Council for management education to assist the Central body.

Legal Education

The suggestions of the NKC to have an independent agency for legal education separated from the BCI is well taken. The author made such a suggestion independently in July 2006 in his Ph.D. Dissertation. However, apart from about 7-8 National Law Universities, there are now 400+ law colleges all over India, most of them of indifferent quality. They are affiliated to respective State Universities. It would be difficult for the Standing Committee to deal with all 400+ colleges directly. There would have to be a State Council for legal education which could deal with the Standing Committee.

Medical Education

The Medical Education Commission as proposed by the NKC in place of the Medical Council of India is of long standing. Once the medical colleges are de-linked from the MCI as well as the affiliating universities, there would be no alternative but to have State Councils for Medical Education. Secondly, the NKC has not dealt with the problems of colleges for para-medical disciplines like physiotherapy. The Standing Committee may have to accommodate such additional disciplines.

Traditional Health Systems

The NKC's recommendations in this area are too general. It is not clear if there would be a separate Standing Committee on AYUSH disciplines and what to do with 'poor colleges' and sub-critical research institutions.

Open and Distance Education

Government has already decided to delink the DEC from the IGNOU and to set it up as an independent council. Some of the recommendations of the NKC in this field are either highly technical or unexceptionable. The issue whether Standing Committee for the ODE should be under the IRAHE or should be free-standing needs to be debated further because the ODE is a mode of education rather than a branch of higher education.

Regulatory Functions in Higher Education

The UGC has reportedly made an issue of the NKC not having consulted it before making proposals for expansion of higher education. On merits, NKC's proposals have elicited highly critical comments. The recommendation that the UGC should be a purely grant giving body and a body for maintenance of Central universities apparently is quite drastic. But it would appear to follow that if the UGC has not been able to do much in the area of determination, maintenance and enhancement of standards, an alternative would have to be thought about.

National Knowledge Commission (NKC) states that in higher education, a regulator performs five functions: (1) Entry: Licence to grant degrees, (2) Accreditation: Quality Benchmarking, (3) Disbursement of Public Funds, (4) Access: Fees or affirmative action, (5) Licence to practice profession. From the way NKC has described functions of the UGC, Medical Council and Bar Council in the post-NKC period, it would appear that NKC would attend to functions at (1), (2) and (4). NKC's recommendation, in regard IRAHE which would perform these functions are, to say the least, simultaneously ambitious and ambiguous. The ambiguity arises from the fact that the NKC has couched its recommendations not so much in general as abstract terms and has not spelt out its implications in practical terms except in regard to the UGC, MCI etc. The present position is that as soon as a State legislature passes an Act, setting up a University, the State Government can go ahead and set up an organization which begins admissions. So also in the case of Central Universities. Constitutionally, education is a concurrent subject. The NKC has impliedly suggested higher education being transformed into a Central subject, what is more, it has suggested an arm's length relationship between the IRAHE and the State. It is highly unlikely that in a federal polity like India, the executive and the legislature at both the Central and State level would agree to such a surrender of powers. Incidentally, while elaborating the point that there are extensive rules after entry, the NKC states " The system is also based on patently irrational principles. The UGC Act Section 3.1.2(a) suggests that permission for receiving grants will be accorded only if the Commission is satisfied that the existing institution in the State are not adequate to serve the needs of the State" (p. 54 of 2006 Report). The author has verified and found that there is no such section.

Regarding autonomous colleges, the NKC identifies the principal-agent problem of providing autonomy as an option, distinguishing between motivations and capabilities of colleges. There may be such colleges which wish to become autonomous, but do not deserve to and colleges that have the capabilities to be autonomous, but do not wish to opt for autonomy. For the former, a filtration mechanism and for the latter, an incentive mechanism are proposed. The NKC has also mooted the idea of conferring autonomy on a cluster of colleges with similar standards or geographical proximity. It realizes that an institutional mechanism in the form of committees will have to be set up.

The solution proposed by the NKC for the problem of affiliated under graduate colleges, which cannot be made autonomous, is three-fold: (1) Remodel undergraduate colleges as community colleges which could provide both vocational education through two-year courses and formal education through three-year courses. (2) Establish a Central Board of under-graduate education along with State Board of under-graduate Education which would set curricula and conduct examinations for under-graduate colleges that choose to be affiliated to them. (3) Affiliate the college with new universities.

There are grave doubts about the viability of the structure envisaged by the NKC in the form of a top heavy IRAHE and Central and State Boards of U-G Education. As in the case of Japan and Korea, India may require a large number of Central and State Universities supplemented by private universities to cope with the problem of reaching the higher GER but a single apex body like the IRAHE for a vast country like India appears to be impracticable. The NKC is not clear regarding the respective jurisdictions of Central and State Boards of under-graduate education. It is not aware of the problems faced by the CBSE in affiliating high schools from various States. An NOC from a State Board is a prerequisite in such cases. It is also felt that the idea of community colleges might not be workable in India and that the best course is to have "affiliating model" universities as set out in the relevant chapter of the Gnanam Report [Chapter XVIII: 280(A)].

In regard to Research Councils, the NKC has advocated the setting up of a single National Science and Social Science Foundation (NSSSF) which, in essence makes sense and compares with the British mechanism of Advisory Board of Research Councils (ABRCs).

Concluding Remarks on the NKC

There is no doubt that the proposals made by the NKC are at once ambitious and ambiguous. But they needed to be debated and discussed across several fora before arriving at a final decision and in particular, along with Yashpal Committee Report on joint review of the UGC and the AICTE which led to the NCHER.

It is unfortunate, that a closure to the points raised by the NKC was sought to be applied by the Education Ministry under leadership Shri Arjun Singh. According to Press Reports (*Times of India*, 11th February, 2008), the NKC report (on higher education) was considered by the CABE and a majority of its recommendations were rejected. The following recommendations, in particular, were named: (1) Public private partnership, (2) Use of surplus land to generate revenue, (3) Differential salary structure, and (4) Creation of Independent Regulatory Authrity for Higher Education. Such a rejection of course, can only be interpreted as symbolic of the tussle between two organizations of the Government which incidentally are headed by Ministers belonging to the same political party (and not an aberration of coalition politics).

It may be noted that the NKC recommendations have not been superseded but rather overtaken by the recommendations of the Yashpal Committee which recommended establishment of the NCHER. The author, therefore, takes up the same.

The Yashpal Committee Report: Prelude to National Commission for Higher Education and Research (NCHER)

The genesis of the proposed NCHER is in the Report of the Yashpal Committee submitted under the catchy title of 'Renovation and Rejuvenation of Higher Education' to the Government of India in May 2009, shortly after the new (UPA II) Government came to power. The newly formed Government had framed an agenda for the First Hundred Days in which the establishment of the NCHER was an important item proposed by the new Minister for HRD (Shri Kapil Sibal).

When one goes into a little detail and especially the terms of reference of the Committee one finds that the prescribed agenda of the Committee was quite different. In particular, the Government Order dated 28th February, 2008 had specifically entrusted to the Committee the task of reviewing the working of the two apex bodies of the UGC and the AICTE and to propose amendments to the respective Acts. To quote:

"2. The following are the terms of reference of the Committee:

(a) To review the functioning of the UGC/AICTE and to critically assess the role of the UGC/AICTE and their preparedness to provide institutional leadership to the emerging demands of access, equity, relevance and quality of higher education/technical education and the university system.

(b) To review the provisions of the University Grants Commission Act, 1956 and the All India Council for Technical Education Act, 1987 and various suggestions for amendments to the said Acts by earlier Committees such as the Prof. Amreek Singh Committee.

(c) The role of the UGC in co-ordinating standards of higher education *vis-à-vis* the functional role of other statutory bodies such as AICTE, MCI, DCI, NCI, NCTE, DEC, etc.

(d) An assessment of the requirements of autonomy of the UGC *vis-à-vis* the Central Government and that of the university system *vis-à-vis* the UGC.

(e) The role of the UGC/AICTE in determining and enforcing standards of higher education/technical education in State Universities and the possibility of introducing a system of incentives and disincentives so that national standards of higher education/technical education are not compromised or diluted.

(f) Recommendations in regard to an effective and efficient mechanism for flow of resources from the UGC to the universities for their timely utilization including a mechanism of feedback thereto.

(g) The requirement of transparency and efficiency in the functioning of the UGC/AICTE.

(h) The role of the UGC *vis-à-vis* declaration of institutions to be deemed universities and recommendations for streamlining the process adopted by the UGC.

(i) Recommendations about the need to change the eligibility criteria for becoming eligible to receive grants under Section 12B of the UGC Act, 1956.

(j) Any other issue arising out of or relating to the above terms of reference and, the functioning of the UGC/AICTE which the Government or the Committee on its own, may desire to look into."

There were 24 Members of the Committee who were headed by Prof. Yashpal, former Chairman of the UGC. The Committee comprised eminent scholars in disciplines like law, economics, Vice-Chancellors, Directors of "IIT/IIM", serving Chairman, UGC, serving Chairman, AICTE, Director, NAAC, Secretaries to Government of India in Finance/Planning Commission, a Secretary of State Government (Tamil Nadu) and Shri Sunil Kumar (Jt. Secretary, Higher Education) : Member-Secretary.

One notices a disconnect between the Terms of Reference of the Committee and the composition of the Committee. Terms of Reference were very specific, viz. the study of the functioning of two apex organizations and suggest amendments, but the Members were very busy persons, who could not be said to be specialists in the working of these organizations. Contemporary newspaper reports indicated that very few Members attended the first meeting of the Committee. The Chairman reportedly met the Minister, HRD (at that time Shri Arjun Singh) on 14th September, 2008 and requested for the change of the nomenclature of the Committee as "Committee to Advise on Renovation and Rejuvenation of Higher Education". According to the Chairman's request, the Committee was suitably named but it is significant to note that in the Government Order dated 14th October, 2008, it was specifically stipulated that "composition and *terms of reference* of the Committee remains unchanged". To this, the Chairman's response was his letter dated 1st November, 2008 in which he stated: "I do not want to be involved in a routine administrative exercise but would be prepared to take on this responsibility only as an effort to go deep into the causes of the malaise in our education system just like the work we did in connection with drafting a curriculum framework at school level, something that led to the NCF 1995" (*sic* 2005)? The Committee appears to have given up the work of the review of the UGC/AICTE and focused on the tasks entailed by the new nomenclature of the Committee.

The Committee submitted its interim report in March 2009 and Final Report in May/June 2009. The Final Report numbers 84 pages, but if one excludes the Foreword and Appendices, it barely numbers

60 pages. The report, as expected, does not at all review the functioning of the UGC and the AICTE, but makes some general points about the university system in India as a background to its basic recommendation about the establishment of the NCHER.

So the basic point to be noted about the Report is that the Yashpal Committee Report departs from its 'Terms of Reference' although the Government had not formally deleted them. The significance of the reference to the NCF 2005 in Chairman's letter of November 2009 appears to be that when the UPA-I Government decided to revise the school curriculum 2000 (of the NDA Government), it had appointed a Steering Committee under the Chairmanship of Prof. Yashpal. This Steering Committee was assisted by the think-tank in the form of the NCERT, which had set up 21 Focus Groups and on the basis of their reports, the NCF 2005 was formulated within about 1½ years. The Yashpal Committee, significantly, did not have the assistance in its work of any think-tank simply because, thanks to the neglect by the UGC of the subject, there was no such think-tank in the form of a Training and Research Institute for Higher Education in India in existence at that time. The Committee was reportedly assisted by a consultant who was a Hindi specialist. The Yashpal Committee Report, therefore, hardly quotes any statistics and research findings in support of its recommendation for setting up the NCHER. It says that there are 13 professional councils (The author has pointed out earlier that the number of councils is much more). It feels that they have fragmented the higher education sector in the country from a policy perspective (Report p. 5). It considers the alternative of co-ordination and rejects it ("co-ordination among agencies which have different views of knowledge in education and which had to treat knowledge within narrow confines is extremely difficult"). It would, it concludes therefore, be necessary to have a single apex body.

On such theoretical foundations and empirical evidence is the Committee's recommendation for establishment of NCHER based. The Commission would be created by a Constitutional amendment. It would have a seven-member board with a full-time Chairman. Of seven members one would be an eminent professional from the world of industry and one with the background of law and consistent to social engagement. All other five members would be academic people of eminence, representing broad areas of knowledge. The Chairman's status would be that of Chief Election Commissioner and that of Members should be comparable to the Election Commission. The Commission would be independent of all the Ministries of the Government of India. The Committee proposed that the job to provide operational frame should be assigned to a competent professional organization as a project on a consultancy basis.

The Yashpal Committee Report (YPC) has been criticized even by sympathetic academics. Thus, Professor Sudhanshu Bhushan (2009) states that YPC Report is based on an idealist concept of the university and ignores the fact that knowledge has an important dimension of commercialization and marketing. We can also not be oblivious to the role played by professional councils in the maintenance of standards (S. Bhushan, 2009: 179-185).

Post Yashpal Committee Report—How NCHER has evolved?

The NCHER Bill as introduced in Parliament on 3rd May, 2010 appears to depart from the YPC Report. Firstly, medical education and agricultural education have been specifically excluded. There is reportedly a move in the Law Ministry to exclude legal education as well. If it succeeds, the ambit of the NCHER would be reduced to the three areas of the UGC, the AICTE and the NCTE which implies that it remains confined to the education sector as controlled by the Ministry of HRD. The reason for exclusion of medical education appears to be that the President of India in her address to the Parliament in 2009 referred to the establishment of a separate apex body for medical education. The reason for exclusion of agricultural education is reported to be that agricultural education is a State subject. It is surprising that the attention of the Government was not invited to the overriding power of the Central Government in Entry 66 of the Central List of the Seventh Schedule of the Constitution which is the basis of continuing funding of the ICAR by the Department of the Agricultural Research and Education (DARE).

One basic provision of the NCHER is to have a collegium of persons of eminence and integrity in academics etc. which would have a perpetual existence. It would advise the NCHER in its functioning and most importantly on the preparation of the National

Registry of potential Vice-Chancellors. It has been pointed out that the way NCHER Bill has been drafted would severely curtail powers of the Central Government and State Governments and would be against the tenets of federalism which is part of the basic structure of the Constitution of India. the NCHER Bill is stated to be a solution worse than the disease (JBG Tilak, 2010, *EPW*, 1st May, 2010).

Other observers have called the proposed NCHER Bill as amounting to a power grab (TCA Anant/B. Venkatesh Kumar, 2010). They have suggested deletion of provisions regarding appointment of Vice-Chancellors and drastic amendment of the Bill in other respects.

Conclusion

The NCHER Bill no doubt would be referred to a Joint Committee of Parliament. But even before the time arrives for such a step, it would be advisable to have a wide ranging consultations on the Bill, which has the appearance of a peculiar brand of academic authoritarianism which is against the spirit of Indian democratic federalist polity.

ANNEXURE 15.1

Summary of the NKC's Recommendations

Higher Education

- Create more universities expanding to around 1500 universities nationwide, to enable India to attain a gross enrolment ratio of at least 15 per cent by 2015
- Establishment an Independent Regulatory Authority for Higher Education (IRAHE)
- Increase public spending and diversify sources of financing
- Promote enhanced quality through measures such as upgrading infrastructure, introduction of salary differentials, etc.
- Establish 50 National Universities as multi-disciplinary exemplars with admission on an all-India basis
- Ensure access for all deserving students through well funded scholarships and affirmative action
- Affirmative action should address multiple dimensions of deprivation
- Reform existing universities to ensure curricula revisions, introduce course credit system, enhance reliance on internal assessment, encourage research, reform governance, etc.
- Restructure the system of affiliated undergraduate colleges
- New undergraduate colleges could be established as Community Colleges and be affiliated with the Central Board of Under-graduate Education or State Boards of Under-graduate Education or with some of the new universities that are established.
- UGC's functions will be delimited to disbursement of grants to and maintenance of public institutions

National Science and Social Science Foundation

- Set up a National Science and Social Science Foundation

(NSSSF) which will look at all knowledge as one seamless entity

- The Foundation to suggest policy initiatives to make India a leader in the creation and use of knowledge, to ensure that science and technology are maximally used for the betterment of the lives of people and to develop the scientific temper in the country

Legal Education

There should be a new regulatory mechanism by way of a Standing Committee for Legal Education under the IRAHE. The Bar Council of India would continue to exercise its powers: (1) to recommend minimum standards required for practice in the courts, (2) to discipline members of the Bar.

The main components of the new mechanisms are:

1. Prioritize Quality and Develop a Rating System
2. Curriculum Development
3. Examination System
4. Measures to attract and retain talented faculty
5. Developing a research tradition in law schools and universities
6. Centres for Advanced Legal Studies or Research (CALSAR) for each region
7. Financing of Legal Education (Fees to meet at least 20 per cent of total expenditure in universities)
8. Dimensions of Internationalization
9. Technology of Dissemination of Legal Knowledge (in which ILI will play a role)

Medical Education

Medical Council of India (MCI) would function only as a professional association with powers to conduct nation-wide examination and to provide licence for those who wish to join the profession. Similar changes would be made in other Councils like Nursing, Pharmacy, Dental and Rehabilitation. A paramedical council (for compounders, dressers and laboratory technicians) should be set up.

The main components of the new mechanisms are:

1. Regulation: Standing Committee of the IRAHE
2. Accreditation
3. Admission: One All-India Common Entrance Test
4. Quality: Curriculum, standards test, internship assessment, continuing medical education to be revamped based on distance/correspondence
5. Faculty development, teaching, research and training
6. Post-Graduate education: 50 per cent reservation for general physicians
7. Regional balance: More institutions in under-served areas: A Centre of Excellence in each State
8. Education for support services—nursing, pharmacy, paramedics.

Traditional Health Systems

There are extensive recommendations on this field including the basic one of establishment of a National Mission on Traditional Health Knowledge. Many of these relate to health delivery, manufacture of drugs etc. The main recommendations regarding Education are:

1. The 450 or so poorly endowed colleges in this area (AYUSH) need to be upgraded by introduction of evidence-based approaches through institutions like AIIMS
2. Establishment of a Network of World-class Research Programmes based on evidence-based approaches in fields like pharmaco-generics, immunology etc.

Management Education

The NKC proposes a Standing Committee for Management Education under the IRAHE, thus decoupling it from the AICTE. Since there is a variety of institutions (e.g. IIMS, University Faculties etc., it chooses to call them Management Education Entities (MEEs).

Other components of the mechanism are:

1. Grading institutions through CRISIL,

2. Accreditation and Branding of accreditation similar to ISO 9001,
3. Improve access (weightage to work experience at admission stage, educational loans),
4. Indigenization (social context)—development of India—specific case studies, Courses for Government officers,
5. Faculty Development,
6. Monitoring by IIMs of 3-4 MEEs,
7. New institutions including for new subjects (Entrepreneurship), by Foreign Universities, etc.,
8. Autonomy,
9. Governance—Board of Governance with 50 per cent independent members,
10. Non-traditional Management Education, e.g. rural managements, faculty management, social sector management, NGO management etc.

Open and Distance Education (ODE)

1. A New Standing Committee on ODE in place of the DEC of the IGNOU with two Advisory Groups: (a) Technical Advisory Group to devise common standards for labelling learning content and (b) Advisory Group on Pedagogical content management,
2. A system for quality assessment.
3. Facilitate convergence with Conventional universities.
4. Set up a Research Foundation to support research activities in the ODE.
5. Overhaul Training Programme for Educators.
6. The most innovative recommendations of a technical nature are:
   (a) Create a national ICT infrastructure for networking ODE institutions and their study centres,
   (b) Set up a National Education Foundation to develop web-based common open resources,
   (c) Establish a Credit Bank to effect transition to a course credit system,
   (d) Establish a National Education Testing Service for assessing ODE students.

16

An Overview and Prospects

It now remains for the author to take an overview of preceding chapters and then to make an assessment of the likely prospects especially in the context of the emerging challenge of globalization.

Chapter I *Introduction* is devoted to methodology and review of literature. The author clarifies that he has attempted what may be termed a *Contemporary* history of higher education in India as distinguished from a history written from a distance. He emphasizes the need for reading documentary sources with full understanding of their politico-administrative dynamics and the dialectics of policy making. The present account is basically of the politico-administrative variety with a mix of socio-economic trends like commercialization of professional education, and liberalization of economic policy in the background of globalization.

The second part of introduction is devoted to a review of literature, under the headings: (1) Textbooks, (2) Government sources (AIU, IIAS, NBT, NCERT, NIEPA, UGC), (3) privately produced compilations, and (4) International Organizations. The absence of histories has much to do with B.Ed. and M.Ed. curricula framed by the UGC, the latest being in 2000, which while recognizing psychological foundations of education as a compulsory subject shuns the term "history" or "historical foundations" and instead uses the vague term "educational developments in India".

Chapter 2 deals with historical background with a focus on evolution of apex institutions in higher education and research including medical education which is characterized by two systems—modern and traditional and multiple disciplines.

Chapter 3 takes an overview of development of higher education in the 1947-2007 period. It is pointed out that there has been several-fold increase in the number of conventional institutions and their enrolment. New types of institutions like Deemed Universities, Institutions of National Importance, single faculty universities, and new modes of imparting education like open universities have also come up. However, age-specific gross enrolment ratio (GER) which was about 0.7 per cent in 1950-51 still remains quite low at about 10 per cent which is less than the average GER of developing countries (11.3%). Moreover, there are some disturbing trends—like secular declining trend in the P-G and research and enrolment in science and technology faculties.

The reasons for growth in enrolment are identified as open door policy in admissions, pressure of social demand, manpower planning approach to technical education and initiation and expansion of ODL courses. The expansion has been accompanied by inequalities along regional, rural-urban, caste community and gender dimensions, some of which are addressed by reservation policies.

The expansion of educational facilities is also accompanied by a perceived fall in standards for which Committees have been appointed and some of their recommendations have been implemented. It would appear that while the UGC has addressed the input side of the quality dimension and the newly set up NAAC has tried to measure the outcomes in terms of grading, the crucial third dimension of quality remains unaddressed, viz. the teaching learning process in which the move for improvement has to come from the teachers.

Four chapters deal with the UGC in one way or the other. This concentrated treatment of the UGC is justified by the fact that the UGC is the prototype body for promotion and co-ordination of university education and for the determination and maintenance of standards of teaching, examination and research in universities, which has been in existence in excess of fifty years.

Chapter Four deals with precedents like UK-UGC and foundations of the UGC, including the establishment of *interim UGC* in December 1953 followed by the *statutory UGC* in November 1956. India, unlike the UK, is a federal polity and therefore, the UGC Act should have provided for regional offices of UGC *ab initio* and also a mechanism to give representation to and ensure participation of the

State governments in the governance of the UGC, which remains a lacuna. The UGC Act has been amended on three occasions (in 1972, 1984 and 1985). The UGC's regulatory and penal powers though limited could have been used more effectively but were not owing to the soft leadership of the UGC. The relationship of the UGC with State Governments and Central Government is considered, followed by a glance at successive Chairmen, Vice-Chairmen and Secretaries of the UGC.

Chapter 5 deals with the activities of the UGC for the period 1956 to 1980. For this period use has been made of the Review Report of UGC (1977), Programme Review Committee (1981) and the PAC Report (1977). It is concluded that the UGC with all its administrative weaknesses and lack of decisive academic leadership in this period was a functioning mechanism with a soul.

Chapter 6 deals with the period 1980 to 2007. In the sub-period 1980-85, UGC's main academic achievement was to have started the Women's Studies programme. In the sub-period 1985-92, UGC was seen to expand by way of setting up of four Inter-University Centres with two IUCs in the pipeline. The UGC was slow to respond to the challenge of establishment of National Open University (1985) by bringing about necessary coordination between the new SOUs and the correspondence course institutes of the conventional universities. The UGC proposed State Councils of Higher Education and set up Gnanam Committee to bring under review the whole gamut of management problems of higher education. The UGC was able to set up in 1994 NAAC for assessment and accreditation of colleges/ universities. Arrangement for co-ordination of OUs was also worked out with the setting up of the DEC under the statutes of the IGNOU. A progressive step was taken with the setting of Regional offices, but the UGC was not able to realize the potential of State Councils of Higher Education. During the Ninth and Tenth Plan periods (1997-2002 and 2002-2007), the UGC became more of a bureaucratic organization lacking a soul, and its autonomy tended to be eroded in different ways. In March 2005, UGC's weakness as a regulatory body was exposed by its inability to rein in "paper" private universities in the State of Chhattisgarh for tackling which, the Supreme Court had to intervene.

Chapter 7 deals with four organizations which are allied with the UGC in different ways—(1) NAAC, which is a quality enhancing Inter-University Centre which showed an impressive achievement in an earlier period but whose recent record is not so good, (2) the Distance Education Council under the IGNOU which has not been able to cope with the problem of quality and coordination in the ODL system, (3) the AIU which evolved out of the IUB which has a longer ancestry (1925) than the UGC, but was able to secure a consultative status with the UGC in 1989, thanks to the intervention of a Parliamentary Committee, and (4) the NIEPA (now renamed NUEPA), which has worked as a supplement to the UGC in the matter of training of non-academic administrators and higher education research.

Chapter 8 entitled Research Councils underlines the rationale of the Dual Funding mechanism for research in Indian higher education which necessitates co-existence of research councils and the UGC. the ICSSR established in 1969 was followed by the ICHR (for History) in 1973 and the ICPR (for Philosophy) in 1980. Generally, research in social sciences/humanities has suffered for want of adequate funding *vis-à-vis* funding of hard S & T research. The attempt to set up an institution similar to the Princeton Institute of Advanced Study in the form of IIAS did not quite make a mark. [More recently, a private National Institute of Advanced Study at Bangalore has come up in the non-profit sector.]

The next part of the book deals with five branches of professional higher education comprising: (1) Technical Education, (2) Teacher Education, (3) Legal Education, (4) Medical Education and (5) Agricultural and Forestry Education. The former two are under the Ministry of Education. Technical Education has a long pedigree going back to the advisory AICTE set up in 1945. It did good work till about 1969, but thereafter lost its élan in the statutory AICTE was set up in 1987 under the NPE 1986. Unfortunately, it has not given a good account of itself with self-financing sub-standard engineering and management colleges having proliferated and with the regional imbalances in the spread of technical education.

Teacher Education dealt with in Chapter Ten, is another weak spot. The Advisory National Council of Teacher Education set up under the NCERT in 1973 did good work in the framing of teacher education curricula expanding in-service teacher training facilities and taking a stand against sub-standard distance education B.Ed. courses. The statutory NCTE which started functioning in 1955 did good preparatory work in the initial four years but has become controversial because of its complicity with proliferation of sub-standard teacher training institutions. It has reportedly been temporarily superseded.

Chapter 11 on Legal Education deals with evolution of all-India Bar through the passing of the Advocates Act in 1961, its complicity with the Bar Council of India being responsible for Under-graduate Legal Education, and the universities for Post-graduate education. There has been resistance to reform by way of a three-year course, five-year integrated course etc. The bright spot is the National Law School University at Bangalore (set up by the Bar Council Trust) and its clones in Hyderabad, Jodhpur, Bhopal, Culcutta (Kolkata) and elsewhere. However, there is shortage of good teachers for these law universities running integrated five-year courses and other innovative programmes. The perception of higher judiciary about its special role in legal education has complicated the situation. The suggestion originally made by Dr. B.R. Ambedkar that a regulatory body for legal education which would deal with the UG and P-G education and research with the Bar Council of India being confined to professional registration and ethics is commended.

Chapter Twelve deals with Medical Education which has certain special characteristics. One problem is lack of integration of AYUSH institutions (Ayurveda, Yoga and Naturopathy, Unani, Siddha and Homoeopathy) with the modern bio-medical education system. The legal framework even of the MCI is outdated. Their is multiplicity of professional bodies like Dentistry Council and bodies for para-professional education courses in Pharmacy and Nursing. The pending proposal of having a UGC-type body both for grants and standards appears to be on the radar. As in the case of technical education, there is large expansion of the system through self-financing institutions. There are also institutions of National Importance. The chapter advocates a new regulatory body coupled with the *Flexner* type revamping which would involve closure of substandard institutions and consolidation of sub-critical institutions.

Agricultural and Forestry Education dealt with in Chapter Thirteen is led by research and has a long ancestry going back to 1905 and 1929. Moreover, this is a sector which can boast of having solved the food problem of India through its scientific advances which led to the Green Revolution in 1968 onwards. The successive reorganization of ICAR in 1966 and 1972 and the setting up of the State Agricultural universities for education, research and extension have been a necessary pre-condition for the break through in agricultural productivity achieved through research. Of late, however, agricultural research establishments have proliferated massively and there is lack of coordination between the Central and State Institutions. The productivity of agriculture has also declined. Hence successive reorganization reports including the proposal to have the PM as the President of ICAR à la CSIR. Forestry Education, since the outset has been a comparative laggard under its highly centralized Indian Council for Forestry Research and Education (ICFRE) set up as late as 1987. The existence of a generalist all-India Forest Service appears to have stood in the way of advance of research. The Supplementary Note on Rural Higher Education clears up confusion about rural universities, agricultural universities and rural higher education.

Chapter 14 deals with three general problems of higher education, viz. (1) Medium of education, (2) Financing, and (3) Super Regulation, earlier called Co-ordination. It is suggested that the solution to the first problem is a regional language as medium till undergraduate education, but reintroduction of English at the level of P-G education and research. This is called Advanced Anglification strategy. The Section on Financing of Higher Education deals with the recommendation of Punnayya Committee and Mungekar Committee which latter has set up a target ratio 1.5 per cent of GDP for investment in higher and technical education. Lastly, the super-regulation of higher education and research as recommended in the NPE 1986 (called there as 'National Council of Higher Education') is dealt with.

Chapter 15 deals with the National Knowledge Commission and how the latest proposal for having a National Commission for Higher Education and Research has evolved from the recommendations of the Yashpal Committee Report.

Prospects: Globalization and Higher Education in India

The account is concluded by referring to the state of preparedness of the Indian higher education system to face the challenge of globalization when the domestic education scene is characterized by Chronic Degradation Syndrome (CDS) and Dysfunctionality.

As pointed out by scholars like Gerald Delanty and Peter Scott, universities/higher education systems are primarily national systems. They provided the dominant elite with a common culture and a means of communication such as the codification of national languages. As such, it was easy for them to serve as instrumentalities for the spread of what may be called internationalization of higher education by receiving students from colonies for higher education and by sending their academic staff for work as experts or explorers in the colonies. Moreover, the universities in the West became massified (in the sense of student enrolment in the age group 17-23 exceeding 15%) in the 1960s and conditions were favourable for strengthening the trend towards internationalization in the four senses of (a) student flows, (b) flows of academic staff, (c) collaboration between different institutions, and (d) flow of ideas. In the 1990s, higher education systems have graduated from 'internationalization' to globalization. As expressed so tellingly by Peter Scott, globalization cannot be regarded simply as a higher form of internationalization, adapting the famous phrase of used by Lenin to the effect that 'imperialism is the highest stage of capitalism'. Rather, their relationship has to be seen as dialectical, mediated by several developments like the demise of the Soviet Union, rise of the Internet and the impact of round-the-clock, round-the-globe financial markets and integrated world markets as part of the phenomenon of the Death of Distance. The commodification of education in the form of GATS (General Agreement on Trade in Services) administered by the WTO (World Trade Organization) since 1993 has placed ex-colonies like India in a particularly vulnerable position. As observed by Nancy Birdsall (2008), there are inherent asymmetries in globalization (defined by her as a process of increased economic integration across borders with expanding flows of goods and services, people, capital and ideas). The asymmetries arise from two fundamental factors: (a) Market imperfections, and failures, and (b) The tendency of the markets to reward those who already have financial assets (financial and human capital). The GATS identified four modes of supply, viz. Cross Border Supply: Mode 1; Consumption abroad: Mode 2; Commercial Presence: Mode 3 and Presence of national persons: Mode 4. For countries like India, the great matter of concern is how to regulate trade in educational services under Mode 1 and Mode 3.

The Present Indian Scenario *vis-à-vis* Globalization

In this background, Indian scenario is as below:

- India has a very large higher education system with 376 Universities and over 20,000 Colleges, a teaching faculty of over 5 lakh and student strength of 1.16 crore. India does not have a mass higher education system in the sense of participation of 15 per cent or more of students of relevant age group in higher education but it may do so in the decade 2010-20 (the target being to achieve 30 per cent of GER by 2020).
- There is a dualism or rather triplism in structure, with a majority of institutions without high standards but a minority of institutions with an international brand name. (Triplism takes account of middling institutions below the level of IITs but above the level of the general run of institutions).
- Higher Technical and Medical Education is commercialized in a *political feudal* rather than a trade sense.
- The system is not open internally because private universities are not allowed to be set up (a Bill is pending in Parliament since 1995) and when State Governments enter the fray as the Government of Chhattisgarh did by allowing private universities to be notified on the basis of project reports, the Supreme Court had to step in to close them because the UGC failed to do so, another example of regulatory failure of the UGC.
- The number of Indian students going for study abroad (consumption abroad) is on the increase especially in the context of liberalization of foreign exchange regime. The flow is towards North America, Australia and Europe in that order. Press reports indicate that the Indian students outstripped the Chinese students as the largest group of overseas students in the USA, though China is expected to overtake India.

- The reliable statistics about foreign students studying in India are not available, but in 1993, the number was estimated to be 13,000 and according to qualified observers, the number is not showing any upward trend, the downward trend being barely stemmed by the enrolment of foreign students with the IGNOU (*Indian Express*, 20th March, 2009).
- Foreign entities have started to establish commercial presence in India.

In this background, what are the thinking/action on the policy front?

Disarray on the Policy Front

Unfortunately, the policy response in India, in the executive Ministries like Commerce and Education leaves much to be desired. The National Policy on Education 1986 does not refer to Globalization. This was not surprising because the term had not come into vogue. But it did refer to a "variety of new challenges and social needs" (para 1.10), and "unprecedented explosion of knowledge" (para 5.25). Most significantly, it stated in para 6.20 that "in the interests of maintaining standards and for several other valid reasons, the commercialization of technical and professional education will be curbed". Domestically, the Cental/State Governments did nothing to curb commercialization till the Supreme Court in the well-known Unnikrishnan case compelled them to do so whose impact has since been diluted by subsequent judgments. Since GATS is a matter of 'international treaty', it will certainly override the dictum in 1986 policy so far as international trade in educational services is concerned, in view of Directive Principles of State Policy, *vide* Article 51(c) which asks the State in India to foster respect for international law and treaty obligations in the dealings of organized people with one another. A Bill for regulation of foreign education service providers was not taken up by UPA-I because of the Leftist opposition.

It is heartening to note that after UPA-II came to power in May 2009, the new Minister HRD has pursued the matter and has introduced in Parliament the Foreign Educational Institutions (FEIs) (Regulation of Entry and Operations) Bill, 2010 on 3rd May, 2010 which seeks to include, within its ambit, foreign educational institutions whether existing and proposed, set up independently or in tie-up with an Indian partner or education provider imparting education resulting in degree, diploma or certificate in India. Distance education has been excluded from its ambit. FEIs proposing to award degrees and diplomas are required mandatorily to seek notification from the Central Government as a foreign education provider subject to meeting specified criteria, which include a corpus of Rs. 50 crore with a bar on repatriation of profits (75 per cent revenues to be used for development and 25 per cent revenues are to be invested in corpus).

The Bill has been criticized both by the Leftists and by the Neo-liberals. The Bill appears to have been introduced merely to comply with India's commitment to GATS in the context of the confusion created by making an initial offer to the GATs and then its withdrawal by the Government of India in the mid-2000s (JBG Tilak, *EPW*, 8th May, 2010). It is believed that the Bill will neither attract first-class foreign universities to India (which are more interested in joint research programmes and attracting Indian students to their domestic campuses), nor would it enable India to solve its problem of access, equity and quality in relation to the student numbers.

To shift perspective, Planning Commission's 2001 Report on India as a Knowledge Super-power deals with the problem in a narrow focus of enhancing India's annual software service exports and on this basis, the report had set before the nation a viable agenda for societal transformation, wealth creation and knowledge protection to be achieved by 2020. There are two problems: Recent events, viz. burst of the dot com bubble and the opposition to BPO (Business Process Outsourcing) in the US, now exacerbated by the financial melt-down since September 2008 necessitates a fresh review. Secondly, the Report does not have to say much about GATS.

The Tenth Plan Document, Vol. I flags the issue of movement of natural persons (the export of Indian education). The only statement about Mode 3 is: On the domestic front, there is need for a regulatory mechanism, based on objective and transparent criteria, so that competence and ability to supply services is given due cognizance. The Tenth Plan Document, Vol. II says in relation to Education Ministry that a Committee on Promotion of Indian Education Abroad (COPIEA) was set up in April 2002 under the Chairmanship of

Secretary, Department of Secondary and Higher Education. The Eleventh Plan document Vol. II does not appear to deal with the issue of globalization at all, in its higher education chapter (pp. 22-30). However, it talks of the intention to set up 14 World-class Universities (WCU) to enable India to become a global knowledge hub. In Vol. I of the document dealing with trade and commerce, there is reference to IT. and IT-enabled services, (*vide* pp. 311-312 of Vol. I) but no reference at all to India's position on education services apparently because of differences in the matter between the Commerce Ministry and the Education Ministry.

There was thus a policy vacuum, which was exacerbated by neglect of available documentation; by over-emphasis on educational exports, which as noted earlier, have shown a falling trend and whose promotion is a long-term process; by reluctance to involve academics, and to set up an independent mechanism as in UK (Universities UK) or Australia. There is some movement since the UPA-II came to power as illustrated by introduction of the FEI regulation Bill, referred to above.

National Knowledge Commission (NKC) has this significant thought to offer on GATS:

> "India is not an attractive destination for international students, not even as much as it used to 30 years ago. It is time for us to make a conscious attempt to attract foreign students to India for higher education. This would enrich our academic milieu, inherent quality and be a significant source of finance. Even 50,000 foreign students charged fees at an average rate of US$ 10,000 per annum would yield US$ 0.5 billion, the equivalent of Rs. 2,300 crore per annum in current prices at current exchange rates. The other side of the coin is even more important. Estimates suggest that there are about 160,000 students from India studying abroad. If their average expenditure on fees and maintenance in US$ 25,000 per student per year, Indian students overseas are spending US$ 4 billion—the equivalent of Rs. 18,400 crores per annum at current prices at current exchange rates. This has an enormous potential as a source of finance for India, if only we could create more opportunities for students with

increased placement and enhanced quality in our system" (NKC, 2006: 53).

By way of comparison, the allocation for selected programmes in higher education in the Union Budget in 2008-09 (BE) was Rs.10,360 crores (*vide* Chapter 13).

The author wishes to revert to his earlier reference to Degradation and Dysfunctionality so far as domestic educational scene is concerned. In this connection, para 7 of the NPE 1986-92 under the heading "Making the System Work" may be recalled. It states: "Education needs to be managed in an atmosphere of utmost intellectual rigour, seriousness of purpose and at the same time, of freedom essential for innovation and creativity. While far-reaching changes will have to be incorporated in the quality and range of education, "the process of introducing discipline into the system will have to be started here and now, in what exists. The first task is to make it work. All teachers should teach and all students study." But for this purpose teachers and students have to be incentised by the political leadership which is perceived to be corrupt and which has spread its corrupt tentacles to the private unaided institutions (This is written at the time of news of resignation of Union Telecom Minister in the context of 2-G Spectrum Scam). The Government has reportedly introduced "Prohibition of Unfair Practices in Technical Education Institutions, Medical Education Institutions and Universities Bill 2010", which seeks to regulate admissions and fees and introduce greater transparency regarding mandatory disclosures about faculty, fees and infrastructure etc. According to some critics the Bill is not stringent enough. It is felt, however, that what is necessary is to take up a *Flexner Type Investigation* into the malpractices in all sectors of higher education preparatory to western type regulation. To repeat what I stated earlier in the Chapter on Medical Education: There is no doubt that Medical Education requires a thorough reorganization including modernization of its complicated legal framework. In the first instance, it requires its Flexner Type Report preparatory to thorough going reforms, the reference being to the Report prepared by Abraham Flexner for the Carnegie Corporation for the Advancement of Teaching in Medical Education in the US and Canada. Published in 1908, it led to the revamping of medical education in the US consequent on closure of a large number of sub-standard medical colleges and similar results may be expected in India also. Nothing short of "Operation Higher Education Clean-up" would do!

Concluding Remarks

The educational policy planners perceive the problematique of Indian education in terms of expansion of access, improvement of *quality* and *reduction of inequality*. The solutions suggested are establishment of more IITs/IIMs and World-class Central Universities (WCU) and increase in GER to 30 per cent by 2020. They fail to suggest any remedy on the quality front and continuously harp on financial limitations of the public sector. The legislative agenda pays lip service to reduction of corruption and to the opening up (*vide* bills about malpractices and foreign universities referred to above). The way out of the impasse is suggested by (1) operation clean-up proposed by the author followed by (2) implementation of the recommendations of the NKC (quoted *supra*).

Bibliography

Abidi, S.A.H., K. Venkatesvaran and R.S. Biradar: 'Fisheries education in India', in Mehta, S.L./B.N. Mathur (Ed.) (2000): pp. 79-84.

Advisory Board for Research Councils (1982): Report of Joint Working Party on the Support of University Scientific Research (London, HMSO).

Agarwal, Pawan (2009): *Indian Higher Education: Envisioning the Future* (New Delhi, Sage Publication).

Agarwal, V.P. (1985): *Forests: Environmental and Production Frontier* (New Delhi, Oxford & IPH).

Agrawala, Rajkumari (2001): Indian Legal Research: An Evolutionary and Perspective Analysis in S.K. Varma and M. Afzal Wasim (Ed.) (2001): *Legal Research and Methodology* (New Delhi, Indian Law Institute).

Agrawala, S.K. (Ed.) (1973): *Legal Education in India: Problems and Prospects* (Esp. articles by S.P. Sathe, Ram Jethmalani and S.K. Agrawala).

Agrawala, S.K. and Mohamad Ghouse (Ed.) (1981): The Report on the Status of Teaching and Research in Law (New Delhi, UGC).

AICTE (Jan 1994): Report of the High Level Committee for Mobilization of Additional Resources for Technical Education (New Delhi).

AICTE (August 1994): All-India Council of Technical Education Act 1987 (New Delhi).

AICTE (1999): Technical Education in Independent India 1947-1997 (New Delhi).

AICTE (2002): *Annual Report 2000-01.*

AICTE (September 2003): *Report of Review Committee of AICTE* (Mimeo).

AICTE (2004): *Annual Report 2002-03.*

AIU (Sept. 1992): *Report of National Colloquium on Right to Education as a Fundamental Right* (New Delhi).

AIU (June 1999): *Report on the Dismissal and So-called Resignations of Vice-Chancellors of Bihar Universities and Dr.H.S. Gaur Vishvavidyalaya, Saugar in 1998.*

AIU (1999): *Appointment of Vice-Chancellors, their Security and Tenure and some related issues* (New Delhi).

AIU (1999): *Diminishing Autonomy of the Universities* (New Delhi).

AIU (2004) *Universities Handbook*, 30th Ed. (New Delhi).

AIU (2006) *Universities Handbook*, 31st Ed. (New Delhi)

AIU (2007): *University News*: Special Issue on National Knowledge Commission Report: Articles by JBG Tilak, VC Kulandai Swamy and Sudhanshu Bhushan.

Amarel Alberto, Glen A. Jones & Berit Karseth (Eds.) (2002): *Governing Higher Education: National Perspectives on Institutional Governance* (Dordrecht, Kluwer Academic Publishers).

Ambedkar, B.R. (Jan. 1936): Thoughts on the Reforms of Legal Education, in the Bombay Presidency (*Government Law College Magazine*, pp. 6-17).

Amrik Singh & Philip Altbach (Ed.) (1974): *The Higher Learning in India* (New Delhi, Vikas).

Amrik Singh (1985): *Redeeming Higher Education: Essays on Educational Policy* (New Delhi, Ajanta).

Amrik Singh (1986): *Asking for Trouble* (New Delhi).

Amrik Singh and G.D. Sharma (1988): *Higher Education in India: The Social Context* (New Delhi, Konark).

Amrik Singh (1989): The Last Two Decades, in Amrik Singh/G.D. Sharma (Ed.) (1989): *Higher Education in India: The Institutional Context* (New Delhi, Konark).

Amrik Singh and G.D. Sharma (1989): *Higher Education in India: The Institutional Context* (New Delhi, Konark).

Amrik Singh (2004)(a): *Fifty Years of Higher Education in India* (New Delhi, Sage).

Amrik Singh (2004)(b): *Challenge of Education* (Hyderabad, ICFAI University Press).

Anant, T.C.A. and B. Venkatesh Kumar (2010): The Draft Higher Education Bill 2010: A Critical Review (*EPW*, 20th March, 2010, pp. 10-13).

Anirudh Prasad (2000): *University Education, Administration and the Law* (New Delhi, Deep & Deep Publishers).

Ashby Eric (1963): *Community of Universities: An Informal Portrait of the Association of Universities of the British Commonwealth* (Cambridge University Press).

Ashby Eric (1966): *Universities—British, Indian, African* (Cambridge, Mass., Harvard University Press).

Awasthi, S.K. (2002): Legal Education: Role of BCI, Judicial Intervention and Suggestions (*Indian Bar Review*, 3 & 4, 2002, pp. 9-30).

Awasthi, Dr. S.K. (2004): Powers of BCI to Improve Standards in legal Education (*Journal of Indian Law Institute*, Jan-March, 2004, pp. 55-78).

Bala, Poonam (1991), *Imperialism and Medicine in Bengal: A Socio-historical Perspective* (Delhi: Sage Publications).

Banerjee Madhulika (2002): Public Policy and Ayurveda: Modernizing a Great Tradition (*EPW*, 23rd March, 2002).

Bapat, Ravi (May 2005): *Summary of Lectures on Public Economics of Medical Education in India* (Mumbai) (Mimeo).

Bar Council of India (2003): Annual Report 2001-2002 (New Delhi)

Basu, Anathnath (1940): *Secondary education in Bengal: A Study,* (Culcutta): Culcutta University Press).

Basu, Anathnath (1944): *University Education in India: Past and Present* (Culcutta : The Book Emporium Ltd.).

Baxi, Upendra (1996): *Judicial Activism: Legal Education and Research in Globalizing India* (New Delhi).

Baxi, Upendra (Ed.) (1977): *Socially Relevant Legal Education* (New Delhi, UGC).

Behar Sharad Chandra (Ed.) (March 2003): *Globalizing Education: Perceptions and Processes* (Pune, Indian Institute of Education).

Bell, Daniel (1973): *The Coming of Post-Industrial Society* (N.Y., Basic Books).

Ben, David Joseph (1968): "Universities" in Sils David L (Ed.): *International Encyclopaedia of Social Sciences*, Vol. XVI, pp. 191-198 (N.Y., Macmillan).

Berdahl Robert (1959): *British Universities and the State* (Berkeley & Los Angeles: University of California Press).

Bhandarkar, S.S. (1975, 1985 2nd Ed.): *Association of Indian Universities: A Short History* (New Delhi, AIU).

Bhardwaj, S.M. (1981): "Homoeopathy in India", in Giriraj Gupta (1981) (*Infra*) (pp. 31-54).

Bhargava, M.L. (1987): *Hundred Years of Allahabad University* (New Delhi, Ashish Publishing House).

Bhatia, K.L. (2006): *Legal Justice Education: Vision Plan for Legal School* (Deep & Deep Publications, New Delhi).

Bhatia, S.L. (Maj. Gen.) (1977): *A History of Medicine with Special Reference to the Orient* (B.C. Roy National Award Fund, MCI, New Delhi).

Bhatt, P.N. (2000): 'Veterinary Education in India, in Mehta, S.I./B.N. Mathur (Ed.) (2000) (*Infra*) pp. 64-78.

Bhattacharya Sabyasachi (Ed.) (1998): *The Contested Terrain: Perspectives on Education in India* (New Delhi, Orient Longman).

Bhave, Savita (1994): *Krishak Krantiche Senani: Annasaheb Shinde* (Pune, Kalpana). (Marathi)

Bhushan, Sudhanshu (2009): *Restructuring Higher Education in India* (Jaipur/New Delhi, Rawat Publication).

Bode, Martin (2007): *Taking Traditional Knowledge to the Market: The Modern Image of Ayurvedic and Unani Industry 1980-2000* (Hyderabad, Orient Longman).

Boman-Behram, B.K. (1944): *Educational Controversies in India: The Cultural Conquest of India under British Imperialism* (Bombay : D.B. Taraporewala Sons & Co.).

Brass, Paul (1972): "The Politics of Ayurvedic Education: A case study of revivalism and modernization in India", in Susanne H. Rudolph and Lloyd I. Rudolph (Ed.): *Infra*.

Burke, Peter (1997): Studying History, in Jeremy B. Black *et al.* (Ed.): *Perspectives on Historical Writing* (London, Macmillan).

CABE (1947): *Compilation of CABE Reports including Report on Agricultural Education* (New Delhi).

CABE (June, 2005): *Report of CABE Committee on Financing of Higher and Technical Education* (New Delhi, NIEPA).

CABE (June, 2009): *Report on Autonomy of Higher Education Institutions* (New Delhi, NBT).

Culcutta University Commission (1917) (Culcutta, Government Central Press) [Chairman: Sir Michael Sadler].

Chagla, M.C. (1974): *Roses in December* (Bombay, Bharatiya Vidya Bhavan).

Chandrakant, L.S. (January 1963): *Technical Education in India Today* (New Delhi, Ministry of Scientific Research & Cultural Affairs).

Chandrakant, L.S. (1971): *Polytechnic Education in India* (Bombay, D.B. Taraporewala Sons & Co.).

Chitnis, Suma & Philip Altbach (Ed.) (1979): *Indian Academic Profession: Crisis and Change in the Teaching Community* (New Delhi, Macmillan Co.).

Chitnis, Suma and Philip Altbach (Ed.) (1993): *Higher Education Reforms in India: Experience and Perspectives* (New Delhi, Sage Publication).

Chowdhary, T.H. (2001): Do we Need the AICTE? (*EPW*, 17th Feb. 2001).

Chowdhury, Subir (1959): *Management Education in India* (Ghaziabad, Institute of Management Technology).

Cobban, A.B. (1975): *The Medieval Universities: Their Development and Organization* (London, Methuan & Co.).

Coleman, James (Ed.) (1965): *Education and Political Development* (Princeton, New Jersey, Princeton University Press).

Committee on Higher Education (1963), Report [Chairman: Robbins] (London, HMSO Cmnd. 2154).

Crawford, D.G. (1914): *A History of Indian Medical Service*, Vols. I & II (Culcutta, Thacker & Spink).

Dahanukar, Sharadini and Thatte Urmila (1989): *Ayurveda Revisited: Ayurveda in the light of Contemporary Medicine* (Bombay, Popular Prakashan).

Dandekar, V.M. (1991): Reforms of Higher Education (*EPW*, 16th Nov. 1991, pp. 2631-36).

Daniel, John (1996): *Mega Universities and the Knowledge Media: Technology Strategies for Higher Education* (London, Kegan Paul).

Das, Sisir Kumar (1978): *Sahibs and Munshis: An Account of the College of Fort Williams* (New Delhi, Orian Publication).

Deb, Sandeepan (2004): *IITians—The Story of a Remarkable Indian Institution and How its Alumni Are Reshaping the World* (Penguin Books, New Delhi).

DEC (1999): *Guidelines for Support to State Open Universities and Correspondence Course Institutes* (New Delhi).

Dental Council of India (1973): *Silver Jubilee History of Dental Council of India, 1948-73* (New Delhi).

Deshpande, J.V. (2000): AICTE as Politicians' Hand Maiden (*EPW*, 2nd Jan. 2000).

Deshpande, J.V. (2000): Education as Business (*EPW*, 15th July, 2000).

DiBona, Joseph E. (1969): Change and Conflict in the Indian University (Duke University, USA).

Dogra, P.D. and R.C. Dhiman (Ed.) (1994): *Forestry Research and Education in India* (New Delhi, Indian Science Academy) (Esp. Articles by D.N. Tewari/P.N.Roy, B.R. Sahni, R.V. Singh and R.C. Dhiman).

Dongerkery, S.R. (1957): *A History of the University of Bombay (1857-1957)* (Bombay, University of Bombay).

(Draft) *Private Universities (Establishment and Regulation) Bill 1995* (Rajya Sabha)(New Delhi).

Flexner, Abraham (1908): Report on Medical Education in USA and Canada (Carnegie Foundation for the Advancement of Teaching).

Gadgil, Madhav and Ramchandra Guha (1990): *Ecology and Equity* (London, Routledge).

Garg, Suresh *at et.*, (Ed.) (2006): *Four Decades of Distance Education in India: Reflections on Policy and Practice* (New Delhi, Viva Book).

Gaudino, Robert L. (1965): *The Indian University* (Bombay, Popular Prakashan).

Geddes, Patrick (1918?): *The Proposed University* (Bombay).

Ghosh, A.B. (1969): *Commerce Education: A Study of Some Aspects* (New Delhi, S. Chand & Sons).

Gnanam, A., David Bradbury and Antony Stella (Ed.)(2003): *Benchmarking Quality of Higher Education: The Indo-UK Perspectives*. (New Delhi, Sterling Publications).

Gopal, S., (1989): Radhakrishnan: A Biography (New Delhi, OUP).

Government of India: (i) (1923): *Quinquennial Review of Progress of Education in India* (QRPE) (1917-22), (ii) (1928) QRPE 1922-27, (iii) (1938) QRPE (1932-37), (iv) (1948): *Progress of Education in India (1937-1947)*, (v) (1953) QRPE (1947-52), (New Delhi).

GoI: Ministry of Education (1948): Report of the University Education Commission (New Delhi).

GoI: Ministry of Law (1953): The Report of Indian Bar Review Committee (New Delhi) (Chairman: Justice S.K. Das).

GoI: Ministry of Education (1957): Proceedings of the 4th Meeting of the National Council for Rural Higher Education held at Sriniketan in March, 1958 (New Delhi).

GoI: Ministry of Science and Cultural Affairs (1958): Scientific Policy Resolution (New Delhi).

GoI: Ministry of Law (1958): 14th Report of the Law Commission of India: (Chairman M.C. Setalvad) (New Delhi).

GoI: Ministry of Education (1961): Report of the Fourth Inter-State Seminar on Rural Higher Education (New Delhi).

GoI: Ministry of Health (1961): Report of Health Survey and Planning Committee (Chairman: A.L. Mudaliar) (New Delhi).

GoI: Ministry of Scientific Research & Cultural Affairs: AICTE (July 1961): Report of the Special Committee on Science Education.

GoI: Ministry of Scientific Research and Cultural Affairs: AICTE (August 1961): Report of the Committee on P-G Engineering Education and Research [Chairman: M.S. Thacker].

GoI: Ministry of Education (1964): Committee of MPs to Review Higher Education (New Delhi). [Sapru Committee]

GoI: Planning Commission (1967): Report of the Committee on Social Science Research [Chairman: V.K.R.V. Rao] (New Delhi).

GoI: Ministry of Agriculture (1973): Report of the ICAR Enquiry Committee [Chairman: Justice P.B. Gajendragadkar] (New Delhi).

GoI: Ministry of Education & Social Welfare (February 1974): Report of the Review Committee of Regional Engineering Colleges (New Delhi) [Chairman: Jaikrishna, then V-C of Roorkee University].

GoI: Ministry of Education & Social Welfare (January 1977): Report of the Review Committee on the UGC (New Delhi) [Chairman: V.S. Jha].

GoI: Ministry of Science & Technology (1983): Technology Policy Statement.

GoI: Ministry of Health & Family Welfare (1985): Compendium of Reports on Health (New Delhi).

GoI: Ministry of Education (1985): Challenge of Education (New Delhi)

GoI: Ministry of Health and Family Welfare (1987): Report of the Expert Committee on Health Manpower Planning, Production and Management (New Delhi) (Chairman: Dr. K.K. Bajaj).

GoI: Ministry of Education (1988): *(Report of the High Powered Review Committee on the REC's)* [Chairman: R.A. Mashelkar] (New Delhi).

GoI: Ministry of Environment & Forestry (1988). National Foresty Policy, (New Delhi).

GoI: Ministry of Education (1989): Report of Review Committee on NIEPA (New Delhi).

GoI: Ministry of Health and Family Welfare (1989): National Education Policy in Health Sciences (New Delhi).

GoI: Ministry of Education (1994): Report of the CABE Committee on Distance Education (New Delhi).

GoI: Ministry of Tourism: Annual Report (1997-98) (New Delhi).

GoI: Department of ISM and Homoeopathy (1998): Indian System of Medicines and Homoeopathy in India (New Delhi).

GoI: Ministry of Education: Annual Reports (from 1998 to 2006) (New Delhi).

GoI: Ministry of Environment & Forestry (1999). National Forestry Action Plan (New Deihi).

GoI: Planning Commission (2000): Mid-Term Appraisal of the Ninth Plan (New Delhi).

GoI: Ministry of Health & Family Welfare (2001): Report of the Working Group on Development of Human Resources for Health (New Delhi).

GoI: Planning Commission (June 2001): India as a Knowledge Super Power: Strategy for Transformation: Task Force Report.

GoI: Ministry of Statistics and Programme Implementation (2001) Report of National Commission on Statistics, Vols. I and II (New Delhi).

GoI: Planning Commission (Dec. 2002): Report of the Committee on India: Vision 2020 (New Delhi).

GoI: Ministry of Science & Technology (May 2002): R & D Statistics 2000-2001 (New Delhi).

GoI: Ministry of Science and Technology (2003): Science and Technology Policy Resolution.

GoI: Planning Commission (April 2003): Towards Excellence in Polytechnic Education—Perspectives for the year 2000 and Beyond (New Delhi).

GoI: Department of Agricultural Research and Education: Ministry of Agriculture (2005): Annual Report 2004-2005 (New Delhi).

GoI: Department of Animal Husbandry and Dairy, Ministry of Agriculture (2005): Annual Report (2004-05) (New Delhi).

GoI: Planning Commission (2005): Mid-Term Appraisal of Tenth Plan (New Delhi).

GoI: Planning Commission (January 2005): Report of the Task Force on Revamping and Refocusing of Agricultural Research [Chairman: M.S. Swaminathan] (New Delhi).

GoI: Planning Commission (Nov. 2006): Toward A More Inclusive Growth: An Approach to Eleventh Plan (New Delhi).

GoI: National Knowledge Commission (2006): Report to the Nation (New Delhi).

GoI: Ministry of Education: Annual Report (2007-08) (New Delhi).

GoI: Ministry of Education (2007): Report of the 11th Plan Working Group on Technical Education (New Delhi).

GoI: National Knowledge Commission (2007): Report to the Nation (New Delhi).

GoI: Planning Commission (December 2007): Eleventh Five Year Plan (2007-2012) Vol. I: *Inclusive Growth*, Vol. 2: *Social Sector Services*,

Vol. 3: *Agriculture, Industry, Services, Physical Infrastructure* (New Delhi).

Golay, W.H. (1974): *The University of Poona 1949-1974* (Poona, Registrar of Poona University).

Guha, Ramchandra (2007): *India After Gandhi* (London, Picador).

Guha, Ramchandra (2008): The Challenge of Contemporary History, *EPW*, 28th June 2008 (pp. 192-203).

Gupta, Giriraj (Ed.) (1981): *The Social and Cultural Context of Medicine in India* (New Delhi, Vikas).

Gupta, Sushma (2006): *History of Legal Education* (Deep & Deep Publications, New Delhi).

Hartog, Sir Philip (1939): *Some Aspects of Indian Education: Past and Present* (London, OUP).

Hebbar Ritambara (2003): Social Science Policy in the New Millennium: A Workshop Report (*EPW,* 31st May, 2003, pp. 2118-2120).

Hehir, Patrick (1923): *The Medical Profession in India* (London, Henry Fraude & Hodder Stoughton).

Homoeopathy Central Council Act, 1973 (Printed in AIR Manual, Vol. 27, Fifth Edition) (Nagpur).

ICAR (1955): Report of the (First) Joint Indo-American Team on Agricultural Research & Education 1954-55 (New Delhi).

ICAR (1960): Report of the (Second) Joint Indo-American Team on Agricultural Education, Research and Extension (New Delhi).

ICAR (1978): Report of the Review Committee on Agricultural Universities [Chairman: M.S. Randhawa] (New Delhi).

ICAR (1988): Report of the ICAR Review Committee (Chairman: G.V.K. Rao) (New Delhi).

ICAR (Aug. 2000): Memorandum of Association (New Delhi).

ICAR (2002): Report of the Committee set up to Review Administrative Structure of the ICAR at headquarters and its linkages with institutions and SAUs (Chairman: Shri Hemendra Kumar) (New Delhi).

ICAR (April 1998): Education for Agriculture: Bridge to Century of Hope on the Farm Front (New Delhi).

ICAR (July 2007): Report of the ICAR Reorganization Committee (Chairman: Dr. R.A. Mashelkar).

ICHR (1982): Report of ICHR Review Committee (New Delhi).

ICHR: Annual Reports: 2003-04 to 2005-06 (New Delhi).

ICPR (2002): *ICPR: A Profile* (New Delhi).

ICSSR (1970): Report on Social Sciences in India: Retrospect and Prospect, Vol. I and Vol. II (First Review Committee Report—Chairman: Malcom Adisheshiah) New Delhi.

ICSSR (1971): Role, Responsibilities, Functions and Organization of ICSSR: Occasional Monogram No. 7 (New Delhi).

ICSSR (1978): Report of the Second Review Committee (Chairman: V.M. Dandelkar) (New Delhi).

ICSSR (1985): Report of Regional Offices Review Committee (Chairman: Prof. Iqbal Narain).

ICSSR (1986): Report of Regional Offices Review Committee (Chairman: Prin. Ram Joshi). (New Delhi).

ICSSR (1986): Report of the Third Review Committee (New Delhi).

ICSSR (1998): Report of Regional Offices Review Committee (Chairman: Prof. Amitabh Kundu) (New Delhi).

ICSSR (2002): Report of Regional Offices Review Committee (Chairman: Prof. T.S. Papola) (New Delhi).

ICSSR News Letter—Several issues of 2004-2007.

Imran, Quadeer & K.K. Narayan (2005): Politics of Pedagogy in Public Health (*Social Scientist*, Jan-Feb 2005). (New Delhi).

Indian Bar Review (Special No. On Legal Profession) (1995) (Nos. 2 & 3) (containing: Report of *Judges* Committee and Bhubaneshwar Resolution of Law Ministers Conference) (New Delhi).

Indian Medicine Central Council Act, 1970 (Amended upto 1st October, 1986) (1987) (Delhi, Controller of Publishing GoI).

Indiresan, Jaya (1993): Quest for Quality: Intervention versus Impact, in Chitnis Suma and Philip Altbach (Ed.).(*Supra*)

Indian Veterinary Council Act, 1984 (1989) (Delhi, Controller of Publication).

Jaggi, O.P. (1979): *Western Medicine in India: Medical Education and Research* (New Delhi, Atma Ram & Sons).

Jain, M.P. (1930): *Outlines of Indian Legal History* (New Delhi, N.M. Tripathi Pvt. Ltd., 5th Ed.).

Jayaram N. (1993): The Language Question in Higher Education: Trends and Issues, in Chitnis/Altbach (1993). *Supra*.

Jeffery, Roger (1988): *The Politics of Health in India* (Berkeley, University of California Press).

Jha, B.K. (2004): Technical Education in UP (*EPW*, 29th May, 2004).

John, V.V. (1969): *Education and Language Policy* (Bombay: Nachiket Publications).

John, V.V. (1969): *Orbiting Professor and other Reflections on Indian Education* (Bombay, Pearl Publications).

John, V.V. (1972): *Light Luggage* (Bombay, Indian Book House).

John, V.V. (1973): *Misadventures in Higher Education* (New Delhi, Young Asia Publications).

John, V.V. (1978): *The Great Classroom Hoax and other Reflections on Indian Education* (New Delhi, Vikas).

Jones Elspeth & Solly Brown (Eds.) (2007): *Internationalizing Higher Education* (London, Routledge).

Karve, R.P. (1938): *History of Government Law College, Bombay* (Bombay).

Kaul, A.K. and V.K. Ahuja (1997): Legal Education in India in 21st Century (All India Law Teachers Congress, Faculty of Law, Delhi University (see Esp. Article by M.C. Narayan—Distance Learning).

Kaul, Rekha (1993): *Caste, Class and Education* (New Delhi, Sage).

Kaur, Kuldeep (2003): *Higher Education in India (1781-2003): Policies, Planning and Implementation* (New Delhi, UGC & Chandigarh, CRRID).

Keswani, N.H. (1970): "Medical education in India since Ancient Times", in ODO'Malley (Ed.): *The History of Medical Education* (Berkeley: University of California Press), pp. 329-366.

Khera, S.S. (1997): *Government in Business* (New Delhi, National Publishers).

Kolhatkar, D.D. (1974): *Commentary on the University Laws in India* (Indore, The Lawyers' Haven).

Kolhatkar, M.R. (1976): Administration and Management of Research Organizations (*Indian Journal of Public Administration*, Jan-March, 1976).

Kolhatkar, M.R. (1984): Administration of Institutions of Higher Learning: Perspectives, Problems and Remedies (*Indian Journal of Public Administration*, Apr-June 1984).

Kolhatkar, M.R. (1988): Education Expenditure in India in relation to National Income: Trends and Implications (*Education & Social Change*: *The Journal of IIE*, Pune, July-Sept, 1988).

Kolhatkar, M.R. (1997): *Educational Planning and National Development—Some Crucial Aspects* (New Delhi, M.D. Publishers).

Kolhatkar, M.R. (2003): A Policy Framework for Higher Education in India: A Missing Dimension in, Dr. K. Venkat Subramaniam (Ed.): *Issues in Higher Education*, Vol. I (Hyderabad, ICFAI, University Press).

Kolhatkar, M.R. (2003): Multiple Inequalities of Globalization and What to do about them in Yazdi Josephine (Compiled): *Globalization and Challenges of Education* (New Delhi, Shipra Publications).

Kolhatkar, M.R. (2005): Globalization & Higher Education Sector in India: A Policy Deficit in S.C. Behar (Ed.) (Pune Indian Institute of Education).

Kumar, Anil (1998): *Medicine and the Raj: British Medical Policy 1835-1911* (New Delhi, Sage).

Kumar, Deepak (1995): *Science and The Raj (1857-1905)* (New Delhi, OUP).

Kumar, Deepak (2005): "Colony under a Microscope: The Medical Works of W.M. Haffkine", in Palit, Chittabrata/Achintya Dutta (2005) *infra*, pp. 177-204.

Kumar, Nita (2000): *Lessons from Schools: The History of Education , Banaras* (New Delhi, Sage Publishers).

Kumar, Nita (2007): *Politics of Gender, Community & Modernity—Essays on Education in India* (New Delhi, OUP).

Law Commission of India (1998): 160th Report on the Amendment of the AICTE Act (New Delhi).

Law Commission of India (2007): 184th Report (New Delhi, Universal).

Lok Sabha Debates—17th December, 1985 on UGC Amendment Bill 1985 (Column 356).

Lok Sabha Secretariat (1966): 102nd Report of the Estimates Committee on Higher Education. (New Delhi).

Lok Sabha Secretariat (1977): Ninth Report of the Estimates Committee on AICTE (New Delhi).

Lok Sabha Secretariat: Public Accounts Committee: 73rd Report on UGC (March 1978).

Lok Sabha Secretariat (1989): 66th Report of Estimates Committee on UGC (New Delhi).

Lok Sabha Secretariat (1990): Report of Action Taken on Supra (N. Delhi).

Maharaj Singh: 'Agricultural Education: Historical perspective', in Mehta S.L./B.N. Mathur (Ed.) (2000), pp. 8-22.

Maharashtra Medical Council Act, 1965 (Amended upto 2nd April, 1992) (Bombay, Directorate of Government Printing & Stationery).

Majumdar, Sulekha (2000): Infrastructure and Educational Administration in Marmar Mukhopadhyaya and M. Parikh (Ed.): *Education in India: The Fifty Years* (New Delhi).

Malcolm, Adisheshiah (1997): Presidential Address in Atal Yogesh (Ed.) *Social Sciences in Asia* (New Delhi, Abhinav).

Malik, S.C. (Ed.) (1971): *Management and Organisation of Indian Universities* (Shimla, IIAS).

Mallick, B.B.: 'West Bengal University of Animal and Fishery Sciences, Culcutta' in Mehta, S.L./B.N. Mathur (Ed.) (2000) pp. 296-299.

Martin, Willam J. (1985): *The Global Information Society* (A Gower Publishers).

Mathew A (1990): *Ministry of Education: An Organizational History* (NIEPA, New Delhi).

Mathur, M.V. & Ramesh K. Arora (Ed.) (1992): *The Vice-chancellors Remember* (New Delhi, Associated Publishing House for Centre for Administrative Change, Jaipur).

Mathur, M.V., Ramesh K. Arora and Meena Sogani (Ed.) (1994): *Indian University System: Revitalization and Reforms* (New Delhi, Wiley Eastern).

McCully, Bruce T. (1940): *English Education and the Origin of Indian Nationalism* (N.Y., Columbia University Press).

McKinsey Consultants (December 2000): *Shaping the Knowledge Economy in India: The Need to set up a National Mission for Technology Education* (New Delhi).

Medical Council Act, 1956 (vide MCI *Bulletin-cum-Directory*, 2001), (New Delhi).

Medical Council of India (1960): *Proceedings of Medical Council 1956-1959* (New Delhi).

Mehrotra Committee Report (1986): Report of the Committee on Revision of Pay-scales of Teachers in Universities and Colleges (New Delhi, UGC).

Mehta, P.L. and Sushma Gupta (2000): *Legal Education and Profession in India* (New Delhi, Deep & Deep Publishers).

Mehta, S.L. and B.N. Mathur (Ed.) (2000): *50 Years of Agricultural Education in India* (New Delhi, ICAR).

Metcalf, Barbara D. (2004): *Islamic Contestations* (New Delhi, OUP).

Misra, B.B. (1961): *The Indian Middle Class* (Delhi, OUP, 1961, Reprint 1978).

Mukerji, D.P. (1948): *Indian Culture: A Sociological Study* (1st published 1948; New Delhi, Rupa Paperback, 2002).

NAAC (2003): *Total Quality Management for Tertiary Education: Government of Karnataka Initiative* (Bangalore).

NAAC (2004): *Guidelines for Establishment of SLQAAC and QACs* (Bangalore).

NAAC: *Annual Reports* 1994-2005 (Bangalore).

Naik, K.C. (1972, 2nd Ed.): *A History of Agricultural Universities* (New Delhi, Oxford & IBH Publishing).

Naik, J.P. (1961): *Role of Central Government in Education* (New Delhi, Ministry of Education).

Naik, J.P. (1965): *Educational Planning in India* [Bombay (Now Mumbai), Allied].

Naik, J.P. and Syed Nurullah (1974): *A Student's History of Education in India* (6th Edition, Bombay (Now Mumbai), Macmillan & Co.).

Naik., J.P. (1977): *Alternative System of Health Care in India* (Bombay, Allied).

Naik, J.P. (1977): *Equality, Quality and Quantity in Higher Education: The Elusive Triangle* (Bombay, Allied).

Naik, J.P. (1982) *Education Commission and After* (1st ed. Bombay: Allied) Reprint (New Delhi, APH Publishing, 1997).

Nair, Sunitha B. (2001): "Social History of Western Medical Practice in Travancore: An Inquiry into the Administrative Process", pp. 215-232, in Kumar Deepak: *Disease and Medicine in India: A Historical Overview* (New Delhi, Tulika Books for Indian History Congress).

Nandi, P.K. (1981): "Cultural Constraints of professionalization: A case of Nursing in India" (pp. 147-161). In Giriraj Gupta (Ed.) (1981) *Supra.*

Narain, Iqbal (1989): *ICSSR: Recent Developments* (New Delhi, ICSSR).

National Council for Teacher Education (1998): *Policy Perspectives in Teacher Education—a Critique and Documentation* (New Delhi).

National Council for Teacher Education Act, 1993 (New Delhi, Law Ministry).

National Health Policy 2002 in Prakash Louis (2003): *Compilation of Policy Documents of Government of India* (New Delhi, Indian Social Institution).

NCTE: *Annual Reports for* 1995-2007 (New Delhi).

NCTE (2000): *Four Years of NCTE* (New Delhi).

National Law School of India Act (Karnataka Act No. 72 of 1986) (Bangalore).

Neave, Guy *et al.* (Ed.) (1991): *Prometheus Bound: The Changing Relationship Between Government and Higher Education in W. Europe* (Oxford, Pergamon Press).

Nelson, Frazer (1902): *Deccan College: A Retrospect, 1851-1901* (Poona).

NIEPA: Annual Reports for 1987-2005 (New Delhi).

Nursing Council of India (2000): *Silver Jubilee Volume of NCI* (New Delhi).

Nurullah, Syed and J.P. Naik (1951): *A History of Education in India* (During the British Period) (2nd edition, Bombay, Macmillan & Co.).

Official Language Act, 1967 and Rules: Compilation (1994) (New Delhi, Controller of Publishing).

Padda, Darshan S. and N.L. Maurya: 'Accreditation in Higher Agricultural Education in India', pp. 125-140, in Mehta, S.L./B.N. Mathur (Ed. (2000), Supra.

Palit, Chittabrata/Achintya Dutta (Ed.) (2005): *History of Medicine in India: The Colonial Encounter* (Delhi, Kalpaaz Publication).

Pandit, C.G. and K. Someswara Rao (1961): *IRFA and ICMR, 1911-1961: Fifty Years of Progress* (New Delhi, ICMR).

Patel, K.M. (2005): *NAAC: Accreditation of Higher Education* (Jaipur: Mark Publishers).

Pathan, S.N. (2005): *Quality Improvement Programmes in Higher Education through NAAC* (Bhopal: Intellectual Book Bureau).

Patrick, Geddes (1918?): *The Proposed University.*

Paul, S. (1982): *The Social Transformation of American Medicine: The Rise of a Sovereign Profession and the making of a Vast Industry* (N.Y., Basic Books).

Pharmacy Act, 1948 (New Delhi, Universal).

Philip, J. and D. Shankar Narayan (March 1989): *Management Education in India* (Bangalore, IIM).

Pinto, Marina (1984): *Federalism and Higher Education* (New Delhi, Orient Longman).

Potts, E. Daniel (1967): *British Baptist Missionaries in India 1793-1837* (Cambridge, Cambridge University Press).

Powar, K.B. (2000): *Higher Education for Human Development* (Papers of a 2000 Conference) (New Delhi, AIU).

Powar, K.B. (2004): Deemed to be Universities: Their Genesis and History, Present Status and Future Prospects (*University News*, 29th March, 2004).

Powar, K.B. (2004): *Indian Higher Education: A Conglomeration of Concepts, Facts and Practices* (New Delhi, Concept).

Prabahavan, R.: (2000) Tamil Nadu Veterinary and Animal Sciences University, Chennai, pp. 279-282 in Mehta, S.L./B.N. Mathur (Ed.) (*supra*).

Presidency College, Culcutta: *Centenary Volume (1956*), (West Bengal Government Press).

Principals of Regional Engineering Colleges (Nov. 1992): Report on Perspectives for Excellence in Regional Engineering Colleges, submitted by Principals of Regional Engineering Colleges.

Rajya Sabha Debates—7th December 1993 (Vol. CLXI, No. 4).

Ramamurti Committee (1989): Perspective paper on 'Towards an Enlightened and Humane Society'.

Randhawa, M.S. (1979): *A History of ICAR* (New Delhi, ICAR).

Rao, K. Sudha (2002): *Educational Policies in India* (New Delhi, NIEPA).

Rao, K. Sudha (2003): *Institutes Deemed to be Universities: Contribution to Higher and Professional Education and Research* (Banasthali Vidyapeeth).

Rashdall, H. (1946): *The Universities in the Middle Ages*, 3 Vols. (2nd edition) (London).

Rastogi Committee Report (May 1993): Report of the Committee to Review the Pay-scales of University and College Teachers.

Raza, Moonis (Ed.) (1991): *Higher Education in India: Retrospect and Prospect* (AIU, New Delhi).

Renold, Leah (2005): *A Hindu Education: Early Years of the Banaras Hindu University* (New Delhi, Oxford University Press).

Report of Health Survey and Development Committee (1946). (Delhi Manager, Government Printing Press) [Chairman: Sir J.W. Bhore].

(73rd) Report of the Public Accounts Committee (April 1978).

(114th) Report of the Public Account Committee (April 1980)

Report of Lord Rothschild (1987): An Enquiry into Social Sciences Research Council (HMSO Cmnd. 8554).

Report of Royal Commission on Agriculture in India (1928) (Culcutta, Government of India Printing Press). [Chairman: Lord Linlithgow].

Report of the Review Committee on the Scheme of University Level Book Production in Indian Languages (1987) (New Delhi, M-HRD). (Mimeo).

Rudolph, Susanne H. and Lloyd I. Rudolph (1972): *Education and Politics in India: Studies in Organization, Society and Policy* (New Delhi, OUP).

Rudolph, Susanne H. and Lloyd I. Rudolph (1983): Rethinking Secularism: Genesis and Implication of the Textbook Controversy 1977-80, in *Pacific Affairs*, 56(1), Spring 1983, pp. 15-37.

Saha, S.N. (2000): *National Academy of Agricultural Research and Management, Hyderabad* (2000) in S. Mehta/B.N. Mathai (Ed.) *Supra*.

Said Edward (1978): *Orientalism* (London, Penguin Books).

Sanyal, Bikas (1995): *Innovations in University Management* (Paris: UNESCO Publishing for IIEP).

Sen, Amartya (1971): "The Crisis in Indian Education" in S.C. Malik (Ed.): *Management and Organisation of Indian Universities* (Simla, Indian Institute of Advanced Study) pp. 248-274.

Sen Committee Report (1973): Report of the Committee on Governance of Universities and Colleges, Part II—Teachers (New Delhi, UGC).

Sen, S.N. (1991): *Scientific and Technical Education in India* (1781-1900) (New Delhi, INSA).

Sethi, R.R. and J.L. Mehta (1968): *A History of the Punjab University, Chandigarh (1947-1967)* (Chandigarh, Publication of PU).

Shonfield Andrew & Albert R. Cherns (1971): *Social Science Research in India: ICSSR Pamphlet No. 20* (New Delhi, ICSSR).

Sharma (Dr.) Kavita A. (2003): *50 Years of UGC* (New Delhi, UGC).

Sharma, G.D. (1989): NIEPA: Instrumentality of Change in Prof. P.R. Panchamukhi (Ed.) *Studies in Educational Reforms in India*, Vol. II (Bombay, Himalaya Publishing).

Sharma, Shaloo (2002): *History & Development of Higher Education in India,* Vol. I to V, (New Delhi, Sarup & Sons).

Shattock, Michael (1994): *The UGC and the Management of the British Universities* (Society for Research into Higher Education and Open University Press, Buckingham).

Shourie, Arun (1998): *Eminent Historians, Their Technology and Their Line—Their Fraud* (New Delhi, ASA).

Singh, Y.P., Udai Pareek and D.R. Arora (1973): *Diffusion of an Inter-discipline: Social Sciences in Agricultural Education.* (New Delhi).

Sivaramakrishna, Kavita (2001): *Old Patrons—New Bottles: Recasting Indigenous Medicine in Colonial Punjab (1850-1945)* (New Delhi, Orient Longman).

Sivaramkrishnan, K. (1999): *Modern Forests, State Making and Environmental Changes in Colonial Eastern India* (New Delhi, OUP).

Snow, C.P. (1957): *The Two Cultures and the Industrial Revolution* (London).

Snow, C.P. (1965): *The Two Cultures and A Second Look* (London).

Social Science Research Council (2002): Social Science Research Capacity in S. Asia (New York).

Stebbing, E.P. (1922, 1923, 1926): *The Forests of India*, Vols. I, II, III (London, John Leage, The Bodley Head Ltd.).

Stebbing, E.P. (1962): *The Forests of India*, Vol. IV (Ed: Harry Champion and F.C. Ormaston) (London, Oxford University Press).

Stella, Antony and A. Gnanam (2001): *Assessment and Accreditation in Indian Higher Education: Issues of Policy and Prospects* (New Delhi, Books Plus).

Tamil Nadu Basic Education Society (1951): *Rural Universities* (Kilamongiladi Chidambaran).

Tarlok Singh (1978): Social Science Movement in India: The Case for Autonomous Forums (*University News*, Vol. 36, No. 20, 18th May, 1978).

The Indira Gandhi National Open University Act (No. 85 of 1985) and Statutes under the same (New Delhi).

Tickoo, Champa (1980): *Indian Universities: A Historical Comparative Perspective* (Madras, Orient Longman).

Tikekar, Aroon (1984): *The Cloister's Pale* (Bombay, Somayya Publication).

Tikekar, Aroon (2007): *The Cloister's pale: Biography of a University* (Mumbai, Popular Prakashan).

Tilak, J.B.G: "Financing of Higher Education in India", in Chitnis Suma/ Philip Altbach (Ed.) (1993) (*Supra*).

Tilak, Jandhyala B.G. (1997): "Inclusive Growth & Education: On the Approach to the Eleventh plan", *EPW*, 22nd Sept., 2007, pp. 3872-3877.

Tilak, J.B.G. (2008): Education in 2008-09 Union Budget (*EPW*, 13th May, 2008).

Tilak, Jandhyala, B.G. (2008): Education in 2008-09 Union Budget, *EPW*, 17th May, 2008, pp. 49-56.

Tilak, J.B.G. (2010): The Proposed NCHER: A Solution Worse Than the Disease? (*EPW*, 1st May 2010: 10-13).

Tilak, J.B.G. (2010): The Foreign Educational Institutions Bill: A Critique (*EPW*, 8th May, 2010: 12-14).

Tocqueville (1966): *Democracy in America*, 2 Vols. (Paperback and Hardback, Harper). (First Published in French, 1835).

Tomlinson, B.R. (1998): Technical Education in Colonial India (1886-1914) Searching for a 'Suitable Boy', in Bhattacharya, Sabyasachi (Ed.) (1988): *Supra.*

Udup Committee Report (1950): Report of the Committee to Assess and Evaluate the Present Status of the Ayurvedic System of Medicine (New Delhi, Government of India).

UGC: Annual Reports from 1953 to 2006-2007.

UGC (1965): Report of the Committee on Standards of University Education (New Delhi) [Chairman: Prof. Govindrajulu).

UGC (1967): Report of the Committee on Colleges (New Delhi) [Chairman: G.S. Mahajani].

UGC (1984): Report of the Committee to Enquire into the working of Central Universities (New Delhi) [Chairman: Madhuri R. Shah].

UGC (1986): Report of UGC Committee on State Council of Higher Education (New Delhi).

UGC (June 1986): Report of the Committee on Framing Regulations under UGC Act for Charging Fees for Colleges (Mimeo).

UGC (1987): Report of the Committee on Accreditation and Assessment Council (New Delhi).

UGC (1990): Report of the UGC Committee on 'Alternate Models of Management' (Towards New Educational Management) (New Delhi) [Chairman: Prof. A. Gnanam].

UGC (1993): Performance and Accountability in Higher Education: Occasional Paper No. 1 (New Delhi).

UGC (1994): UGC Funding of Institutes of Higher Education—Report of 1992-93 (Chairman: Justice Punnayya).

UGC (June 1996): Report of the Working Group on Higher Education—Ninth Five Year Plan (New Delhi).

UGC (2000): Guidelines for considering proposals for declaring an institute as deemed to be university u/s 3 of UGC Act (New Delhi).

UGC News (Issues in 2003-2005).

UGC (2007): Draft Report of UGC on 11th Five Year Plan.

University News (2007 and 2008) (Articles on Teacher Education in several issues).

University of Madras (1957): History of Higher Education in Southern India, Vol. I (Madras, Government of Madras Printing Press).

Vaidyanathan, A. (2008): Fourth Review of ICSSR: An Overview (*EPW*, 2nd Feb., 2008, pp. 21-24).

Varma, L.R., P.K. Khosla and R.N. Sehgal: 'Status of Forestry Education and Training in India', pp. 37-46, in Mehta, S.L./B.N. Mathur (Ed.) (2000), *Supra*.

Vashishtha, K.K. (2002): *Association of Indian Universities* (New Delhi, AIU).

Kulandai Swamy, V.C. (1991): Distance Education: Status and Prospects, in Moonis Raza (Ed.) *Supra*.

Ved Prakash (2007): Trends in Growth and Financing of Higher Education in India, *EPW*, 4th August, 2007, pp. 3249-3258.

Wiener, Myron (1962): *The Politics of Scarcity: Public Pressure and Political Response in India* (University of Chicago, Indian reprint by Asia Publishing in Bombay).

World Bank (1999): *The World Development Report 1998-99* (Washington, DC).

Yadav, M.S. and Santosh Panda (1997): Open and Distance Higher Education: Policy and Development, in Panda Santosh (Ed.): *Open and Distance Education* (New Delhi, Aravali Books International Pvt. Ltd.).

Zastoupil, Lynn and Martin Moir (Ed.) (1979): *The Great Indian Education Debate: Documents relating to the Orientalist—Anglicist Controversy, 1781-1843* [Surrey, Richmond (UK), Curzon Press].

List of Cases Cited

Ashok Kumar Thakur *v*. Union of India (2008) JT (5) SC 1.

Bhartidasan University *v*. AICTE (2001 AIR, SC 286) decided on 24th Sept. 2001.

Dental Council of India *v*. SRM Institute of S & T (2004) 9 SCC 676.

Dr. Preeti Srivastava *v*. State of AP (1999) 7 SCC 720.

Gopal Krishna Chatre *v*. BCI (2001) AIR P & H (41).

Indian Council of Legal Aid and Advice *v*. BCI (1993) AIR SC 65.

Islamic Academy of Education *v*. State of Karnataka (2003) 6 SCC 697.

J.P. Unnikrishnan *v*. State of A.P. (1993) 1 SCC 649.

M.P. Vashi *v*. State of Maharashtra (1995) 5 SC 730.

Mohini Jain *v*. State of Karnataka (1992) 3 SCC 666.

O.N. Mahendru v. Bar Council of India (1968) AIR SC 888.

Osmania University Teachers' Association *v*. State of A.P. (AIR 1987) SC 2034.

State of Tamil Nadu *v*. Abhiyaman Education and Research Institute (1995) 4 SCC 104.

TMA Pai Foundation *v*. State of Karnataka (2002) SSC 1481.

V. Sudeer *v*. Bar Council of India (1987) AIR SC 1967.

Yashpal *v*. State of Chhattisgarh (2005) AIR SCW 1168.

Index